D1666506

European Yearbook of International Economic Law

EYIEL Monographs - Studies in European and International Economic Law

Volume 12

Series Editors

Marc Bungenberg, Saarbrücken, Germany

Christoph Herrmann, Passau, Germany

Markus Krajewski, Erlangen, Germany

Jörg Philipp Terhechte, Lüneburg, Germany

Andreas R. Ziegler, Lausanne, Switzerland

EYIEL Monographs is a subseries of the European Yearbook of International Economic Law (EYIEL). It contains scholarly works in the fields of European and international economic law, in particular WTO law, international investment law, international monetary law, law of regional economic integration, external trade law of the EU and EU internal market law. The series does not include edited volumes. EYIEL Monographs are peer-reviewed by the series editors and external reviewers.

More information about this subseries at http://www.springer.com/series/15744

Seyoum Yohannes Tesfay

International Commercial Arbitration

Legal and Institutional Infrastructure in Ethiopia

 Springer

Seyoum Yohannes Tesfay
GeTS Law Office
Addis Ababa, Ethiopia

ISSN 2364-8392   ISSN 2364-8406   (electronic)
European Yearbook of International Economic Law
ISSN 2524-6658   ISSN 2524-6666   (electronic)
EYIEL Monographs - Studies in European and International Economic Law
ISBN 978-3-030-66751-1   ISBN 978-3-030-66752-8   (eBook)
https://doi.org/10.1007/978-3-030-66752-8

This Springer imprint is published by the registered company Springer Nature Switzerland AG.
The registered company address is: Gewerbestrasse 11, 6330 Cham, Switzerland

To my late uncle, Abba Yoseph Tesfay,
because I owe it all to him.

Acknowledgments

This book originated from a doctoral dissertation written at Martin-Luther-Universität Halle-Wittenberg. Many people contributed, in one way or another, to its successful completion. A special mention, however, goes to Prof. Dr. Matthias Lehmann, my advisor, not only for providing insightful academic guidance but for being a friend and a mentor all-in-one. The book would not have seen the light of the day without his understanding and encouragement.

I would also like to thank Prof. Dr. Christian Tietje for the discerning feedback he gave me during doctoral workshops and for being the driving force behind the partnership between Martin-Luther-Universität and Addis Ababa University which lead to the PhD program. Dr. Fikremarkos Merso too deserves appreciation for his tireless involvement in the partnership between the two universities. I also owe a debt of gratitude to Deutscher Akademischer Austauschdienst (DAAD) for the generous financial support.

I was really fortunate to have been surrounded, from the get-go, by friends who are able and willing to help. They contributed intellectually, emotionally, and financially. I am, particularly, indebted to Dr. Tadesse Kassa, Tewodros Meheret, Gebreamlak Gebregiorgis, Yazachew Belew, Dr. Muradu Abdo, Aman Assefa, Manyawkal Mekonnen, Zewugeberhan Zegeye, Birhanu Tsigu, and Yospeh Mulugeta.

I greatly appreciate the valuable time and effort spent by those who agreed to be interviewed and filled in questionnaires. Their insights were priceless. They deserve a big thank you.

Finally, I would like to say thank you to my family and siblings who have been by my side throughout this project. I am grateful, in particular, to my mother Adhanet, my brother Asrat, and my sister Meazu for their moral and emotional support. I also thank Senay, my son, for being such a good boy. Last but not least, special thanks go out to Dominika, Sabine, and Helga Bouchon for their understanding and generosity all along the way.

Contents

Abbreviations

AAA	American Arbitration Association
AACCSA	Addis Ababa Chamber of Commerce and Sectoral Associations
AACCSA AI	Addis Ababa Chamber of Commerce and Sectoral Associations Arbitration Institute
AAWSA	Addis Ababa Water and Sewerage Authority
AU	African Union
FAA	Federal Arbitration Act of the United States of America (1925)
FDRE	Federal Democratic Republic of Ethiopia
EC	European Council
EC	Ethiopian Calendar
ECJ	European Court of Justice
ETB	Ethiopian Birr
EU	European Union
GDP	Gross domestic product
HDI	Human Development Index
IBA	International Bar Association
ICC	International Chamber of Commerce
LCIA	London Court of International Arbitration
OPEC	Organization of the Petroleum Exporting Countries
UK	United Kingdom
UNCITRAL	United Nations Commission on International Trade Law
U.S.	United States
USA	United States of America
ZPO	Civil Procedure Code of Germany

Chapter 1
Ethiopia and Its Legal System: The Context

1.1 The State, Its People and Economy

1.1.1 Geography, Population and Organization of the State

Ethiopia is a landlocked country in the Horn of Africa. At 1,127,127 Sq km its land area is almost as big as France, Germany and the United Kingdom put together.[1] The country is bisected by the Great Rift Valley into northern and southern highlands each of which is surrounded by lowlands. Ras Dashen, the highest peak, is 4620 m above sea level. The Danakil Depression, which is located in the Great Rift Valley, is as low as 115 m below sea level at some locations, and is one of the hottest places on Earth.[2]

The conduct of census or even a systematic estimation of the population is a recent phenomenon in Ethiopia. The first estimate of the country's population was made in the 1930s while the very first census was conducted in 1984. The second and third censuses were carried out in 1994 and 2007 respectively.[3] The 1984 census showed that the country had a population of 42.6 million. The population had reached 53.5 million by 1994 and climbed to 73.8 by the time of the 2007 census. Over the period of three decades in between the three censuses, while the population grew steadily, there was a slight decline on the rate of birth. The population grew annually by 3.1% in 1984; 2.9% in 1994 and 2.6% in 2007.[4] The 2017 United

---

[1]World Atlas, Countries of the World by Land Area: Available at: http://www.worldatlas.com/aatlas/populations/ctyareal.htm, accessed on May 7, 2017.

[2]Library of Congress-Federal Research Division, Country Profile: Ethiopia, available at: http://lcweb2.loc.gov/frd/cs/profiles/Ethiopia.pdf, accessed on May 7, 2017.

[3]Central Statistics Agency [Ethiopia] and ICF International, Ethiopia Demographic and Health Survey 2011 3 (Addis Ababa and Calverton, 2012), available at: https://www.usaid.gov/sites/default/files/documents/1860/Demographic%20Health%20Survey%202011%20Ethiopia%20Final%20Report.pdf, accessed on 25 September 2017.

[4]*Id.*

© The Author(s), under exclusive license to Springer Nature Switzerland AG 2021
S. Y. Tesfay, *International Commercial Arbitration*, European Yearbook of International Economic Law 12, https://doi.org/10.1007/978-3-030-66752-8_1

Nations estimate of the country's population is 105 million, making the country the 12th biggest country by population size.[5]

With only twenty per cent of its people living in cities and towns, Ethiopia is one of the least urbanized countries of the world.[6] Most of the people of the country live in the highlands, and mainly engage in farming. The rest inhabit the lowlands, and are pastoralists that move from place to place in search of water and grass for their herds.[7]

Coming to the organization of the state, a constitution establishing a federal form of government along more or less ethnic lines was adopted in 1995. This Constitution, which is still in force, divides the country into nine regional/federal states and two cities. The federal states are Tigray, Afar, Amhara, Oromia, Somali, Benshangul-Gumuz, Gambella, Harari and, a state curiously named as, Sothern Nations Nationalities and Peoples State. Sidama was officially created, as the tenth state on 18 June 2020 from the Southern Nations, Nationalities and Peoples' state.[8] The two cities that are administered by the Federal Government of Ethiopia, with limited autonomy of their own, are Addis Ababa and Dire Dawa.[9]

1.1.2 The Economy

The Ethiopian economy of the last 120 years can best be understood by looking at it in five different periods.[10] The first is the period from the turn of the twentieth century to 1936. In this period, the political boundary of the state on which rests the political economy of the same was well established. Moreover, the landed aristocracy consolidated its powers, thus, becoming an undisputed ruling class. Other concomitant developments of economic significance were the completion of the Addis Ababa-Djibouti railway and the growth of Addis Ababa itself and some other towns.[11]

The second period, the duration of the Italian occupation (1936–41), witnessed some industrial activity. This, however, was not a profound phenomenon. The most enduring feature of this period was the construction of over 6000 km of roads that

---

[5] www.worldometers.info/world-population/ethiopia-population, accessed on September 25, 2017.
[6] *Id.*
[7] Central Statics Agency, *supra* note 3.
[8] https://www.thereporterethiopia.com/article/sidama-embarks-statehood,   accessed   on 24 Sep. 2020.
[9] Constitution of the Federal Democratic Republic of Ethiopia, Proclamation 1/1995, Article 47(1), Federal Negarit Gazeta, 1st year, No. 1.
[10] Eshetu (1995), p. 194.
[11] *Id.*

formed the backbone of the country's transportation system in the decades that followed.[12]

The third period, the years between the restoration of the monarchy in 1941 and its demise in 1974, represents both continuity and change in the structure of the Ethiopian economy. There was no fundamental departure from the previous two periods in that the period did not bring about industrialization and commerce that was significant enough to transform the structure of output and employment in the economy.[13] The subsistence sector was almost completely dependent on rain, thus, minor aberrations in climatic conditions resulted in mass starvation and the deaths of thousands of peasants. The monetized sector formed linkages with the global economy. Nevertheless, the exports being a limited quantity of primary products that suffered owing to persistent deterioration in the terms of trade, there was very little room for trade, be that domestic or international.[14] The period does, however, represent change in that whatever level of industrialization that the country had come to achieve before the 1990s has its roots in this particular epoch.[15] Commerce too started to take modern form in this period. Encouraging results started to be registered particularly in the power, transport and manufacturing sector though starting from an extremely low base.[16]

Overall, though there was some development in certain sectors of the economy, the general picture was that economic progress was too sluggish and erratic.[17] For instance, between 1961 and 65, relatively good years, the economy grew at the rate of 4% and the GDP reached 2861.9 million Ethiopian Dollars. That means even assuming a very low population increase of 2% per year, the increase in per capita income was just about 2% for these relatively "fat" years.[18]

In sum, the Ethiopian economy of the pre-1974 period was a traditional subsistence economy. That only 15% of the produce entered the market is a testament to this fact. The economy was characterized by structural problems such as a feudal land tenure system. Moreover, at about 7% the adult literacy rate was an obstacle to meaningful economic development.[19] Making things worse was that there seemed to be "a conspicuous absence of the will to develop in the government itself."[20]

---

[12]*Id.*, p. 195.

[13]*Id.*

[14]*Id.*, p. 4.

[15]*Id.*, p. 195.

[16]Assefa and Eshetu (1967), p. 4.

[17]*Id.*, p. 2.

[18]Eshetu (2004), p. 80. Eshetu indicates the annual rate of growth of per capita production for the agricultural sector which formed the back bone of the economy was only 0.5% during 1961–65. In contrast, significant progress was registered in the transport, power and manufacturing sectors. The latter for example grew by 16.2% during the said period.

[19]*Id.*, p. 88.

[20]*Id.*, p. 92.

The sluggish economic growth, an outbreak of famine in 1973/74, and the high price of fuel, among other things, helped the disaffected masses and political forces rise in revolt in unison. At the same time various mutinies were taking place by soldiers and junior officers. The culmination of all these things was a revolution that brought the military to power in 1974.[21]

This brings us to the fourth period in the economic history of Ethiopia: the military or "socialist" era, 1974–91.[22] On 20 December 1974, the military declared that socialism would be the guiding ideology. In line with this declaration, it issued the Economic Policy of Socialist Ethiopia in February 1975. The policy sought to delineate the role of the private sector and the state in the economy giving the latter a salient role.[23] By way of implementation of this policy, all banks, insurance companies, commercial as well as industrial firms were nationalized in early 1975. Moreover, a proclamation that made all rural land "the collective property" of the Ethiopian people was issued in March 1975. This was followed by the nationalization of urban land and 'extra houses'. Each family was allowed to have only one dwelling house. All rented out houses were transferred to state ownership.[24]

The overall economic performance of the socialist era was dismal despite drastic measures such as the termination of feudal relations of agricultural production. Endless war, poorly planned and executed command economy, demographic pressure exerted by a significant birth rate, shortage of investment, use of rudimentary or obsolete technology in almost every sector and external economic environment rendered the period of military rule an utter failure in economic terms.[25] In fact, the per capita income of Ethiopians had declined by 0.8% at the end of the military's 17 years of rule compared to 1974 when they took power.[26] One noteworthy achievement of this period was the reduction in the rate of illiteracy to 38% as the result of a sustained "Literacy Campaign."[27]

The fifth period starts in 1991, when the Ethiopian Peoples' Revolutionary Democratic Front (EPRDF), a coalition of rebel forces, ousted the military after years of war that inflicted untold misery on the population and sapped the resources of the country.[28] The transitional government that the EPRDF and other rebel forces formed embarked on major economic reforms in agreement with the World Bank and the International Monetary Fund, IMF. The outcome was the adoption of Policy Framework Paper (PFP) by 1992. Some of the more important measures to be taken

---

[21]Dessalegn (2009), pp. 295–296.

[22]Eshetu (2004), p. 100.

[23]Id., pp. 100–101.

[24]Id.

[25]Id., pp. 117–123.

[26]Id., at 104.

[27]Mamo KS. Ethiopia: where and who are the World's Illiterates? Available at: http://unesdoc. unesco.org/images/0014/001460/146064e.pdf, last visited on 20 September 2018.

[28]Eshetu (2004), p. 265.

according to the PFP included revision of investment, labour and tax laws.[29] Further the PFP envisaged the "elimination of controls in price and distribution; reforms in trade and exchange policy; formulation of banking and financial laws; guarantying rights to use of land; introducing autonomy in public enterprise management; privatizing some state enterprises; and civil service reform."[30]

The economy of Ethiopia did not improve significantly in spite of these reform measures. There would be some years of modest success and years of regression. Hence, in a decade between 1991 and 2001 the GDP per capita increased only by 1.7% annually.[31] Though this may be on account of many reasons, that the period between 1991–2 was an abnormal time at the end of a civil war, that a war broke out between Eritrea and Ethiopia in 1998 and lasted till the end of 2000, and that the country was hit by severe drought during some of the years did certainly contribute to the poor economic performance of the country.

The economy started to expand in a robust and sustained manner only since 2004. The World Bank indicates that the Gross Domestic Product (GDP) of the country expanded by about 10.3% annually in the decade that ended on 31 December 2016.[32] According to the Economist, Ethiopia was Africa's fastest growing non-oil economy particularly between 2006 and 2011.[33] In June 2017, the World Bank predicted an economic growth of 8.3% in 2017 making the country's economy the most expansive in Africa.[34]

Going beyond growth in GDP the country has also registered remarkable success in areas like life expectancy and education. This is attested to, for example, by the Human Development Index (HDI), released by the United Nations Development Program (UNDP). The 2013 report identifies Ethiopia as one of the 14 countries in the world that managed to score HDI gains of more than 2% annually between 2000 and 2013. In fact, Ethiopia is a leader even in this pack. Having scored an annual average of 3.1% increase in its HDI during that period, Ethiopia has achieved the 3rd

---

[29]Id.

[30]Id.

[31]The World Bank, Ethiopia at a Glance 2011, http://devdata.worldbank.org/AAG/ethaag.pdf, accessed on May 12, 2016.

[32]The World Bank Group, 5th Economic Update for Ethiopia, available at, www.worldbank.org/en/news/press-release/2016/12/06/world-bank-group-launches-its-5th-economic-update-for-ethiopia, accessed on 25 September 2017.

[33]The Economist, "Investing in Ethiopia: Frontier Mentality", May 12th, 2012 edition, available at http://www.economist.com/node/21554547, accessed on May 1, 2016.

[34]The World Bank, Global Economic Prospects: A Fragile Recovery, available at http://www.products.worldbank.org/en/710231493655506452/Global-Economic-Prospects-June-2017-Regional-Overview-SSA.pdf, accessed on 25 September 2017.

highest gain in HDI.[35] That being said, the country still ranks very low scoring 0.448 on a scale of 1, according to the 2016 report of the UNDP.[36]

1.2 The Legal System of Ethiopia

An examination of the legal history of Ethiopia reveals that there is a watershed period in the development of the legal system of the country. Particularly, the way laws were conceived, issued, communicated and implemented varies markedly before and after the Second World War. Similarly, the institutional infrastructure for the issuance, interpretation and application of laws took a sharp turn after the Second World War. Hence, the best way to look at the legal system of the country is by dealing with the pre-war and post-war periods separately.

1.2.1 The Pre-World War Two Period: A Rudimentary 'Legal System'

Though Ethiopia existed as a state for centuries, one is hard pressed to show that it had a 'legal system' in the sense of a *corpus* of laws with formal source that was applied methodically, consistently and throughout its jurisdiction. Although it does appear that legal institutions of some sort and 'rules of law' did exist for a very long time, people tended to look to the ruler rather than these for justice.[37] This is not unique to Ethiopia. In many societies in early stages of legal development it is difficult to separate the law from the ruler who administers it.[38] Hence, the ruler is above the law, the only limitation being that imposed on him by the people's sense of injustice rather than the rule of law. A ruler that is arbitrary and unfair in the administration of justice will likely face the indignation of his subjects. Generally, this is the only 'limitation' on him.[39]

The contention by some quarters that the *Fetha Negast* (Law of the Kings), which was introduced sometime between the fourteenth and sixteenth century, was the law of the land, is not tenable. According to Vanderlinden, there is no evidence that the

---

[35] UNDP, The 20013 Human Development Report, "The Rise of the South: Human Development in a Diverse World" available at: http://www.undp.org/content/ethiopia/en/home/presscenter/articles/2013/03/15/human-development-report-2013-puts-ethiopia-as-third-top-movers/ accessed on May 7, 2013.

[36] UNDP, Human Development Report 2016, available at: http://hdr.undp.org/sites/default/files/hdr_2016_statistical_annex.pdr, accessed on 24 October 2017.

[37] Redden (1968), pp. 41–43.

[38] *Id.*, p. 43.

[39] *Id.*

Fetha Negast was promulgated by any of Ethiopian emperors or kings. Hence, it lacked formal authority.[40] It, thus, remained a private compilation[41] that derived its "authority from the fact that it was unique and that it was constantly referred to in the most important cases."[42] The assertion by Vanderlinden that the *Fetha Negast* was never promulgated is not correct. It was formally incorporated into Ethiopian law but only as recently as in 1908.[43] But this formal incorporation by the turn of the twentieth century does not really refute the crux of the contention of those that hold the *Fetha Negast* lacked formal authority for it had been centuries since its introduction to Ethiopia by 1908.

Apart from the *Fetha Negast*, formally adopted only as recently as in 1908, Ethiopian laws with formal sources were scarce even by the turn of the twentieth century. Legislation started to play part in the country only by the beginning of the twentieth century.[44] Emperor Menelik II was the first to order the systematic description of laws and the creation of governmental institutions on a European model. Particularly, he ordered that judicial decisions be recorded. Before that decisions were given only orally.[45] This trend was consolidated during the reign of Hailesellasie I. A penal 'code' seeking to carefully balance the rules from *Fetha Nagast* with modern principles of criminal law was issued on the day of the coronation of the Emperor in 1930.[46] On 23 July 1931 the new Emperor 'granted' the very first constitution to the people of Ethiopia.[47] This constitution was modelled on the 1889 *Meji* Constitution of Japan.[48] It was essentially an instrument of centralization aimed at reinforcing the control of the Emperor over the provincial nobility. Its provisions on the rights of the subjects were of little actual relevance in

---

[40]Vanderlinden (1967), p. 251.

[41]There is a general consensus that the immediate source of the Fetha Negast is a compilation made in Arabic from its original in Greek by a Christian Egyptian jurist known as Ibn Al'- Assal for the use of the Egyptian Coptic Church in the thirteenth century. *See* Paulos (2009), p. XXXiV.

[42]Vanderlinden (1967), p. 251.

[43]The law issued in 1908 by Emperor Minilik to establish Ministries and define their powers and duties indicates as one of the powers of the Minister of Justice "He shall control whether any decision has been given in accordance with the rules incorporated in the Fetha Negast". *See* Paulos (2009), p. XXXiV.

[44]Vanderlinden (1967), p. 252.

[45]Singer (1970), p. 76. At the outset the reforms were little more than changes in form and names. The Ministries that were established had no functional difference from office holders that preceded them. Change was gradual. As regards how the functions of the Ministry of Justice evolved, for example, see pp. 76–77.

[46]*Id.* at 79.

[47]*Id.* at 78.

[48]Paul and Clapham (1972), pp. 340–341. This Constitution was drafted by the foreign educated Minister of Finance, Bajerond Tekle-Hawariyat. According to Tekle-Hawariyat, when he urged the Emperor to grant a constitution to the country, the Emperor ordered him to draft one. The Minister who had no background in law relied heavily on a copy of the Imperial Japanese Constitution of 1889 that was supplied to him.

that time and could be easily ignored.[49] Overall, it can only be said that in the pre-World War II period, some rudimentary measures were taken in the direction of the development of substantive law of the country.

One should, however, underscore the fact that any law, be that foreign influenced or the *Fetha Negast*, gave way to the imperatives of 'justice' in the period preceding the Second World War. Particularly, civil adjudication was based on the main on equity and the custom that prevailed in the locality concerned.[50] Besides, the laws issued in the pre-war period had little impact, if any, on the development of the legal system of the country in the post-war period. Hence, they can safely be ignored.[51] In sum, until the 1950s the laws of Ethiopia were only an amorphous mix of statutes and decrees mostly focusing on the public law sphere. Social and private relations were governed on the main by the traditions and customs of the various ethnic, tribal and religious groupings.[52]

1.2.2   The Post-World War II Period: An Era of Laws and Institutions

In the years following the end of the Second World War, the Ethiopian state was increasingly modernized as far as legal development is concerned. The administrative structure of a modern state was progressively established. Particularly, a comprehensive court system was officially established in all political subdivisions of the state for the first time. Judges were dispatched to as many of these newly established courts as possible. Where that was not possible, the governor continued to discharge the responsibilities of a judge.[53] Legislations were consistently published in the *Negarit Gazeta,* a legal gazette established in 1942.[54] A revised constitution was adopted in 1955, according to the Emperor, with a view to enabling the people 'enjoy direct representation and participation in the business of Government.'[55] This was done, again according to the Emperor, despite 'objections and opposition.'[56] Whatever the process of its issuance, the 1955 Revised Constitution was a relatively modern constitution at least in form.[57]

---

[49]*Id.*

[50]Redden (1968), pp. 44–45.

[51]Vanderlinden (1967), p. 253.

[52]Beckstrom (1973), p. 559.

[53]Singer (1970), p. 79.

[54]Vanderlinden (1967), p. 255.

[55]Singer (1970), p. 78.

[56]*Id.*

[57]Paul and Clapham (1972), p. 387. The constitution of 1931 that was in force till 1955, contrasted unfavorably with the liberal constitution that was bestowed on Eritrea by the United Nations. Since Eritrea was federated to Ethiopia by the United Nations, having two constitutions, within one

1.2.2.1 The Codification of Laws: Any Local Content?

In the period between 1955 and 1965 Ethiopia undertook the codification of its laws. Six codes that can be regarded as such in the fullest sense of the term were promulgated.[58] The codes that were adopted are: the Civil Code (1960), Commercial Code (1960), Maritime Code (1960), Civil Procedure Code (1965), Penal Code (1957) and Criminal Procedure Code (1961).[59]

As regards the content and sources of the laws, some maintain that the drafting of the substantive codes benefited from input by Ethiopian legal experts. Once the expert draftsperson finished drafting a certain portion of the code concerned, the draft would be submitted for deliberation by the Codification Commission. Though the contribution of the Ethiopian members of this Commission was limited on technical matters they would ensure that their views were understood. In certain fields they managed to have the drafts essentially modified. Cases in point are parts of the Civil Code dealing with marriage, successions and property. There were also instances in which the Parliament introduced significant changes such as in the part of the Penal Code dealing with corporal punishment.[60]

Others dispute that the new laws, even the substantive codes, had any meaningful Ethiopian content. Pre-existing laws were repealed in some cases explicitly and in others by implication. As for the customs of the country, there was not much for the drafters to rely upon as there was no systematic survey of the customs of the country in existence at the time.[61] Paul Brietzke maintains that the customs that were consulted, to the extent any were consulted, are those that coincided with the interest of the 'landed, state-supporting, westernized, urbanized minority that practiced rudimentary form of capitalism and dominated the Parliament.'[62]

---

country, that are markedly different in rights they vest in citizens created anomaly. This was one of the driving causes for the adoption of the 1955 Constitution.

[58]The decision to comprehensively reform the legal system and codify were taken in late 1953. A plan was drawn and continental experts were sought. The experts that were chosen were: for the drafting of Civil Code and Civil Procedure Code Professor Rene David, Professor of Comparative Law at the University of Paris; for Penal Code and Criminal Procedure Code, Professor Jean Graven of the University of Geneva; for Maritime and Commercial Codes, Professor Jean Escarra of the University of Paris. There were however changes in the process. Thus for example, Professor David did not draft the Civil Procedure Code. Similarly, the Criminal Procedure Code was not drafted by Professor Graven. Professor Escarra died before he could complete the drafting to the Commercial Code thus Professor Jauffret had to finalize the drafting of the Code.

[59]Beckstrom (1973), p. 559.

[60]Vanderlinden (1967), p. 259.

[61]Beckstrom (1973), pp. 559–560. Lending credence to this observation, the drafter of the Civil Code says his draft was substantially modified to impose punishment of extreme severity on persons who sawed seeds, planted trees and erected buildings on the property of others. He further says Parliament introduced into the draft 'modifications constantly favorable to owners' in the part of the Code regulating the relationship between farmers and owners of land. See David (1963), p. 200.

[62]Brietzke (1974), pp. 152–154.

Others go further and emphatically hold that the very purpose of the codification was at odds with the consolidation of existing customs. What Ethiopia sought was not a 'methodical and clear statement' of actual customary rules. According to the drafter of the Civil Code at least, what the Ethiopians wanted was to use the codes as 'a program envisaging a total transformation of society' so as to have new rules for 'the society they wish to create' while maintaining some traditional values.[63]

The foregoing being how the drafters understood their task one can safely conclude that the codes adopted by Ethiopia are essentially foreign in content. In fact, Professor Krzeczunowicz, a leading authority on the Ethiopian Civil Code, holds the Civil Code of Ethiopia is characterized by its detailed and comprehensive regulation on the one hand and by the general repeal of all prior rules and customs on the other. Indeed, for him, the Civil Code of Ethiopia is unprecedented in its sweeping repeal of custom anywhere in the world, at least in the recent past.[64] Brietzke concurs. He says especially the Civil Code made short work of traditional laws.[65] The code itself clearly says, '[u]nless otherwise expressly provided, all rules whether written or customary previously in force, concerning matters provided for in this Code shall be replaced by this Code and are hereby repealed.'[66]

So, overall, it is safe to conclude that the content of the laws, especially those that are of relevance to commerce and international commercial arbitration is essentially foreign, to say the least. This raises the question of the foreign sources and their contribution addressed in the following sub-section.

---

[63]David (1963), pp. 193–195. Professor David says only those customs that correspond to the profound sentiment of justice of Ethiopians and those that are too profoundly rooted were taken into account. He adds that these were not many given the society had been frozen for centuries and many spheres of social and economic life were at their rudimentary level. He says, the concept of contract, for example, was not known and 'the entire matter of contract in the Code is a new thing' because these things were not know to the Ethiopian society at that time and hence no custom occupied the field. Others vehemently challenge the foregoing assertions by Professor David. Paul Brietzke, for instance says, Professor David simply attributes his own assumptions to Ethiopians. In reality he alleges the drafters of the Civil Code and the Commercial Code were following the colonial legal thinking that 'good law in one place is good law in any place else'. He says some basic assertions made by the two drafters are false or disingenuous. For instance he challenges the assertion by the two drafters that there were no custom in Ethiopia regarding commercial matters and particularly contracts. He maintains even substance trade is contractually regulated and hence such customs exist everywhere let alone in Ethiopia that practiced commerce for thousands of years. *See* on this Brietzke (1974), pp. 150–151.

[64]Krzeczunowicz (1963), p. 175. Professor Krzeczunowicz published commentaries on contracts and torts besides publishing numerous articles on different areas of the Civil Code. To date, his books are used as texts in law schools in Ethiopia.

[65]Brietzke (1974), p. 154.

[66]Civil Code of the Empire of Ethiopia, Proclamation No. 165/1960, *Negarit Gazeta*, 19th Year No. 2, Article 3347(1).

1.2.2.2 The Contribution of the Civil Law and the Common Law Traditions

Coming to the system from which the borrowing took place, we see that the substantive laws generally followed Romano-Germanic legal doctrines. In drafting the Civil Code, for example, French law had the most pervasive influence, though the laws of diverse jurisdictions were consulted.[67] The laws that were consulted include those of Egypt, Greece, Switzerland, South Africa, Turkey, Portugal, Israel, and even the Soviet Union in the field of collective exploitation.[68] Pertinent laws of some Common Law jurisdictions like India, England and the Restatement of American Laws were also considered, though their contribution was not as profound as the Civil Law jurisdictions.[69]

The approach taken was totally different when it comes to the procedural laws.[70] The Civil Procedure Code, for instance, was drafted by an Indian trained Ethiopian, Mr. Nirayo Esayas, Assistant Minister of Justice, and was manifestly influenced by the Indian Code of Civil Procedure.[71] It was issued only as a decree of the Emperor 'on the advice of the Council of Ministers.' So, there was no opportunity for the Parliament to discuss and give it even some local appearance let alone supply meaningful local content.[72] Professor Réne David says he was requested to prepare a preparatory plan for the Civil Procedural Code but had to decline the offer.[73] So, it does seem that the modelling of the procedural law on a common law country was not by design.

Similarly, the Criminal Procedure Code was drafted by Sir Charles Mathew, a Brit who was a judge in Ethiopia at the time. This Code was modelled after Malayan Criminal Procedure Code.[74] Therefore, clearly the adjective laws have been influenced, to say the least, by common law doctrines, unlike the substantive laws. Hence, we find a dichotomy between substantive and procedural laws in Ethiopia, when it comes to their sources.

This raises the questions why Ethiopia decided to codify and why substantive laws were all drafted by continental lawyers in French, in an English speaking country[75] when it was known all the Codes had to be translated twice, into English

---

[67]Singer (1970), pp. 88–89.

[68]Id.

[69]Id.

[70]Sand (1971), pp. 5–6.

[71]Id., p. 11.

[72]Civil Procedure Code Decree No. 52/1965, *Negarit Gazeta*, 25th Year, No. 3. See the Preamble. According to some who are familiar with the Code, it is more or less a translation of the Civil Procedure Code of India that was in force during that era. In fact, colleagues teaching the course heavily rely on a commentary on Indian Civil Procedure Code in teaching the course.

[73]David (1963), p. 204.

[74]Vanderlinden (1967), p. 257.

[75]French, that had been the more familiar language in pre-war period, was replaced by English after the return of the Emperor from exile in 1941 because of significant influence of the British and the

and Amharic. Professor David says the decision to codify was apparently based on the belief that codification by itself represented progress. He adds that was a justified view given the context in Ethiopia though he acknowledges the existence of many advanced legal systems without codified laws.[76]

As regards the choice of continental experts he hypothesizes that this could be more owing to the political and cultural order than juridical arguments. First, he says, the *Fetha Negast*, which was highly venerated in Ethiopia for centuries, has its roots to some extent in the Byzantine legal tradition which in turn can be deemed an heir to the Roman legal tradition. The Romano-Germanic legal system and experts from the same were, therefore, chosen in a bid to ensure historical continuity in the Ethiopian legal tradition.[77] Secondly, Ethiopia wanted to counter the increasingly pervasive influence of the British and the Americans in the post-war period in the affairs of the Ethiopian state. One way of doing that was picking continental experts.[78]

Others contest the above hypothesis of Professor David. Singer, for example, says Ethiopia preferred a 'clear, systematic, compact, complete and authoritative state-ment of law' for the drafting of which common-law lawyers were believed to be less suitable. He, however, contends the controlling reason for the choice of continental experts was the basic orientation of the Emperor who made the decision. Since the Emperor spoke French and was exposed to that tradition from early age, he preferred people with whose culture he was more conversant than English or American experts for the drafting job.[79]

Whatever the reasons behind Ethiopia's importation of substantive laws and procedural laws from two different legal traditions, this is not without its downside. The consequence is the aggravation and further complication of the problems that arise when a country imports a single legal system.[80] As if judges, law teachers and civil servants etc...do not face enough difficulty in understanding, teaching and

---

Americans in the country in the post-war period. English was the language of instruction especially at collage level at the time of the codification though Amharic remained the official language in all other aspects of public life.

[76]David (1963), pp. 188–189. The advanced legal systems that do not have codified laws have various things that compensate for the absence of a code ranging from many written laws that are not named codes, well-developed jurisprudence articulated by highly competent judiciary that is available in various digests etc... Ethiopia in late 1960s had nothing of this sort and the only way to mitigate arbitrariness was to codify laws according to him. The modernization of Ethiopia required the adoption of "ready-made" system as Ethiopia had no luxury of waiting for three to five hundred years to slowly develop its laws from practice relying on empirical experience. What was needed in Ethiopia was ensuring minimum security in legal relations as quickly as possible. Hence, codifica-tion was progress by itself in the Ethiopian context, according to Professor David.

[77]*Id.* at 192. Despite the disparity between the rules contained in the Fetha Nagast and the actual solutions to legal problems it was constantly considered in Ethiopia "nearly sacred to which it would have been desirable to conform". The Fetha Nagast had parts which may be deemed church law while the rest was governing many things including private relations.

[78]*Id.*

[79]Singer (1970), pp. 82–83.

[80]Sand (1971), p. 18.

applying laws and concepts developed in a foreign social, cultural and economic context and coined in a foreign language, the adoption of laws from multiple legal systems multiplies the challenges they face.[81]

Moreover, the difficulty the legislator faces in keeping up with current changes in a single parent system of laws is exacerbated when laws are adopted from multiple systems. The legislator is expected to keep abreast of simultaneous developments in multiple legal systems.[82] Sand contends that the worst effect of reception of laws from multiple systems is that in such cases there will be no special or 'genetic' relationship with a single 'law-donor'. He maintains that within a 'legal-family' it is feasible for younger members to look for clues and developments in the parent country for interpretation. This is not the case when the borrowing is from multiple legal systems. He concludes that 'eclectic legislations produce orphan laws.'[83]

Though the observations of Sand are essentially correct, the full impact of the problem is not felt in cases where the importing country makes sure that eclectic approach is not followed within a single branch of law. For example, given that the procedural laws were taken almost in their entirety form the common-law system, the observations of Sand apply in Ethiopia only with regard to borrowing made from different jurisdictions within the common law system. Assuming the variations within the common-law system are not dramatic the problems caused by borrowing from different countries within the same family of laws are less fundamental.

1.2.2.3   The Continuing Competition Between the Civil Law and Common Law Traditions

Despite the codification of the substantive laws of Ethiopia, mainly along the lines of continental legal tradition, the competition between the common law and civil law traditions has not come to an end. Foreign judges, mostly British, were appointed to the newly established courts with equal authority as Ethiopian judges, at the time of the codification.[84] This opened the door for common law influence in the judiciary. The new codes had to be interpreted by a judiciary with essentially common law background. Their influence was reinforced by the Ethiopian tradition that accorded precedence to justice and equity rather than strict adherence to the letter of the law in the administration of the law, according to one view.[85]

Others, however, contend that the judges from common law background did not have significant impact on the nature of the system. Among others things, the fact that the judges from the common law background had to sit with Ethiopian colleagues with whom little communication was possible owing to language barrier,

---

[81]Id.

[82]Id.

[83]Id., at 19.

[84]Vanderlinden (1967), p. 255.

[85]Id., p. 261.

their difference in background, and the absence of communication within the judiciary in more systemic ways hindered the common law influence from taking roots and leaving behind a dominant footprint.[86] That being said, though people may disagree on the reach and depth of the impact that these judges had, they must have influenced the Ethiopian system, to some extent.

The common law tradition came to exert further influence when the first law school was established in 1963 and Ethiopian law started to be taught by means of the case method by the numerically dominant American teaching staff. The outcome was that enough emphasis was not placed on the 'analysis of the inner structure of the codes and the necessary links which exist between each of their parts.'[87] Hence, many students treated the codes as a 'corpus of articles from which the party tries to fish a suitable argument' by making some analogy between the facts of the case at hand and the article of the code concerned in disregard of the exact place of the article in the overall structure of the code(s).[88]

Even today, over fifty years after the establishment of the first law school in the country, one is struck by the lack of strict articulation of teaching methods in Ethiopia though teaching staff are almost exclusively Ethiopian. There is still a lingering effect of the case law method perhaps owing to overdependence on texts authored by the mostly American faculty before their departure in the mid-1970s.

Not only were most of the early professors Americans, but many who taught ever since in Ethiopian law schools have pursued their graduate studies in common law jurisdictions. The possibility of studying in France or other civil law countries is limited owing to, among others, the language barrier. This is yet another route for common law influence to find its way into Ethiopian laws. Alan Watson says that where jurists of a periphery state study has significant impact in the development of the laws of that country.[89] These students became leading lights in law in their respective countries. They have significant potential of affecting where further borrowing takes place because of their exposure to the laws of the jurisdiction in which they studied in their formative stage, books they bring back and network they establish.[90] He illustrates this by the significant impact Scots law has on the laws of Botswana, Swaziland and Lesotho because the early jurists of these countries studied in the University of Edinburgh between 1966 and 1986.[91]

The need to cite authority when confronted with new issues could be yet another route for common law to influence Ethiopian law. Watson says that 'all law making,

---

[86]*Id., p.* 256.

[87]*Id.,* p. 263.

[88]*Id.*

[89]Watson (1996), pp. 340–341.

[90]*Id.,* pp. *339–341.*

[91]*Id.* He says a total of 240 LL.B student s from these countries were sent to the University of Edinburgh to spend two years studying there. In consequence, the impact of Scots law in these countries is evident according to Watson.

apart from legislating, desperately needs authority.'[92] He says that legal transplantation may result from the fundamental 'need to cite authority' that jurists, judges and all other lawmakers except parliament itself feel. When confronted with a new situation or case that is not covered by the local laws, Watson says, judges, for example, 'cite with all apparent seriousness what are regarded as the appropriate authorities', even where these may be actually unhelpful or irrelevant.[93] One may imagine Ethiopian jurists, for example, confronted with new issues, look to continental legal sources for authority. This would make sense because diffusion is generally driven 'by the emulation of others who are perceived as fundamentally similar and who are hence perceived to be facing the same problems.'[94] The problem is, few, if any, Ethiopian lawyers are fluent in French, German, Spanish or other continental European languages and able to understand legal texts written in them. Besides, material from civil-law tradition countries is not readily available. Hence, it is very likely that most borrowing today by Ethiopian judges as well as lawmakers is from English speaking jurisdictions, especially, the United States and England.

Besides, there is a relatively recent legislative development that introduces a common law feature into the Ethiopian legal system. We now have a law that gives the power of precedent to the decisions of the Cassation Bench of the Federal Supreme Court. It provides that any 'interpretation of law' by no less than five judges seating in the Cassation Bench of the Federal Supreme Court 'shall be binding' on all courts in Ethiopia, whether they are federal courts or state courts.[95]

1.2.2.4 Absorption of the Transplanted Laws

The question of significance that comes to mind regarding these, almost entirely transplanted, laws concerns the extent to which they have been absorbed by the Ethiopian society. The answer to this question is a reflection of several factors. Generally, it can be said that laws that have not been adapted to local conditions are not easily absorbed.[96] This is due in part because it takes time for the population to be familiar with the transplanted law. In consequence, the initial demand for using the transplanted laws remains weak.[97] As seen under Sect. 1.2.2.1 above, the codes adopted by Ethiopia had little, if any, local content. They were essentially programmatic. This must have impacted negatively their absorption.

Another factor that affects the absorption of transplanted laws is the extent to which lawyers, judges, and those in administrative agencies entrusted with the

---

[92] *Id.*, p. 346.

[93] *Id.*, p. 350.

[94] Spamann (2009), pp. 46–47.

[95] A Proclamation to Reamend the Federal Courts Proclamation No. 25/1996, Proclamation No. 454/2005, NEGARIT GAZETA, 11th Year, No.42, Article 2(1).

[96] Berkowitz (2003), pp. 168–169.

[97] *Id.*

interpretation and implementation of the laws have understood, accepted and applied them. In other words, the people will not conduct their affairs in ways that represent changes attributable to the new laws where the foregoing actors do not understand, accept and apply the new laws.[98] There were challenges in this regard because the country did not have a sufficient number of qualified lawyers, judges etc... to understand and apply these new laws. The very first Law School in Ethiopia was opened in 1963, three years after the adoption of the Civil Code.

Overall, owing to the foregoing reasons, among others, ten years after the adoption of the codes Beckstrom found many provisions of the Commercial Code were not applied. For instance, those dealing with bankruptcy, keeping of books and accounts by traders, negotiable instruments were unapplied.[99] He predicted that the application of the Commercial Code provisions like the foregoing would be unlikely even in decades ahead owing to the absence of economic development that calls for their application, lack of efficient bureaucracy that could apply them and the overall absence of a good grasp of the rules.[100]

Beckstrom really put his finger on the fate of a large chunk of the Commercial Code provisions, and the Civil Code for that matter. Even fifty years after the adoption of the Commercial Code, in the estimate of colleagues[101] that practiced law for over a decade, about 50% of the provisions of the Commercial Code remain either totally unapplied or misapplied. For instance, the provisions of the Code on negotiable instruments such as on bills of exchange and those on banking, particularly those on 'current accounts', remain totally unapplied.[102] Provisions of the Code on checks[103] and bankruptcy, especially the latter are misapplied fundamentally.[104] As regards the Civil Code, provisions on registration of status, particularly, birth, marriage and death remained totally unapplied for 56 years even in big cities like Addis Ababa. This is despite the Revised Family Code issued in 2000 re-requiring

---

[98]Beckstrom (1973), p. 568.

[99]*Id.*, at 570.

[100]*Id.*

[101]Discussion with Mr. Tewodros Meheret, formerly head of Legal Services of Abyssinia Bank, Currently Head of Legal Services of Addis Ababa University and Lecturer. Also Mr. Yazachew Belew, formerly judge in the Supreme Court of the Oromia Regional State and currently lecturer at Addis Ababa University. Discussion was held with the two on November 26, 2013 at the main campus of Addis Ababa University.

[102]*Id.*

[103]Because banks, as a matter of practice do not accept presentment of postdated checks, business people obtain credit from fellow businessmen by drawing a postdated check, for the amount borrowed and often egregiously high interest in return. This happens despite the fact that issuing a check without cover is a criminal offence, and in spite of the existence of a lawful mechanism that could exactly serve the same purpose, the issuance of bills of exchange. Those giving credit prefer getting a post-dated check because they use the criminal sanction as an additional leverage to get back the money they lend besides the Civil Procedure Code provisions on summary procedure for recovery of debt supported by a check. *See* Brietzke (1974), p. 164, The Civil Procedure Code of Ethiopia (1965), Art 284.

[104]Interview with Mr. Tewodros and Yazachew.

the government to set up the institutional set up necessary for this purpose within six months form the issuance of that law.[105] Registration of birth, marriage, divorce and death started only as recently as July 2016.[106]

The incompetence and neglect of duty by judges as well as the insufficient attention given by the state to the judiciary as an institution is one of the many reasons why the laws of Ethiopia are not fully and properly applied. In 1974, nearly fifteen years after the adoption of the codes, Brietzke observed 'judges typically cite irrelevant provisions of the codes to 'dress up' their opinion and make little attempt to explain how exactly the Code provisions apply to the facts at hand.[107] Sadly, today, over fifty years after the adoption of the codes, this same problem remains entrenched even at the highest court in Ethiopia. Though the right to have reviewed on cassation a final decision of a court that suffers a 'basic error of law' is a constitutional right[108] and it is legitimately expected that courts are to give reasoned decisions[109] the Cassation Bench of the Federal Supreme Court routinely uses a 'standard form' in rejecting applications for review on cassation.[110] And even when the Cassation Bench does, in fact, review decisions and reverses them, one is really shocked looking at how brief, insufficiently reasoned, and even self-contradictory its decisions are.[111] A typical decision of the Cassation Bench is five pages long.[112] That is hardly enough to provide a comprehensible summary of the facts of the case,

---

[105]The Revised Family Code Proclamation, FEDERAL NEGARIT GAZETTA, 6TH Year, Extraordinary Issue No. 1, Article. Article 321(1) requires the Federal Government to issue laws for the implementation of the registration of civil status and establish the institutions necessary for this purpose within six months from the coming into force of the Code in 2000. Yet such institutions were not established till 2016.

[106]*Id.*

[107]Brietzke (1974), p. 157.

[108]The Constitution of the Federal Democratic Republic of Ethiopia, Proclamation No. 1/1995, *Federal Negarit Gazetta*, 1st Year, No. 1, Art. 80(3).

[109]Civil Procedure Code (1965), Art 182(1).

[110]This has been an official policy of the Cassation Division for over a decade now. The official reason being the Court need not waste time when it finds the decision sought to be reviewed for fundamental error of law suffers none and hence reasoning out would be only reproducing the decision that was sought to be reviewed.

[111]Though Courts in Ethiopia do not generally follow precedent they are by law required to follow the interpretation of laws by the Cassation Division of the Federal Supreme Court so laws are understood and applied uniformly throughout the country. *See*, Federal Courts Reamendment Proclamation No. 454/2005, Art, 2. So, one would assume that the Division of the Supreme Court entrusted with such a lofty goal, akin to law making, though not directly so, would make reasoned and consistent decisions that analyze the law in view of the facts in the case. But for a variety of reasons that go beyond the scope of this dissertation it routinely makes decisions which are one or two pages long. Sometimes they are even shorter thus making it impossible to figure out what the legal issue at hand was and what the reasoning of the court is.

[112]For instance, Cassation Court Report, Volume 20, published in May 2017 reproduces 88 Cassation Court decisions in 444 pages. That makes the average length of the decisions 5 pages. Of the five pages a total of one page is dedicated to description of the court, name of judges and the orders issued by the Cassation Bench in the end. So, about four pages only are

its procedural history and the reasoning of the lower courts let alone provide additionally a sufficiently reasoned decision, and dissenting opinions, if any.

1.3 Does Ethiopia Have a Special Legal Regime for Arbitrations That Are 'International'?

Some states like France, Switzerland and Singapore distinguish between domestic and international arbitration and apply different sets of rules to them.[113] The rationale for this distinction is that considerations that apply to domestic and international arbitration could differ. For instance, parties to an international arbitration are generally, though not necessarily, businesses or financial corporations. In contrast, parties to a domestic arbitration will more often be private individuals. In consequence, consumer protection will most likely be a consideration in domestic arbitration unlike in international arbitration.[114] Whatever the rational for the dichotomy, accurate determination of which arbitration is international and which domestic becomes critical in jurisdictions that make this distinction.

Three yardsticks are used to determine whether arbitration is 'international'. These are the objective criterion, the subjective criterion and the combined criterion.[115] Proponents of the objective criterion zoom in on the transaction leading to arbitration. They focus on the subject matter of the dispute to determine whether international commercial interests are involved, or whether the underlying contract has cross-border element.[116] If the answer to the foregoing is in the positive the arbitration is characterized as 'international.' The French legal system follows this approach. It focuses on the economic reality of the process leading to arbitration.[117] Other jurisdictions that follow the same approach deem arbitration international if the underlying transaction had some 'foreign element'. This term is used, for instance, in the Romanian Code of Civil Procedure. It is adequately wide and less problematic than the 'international commercial interest' criterion used in French law.[118] That the parties have referred the dispute to an arbitration institution of international standing such as the ICC, or the LCA is a sufficient reason, according to some authors, to treat the arbitration as 'international.'[119] This approach is regarded as yet another sub-category of the objective criterion.

---

dedicated to the summary of the facts of the case, its procedural history, the reasoning of the lower courts and the Cassation Bench's own holding and reasoning.

[113]Blackaby et al. (2015), p. 8.

[114]*Id.*, at 7.

[115]Lew et al. (2003), p. 58.

[116]*Id.*

[117]*Id.*

[118]*Id.*, p. 59.

[119]*Id.*, p. 58.

The subjective criterion, in contrast, focuses on the actors involved in the process rather than the subject matter of the transaction. According to this criterion, arbitration is 'international' where the parties, be they individuals or companies, come from different jurisdictions. The focus is on such things as the nationality, place of residence or business and the domicile of the parties to the arbitration agreement.[120] If two companies have their principal place of business in the same country, the arbitration between them is characterized as domestic according to this criterion. This is so even where the transaction that gave rise to the arbitral proceedings had been concluded and performed in another country or even involved a number of other countries. Switzerland follows this approach.[121]

The third approach combines the objective and subjective criteria above, and hence is known as the combined criterion. In this approach, either the identity of the parties to arbitration or the subject matter of the underlying transaction renders arbitration 'international.'[122] The *UNCITRAL Model Law* of 1985 and its 2006 revised version exemplify the combined approach. Article 1(3) defines arbitration as 'international' if 'the parties to an arbitration agreement have, at the time of the conclusion of that agreement, their places of business in different States' thus reflecting the subjective criterion.[123] The *Model Law* then broadens the grounds for regarding arbitration as 'international' by adding objective criteria. It provides that arbitration is also deemed international if the place of arbitration or the place of the subject matter of the dispute, e.g., the place of contract performance, is situated outside the state where the parties have their place of business.[124]

The *Model Law* arguably goes even beyond the subjective and objective criteria by vesting in the parties themselves the freedom to characterize the subject-matter of the arbitration as going beyond one country. It provides that arbitration is also to be considered as international where 'the parties have expressly agreed that the subject-matter of the arbitration agreement relates to more than one country.'[125] Evidently, the *Model Law* takes a very broad view of when arbitration can be deemed international by alternatively using the subjective and the objective criteria and even going beyond the two by allowing the parties themselves to characterize the arbitration as such. Some have criticized Article 1(3)c of the *Model Law* for allowing the parties to 'internationalize' their dispute even where neither the transaction nor the parties have any apparent link to a third country.[126]

---

[120]Blackaby (2015), p. 9.

[121]*Id.* Under Swiss law, arbitration is 'international,' if one of the parties was not domiciled or a habitual resident of Switzerland at the time of the conclusion of the arbitration agreement.

[122]Lew (2003), p. 60.

[123]UNCITRAL Model Law on International Commercial Arbitration 1985 with amendments as adopted in 2006, General Assembly Resolution 40/72 of 1985 and General Assembly Resolution 61/33 of 2006, Article 1(3)a.

[124]*Id.*, Article 1(3)b.

[125]*Id.*, Article 1(3)(c).

[126]Lew et al. (2003), p. 61. Incidentally one notes that the UNCITRAL Arbitration Rules as Revised in 2010 do not define when arbitration is international though they are aimed at international

Ethiopian does not have two completely separate regimes for domestic and international arbitrations. By and large, the same rules apply to all commercial arbitrations. What this book does is, therefore, dwell on aspects of Ethiopian arbitration law that are of particular importance to international arbitration. Hence, most of the topics covered in this work are also relevant to domestic commercial arbitration.

That being said, given that the aim of this work is to examinee the sufficiency of the legal and institutional infrastructure in Ethiopia for international arbitration, we need to have a working definition of what is meant by 'international' arbitration. Thus, we take the broad understanding of what makes arbitration international along the lines of the *UNCITRAL Model Law,* with one important exception. Arbitration is international for our purpose if either the subjective or the objective criterion above is met. In other words, if parties to arbitration are different nationals, have different domicile or principal place of business in different countries, the arbitration is deemed international for our purpose. Similarly, we regard arbitration as 'international' where the transaction that resulted in the arbitration has some foreign element, for instance, if it is concluded or performed in different countries or involves flow of funds, goods or services across different countries. We do not, however, regard arbitration as 'international' just because the parties characterized it as international despite the absence of subjective or objective link to a third country. Leaving this characterization to the whims and caprices of the parties to arbitration risks rendering the dichotomy devoid of any substantive meaning.

1.4   Conclusion

This chapter aimed at providing the context in which the laws and institutions of relevance to international commercial arbitration operate. Particularly, attempt was made to introduce the legal system of Ethiopia to those who might be unfamiliar with that. It showed that the way laws are conceived, communicated, interpreted and implemented in Ethiopia changed fundamentally after the Second World War. Ethiopia had a very rudimentary legal system focusing more on the area of public

commercial arbitration. *See,* UNCITRAL Arbitration Rules as Revised in 2010, General Assembly Resolution 65/22, Preamble and Article 1. Coming to Africa, the law in South Africa makes distinction between domestic and international arbitration. The International Arbitration Bill, Bill No.10/2017 published in Government Gazette No. 40687 applies to international arbitration while Act No. 42 of 1965 applies to domestic arbitration. The preamble of the International Arbitration Bill states its purpose is, among others, to 'provide for the incorporation of the Model Law on International Commercial Arbitration' as adopted by the UNCITRAL into South African law. Article 3 and 4 of the International Arbitration Bill indicate that the Arbitration Act of 1965 remains in force but does not apply to international arbitration except in relation to certain provisions that have been specifically indicated under the 2017 Bill itself. The South African Bill incorporates verbatim the criteria of the Model Law on what makes an arbitration international. It reproduces the Model Law as annex I to the Bill, in which Article 1(3) of the Model Law is simply reproduced.

law in the pre-war period. Several codes were adopted in about two decades following the war. The codes had very little, if any, local content. All the substantive codes were drafted by continental European experts along the lines of the Civil Law tradition. In contrast, the procedural codes were essentially taken from the Common Law tradition. Beyond this the Common Law tradition continues to influence the legal system of the country. Further borrowing tends to be more from the English speaking world. This is so because of the continued exposure of Ethiopian lawyers to that system and serious language barrier that limits access to new developments in the Civil Law System.

In sum, it may be said that though Ethiopia has a fairly advanced body of transplanted commercial laws, their absorption and application has been modest, at best. Particularly, Ethiopia has yet to grow into a significant part of its commercial laws. This is, of course, not to imply that some of the commercial laws have not fallen obsolete 60 years after their adoption.

References

Assefa B, Eshetu C (1967) The state of the Ethiopian economy: a structural survey (Unpublished material available at the Institute of Ethiopian Studies AAU)

Beckstrom JH (1973) Transplantation of legal systems: an early report on the reception of western laws in Ethiopia. Am J Comp Law 21:559

Berkowitz D et al (2003) The transplant effect. Am J Comp Law 5:168

Blackaby N et al (2015) Redfern and Hunter on international arbitration, 6th edn. Oxford University Press

Brietzke P (1974) Private law in Ethiopia. J Afr Law 18(2)

Central Statistics Agency [Ethiopia] and ICF International, Ethiopia Demographic and Health Survey 2011 3 (Addis Ababa and Calverton, 2012). Available at: https://www.usaid.gov/sites/default/files/documents/1860/Demographic%20Health%20Survey%202011%20Ethiopia%20Final%20Report.pdf. Accessed 25 Sep 2017

David R (1963) Civil Code for Ethiopia, considerations on the codification of the civil law in African countries. Tul Law Rev 37

Dessalegn R (2009) The peasant and the state: studies in agrarian changes in Ethiopia 1950s-2000s. Addis Ababa University Press, Addis Ababa

Economist, "Investing in Ethiopia: Frontier Mentality", May 12th, 2012 edition, available at http://www.economist.com/node/21554547. Accessed 1 May 2016

Eshetu C (1995) Running to keep in the same place: industrialization 1941–74. In: Bekele S (ed) An economic history of Ethiopia: the Imperial era 1941–1974. OSSREA, Addis Ababa

Eshetu C (2004) Underdevelopment in Ethiopia. OSSREA, Addis Ababa

https://www.thereporterethiopia.com/article/sidama-embarks-statehood. Accessed 24 Sep 2020

Krzeczunowicz G (1963) The Ethiopian Civil Code: its usefulness, relation to custom and applicability. J Afr Law 7(3)

Lew J et al (2003) Comparative international commercial arbitration. Kluwer Law International, The Hague

Library of Congress-Federal Research Division, Country Profile: Ethiopia. Available at: http://lcweb2.loc.gov/frd/cs/profiles/Ethiopia.pdf. Accessed 7 May 2017

Mamo KS, Ethiopia: where and who are the World's Illiterates? Available at: http://unesdoc.unesco.org/images/0014/001460/146064e.pdf, last visited on 20 September 2018

Paul, Clapham (1972) Ethiopian constitutional development: a source book, vol I. Haileselassie I
    University, Addis Ababa
Paulos T (translator) (2009) The Fetha Negast: the law of the kings. Carolina Academic Press,
    Durham.
Redden KR (1968) The legal system of Ethiopia. The Michie Company Law Publishers,
    Charlottesville
Sand PH (1971) Current trends in African legal geography: the interfusion of legal systems. Afr
    Law Stud 5
Singer N (1970) Modernization of law in Ethiopia. Harv Int Law J 76
Spamann H (2009) Contemporary legal transplants- legal families and the diffusion of (corporate)
    law. Harvard, John M. Olin Center for Law, Economics and Business Fellows' Discussion
    Paper No. 28
UNDP, Human Development Report 2016. Available at: http://hdr.undp.org/sites/default/files/hdr_
    2016_statistical_annex.pdr. Accessed 24 Oct 2017
UNDP, The 20013 Human Development Report, "The Rise of the South: Human Development in a
    Diverse World". Available at: http://www.undp.org/content/ethiopia/en/home/presscenter/
    articles/2013/03/15/human-development-report-2013-puts-ethiopia-as-third-top-movers/.
    Accessed 7 May 2013
Vanderlinden J (1967) Civil law common law influences on the developing law of Ethiopia. Buff
    Law Rev 16
Watson A (1996) Aspects of reception of law. Am J Comp Law 44:335
World Atlas, Countries of the World by Land Area. Available at: http://www.worldatlas.com/aatlas/
    populations/ctyareal.htm. Accessed 7 May 2017
World Bank, Ethiopia at a Glance 2011. http://devdata.worldbank.org/AAG/ethaag.pdf. Accessed
    12 May 2016
World Bank, Global economic prospects: a fragile recovery. Available at http://www.products.
    worldbank.org/en/710231493655506452/Global-Economic-Prospects-June-2017-Regional-
    Overview-SSA.pdf. Accessed 25 Sep 2017
World Bank Group, 5th economic update for Ethiopia. Available at www.worldbank.org/en/news/
    press-release/2016/12/06/world-bank-group-launches-its-5th-economic-update-for-ethiopia.
    Accessed 25 Sep 2017
www.worldometers.info/world-population/ethiopia-population. Accessed 25 Sep 2017

Chapter 2
Arbitration Agreement: Validity, Lapse and Interpretation

2.1 Arbitration Agreement: Meaning and Relevance

An arbitration agreement is a contract by which two or more parties undertake to resolve their dispute, if any, by arbitration. It has a number of purposes. The first is to oust the state court which would otherwise have jurisdiction to resolve the dispute. The second is empowering an arbitral tribunal to resolve the same, in *lieu* of the court.[1] Third, the parties usually choose the law governing the substance of the contract and the arbitral procedure in this contract itself.[2] Owing to these reasons, among others, the agreement to arbitrate is an indispensable precondition for commercial arbitration.[3]

An agreement to arbitrate may be entered into as regards future disputes or disagreements that have already occurred. The former type is usually contained in the main contract between the parties to a transaction. It is commonly known as an arbitration clause. It is usually brief because the parties do not know, at this point in time, that a dispute will arise.[4] The latter type is called a submission agreement. It is concluded after a dispute has arisen and the parties have made their mind as to how

---

[1]Greenberg et al. (2011), p. 144.

[2]*Id.*, p. 101. In 2009, for example 88% of parties to arbitration before the International Chamber of Commerce, ICC made their choice of the applicable law.

[3]Redfern and Hunter (2004), p. 131. As a matter of exception parties may be deemed to have agreed to arbitration without there being an arbitration agreement. This is, for instance, the case if estoppel or similar other doctrine in a jurisdiction precludes a party from objecting to arbitration because of its failure to raise the absence of arbitration agreement early in the arbitration process. In some jurisdictions there may even be a statutory provision to the same effect as estoppel. *See* Greenberg et al. (2011), p. 145. The question is can such an award be enforced outside the jurisdiction in which it is made given the New York Convention Art II and IV(1)b require proof of a written agreement to arbitrate. The answer is no unless the country in which recognition and enforcement is sought has less stringent requirements than those in the Convention.

[4]Redfern and Hunter (2004), p. 131.

© The Author(s), under exclusive license to Springer Nature Switzerland AG 2021
S. Y. Tesfay, *International Commercial Arbitration*, European Yearbook of International Economic Law 12, https://doi.org/10.1007/978-3-030-66752-8_2

best to resolve the disagreement. Hence, submission agreements tend to be more detailed.[5] The vast majority of commercial arbitrations result from arbitration clauses. Yet, they are often 'midnight clauses' drafted at the very end of negotiations with minimum thought and effort, partly because, at this point in time, the parties are uncomfortable to contemplate falling into a dispute. As a result, wrong choices such as regarding the law applicable to the substance of the dispute tend to be made.[6]

Ethiopian law deals with arbitration agreements in the Civil Code under title XX: 'Compromise and Arbitral Submission'. More specifically, Articles 3325 to 3346 deal with the arbitration agreement *albeit* under the title of 'arbitral submission.'[7] The Civil Procedure Code supplements these provisions. Particularly, some of its provisions deal with the arbitration agreement itself.[8] That being said, it is the Civil Code that defines arbitration and lays down the most important principles of relevance to arbitration agreements.

The law defines an 'arbitral submission' as 'a contract whereby the parties to a dispute entrust its solution to a third party, the arbitrator, who undertakes to settle the dispute in accordance with the principles of law.'[9] Despite the use of the term 'arbitral submission' that suggests otherwise, the Civil Code does indicate that both existing and future disputes may be referred to arbitrators for resolution.[10] Overall, one can conclude that in the parlance of the Ethiopian law, the term 'arbitral submission' is equivalent to arbitration agreement. It is not limited to an agreement to arbitrate a dispute that has already arisen as is the case in the usage of many commentators. In other words, the term 'arbitral submission' in Ethiopia also covers an 'arbitration clause' aimed at resolving a future conflict, if any, by arbitration. Therefore, on this point Ethiopian law has kept pace with global developments in

---

[5]*Id. at 131–132.* Submission agreements tend to deal with details of the arbitration such as place of arbitration, applicable substantive law, name of the arbitrators, specifics about matters in dispute, and may even deal with procedures that the arbitration is to follow such as exchange of written submissions, deadlines etc. . .., where such details are deemed desirable by the parties.

[6]*Id.,* at 132.

[7]Civil Code of the Empire of Ethiopia, Proclamation No. 165/1960, *Negarit Gazeta*, 19th Year No. 2.

[8]Civil Procedure Code Decree No. 52/1962, *Negarit Gazeta*, 25th year, No. 3, Articles 315 to 318.

[9]Civil Code Proc. No. 165/1960, Article 3325(1). Under Sub article (2) of the same Article the Law indicates that an arbitrator may also be entrusted with establishing only a point of fact without deciding on the legal consequences flowing from those facts.

[10]*Id.* Article 3328 titled "object of contract and arbitration clause" provides under sub article (1) an existing dispute could be referred to arbitration while sub article 2 of the same provides parties "may also submit to arbitration disputes which may arise out of the contract in the future." That sub article 2 of this article dealing with disputes which may arise in the future singles out those that 'arise out of a contract' does not mean future disputes that do not arise from contract may not be resolved by arbitration. Sub article 3 of the article clearly indicates that submission agreements regarding future disputes are valid so long as they arise from other 'specific legal obligations.'

arbitration law.[11] The definition is also at par with or even relatively more specific in its articulation of the elements of arbitration.[12]

2.2 Arbitration Agreement: Validity Requirements

The requirements which an arbitration agreement must fulfil are determined by domestic law. That said, one cannot overemphasize the relevance of international requirements if the arbitration agreement deals with an international commercial dispute. Where the latter requirements are not met neither the arbitration agreement itself nor any award made under it will qualify for international recognition and enforcement.[13]

2.2.1 Validity Requirements Under the New York Convention

In seeking to establish the 'international requirements', what comes to mind immediately is the New York Convention, to which Ethiopia acceded on 24 August 2020,[14] as it is 'the single most important pillar on which the edifice of international arbitration rests.'[15] A scrutiny of the validity requirements for an arbitration agreement under the Convention reveals that they pertain to the elements of an enforceable contract. That the Convention takes into account the elements of a valid contract comes as no surprise. The law of contracts generally recognises certain values which take precedence over the value of the freedom of contract. So, where a transaction infringes on values which are deemed of paramount importance, it may be denied contractual force. The objective is preserving the society from the market by denying

---

[11]It is to be noted that, in earlier times many jurisdictions did not enforce arbitration clauses subjecting future disputes to arbitration. Agreement to arbitrate could only be concluded as regards disputes that had already arisen. This was the case, for example, under the Napoleonic Codes of France. *See* Hosseraye et al., p. 333.

[12]The Arbitration Act (of England) 1996, Section 6(1) defines an "arbitration agreement" as an agreement to submit to arbitration present or future disputes (whether they are contractual or not). Article 7 of the Model Law defines an arbitration agreement as 'an agreement by the parties to submit to arbitration all or certain disputes which have arisen or may arise between them in respect of defined legal relationship, whether contractual or not.' *See* UNCITRAL Model Law on International Commercial Arbitration 1985 with Amendments as Adopted in 2006, General Assembly Resolution 61/33 of 2006. The German Law, Section 1029 of the ZPO, defines an arbitration agreement (*Schiedsvereinbarung*) in an essentially the same way as the UNCITRAL Model Law.

[13]Redfern and Hunter (2004), p. 132.

[14]Convention on the Recognition and Enforcement of Foreign Arbitral Awards 1958), commonly referred to as the New York Convention has been ratified by 165 countries as at 23 September 2020. Available at: http://www.newyorkconvention.org/countries, accessed on September 23, 2020.

[15]Redfern and Hunter (2004), p. 133.

enforcement to, for example, oppressive contracts. Besides, even safeguarding the market itself from anti-competitive behaviour of certain economic actors requires denying enforcement to certain contracts.[16]

In any case, the requirements of the New York Convention for the validity of an arbitration agreement can be grouped into those that pertain to the legal capacity of the parties, consent that is sustainable at law, validity of the object of the contract and formality. Particularly, a cumulative reading of Article II (1)(3) and Article V(1)a shows the requirements under the Convention are that:

a) the parties to an arbitration agreement must have the necessary legal capacity under the law applicable to them;[17]
b) the arbitration agreement must be 'valid' under the law to which the parties have subjected it, or in the event the parties have made no stipulation regarding the matter, under the law of the country where the award was made;[18]
c) the arbitration agreement should deal with existing or future disputes, the disputes in question must pertain to a defined legal relationship whether contractual or not, the agreement must not be inoperative or incapable of being performed or 'null and void', and the subject matter of the dispute must be capable of settlement by arbitration;[19] and
d) The agreement must be in writing.[20]

The foregoing requirements must be considered regarding arbitration agreements now that Ethiopia has acceded to the New York Convention. These are the minimum requirements that must be met to trigger the application of the New York Convention.

2.2.2 Validity Requirements Under Ethiopian Law

The New York Convention does not provide in full the requirements for the validity of an arbitration agreement, as can be gathered from the discussion under Sect. 2.2.1 above. In fact, it clearly states that validity requirements are determined by reference

---

[16]Deakin, 'CAPACITAS': Contract Law and the Institutional Preconditions of a Market Economy, Center for Business Research, University of Cambridge Working Paper No. 325, at p. 1. Available at: https://core.ac.uk/download/pdf/7151443.pdf, last visited on 20 October 2018.

[17]This is what one gathers from reading in the positive Article V(1)a of the New York Convention which authorizes denial of recognition and enforcement of an arbitral award where the parties to the arbitration agreement were under some incapacity under the law applicable to them.

[18]These are requirements under Article V(1)a and Article II(3) of the Convention converted into positive formulation. These requirements can be invoked when a party believes his consent was vitiated.

[19]These are requirements that one reads under Articles II(1)(3) and V(1)a of the Convention. All of them focus on the object of the arbitration agreement.

[20]Convention on the Recognition and Enforcement of Foreign Arbitral Awards, Article II(1).

to national laws. The requirements under Ethiopian law can be gleaned from reading Articles 3325 to 3346, part of the Civil Code dedicated to arbitration, and Articles 1678 to 1730, provisions of the same code dealing with the validity of contracts in general. In the part which deals with contracts in general the Civil Code states:[21]

> No valid contract shall exist unless:
>
> a)   The parties are capable of contracting and give their consent sustainable at law
> b)   The object of the contract is sufficiently defined and is possible and lawful
> c)   The contract is made in the form prescribed by law, if any.

The foregoing basic prerequisites for the validity of a contract are an articulation of the values that outweigh the need for recognising and enforcing contracts in Ethiopia. They are similarly stated or otherwise provided for in most jurisdictions around the world.[22] Hence, they need not be discussed in depth. Therefore, in what follows we will dwell on them only in so far as that is necessary for the discussion of the validity requirements of arbitration agreements, especially in view of the requirements of the New York Convention.

2.2.2.1   Legal Capacity and Arbitration Agreement

The capacity to conclude an arbitration agreement may be raised in different contexts and senses. Particularly, capacity may be an issue in relation to physical persons and business organisations. The term 'incapacity' is also used sometimes to refer to a manager or agent acting in excess of his powers, but it is a misnomer in such cases. In what follows attempt will be made to throw some light on Ethiopian law regarding these issues.

2.2.2.1.1   Capacity of Physical Persons

Capacity is a fundamental precondition to the formation of a contract, be that arbitration agreement or otherwise. The term capacity could be understood in two distinct ways. In one sense it is used to refer to the ability to hold rights, which in effect means the right to be treated as the subject of rights rather than a mere object of legal relations. Today the law recognises human beings as subjects of rights from birth. So in the sense of holding rights every human being has capacity.[23] In its second sense the term goes beyond holding rights. It refers to the ability to exercise the rights one holds. When the term capacity is used in the context of the law of

---

[21]Civil Code Proclamation No. 165/1960, Art 1678.

[22]See, Deakin, at p. 1. In common Law jurisdictions, for example, they fall under a rubric of 'public policy'. Though this notion can be deemed to have frozen in its nineteenth century stage of development, social and regulatory legislations have come to complement its objectives.

[23]*Id.*, p. 3.

contract, almost invariably we are using it in this second sense.[24] It is in this second sense that capacity becomes relevant when dealing with arbitration agreements.

In Ethiopia, mostly the full exercise of rights and duties coincides with the capacity to hold rights. As far as physical persons are concerned, the fundamental principle is that capacity is the norm. There must be an explicit legal declaration to that effect for a physical person to be deemed incapable.[25] The Civil Code itself makes this point when it says, '[e]very physical person is capable of performing all the acts of civil life unless he is declared incapable by the law.'[26] Since capacity is presumed, in all spheres of civil life, a person may assume he is dealing with an equal who has full capacity to exercise his rights.[27] In other words, a party to an arbitration agreement who wants to challenge the validity of the contract on grounds of incapacity shoulders the burden of proof.

There are five grounds for incapacity under Ethiopian law. The conditions from which incapacity arises are: minority, judicial interdiction, legal interdiction, nationality and special functions.[28] Yet, two of these grounds exist in name only. Particularly, despite recognising them as grounds for incapacity, the Civil Code does not provide for circumstances in which incapacity results from special functions and legal interdiction. The grounds for the latter were supposed to be provided for under the Penal Code. Yet, the 1957 Penal Code did not impose as penalty limitation on a convict's right to conclude contracts.[29] The Revised Criminal Code of 2004 follows the same approach. It lists down the permissible secondary punishments.[30] Particularly, it provides for the deprivation of only certain civil and family rights and the prohibition on the exercise of a trade or profession where license or authority is required to exercise such trade or profession.[31] It does not impose restrictions on the right to conclude contracts. So, the three grounds for incapacity remain minority, judicial interdiction and foreign nationality, of which the last applies in very rare situations.[32]

---

[24]*Id.*

[25]Vanderlinden (1969), p. 59.

[26]Civil Code Proclamation No. 165/1960, Article 192. The law declares certain categories of persons as incapable on grounds of minority, insanity or infirmity, the exercise of certain functions, foreign nationality and legal interdiction. See on these the Civil Code Articles 194,198, 339, 340–342, 380 and 389.

[27]Vanderlinden (1969), p. 59.

[28]*Id.* at 69.

[29]*Id.*

[30]Criminal Code of the Federal Democratic Republic of Ethiopia Proclamation No. 414/2004, Articles 121 to 128.

[31]*Id.*, Article 123 This Article states that a court may deprive a criminal who has shown himself to be unworthy of the exercise of his civil rights, namely, of the right to vote, to be elected to public office, be a witness, surety and assessor. Similarly, such a convict may be deprived of his family rights, particularly, guardianship and tutorship.

[32]Civil Code of Ethiopia Proclamation No. 165/1960, Articles 194 cum 389 to 393. Foreigners have full capacity in so far as rights and duties under the Civil Law are concerned. The only limitation

In most jurisdictions the rules on incapacity aim at the protection of persons who are deemed to lack the ability to look after their own interests.[33] In Ethiopia too the rules on incapacity of minors and judicially interdicted persons, the only grounds of incapacity that are of significance, have this purpose. The law in Ethiopia provides for the protection of minors and the judicially interdicted by establishing organs of protection that control each other and prevent any abuse.[34] In regard to minors, persons who have not attained the full age of eighteen years, the primary organs of protection are guardians and tutors. The court and a tutor *ad hoc* play specific roles assigned to them by the law to prevent dereliction of duty and abuse by the former two.[35] As a rule, judicially interdicted persons are subject to the same rules of protection as minors in respect of their pecuniary interests.[36]

The law protects minors and persons suffering from mental illness or infirmity by providing for the invalidation of transactions concluded by them. It tries to balance the need to protect minors and the judicially interdicted on the one hand and the protection of third parties in good faith on the other. Likewise, the law seeks to guaranty the safety of legal transactions generally. As regards minors, the law recognises a sphere of activity that is not subject to nullity such as in respect of disposal of income from their own work and acts of everyday life with a view to protecting the rights of third parties that transact with them.[37] The law accords only limited protection to the mentally ill or infirm, if they do not submit to judicial interdiction.[38]

The modality in which protection is accorded to the incapable differs from jurisdiction to jurisdiction. For instance, in Germany the contract is void whereas in England and Wales the contract is mostly void where a minor is involved but it is only voidable in case of mental illness. In France, the contract can be avoided by the court while in the Netherlands even an extrajudicial declaration is sufficient to annul a contract on grounds of incapacity.[39] In Ethiopia, the person affected by incapacity can request the invalidation of the contract. The other party to the contract cannot similarly seek invalidation on grounds of incapacity.[40]

---

pertains to ownership of immovable by foreigners. Under the Civil Code, they are not entitled to own immovable property or have rights that can be assimilated to ownership over such property. Laws issued after the Code have eroded this prohibition. Particularly foreign investors, foreign nationals treated as domestic investors and foreigners of Ethiopian origin may now own immovable property in Ethiopia. See on this Article 24 of the Investment Proclamation No. 769/2012, Federal Negarit Gazeta, 18th Year, No. 63.

[33]Deakin, pp. at 3–4.

[34]Vanderlinden (1969), p. 69.

[35]The Revised Family Code Proclamation No 213/2000, Articles 215, 216, 234, 244 and 245.

[36]Civil Code of Ethiopia Proclamation No. 165/1960, Articles 358, 373 and 375.

[37]The Revised Family Code Proclamation No. 213/2000, Article 263,(2),292, 293 and 301.

[38]Civil Code of Ethiopia Proclamation No. 165/1960, Articles 345, 346(1), 347.

[39]Hesselink (2005), pp. 2, 10, 12 and 13.

[40]Civil Code of Ethiopia, Proclamation No. 165/1960, Article 1808(1).

The actors that engage in international economic transactions are mostly business organisations. Hence, the grounds for the incapacity of physical persons, such as minority and mental illness or infirmity are unlikely to be recurrent issues in the context of international commercial arbitration. So, if the issue of incapacity arises the *ultra vires* doctrine is the more likely ground. We, therefore, dwell on that below.

2.2.2.1.2 *Capacity and* the *Ultra Vires Doctrine*

Though used in slightly different senses, the *ultra vires* doctrine holds that a company has no contractual capacity to engage in transactions that go beyond the objects clause of its statute. Starting with the introduction of limited liability in the mid-nineteenth century, a contract concluded by a company would be invalid if found to be incompatible with the type of business its memorandum shows as the company's business purpose. Not even a unanimous approval by the shareholders would set right this invalidity.[41] The transaction would be void and the contracting party could not enforce such contract against the company. Hence, this doctrine was a pitfall for people dealing with companies especially in jurisdictions whose laws are inspired by English law.[42]

After significant erosion by judicial decisions, this doctrine was given a mortal blow, at least in Europe, by the First Council Directive 68/151 of the European Economic Community of 9 March 1968. This Directive required member states to abolish the *ultra vires* rule to avoid the risk of cross border transactions failing because of its application.[43] The Directive provided: '[a]cts done by the organs of a company shall be binding upon it even if those acts are not within the objects of the company, unless such acts exceed the powers that the law confers or allows to be conferred on those organs.'[44] Overall, this is a dead or at best a dying doctrine in most jurisdictions of significance to commerce. Therefore, today the capacity of a company is not contingent on the objects clause of its memorandum. It is comparable to the capacity of a physical person. Like in the case of physical persons, it is only the law that can impose incapacity, and not a company's own statute.[45]

In Ethiopia, the law requires a company, and even a partnership, to specify in its memorandum of association or partnership agreement, as the case may be, the object

---

[41]Egert (1986), p. 73, The concept was used in two senses: a 'narrower' and 'wider' sense. In the 'narrower' sense a transaction would be *ultra vires* where it is outside the scope of the object expressed in the memorandum of association or which could reasonably be implied as incidental for the attainment of the objects set out in the memorandum. In the 'wider' sense, it was invoked by lawyers to invalidate transactions that do fall within the objects of the company but were actually concluded in furtherance of some other goals.

[42]Yadav (2012), p. 10.

[43]Mitchel and Richard (2010), p. 464.

[44]Griffin (1998), p. 18.

[45]*Id.* Read generally.

or the business purpose of the firm concerned.[46] Ethiopian law is silent on whether a firm can challenge the validity of its own acts on grounds of the *ultra vires* doctrine.[47] The nearest that the law comes to the application of the *ultra vires* doctrine is when the Commercial Code provides in relation to a private limited company, '[w]ithin the limits of the objects of the company, managers shall have full powers.'[48] One may contend that this provision implies exclusion of a company's liability for any act that goes beyond its objects because the company lacks capacity to engage in anything that is beyond its object. In other words, it may be argued that such an act is an *ultra vires* act, not binding on the company. An opposing argument could be made though. Since Article 528 is titled 'powers of managers', and does not mention the capacity of the company itself, and sub-article 2 of the same Article goes on to say that restrictions on the 'powers of managers' cannot be invoked against third parties that transacted with the managers concerned even where the articles of association had been properly publicised, Article 528 does not introduce the *ultra vires* doctrine. It is dealing with the powers of managers rather than the capacity of the company itself. Interpreting this Article as embracing the *ultra vires* doctrine would be reading too much into it.

Even if Ethiopian law embodied the *ultra vires* doctrine, this would not affect arbitration clauses. Submitting disputes to arbitration in and of itself cannot be regarded as the object of a business firm. This is only a dispute settlement mechanism aimed at facilitating the attainment of the business purpose. Submission to arbitration can, in fact, be regarded as reasonably implied in any business purpose. So, even where a contract which contains an arbitration clause otherwise goes beyond the object of a company, say involves engaging in an economic activity not envisaged by the objects' clause, the arbitration clause should stand. This should be the case despite Article 3330 of the Civil Code that in principle denies arbitrators the power to decide on their own jurisdiction.[49] The limitation on arbitrators' powers is when the challenge is directed against the validity of the arbitration clause itself and not the validity of other terms of the contract.[50]

---

[46]Commercial Code of the Empire of Ethiopia Proclamation No. 166/1960, *Negarit Gazeta*, 19th Year No. 3, Articles 284(4), 298, 313(4) and 517(c).

[47]*Id.*, Article 363(1) dealing with the powers of directors of a share company provides that directors shall have powers conferred on them by the law, memorandum of association or meeting of shareholders. Sub-Article 3 of the same provision reads ". . . . Any restrictions on their (directors') powers shall not affect the rights of third parties acting in good faith." As regards the powers of the managers of a private limited company Article 528(.

[48]*Id.* Article 528(1).

[49]Civil Code of Ethiopia, Proclamation No. 165/1960, Article 3330(3) reads "[t]he arbitrator may in no case be required to decide on whether *the arbitral submission* is or is not valid." (Emphasis added) This issue of separability and competence-competence will be discussed elsewhere in detail. Suffice it to say, for the moment, that the prohibition on this point which lags modern arbitration principles does not have the implication of nullifying an arbitration clause just because the main contract is challenged on grounds of the *ultra vires* doctrine.

[50]Separability of the arbitration clause and the rest of the contract is a subject we discuss at length under Chap. 6.

2.2.2.1.3 'Incapacity' as a Misnomer for Lack of Authority to Submit to Arbitration

The term 'capacity' is used in the parts of the Civil Code and Civil Procedure Code dedicated to arbitration in a way that deviates from its core meaning, i.e., the legal ability to hold and exercise rights. Article 3326 of the Civil Code titled 'capacity and form' reads in the relevant part '[t]he *capacity* to dispose of a right *without consideration* shall be required for the submission to arbitration of a dispute concerning such right.'[51] (Emphasis added). The Civil Procedure Code, on the other hand, drops the requirement that the person be able to dispose of the right gratis but still states, '[n]o person shall submit a right to arbitration unless he is capable under the law of disposing of such right.'[52] Despite the use of the term 'capacity' these provisions are not really aimed at protecting persons who have no capacity under the law to exercise their own rights. Rather two other possible purposes come to mind. The first is that these provisions may be understood as dealing with the issue of arbitrability, restricting arbitrable matters to rights that a person may dispose of. In this line of thought, the provisions are meant to state that matters with regard to which only the courts have jurisdiction to decide may not be submitted to arbitration. For instance, under Ethiopian law only the courts may decide on marriage and its effects. The same is true with divorce and its effects.[53] These are not rights a person can dispose of under the law. Therefore, it may be said that a couple have no 'capacity' to submit these matters to arbitration since these are inarbitrable matters. We need not delve into arbitrability here since the next chapter is dedicated to that subject.

The second possible purpose of these provisions seems to be ensuring that an agent, or a person who otherwise act on behalf of others, does not submit to arbitration without a clear authorisation to that effect from his principal. The provisions of the Civil Code and Commercial Code that deal with the powers of agents and managers where power to act on behalf of the principal vested in them is 'expressed in general terms' support this interpretation. In such cases, the agent or manager, as the case may be, will have only the power to discharge 'acts of management.'[54] Particularly, such agent has no powers to effect settlement or

---

[51]*Id.*, Article 3326(1).

[52]*Id.*, Article 315(3) (Civil Code).

[53]Revised Family Code, Proclamation No. 213/2000, Articles 115 and 17. Arbitrability is to be discussed in more depth in Chap. 3.

[54]Civil Code of Ethiopia, Proclamation No. 165/1960, Articles 2203, 2204 and 2204 and Commercial Code Articles 33, 34, 35, 233, 234, 235, 348 deal with this matter. Under the Civil Code 'acts of management' are either acts that are aimed at conservation of property or minor transactions that are deemed of no far reaching consequence on the principal. Particularly, Article 2204 lists as acts of management, '[a]cts for the preservation or maintenance of property, lease for term not exceeding three years, the collection of debts, the investment of income, the discharge of debts' as well as 'sale of crops, goods intended to be sold or perishable commodities.' Though the Commercial Code is not that clear on this point it can be held that 'acts of management' imply more

consent to arbitration under the Civil Code. Express authorisation or 'special agency', in the parlance of the Civil Code, is required for the agent to submit to arbitration.[55]

Where an agent, or a person who otherwise has legal authority to act on behalf of another, has expansive powers so much so that he can dispose of the right for free, he should be able to submit to arbitration. This is what one can gather from the law.[56] The right to dispose of a right for free, being the widest possible right, power to submit to arbitration in regard to that right is implied. In any case, lack of authority to conclude an arbitration agreement on behalf of another person should be treated just as such. It should not be confused with 'incapacity', which is inability to hold or exercise rights emanating from the law.

Regarding 'incapacity' in the sense of lack of authority to submit to arbitration on behalf of another person, the federal courts have taken conflicting positions. In one case, a share company formed by conversion from a public enterprise to facilitate privatisation was involved in a dispute with GTT Trading, its supplier.[57] The contract for the supply of iron bars contained an arbitration clause. A dispute arose and an amicable solution could not be reached. Therefore, GTT petitioned the Federal First Instance Court to compel the share company to appoint its arbitrator per the arbitration clause. The share company contended that neither the company itself nor its representative had capacity to submit to arbitration under the law and the articles of association of the company. A representative of a company needs under the law a special authority to submit to arbitration, the company asserted. Hence, it maintained that there was no enforceable arbitration agreement between the parties. GTT Trading countered this by pointing to Article 12(2) of the articles of association of the share company that vested in the general manager 'power to run the day-to-day affairs' of the company. It argued this provision confers on the general manager sufficient powers to submit to arbitration.

The Federal First Instance Court ordered the company to appoint its arbitrator. According to the court, there is no law which prohibits a share company from

---

powers in the Commercial Code than in the Civil Code. Article 33 of the Commercial Code defined a manager as '. . . a person who has been authorized, expressly or tacitly to carry out acts of management and to sign in the name of the trader.' Article 35 of the same Code states 'in relation to third parties, the manager shall be deemed to *have full power to carry out all acts of management connected with the exercise of the trade*, including the power to sign negotiable instruments.' Emphasis added. Note here that the yardstick for the determination of whether an act is an act of management is whether the act is connected with the exercise of the trade the manager runs and not whether the act is urgent or of no far reaching consequence. The Commercial Code, under Article 235, categorizes an act that 'goes beyond normal partnership practice' as a 'special act' and makes carrying out such act beyond the powers of a manager. This provision lends credence to the position that acts of management mean more in the context of the Commercial Code.

[55]*Id.*, Article 2205(2). (Civil Code).

[56]*Id.*, Article 3326(1).

[57]GTT Trading v. Ethiopian Mineral Development Share Company, Federal First Instance Court, Case No. 59068, (17 February (Yekatit) 1998 Ethiopian Calendar).

submitting to arbitration and the agreement concluded was valid.[58] On appeal, the Federal High Court confirmed the decision of the First Instance Court.[59] Although the two courts did not articulate this point, they found, it seems, power to submit to arbitration is reasonably implied in the 'power to run the day-to-day affairs' of a company.

Discontented with the findings of the courts, the share company petitioned the Cassation Bench of the Federal Supreme Court for review on the ground that the lower courts committed a 'basic error of law.'[60] The Cassation Bench framed the issue as whether the general manager of the company had the power to conclude the agreement to arbitrate. It held that he had no such powers. It reasoned Article 12 (2) of the articles of association of the company that confers on the general manger powers to run the day-to-day affairs of the company is not a sufficient basis to submit to arbitration. Though the powers given imply that the general manger can conclude contracts, they fall short of enabling him to submit disputes to arbitration. This is particularly the case, the Cassation Bench continued, given that the share company had been created pursuant to Article 5(1) of the Privatisation of Public Enterprises Proclamation,[61] and not fully established pursuant to the Commercial Code of Ethiopia. Hence, according to the Cassation Bench, the decisions of the lower courts compelling the company to arbitrate are at variance with the articles of association of the company and the proclamation providing for privatization.[62]

Though the conclusion of the Cassation Bench that the manager had no power to submit to arbitration is correct, the reasoning is less than convincing. The Cassation Bench seems to imply that the general manager would have had sufficient power to submit to arbitration, had this been a company formed under the Commercial Code, and not by the conversion of a public enterprise into a share company. This reasoning is not cogent on two counts. First, as seen above, to submit to arbitration a manger needs either an express authorisation to this effect or power that can be implied from an expansive authority. In other words, if a manager is given power to dispose of rights *gratis* then the power to submit to arbitration in regard to such rights can reasonably be implied from such power.[63] In this case, the manager had not been given power to dispose of rights of the state owned company for free. Secondly, the distinction that the Cassation Bench attempts to draw between different types of share companies on the basis of how they came into existence has no legal basis. Proclamation 146/1998, on which the Cassation Bench purportedly

---

[58]*Id.*

[59]Ethiopian Mineral Development Share Company v. GTT Trading, Federal First Instance Court, Case No. 46254 (February 29, 1999 Ethiopian Calendar).

[60]Ethiopian Mineral Development Share Company v. GTT Trading, Federal Supreme Court, Cassation Case No. 30727 (19 Ghinbot/May 2000 EC).

[61]Proclamation to Provide for the Privatization of Public Enterprises, Proclamation No. 146/1998, Federal *Negarit Gazeta*, 5th Year, No. 26.

[62]Ethiopian Mineral Development Share Company v. GTT Trading Case No. 30727.

[63]This is what we can imply from the Civil Code Provision, Article 3326(1) that says 'capacity' to dispose of the right gratis is necessary for one to validly conclude agreement to arbitrate.

relies, does not stipulate that the general manager of a share company that results from conversion of a public enterprise wields lesser powers than his counterpart in a share company formed under the Commercial Code. In fact, Article 5(1)(3)&(4) of the proclamation clearly stipulate that all the provisions of the Commercial Code apply to such company *mutatis mutandis* except Articles 312(1)(b), 315, 307(1), 311, 347(1), 349. The provisions of the Commercial Code that have been listed as inapplicable to such share company do not have anything to do with the general manger of such company.[64]

At this juncture, it should be emphasised that the Cassation Bench only implied that a general manager of a share company formed under the Commercial Code of Ethiopia would have power to submit to arbitration despite the articles of association only conferring on him 'power to run the day-to-day affairs of the company.' The statement regarding the powers of a general manager of a share company formed under the Commercial Code can only be regarded as an *obiter dictum*. The company in question was not formed under the Commercial Code, according to the Cassation Bench, and the decision was not based on the rules in the code. Therefore, the binding effect of this decision of the Cassation Bench is limited only to share companies formed by conversion from a public enterprise. As a *dictum* it has no binding effect as regards a share company formed under the Commercial Code. So, as the law stands now a manager or agent needs to have either an express authorisation to submit to arbitration or power to dispose of a right for free. Anything short of these does not confer authority to submit to arbitration. There will be 'incapacity' for purposes of concluding arbitration agreements.

2.2.2.2   Consent That Is Sustainable at Law

Unlike courts that derive their decision making authority from the state and vigilantes whose role in doing justice is self-generated, the arbitrator's power emanates from the consent of the parties that are involved in a particular dispute to confer on the arbitrator the power necessary to resolve the dispute.[65] Without a voluntary renunciation, by the parties, of their right to get justice through state courts an arbitrator will have no power in the context of commercial arbitration.[66] For this reason, the consent of the parties to have their dispute resolved by arbitration is an essential element of a valid arbitration agreement.

---

[64]Privatization of Public Enterprises Proclamation No. 146/1998, *Negarit Gazeta*, 5th Year No. 26 and the Commercial Code of Ethiopia Proc. 166/1960. The Commercial Code provisions which the Proclamation makes inapplicable deal with minimum number of founders or shareholders (Art 307(1) & 311(1)), deposit of 25% of par value of cash shares when forming a new company (Art 312(1)b), valuation of contributions in kind (Art 315), and persons who are eligible to become directors and the qualification shares directors should deposit with the company as security for proper discharge of their duties (Art 347(1)&349).

[65]Park (2012), p. 191.

[66]*Id.*

The Civil Code of Ethiopia states that consent which is sustainable at law is a prerequisite for an arbitration agreement, for that matter any contract.[67] The Code reiterates this point when it reads, '[a] contract shall depend on the *consent of the parties,* who define the object of their undertaking, and *agree to be bound thereby.*'[68] We gather from this provision that an agreement to arbitrate must be accompanied by consent to be bound by such agreement. Unless expressly excluded the intention to be bound or *intentio obligandi* should be presumed to exist. Agreements should be presumed to be actionable rather than 'gentlemen's agreements.' The person who alleges he had no intention to be bound, for example, by an agreement to arbitrate, should prove that the agreement was a non-binding type by pointing to circumstances that prove this. Requiring claimants, rather than the defendants, to prove the intention to be bound every time would hinder everyday transactions.[69] That said, the Civil Code does not lay down this presumption. Professor Krzeczunowicz contends judges are free to apply this presumption "by common sense, as a presumption 'of fact', whereby an ordinary contract may be taken, *prima facie* to include the intention to be bound which then need not be proven by the claimant but must be disproved by the defendant."[70]

Consent to be bound by an undertaking to submit to arbitration must be sustainable at law for it to be binding. The consent must be free from vices of consent. If there is discordance between a declaration to submit to arbitration and true will, and such discordance is 'fundamental', then the contract may be invalidated at the request of the party whose consent is defective.[71] The Civil Code regards as 'fundamental' vices of consent: 'mistake', 'fraud' and 'duress'.[72] On top of these, where justice requires that in an exceptional situation, a contract may be invalidated as 'unconscionable' if the consent of the injured party was obtained by 'taking advantage of his want, simplicity of mind, senility or manifest business inexperience."[73] The underlying moral postulate of the foregoing rules is that consent should be true. Other than with regard to an unprovoked basic mistake, the right to invalidate such contract vested in the victim is justified by the other party's immoral behaviour such as misleading the victim by fraudulent behaviour, threatening and exploiting the desperate situation in which the victim finds himself.[74]

Dwelling on consent and vices of consent any further is not necessary as the rules in Ethiopia widely reflect the rules elsewhere in the world on this point. Moreover, these rules are not peculiar to arbitration agreements. They generally apply to contracts, nominate or otherwise.

---

[67]Civil Code of Ethiopia Proclamation No. 165/1960, Article 3325(1) and 1678(a).

[68]*Id.,* Article 1679.

[69]Krzeczunowicz (1996), p. 12.

[70]*Id.*

[71]Civil Code of Ethiopia Proclamation No. 165/1960, Article 1808(1).

[72]*Id.,* Articles 1696, 1698, 1704 and 1706.

[73]*Id.,* Article 1710(2).

[74]Krzeczunowicz (1996), p. 32.

2.2.2.3 Object of the Arbitration Agreement

The object of a contract is the obligation it creates, varies or extinguishes. It is what comes as an answer to the question what a party to a contract owes to the other party. This could be an obligation to procure something, to do or not to do something etc.[75] Therefore, the object of an arbitration agreement is the obligation to submit disputes, if any, between the parties to arbitration. Under Ethiopian law a contract is said to have an effective object if the obligation the agreement creates is defined, possible and lawful. We discuss these below in view of the object of an arbitration agreement one at a time.

2.2.2.3.1 Object of Agreement Must Be 'Defined'

The object of a contract is 'defined' in the sense of the Civil Code if the obligation of the parties can be ascertained 'with sufficient precision.'[76] If the obligation assumed by each party cannot be determined with sufficient precision from the 'terms expressed in the contract and by implication from suppletory law, custom, equity and good faith' the object is not defined.[77] If a contract does not have an effective object it is deemed non existent or void.[78] In such case, no contract exists according to Article 1714 of the Civil Code.

As regards an arbitration agreement, the Civil Code provides that an 'arbitral submission' dealing with a future dispute is valid only if the dispute arises from a 'contract or other *specific legal obligation.*'[79] In a similar language, UNCITRAL Model Law defines an arbitration agreement as a contract for the settlement of a dispute that arises from a 'defined legal relationship whether contractual or not.'[80] On this point the law in Ethiopia is also identical with the New York Convention. The Convention clearly indicates that the 'differences' that may be submitted to arbitration should arise 'in respect of a defined legal relationship, contractual or otherwise.'[81]

The requirement that an arbitration agreement must relate to a specific legal relation, one may hold, is a manifestation of the general rule of the law of contracts that requires the object of a contract be defined. An agreement to submit to

---

[75]*Id.*, at 8.

[76]Civil Code of Ethiopia Proclamation No. 165/1996, Article 1714(1).

[77]Krzeczunowicz (1996), p. 62. Civil Code of Ethiopia Article 1713 reads, "(t) parties shall be bound by the terms of the contract and by such incidental effects as are attached to the obligations concerned by custom, equity and good faith, having regard to the nature of the contract."

[78]*Id.*, at 57.

[79]Civil Code of Ethiopia Proclamation No. 165/1996, Article 3328(3).

[80]UNCITRAL Model Law as amended in 2006, Article 7(1).

[81]UN Convention on the Recognition and Enforcement of Foreign Arbitral Awards (1958), Article II(1).

arbitration any and every future dispute without any regard to the relationship from which it may stem lacks clarity of object required from contracts to be valid. One of the very purposes of an arbitration agreement is to oust the jurisdiction of a national court which would otherwise be competent to resolve the dispute. The requirement of the law that the dispute be related to a contract or specific legal obligation emanates from the need to ensure that the parties have sufficiently clear awareness regarding the waiver of their judicial redress that they make when they conclude an arbitration agreement.[82] One can hold that similar considerations underpin the Civil Code of Ethiopia, the New York Convention and the UNCITRAL Model Law in this respect.

2.2.2.3.2   Obligation to Submit to Arbitration Must Be Possible

Besides being sufficiently clear, the obligation created by a contract must be possible to perform. If "... the obligation of the parties or of one of them relate to a thing or a fact which *is impossible* and such impossibility is absolute and insuperable" then the contract is of no effect.[83] This provision is an embodiment of the Latin maxim *impossibilium nulla obligatio est*—an impossible obligation is no obligation.[84]

The law in Ethiopia treats the impossibility of a contract's object in two distinct ways depending on when exactly the impossibility comes into the scene. In this regard, one takes note of the phrase 'is impossible' in Article 1715(2) cited above. If the obligation cannot be performed already at the time of the conclusion of the contract, then the contract is of no effect. It is simply a void contract. No right can be claimed by either party on the basis of such contract. We may have this kind of impossibility in the context of an arbitration agreement if an arbitrator named in the contract is already dead at the time of the conclusion of the contract unbeknownst to the parties. This agreement simply has no effect and nothing can be done to remedy this situation. Of course, the parties can, if they so wish conclude another agreement appointing a new arbitrator, but that is a totally different story.

Similarly, if the contract provides for arbitration under the auspices of a named arbitration institution that does not exist at all at the time of the conclusion of the contract such agreement will be void or of no effect in Ethiopia. This follows from the provision of the Civil Code that reads '[a] contract shall be *of no effect* where the obligations of the parties or one of them relates to a thing or *fact* which *is impossible* and such impossibility is absolute and insuperable."[85] It is impossible for the parties to discharge their 'contractual obligation' to submit a dispute to arbitration under the auspices of an institution that was not in existence at the time of the contract. No matter what they do or how much effort they exert, an arbitral institution that was not

---

[82]Schramm et al. (2010), p. 50.

[83]Civil Code of Ethiopia Proclamation No. 165/1960, Article 1715(2).

[84]Krzeczunowicz (1996), p. 63.

[85]Civil Code of Ethiopia Proclamation No. 165/1960 Article 1715(2).

in existence will not come into existence. The impossibility is absolute and insuperable.

This must, however, be distinguished from a situation where the arbitration institution is not clearly stipulated or there is ambiguity as to its identity. In such a case, the contract should not be deemed as void just because of this like in some foreign jurisdictions.[86] Attempt should be made to dispel the ambiguity and give effect to the agreement to arbitrate by following the rules of interpretation embodied in the Civil Code.[87] Particularly, the contract should be interpreted with a view to giving effect to the arbitration clause 'in accordance with good faith, having regard to the loyalty and confidence which should exist between the parties according to business practice.'[88] To this end, the 'common intention of the parties should be sought' taking into account the 'conduct of the parties before and after' reaching the agreement to arbitrate.[89] Their 'conduct' regarding the identity of the arbitration institution whose identity is now ambiguous could consist of what they said, wrote, or did before the conclusion of the contract or thereafter.[90] For instance, pre-contractual or post dispute email correspondence may shed light on the common intention of the parties regarding the identity of the arbitral institution.

Impossibility may also be supervening as opposed to original impossibility analyzed above. Where the performance of an obligation that was possible at the time of the conclusion of the contract subsequently becomes impossible we have a supervening impossibility. The contract is not void or of no effect in such a case. The remedy that the law gives is cancellation. According to the Ethiopian law:[91]

> [a] party may declare the contract cancelled, even before the obligations of the other party fall due, where the performance of the contract by the other party has become impossible, or where it is delayed to such an extent that the very basis of the contract is affected thereby.

We find that, in essence, the Civil Code adopts this rule in regard to arbitration agreements too. This can be gathered from a cumulative reading of Article 3337 and 3336. According to the latter, '[w]here an arbitrator refuses his appointment, dies, becomes incapable or resigns, he shall be replaced by the procedure prescribed for his appointment . . . .'[92] Article 3337 clarifies the application of this rule for cases in which the arbitrator is actually named in the arbitration agreement itself. In such a case, the 'arbitral agreement shall lapse' unless the parties manage to reach an

---

[86]Weidong (2010), p. 58. The Chinese Arbitration Law not only requires arbitration agreements to designate arbitration institution as a condition for the material validity of the arbitration agreement but also regards the arbitration agreement invalid if the arbitration agreement is uncertain due to inaccuracies or ambiguities in the naming of the arbitral institution unless the parties choose to conclude an agreement to clarify this ambiguity.

[87]Civil Code of Ethiopia Proclamation No. 165/1960, Articles 1732 to 1739.

[88]Id., Article 1732.

[89]Id., Article 1734.

[90]Krzeczunowicz (1996), p. 85.

[91]Civil Code of Ethiopia Proclamation No. 165/1965, Article 1788.

[92]Id., Article 3336(1).

agreement on a replacement, according to Article 3337(1). So, the parties will not be under an obligation to submit their dispute to arbitration if an arbitrator that had been designated in the arbitration agreement itself dies, or becomes incapable of discharging that function after the conclusion of the agreement. The same results ensue if he refuses to accept the position or resigns.

The UNCITRAL Model law takes a similar position when it provides that an arbitrator's mandate 'terminates', '[i]f an arbitrator becomes *de jure* or *de facto* unable to perform his functions or for other reasons fails to act without undue delay ....'[93] The same holds true for the 'withdrawal' of the arbitrator under the Model Law.[94] One can reach this conclusion from the fact, that like the Civil Code of Ethiopia, the UNCITRAL Model Law provides that an arbitrator is to be substituted, in cases where the legal grounds for that are fulfilled, 'according to the rules that were applicable to the appointment of the arbitrator being replaced.'[95] That means, where an arbitrator had been designated in an arbitration agreement itself, a replacement will be appointed only if the parties are able to agree on the substitute. The law cannot force people to agree. Hence, the arbitration agreement itself lapses, if the parties do not agree on the replacement.

In this connection one notes that while Article 3336 of Civil Code uses the term where the arbitrator is 'incapable' the Model Law uses the phrase if the arbitrator is '*de jure* or *de facto* unable to perform his functions.' The word 'incapable' in Article 3336 of the Civil Code should be understood in a broad sense to include not only cases where the arbitrator is legally incapable but also factually in no position to act as an arbitrator, say, owing to serious illness or other personal challenges. Such an interpretation is consonant with the very purpose of unilateral cancellation for supervening impossibility as embodied in Article 1788 seen above. Particularly, a delay that affects 'the very basis of the contract' is a sufficient condition for the cancellation of a contract under this provision. If an arbitrator designated in an arbitration agreement is bedridden and is, therefore, in no position to discharge his responsibly without delay that affects the very purpose of the arbitration agreement, then he should be deemed incapable within the meaning of the Civil Code for our present purpose.

Another noteworthy distinction between Article 3337(2) of the Civil Code of Ethiopia and the Model Law is that the latter provides for how exactly a controversy regarding *de jure* or *de facto* inability of an arbitrator to perform his functions should be handled. According to the Model Law, any of the parties may apply to the court or another organ that may have been vested with such powers by law 'if controversy remains concerning any of these grounds' for the termination of the mandate of the arbitrator. No appeal lies from the decision of such a court or competent authority on

---

[93]UNCITRAL Model Law, as amended in 2006, Article 14(1).

[94]*Id.*

[95]*Id.* Article 15.

the termination of the mandate of the arbitrator.[96] The Civil Code of Ethiopia says nothing about that.

All the same, if there is a controversy regarding the grounds for the cancellation of the arbitration agreement under Article 3336, i.e., if that the arbitrator declined to act as one or resigned or that he is incapable is contested, then the matter will go to court. That a party to an arbitration agreement can declare cancelation of the contract under specified conditions does not mean that he can act as a judge in his own case, if the grounds for the declaration of cancellation themselves are disputed. Hence, it would be good if the law in Ethiopia provided for how that dispute should be handled by courts. Particularly, it is suggested that the law in Ethiopia should provide that the decision of the court on this point is final, along the lines of the Model Law. This would make sense given that the party that loses in regard to the objection above retains the right to challenge the award on grounds of the lapse of the arbitration agreement even after an arbitral award is made, as will be discussed in the fullness of time. Anyway, the alternative defeats the very purpose of arbitration agreements. It makes a full-fledged litigation lasting potentially for years at the various levels of the court hierarchy a precondition for arbitration.

To go back to the effect of a supervening impossibility, particularly, where the arbitrator is nominated in the arbitration agreement, the Cassation Bench of the Federal Supreme Court has taken the position that the arbitration agreement is cancelled. In Ethiopian *Maritime Transit and Logistics Enterprise v. D.M.C Construction PLC*[97] the parties had concluded a contract for the construction of a building. The contract contained an arbitration clause. Particularly, Article 67 provided that, the Ministry of Works and Urban Development would either act as an arbitrator or designate one for the parties. At the time of the conclusion of the contract the ministry did provide this kind of service. The ministry no longer provided this kind of service when the dispute actually arose. Hence, *D.M.C. Construction* petitioned the Federal First Instance Court to appoint an arbitrator.

The First Instance Court ruled that the parties should appoint arbitrators anew. It reasoned that Article 3336(1) provides another arbitrator is to be chosen in his place, 'where a person appointed as an arbitrator dies or is no longer capable'. . In this case, the court continued, since the entity appointed as an arbitrator no longer renders such service the matter has to be resolved by a different arbitrator. The court further instructed its own Registrar's Office to appoint arbitrators for the parties in case the parties themselves fail to agree on new arbitrators.[98] The Federal High Court confirmed the decision of the First Instance Court. Hence, the *Maritime Transit and Logistics Enterprise* petitioned the Cassation Bench of the Federal Supreme

---

[96]*Id.*, Article 14(1).

[97]Ethiopian Maritime Transit and Logistics Enterprise v. D.M.C. Construction PLC, Federal Supreme Court Cassation Bench, Cassation File No. 80722, (9 January 2013).

[98]D.M.C *Construction PLC v. Ethiopian Maritime Transit and Logistics Enterprise.*

court to review this ruling on the ground that the lower courts committed a 'basic error of law'.

The Cassation Bench found the lower courts committed a 'basic error of law.' It ruled that the courts cannot appoint a replacement arbitrator where the parties had named a particular arbitrator or institution in their arbitration agreement.[99] The more appropriate provision to this particular case is Article 3337 rather than 3336 on which the lower courts relied, the Cassation Bench reasoned. As the arbitration clause indicates a particular arbitrator, and since the fact that the appointed entity no longer provides such service is not contested, the replacement arbitrator can only be appointed if the parties agree to this effect. This has been clearly provided under Article 3337 of the Civil Code. Besides, the Cassation Bench continued, the fact that the parties appointed specifically the Ministry of Works and Urban Development or its designate indicates that they considered this particular entity to have the necessary expertise and knowledge regarding the subject matter. Hence, the appointment of a replacement by the court would be inappropriate.[100] The Cassation Bench's finding and reasoning is consistent with the law in Ethiopia.

An interesting issue that raises its head in relation to an arbitrator's inability or unwillingness to act as an arbitrator is the consequence of such inability or unwillingness on the future of the arbitration clause itself. Since multiple disputes may arise in relation to a single contract, the question arises as to what happens if the impediment to an arbitrator has ceased to exist by the time of, say, the second or third dispute.[101] For example, a person named an arbitrator in the arbitration clause of a contract may be 'incapable' at the time of a specific dispute or may refuse to act as an arbitrator or resign after his appointment as an arbitrator but these circumstance may change when another dispute occurs regarding the same contract. The Civil Code addresses this issue. It provides the arbitration agreement 'shall remain valid in respect of a future dispute where, at the time when it arises, the impediment of the arbitrator has ceased.'[102] That means in regard to such temporary impediments there is no impossibility that warrants the unilateral cancelation of the arbitration clause itself for good. In other words, a party dissatisfied by such temporary impediment to the arbitrator or for that matter the latter's unwillingness to act as an arbitrator or resignation in regard to a specific dispute does not have the right to unilaterally

---

[99] *Ethiopian Maritime Transit and Logistics Enterprise v. D.M.C Construction PLC*, Cassation File No. 80722.

[100] *Id.* The Cassation Bench goes further and says this having been the intention of the parties at the time of the contract, appointment of a different arbitrator by a court would violate Article 3329 of the Civil Code which provides arbitration agreements regarding the jurisdiction of arbitrator are to be construed restrictively. Note though the Cassation Court was right in its finding and reasoning for the most part this last attempt to find yet another justification for its conclusion is wrong. Article 3329 it cites is about the scope of the powers of arbitrators or 'jurisdiction of the arbitrators' in the wording of the said Article. It does not deal with the appointment of arbitrators.

[101] Some of the impediments to an arbitrator named in the arbitration agreement, indicated under Article 3336(1) of the Civil Code are temporary.

[102] Civil Code of Ethiopia Proclamation No. 165/1960, Article 3337(2).

cancel the arbitration clause. The requirements of Article 1788 of the Civil Code are not fully met in such cases. The 'impossibility' exists only in relation to a specific dispute, not future disputes that may arise in respect of the same contract.

2.2.2.3.3   Object of Contract Must Be Lawful

Under Ethiopian law, for a contract to be valid, the obligation that it creates must be 'lawful.' This is a clear implication of the provision that reads, in relevant part, '[n]o valid contract shall exist unless . . . the object of the contract is . . . *lawful.*'[103] That being said, since the object of a contract is freely determined by the parties them-selves the object will be deemed unlawful only when the obligation created by the contract is in contravention of legal restrictions or prohibitions.[104] In other words, since the law presumes freedom of contract, the obligation created by a contract is deemed unlawful only when it is contrary to the rules of public law or mandatory rules of private law. The object of a contract is not deemed unlawful just because it is contrary to the suppletory provisions of the law, 'which may lawfully be set aside by the parties.'[105]

The law in Ethiopia treats a contract with an 'immoral object' in the same way as a contract whose object is unlawful. It states, '[a] contract shall be of no effect where the obligations of the parties *or of one of them* are unlawful or *immoral.*'[106] For the contract to be of no effect, it is sufficient that the obligation assumed by *only one of the parties* is immoral or unlawful. That said, the law does not aim at enforcing all the diverse moral norms of various weight. It is concerned only 'with such a *minimum of morality* in contracts as may be required by common opinion as to what is decent conduct.'[107] One can gather this from the fact that the French master-version does not say 'immoral' obligations but obligations that are contrary to 'good morals' or moral customs which is equivalent to the *boni mores* of the Roman law.[108] Assimilating all moral norms with legal rules would not only be impractical but also would mix up two sets of norms which are not meant to be coextensive.

In sum, an obligation to arbitrate will be of no effect if it is contrary to the law or 'immoral.' In what follows, we will look at specific situations in which an arbitration

---

[103] *Id.*, Article 1678(b).

[104] *Id.*, Article 1711.

[105] Krzeczunowicz (1996), p. 65 KRZECZUNOWICZ. *See also* Civil Code of Ethiopia Proclamation No. 165/1996, Article 1731(2).

[106] Civil Code of Ethiopia Proclamation No. 165/1996, Article 1716(1). For the application of this rule look at sub 2 of 1716 that provides obligations that are perfectly legal taken independently may be unlawful or immoral when they are interrelated or when one obligation is assumed in consideration of another obligation. Also look at Articles 1717 and 1718 of the Civil Code on 'motive' of the parties and how it affects the lawfulness or moral standing of the obligation assumed.

[107] Krzeczunowicz (1996), p. 66.

[108] *Id.*, '*Boni mores*' is a Latin term that broadly denotes 'good public policy or proper moral sentiment.' *See*, Fellmeth and Horwitz (2011).

agreement is deemed unlawful or 'immoral' and hence of no effect under Ethiopian law.

A Party Privileged in Appointment of Arbitrator

Parties to arbitration generally expect the arbitrators to be impartial and independent. Owing to this expectation laws and even institutional rules of arbitration require impartiality and independence from arbitrators. For instance, under UNCITRAL Model Law an arbitrator is expected to be independent and impartial.[109] In countries that have adopted this Model Law rule impartiality and independence are, therefore, legal requirements. Similarly, institutional rules of arbitration such as the Arbitration Rules of LCIA[110] and the rules of arbitration of the American Arbitration Association require arbitrators to be 'impartial and independent from parties.'[111] The ICC Rules too require independence from parties.[112] These requirements are manifestations of the fundamental value that underpins adjudication in general and arbitration in particular—justice.

Where a party to an arbitration agreement is in a privileged position and hence can, for example, pick and choose all the arbitrators the other party is unlikely to expect impartiality and independence. At least, there will be perception of partiality and lack of independence. Ethiopian law provides that '[t]he arbitral submission shall not be valid where it places one of the parties in a privileged position as regards the appointment of the arbitrator,'[113] probably to avoid real and perceived partiality and lack of independence. This brings to mind the discussion regarding a contract with an immoral object. As discussed in relation to Article 1716 (Sect. 2.2.2.3.3 above), a contract that has as its object an obligation that is contrary to a minimum standard of morality expected in the context of contracts is of no effect. An arbitration agreement which, for instance, requires a party to submit to arbitration before a single arbitrator handpicked by the other side or before arbitrators who are all appointed by one party to the dispute will most likely be found, immoral by the standard of the community. Clearly, people will have reason to suspect that justice will not be done in such a case. Hence, this provision which denies validity to an arbitration agreement that puts one of the parties in a *privileged position* as regards the *appointment of arbitrators* can be deemed to be a reflection of the general rule of contracts embodied in Article 1716 of the Civil Code.

---

[109]UNCITRAL Model Law as amended in 2006, Articles 11(5) and 12(2).

[110]The London Court of International Arbitration Rules, (as adopted to take effect commencing on 1 January 1998), Article 5(2).

[111]ICDR International Dispute Resolution Procedures – Arbitration Rules, as amended and effective from September 15, 2005, Article 7(1).

[112]Rules of Arbitration of the International Chamber of Commerce (effective 1 January 1998) Art 7 (1) and 11(1).

[113]Civil Code of Ethiopia of Ethiopia Proclamation No. 165/1996, Article 3335.

Though not framed in an identical language, this kind of rule or sets of rules with similar effect do exist in other jurisdictions. For example, though the Model Law does not directly deal with arbitration agreements that place a party in a privileged position as regards the appointment of arbitrators, it contains a set of rules the interplay of which can arguably have the same effect. On the one hand, it provides for the removal of an arbitrator where '*circumstances* exist that give rise to *justifiable doubts* as to his impartiality and independence.'[114] On the other hand, it provides that where an arbitrator's mandate is terminated on any ground '... a substitute arbitrator shall be appointed according to the rules that were applicable to the appointment of the arbitrator.'[115] Where the basis of the challenge itself is a lack of impartiality or independence because of the very manner in which the arbitrator was appointed, the only certain way to prevent impartiality and lack of independence is to regard the agreement itself invalid. The alternative is to keep on challenging the arbitrator so appointed by one side in the hope that the privileged party finally comes up with an arbitrator about whom no 'justifiable doubts' of impartiality or independence can arise despite such method of appointment. This is not realistic, though not totally impossible.

In some other jurisdictions too an arbitration agreement which gives a privileged position to one of the parties in the appointment of arbitrators would be disregarded. In Germany, for example, a party that finds himself in a disadvantaged position with regard to the composition of the arbitral tribunal because of an arbitration agreement that gives preponderant right to the other party may request a court to intervene. The court may appoint the arbitrator(s) in 'deviation from the nomination made, or from the agreed nomination procedure.'[116] It seems US courts too would intervene where a party is in a privileged position in the appointment of arbitrators. US courts invalidate an arbitration clause where the clause is deemed 'unconscionable' taking into account all factors surrounding it such as the circumstances under which it was concluded, the presentation of the clause itself and the consequences of applying the clause.[117] Particularly, in the Common Law tradition, what constitutes an 'unconscionable' contract is not certain. Hence, it may cover situations where 'the dispute resolution clause designates an unfriendly/hostile jurisdiction, a clause provides biased conditions between the parties and one party is obviously in a disadvantaged situation compared to another. ...'[118]

In sum, one may contend that jurisdictions of significance to international arbitration do not permit a party to be in a privileged position in the appointment of arbitrators. Hence, the Ethiopian Civil Code provision that regards an arbitration

---

[114]UNCITRAL Model Law as amended in 2006, Article 12(2).

[115]*Id.* Article 15.

[116]German Code of Civil Procedure (*ZPO*) of 1998, Section 1034(2), The aggrieved party must make his request to the court within two weeks from the time it became aware of the constitution of the arbitral tribunal on pain of losing this legal redress.

[117]Tang (2014), p. 59.

[118]*Id.*

clause invalid where one of the parties to it is privileged in the appointment of arbitrators is in alignment with the state of the law in other jurisdictions. In any case, this rule is not an impediment to a legitimate commercial arbitration.

2.2.2.4   Form Requirements for Arbitration Agreement

The Civil Code of Ethiopia is indirect in stating the form requirements for an arbitration agreement. The relevant article reads, '[t]he arbitral submission shall be drawn up in the form required by law for disposing without consideration of the right to which it relates.'[119] Hence, having a full picture of form requirements under Ethiopian law of contracts in general and special rules applying to donation is imperative to make sense of this rule. Therefore, attempt will be made to give a synopsis of the state of the law on form requirements regarding these areas in what follows.

The law of contracts starts off with the presumption of *freedom* of form. In the absence of a contrary legal or contractual stipulation a contract exists by a mere agreement provided other requirements in regard to capacity and object are fulfilled.[120] The law indicates this most clearly under Article 1719(1) that reads, 'unless otherwise provided, no special form shall be required and a contract shall be valid where the parties agree.'[121] The law further underscores freedom of form when it says, 'where a special form is *expressly* prescribed by law such form shall be observed.'[122] The use of the term 'expressly' in this provision indicates that any doubt as regards form requirement must be resolved in favour of freedom of form. Form prescribing rules must be construed restrictively.[123]

The foregoing being 'form' requirement, in general, we need to look at the law of donation in Ethiopia. This is necessary because an arbitration agreement is to be drawn in the 'form required by law for *disposing without consideration* of the right to which it relates.'[124] Now, the law dealing with donation states, 'donation relating to an immovable or a right on an immovable is of no effect unless made in the form governing public will (Articles 881–883).'[125] A public will must be written.[126] Moreover, a public will is of no effect unless the person making the will and two witnesses sign it or affix their thumb mark on it.[127] Significantly, one of the two

---

[119]Civil Code of Ethiopia Proclamation No. 165/1960, Article 3326(2).

[120]Krzeczunowicz (1996), p. 71.

[121]Civil Code of Ethiopia Proclamation No. 165/1960, Article 1719(1), *See also* Article 1678(c) of the Civil Code which makes the same point though less emphatically.

[122]*Id.*, Article 1719(2).

[123]Krzeczunowicz (1996), p. 71.

[124]Civil Code of Ethiopia Proclamation No. 165/1960, Article 3326(2).

[125]*Id.*, Article 2443.

[126]*Id.*, Article 881(1).

[127]*Id.*, Article 881(2)(3) and 882.

witnesses must be a registrar or a notary acting in discharge of his duties.[128] The bottom line: an arbitration agreement that pertains to an immovable property or rights on an immovable property must be signed by the parties concluding the arbitration agreement and two witnesses one of whom must be a public official entrusted with this task. Furthermore, the arbitration agreement must be contained in a single document as the law on public will envisages a document that is read to witnesses and signed forthwith.

As regards rights not pertaining to an immovable property the law of donation stipulates, 'other rights and credits may be donated in the *form* governing their *assignment for consideration.*'[129] This brings us back to the law of contracts in general, which as seen above, assumes freedom of form and lists down exceptions to this principle under Articles 1723 to 1725. According to these provisions, any contract relating to an immovable property must be in writing.[130] This provision actually only reiterates the rule we arrived at from the law on donation. It adds very little, if any, to that. The law also requires, '[a]ny contract *binding* the Government or public administration' be in writing and registered with the notary.[131] Similarly, contracts of guarantee and insurance contracts must be concluded in writing.[132] On top of these, memorandum and articles of association of business organizations as well as statutes of associations must be concluded in writing, according to the law providing for authentication of documents.[133] Besides these, where the parties themselves stipulate a written form for the conclusion of a contract, in the absence of a legal requirement to that effect, then the contract 'shall not be deemed to be completed until it is made in the agreed form.'[134]

In sum, the written form is required, under the Civil Code, with respect to contracts pertaining to immovable property, guarantee, insurance, and contracts with Government or public administration. Memoranda and articles of association of business organisations and statutes of other associations too are required to be in the written form owing to another law as discussed. Of these, statutes of not-for-profit associations are not relevant to commerce. Contracts with Government may be relevant to international commerce but they are not that common. So, we can conclude that written form is required for arbitration agreements under the Civil Code in cases of little relevance to international commerce.

---

[128]*Id.*, Article 882.

[129]*Id.*, Article 2445(1).

[130]*Id.*, Article 1723(1) says '[a] contract creating or assigning rights in ownership or bare ownership on an immovable, or a usufruct, servitude or mortgage on immovable shall be in writing and registered with a court or notary. Further sub article 2 of 1723 states that '[a]ny contract by which an immovable is divided and any compromise relating to an immovable shall be in writing and registered with a court or notary.'

[131]*Id.*, Article 1724.

[132]*Id.*, Article 1725(a)&(b).

[133]Authentication and Registration of Documents Proclamation No. 334/2003, Article 5(1), FEDERAL NEGARIT GAZETA, 9th Year, No. 54 (2003).

[134]Civil Code of Ethiopia Proclamation No. 165/1960, Article 1726.

It follows that Ethiopian law is more liberal than the New York Convention and even the Model Law when it comes to the requirement of the written form in regard to an arbitration agreement. Neither the Convention nor the Model Law recognizes an arbitration agreement that is not in 'writing' in respect of any type of transaction. The Convention requires states party to 'recognise agreement in *writing* under which parties agree to submit to arbitration . . . .'[135] The Model law, similarly, requires that an arbitration agreement be in 'writing.'[136] Incidentally, even where the applicable law is Ethiopian, parties to an arbitration agreement are well advised to make the agreement in 'writing' as required by the New York Convention. This is important on two counts. First, playing it safe requires that, especially, if there is some prospect of having to invoke the arbitration agreement outside Ethiopia, for instance, in relation to recognition of the award. Secondly, Ethiopia's obligation under the New York Convention is to recognize agreement in "writing." Sticking to this rule will help the parties avoid costly litigation on the issue of the interplay between the New York Convention and the Civil Code requirements on this subject.

Though Ethiopian law seldom requires the written form, as discussed already, the Civil Code is way more stringent than the New York Convention and Model Law when it comes to the meaning it ascribes to the written form. An agreement that is required to be in writing, it says, 'shall be supported by a special document *signed* by *all* the parties *bound* by the contract.'[137] Besides, it must be attested by two witnesses.[138] These two requirements under the Civil Code made the conclusion of a contract by correspondence of any type, including exchange of offer and acceptance by letters impossible.[139] In particular, it became incompatible with the way business is done in the epoch of electronic exchanges that have become so common with the advent of the internet. Hence, the Ethiopian Parliament passed a 'proclamation to provide for electronic signature' in February 2018. This law states in its preamble that its issuance was necessitated by the need 'to create conducive legal framework to promote electronic commerce . . .' and 'to provide legal recognition to the exchange of electronic messages. . . .'[140] The proclamation recognises electronic messages. The pertinent provision reads '[w]here any law requires that information shall be in writing, such requirement shall be deemed to have been satisfied if such information is rendered or made available in an electronic form and accessible so as to be usable for subsequent reference.'[141] The controlling Amharic version reads where any law requires that any *matter* be in writing rather than any information be in writing. It appears that the Amharic version is broader in scope

---

[135]The New York Convention of 1958, Article II(1).

[136]UNCITRAL Model Law as amended in 2006, Article 7(2).

[137]Civil Code of Ethiopia Proclamation No. 165/1960, Article 1727(1).

[138]*Id.*, Article 1727(2).

[139]Krzeczunowicz (1996), p. 75.

[140]Electronic Signature Proclamation No. 1072/2018, FEDERAL NEGARIT GAZETTE, 24th Year No. 25.

[141]*Id.*, Article 5(2).

than the English version. Arguably, it dispenses with the requirements of the Civil Code that an agreement in 'writing' be contained in a 'special document' signed by all the parties to it and attested by two witnesses. This reading of the proclamation brings Ethiopian law in line with the New York Convention. Under the Convention, an arbitration agreement is deemed to have been made in 'writing' if it is contained in a contract signed by the parties or even if 'contained in an exchange of letters or telegrams.'[142] Ethiopia's accession to the New York Convention has obviated any confusion on this point as far as international commercial arbitration is concerned. An agreement in an exchange of letters or telegrams can be considered as an agreement in 'writing' despite the Civil Code requirements as regards the written form.

The Model Law is even more liberal than the Convention in this regard. An arbitration agreement is deemed to be in 'writing' if 'its content is *recorded* in any form, whether or not the arbitration agreement or contract has been concluded *orally, by conduct*, or by *other means*.'[143] Furthermore, the Model Law provides that an arbitration agreement can be concluded by correspondence of every sort, generously expanding the limited possibilities the New York Convention recognises in this regard. The relevant provisions read as follows.[144]

(4) The requirement that an arbitration agreement be in writing is met by an electronic communication, if the information contained therein is accessible so as to be usable for subsequent reference; 'electronic communication' means any communication that the parties make by means of data messages; 'data message' means information generated, sent, received or stored by electronic, magnetic, optical, or similar means, including, but not limited to, electronic data interchange (EDI), electronic mail, telegram, telex or telecopy.

(5) Furthermore, an arbitration agreement is in writing if it is contained in an exchange of statements of claim and defence in which the existence of an agreement is alleged by one party and not denied by the other.

The UNCITRAL Model Law considers so many things as being in writing that some have dubbed this the 'fiction of written orality.'[145] In fact, this seems to be an understatement since the Model Law goes even beyond oral agreements in recognising agreement by *conduct* as agreement in writing. The 'writing' requirement is effectively fulfilled, according to the Model Law, by certain conduct even at the stage of litigation. Failure to object to the jurisdiction of an arbitral tribunal in a timely manner amounts to an 'agreement in writing' to arbitrate.[146] Effectively, waiver of the right to object to arbitral jurisdiction in and of itself creates an

---

[142]The New York Convention 1958, Article II(2). That means under the Convention the arbitration agreement need not be contained in a single document. It is possible to agree to arbitrate through telegrams or exchange of letters, particularly.

[143]UNCITRAL Model Law as amended in 2006, Article 7(3).

[144]*Id.*, Article 7(4)&(5) (UNCITRAL Model Law as amended in 2006).

[145]Uzelac (2001), pp. 83–85.

[146]UNCITRAL Model Law as amended in 2006, Article 7(5).

arbitration agreement in 'writing.'[147] Given all these things, one may conclude that there is a clear shift, when it comes to the 'writing' requirement, from validity requirement to evidentiary function in the Model Law.[148]

2.2.2.4.1   Effect of Non-Compliance with Form Requirement

If an arbitration agreement must be concluded in a written form because it falls within the few exceptions to *freedom* of form, then, the prescribed form has to be complied with under the sanction of nullity. The law makes this point clear when it says, '[w]here a special form is prescribed by *law* and not observed, *there shall be no contract* but a mere draft of a contract.'[149] Therefore, an arbitration agreement legally required to be in writing will be null and void if it does not conform. The written form is prescribed by Ethiopian law *ad validitatem* and not simply for purposes of proof.[150]

The same result follows where the arbitration agreement is required to be in the written form by the parties themselves. The law states, '[a] contract which the parties agree to make in a special form not required by law shall not be deemed to be completed until it is made in the agreed form.'[151]

2.3   Interpretation of Arbitration Agreements

Parties to arbitration agreements have broad autonomy in drafting and adopting them under virtually all developed arbitration laws and the New York Convention.[152] This party autonomy results in a wide range of arbitration clauses with varying degrees of clarity.[153] Courts and arbitrators alike are, thus, confronted with questions concerning the existence, validity and scope of arbitration clauses.[154] That being

---

[147]Uzelac (2001), p. 85.

[148]*Id.*, at 84.

[149]Civil Code of Ethiopia Proclamation No. 165/1960, Article 1720(2). Note that non-compliance with fiscal provisions such as provisions that require that a stamp evidencing payment of stamp duty be affixed to a contract or failure to pay registration fee do not render the contract null and void, according to Article 1720(2) of the Civil Code.

[150]Krzeczunowicz (1996), p. 172.

[151]Civil Code of Ethiopia Proclamation No. 165/1960 Article 1726.

[152]Born (2001), p. 297.

[153]*Id.*

[154]*Id.*, at 165–166 and 298–299. Other issues that may necessitate interpretation include: whether parties have agreed to arbitration or some other form of dispute settlement like conciliation, mediation etc...; whether or not arbitration is the only and mandatory dispute settlement mechanism or parties are free to resort to litigation in courts; and the question of applicable substantive law.

said, the most common disputes pertain to the scope and coverage of arbitration agreements.[155] This is mostly the case because arbitration clauses of contracts tend to be midnight provisions that are hastily drafted and hence lack clarity. Besides, even seemingly clear clauses generate lots of controversy once conflicts arise.[156] These problems raise the issue of principles of interpretation to be followed concerning arbitration agreements.[157] Hence, arbitration laws and courts in many jurisdictions enunciate some principles of interpretation to be followed in the construal of arbitration agreements.

In Ethiopia too the law embodies a fundamental rule of interpretation applicable to arbitration agreements. The Civil Code states, '[t]he provisions of the arbitral submission relating to the jurisdiction of the arbitrators shall be interpreted *restrictively.*'[158] The implication of this provision is that any doubt regarding the existence, validity and scope of an arbitration agreement is to be resolved in favour of adjudication rather than arbitration. This was the typical approach in the era the Civil Code of Ethiopia was promulgated.[159]

Coming to the construction of arbitral clauses by courts the Cassation Bench of the Federal Supreme Court had to interpret a poorly drafted 'arbitration clause' in *Zemzem Private Limited Company (PLC) v. Illubabour Zone Education Department.*[160] Article 24 of the contract read, 'where the parties cannot resolve their differences amicably a party can get redress by law or arbitration'.[161] When the *Illubabour Zone Education Department* brought legal action before the Illubabour Zonal Court of Oromia Regional State, *Zemzem PLC* objected on the ground that the court lacked jurisdiction because of the arbitration clause. The court rejected the objection. It reasoned that the contract did not stipulate arbitration as the sole dispute settlement mechanism. Hence, it continued, the party that sought judicial redress could not be compelled to arbitrate. The Supreme Court of Oromia Regional State confirmed this decision. *Zemzem* PLC, hence, sought review on cassation alleging the state courts committed a fundamental error of law. The Cassation Bench of the

---

[155]Tang (2014), p. 60. *See also* Born (2001), p. 298.

[156]Delaney and Lewis (2008), p. 344. Moreover even courts could not be consistent on the meaning of identical phrases. For instance, in *Heyman v. Darwins Ltd* the House of Lords concluded arbitration clauses that provided for settlement of disputes arising 'under' a contract as narrower than arbitration clauses that provided for settlement of disputes arising 'out of' a contract. In contrast the House of Lords could not see any difference between the same terms.

[157]Tang (2014), pp. 61–62.

[158]The Civil Code of Ethiopia Proclamation No. 165/1960, Article 3329.

[159]Born (2001), pp. 156–157. Before the sweeping liberalization of 1980s and 1990s resulted in a pro-arbitration consensus, arbitration was deemed an exception to which litigation in courts was generally preferred by lawmakers in most parts of the world.

[160]*Zemzem Private Limited Company (PLC) v. Illubabour Zone Education Department*, Federal Supreme Court of Ethiopia, Cassation Bench, File No. 16896 (1998 EC). The underlying contract was for the construction of a primary school. The dispute that gave rise to this case pertains to the execution of this contract.

[161]*Id.*

Federal Supreme Court found in favour of *Zemzem* PLC. It decided that the state courts committed a fundamental error of law in taking jurisdiction. According to the Cassation Bench's understanding of Article 24, what the parties agreed is, 'to make effort to settle disputes, if any, amicably, and if unsuccessful in that, by arbitration.' This being the agreement between the parties, the state courts wrongly assumed jurisdiction, the Cassation Bench concluded.

Despite its appearance, the foregoing decision of the Cassation Bench does not stand for a broad interpretation of arbitration clauses. The Cassation Bench simply had a different take on the meaning of the arbitration clause from that of the state courts. It did not indicate why exactly its interpretation was correct while that of the state courts was wrong. It, for instance, neither quotes nor even summarises the language of the disputed clause. More significantly, it makes no mention of the Civil Code provision that calls for a restrictive interpretation of arbitration clauses. Hence, it is difficult to maintain that this decision introduces a different understanding as regards the construction of arbitration agreements from that embodied in the Civil Code. It is therefore still correct to conclude that arbitration clauses are interpreted restrictively in Ethiopia.

Ethiopian law is at variance with the laws of the overwhelming majority of states when it comes to the principle of interpretation of arbitration agreements. In states that have adopted the Model Law, for example, arbitration clauses are construed broadly. The Model Law states, '[a] court before which an action is brought in a matter which is the subject of an arbitration agreement *shall ... refer* the parties to arbitration *unless it finds that the agreement is null and void, inoperative or incapable of being performed.*'[162] Some contend, based on this language that any doubt regarding, at least, the scope of arbitration agreements is to be resolved in favour of arbitration, rather than adjudication. Some others go beyond this, and read into the Model Law language a general pro-arbitration bias in the construction of arbitration agreements.

Coming to specific jurisdictions, in Germany, a Model Law country, the Federal Supreme Court (BGHZ) has adopted a broad interpretation at least as regards an arbitration clause underlying a foreign award sought to be enforced in Germany.[163] Similarly, in the United States, the Federal Supreme Court has been generally pro-arbitration in its interpretation of arbitration clauses. In *Moses H. Cone Memorial Hospital v. Mercury Construction Corp.*, it read Section 2 of the Federal Arbitration Act[164] as indicative of a general federal policy favouring arbitration to

---

[162]UNCITRAL Model Law as amended in 2006, Article 8(1) and explanatory note to the same law para. 21.

[163]Raeschke-Kessler (2014), p. 252.

[164]The United States Arbitration Act, Pub.L. 68–401, 43 Stat. 883, Feb. 1925, Article 2 of the Federal Arbitration Act reads in relevant part '... an agreement in writing to submit to arbitration ... shall be valid, irrevocable, and enforceable, save upon such grounds as exist at law or in equity for the revocation of any contract.'

adjudication. It, therefore, ruled that any doubt as to whether a claim falls within the scope of an arbitration clause should be resolved in favour of arbitration.[165]

In matters of international arbitration, some United States courts have relied on Article II of the New York Convention which, according to them, embodies even weightier pro-arbitration bias than the Federal Arbitration Act.[166] The New York Convention states, '[e]ach contracting party *shall recognise* an agreement in writing under which parties undertake to submit to arbitration all or any differences which have arisen or which may arise between them. . . .' Owing to this pro-arbitration bias, it may be argued that:[167]

a) doubts will be resolved in favour of the existence of an arbitration agreement;
b) doubts will be resolved in favour of the validity and legality of an arbitration agreement and
c) doubts will be resolved in favour of interpreting the scope of an arbitration agreement to cover borderline disputes.

Similarly, arbitration agreements are now interpreted broadly in the United Kingdom, unlike in Ethiopia. The UK House of Lords put an end to interpretation techniques that rely on nuanced semantics in the Fiona Trust case.[168] According to the House of Lords, the focus should be instead 'on the commercial purpose of the arbitration agreement and the likely intention of rational businessmen.' This, according to the House of Lords, calls for a presumption in favour of 'a one-stop method of adjudication' . . . that can only be rebutted by clear words to the contrary.'[169] This should be the case, more particularly, in relation to international commercial arbitration. Lord Hoffmann stresses this point when he writes,[170]

> . . . [p]articularly in the case of international contracts, they [parties] want quick and efficient adjudication and do not want to take the risks of delay and, in too many cases, partiality, in proceedings before a national jurisdiction. If one accepts that this is the purpose of arbitration clause, its construction must be influenced by whether the parties, as rational businessmen, were likely to have intended that only some of the questions arising out of their relationship were to be submitted to arbitration and others were to be decided by national courts. . . A proper approach to construction requires the court to give effect, so far as the language used by the parties will permit, to the commercial purpose of the arbitration clause.

---

[165]Koplowitz (2012), pp. 566–567 (2012).

[166]Born (2001), p. 165. Gary B. Born cites the following US cases as examples of pro-arbitration bias banking on the New York Convention: *Riley v. Kingsley Underwriting Agencies Ltd*, 969 F.2nd 953, 960 (10th Cir. 1992) ("null and void' exception is to be narrowly construed"); *Rhone Mediterranee* 712 F. 2nd at 53–54 ("the Policy of the Convention is best served by an approach which leads to the upholding of agreements to arbitrate."); *Samson Resources Co. v. Int'l Business Partners, Inc.*, 906 F. Supp. 624 (N.D. Okla. 1995)("The policy favouring arbitration is 'even stronger in the context of international business transactions.").

[167]*Id.*, at 165 to 166.

[168]Delaney and Lewis (2008), p. 342.

[169]*Id.*

[170]*Id.*, at 345.

The House of Lords underscored that liberal interpretation of arbitration clauses is the norm in international practice. Moreover, Lord Hope emphasised that one should consider the practice in the rest of the world when it comes to international commerce and interpretation of arbitral clauses in the field. In support of this position, he quoted the decision of the Australian Federal Court in *Comandate Marine Corp v Pan Australia Shipping Pty Ltd.* in which the Australian court said that:[171]

> ... a liberal approach to the words chosen by the parties was underpinned by the sensible commercial presumption that the parties did not intend the inconvenience of having possible disputes from their transaction being heard in two places, particularly when they were operating in a truly international market. This approach to the issue of construction is now firmly embedded as part of the law of international commerce. ...

The bottom line is that the Ethiopian law that requires a restrictive interpretation of arbitration clauses is ill-suited to the needs of commerce, especially in the context of international transactions. Hence, Ethiopia needs to align its law on this point with the laws of jurisdictions of significance to international commerce. Particularly, Article 3329 of the Civil Code should be amended to allow liberal interpretation of arbitration clauses to the extent the language of the arbitration clauses permit. This approach poses no grave risk because there are post award remedies, discussed in Chap. 6, in case the arbitration lacks legitimacy because of invalidity or nonexistence of the arbitration clause or the arbitrators exceed their powers. Moreover, recognition and enforcement is not extended to an award that is not based on a valid arbitration agreement or not contemplated by an arbitration agreement under the New York Convention.[172]

2.4 Conclusions and Recommendations

The aim of this chapter has been to discuss the arbitration agreement, and the legal requirements it must meet in Ethiopia. It finds the parties to an arbitration agreement must be capable of contracting and give consent that is sustainable at law. Besides, the object of the contract must be sufficiently defined, possible and lawful. Additionally, the contract must be made in the form prescribed by law, if any. These are pretty much standard requirements for the validity of a contract in many parts of the world. On top of the foregoing, there are validity requirements and rules of

---

[171] *Id.,* at 346.

[172] Civil Procedure Code of Ethiopia Proclamation No. 165/1960. Cumulative reading of Articles 356(a) and 355(1) shows that a party may apply to a court to set aside an award where '... the arbitrator decided matters not referred to him...' Similarly, recognition and enforcement will be denied under the New York Convention 'where the award deals with a difference not contemplated by the parties or not falling within the terms of the submission to arbitration...' according to Article V(1)C.

interpretation that are peculiar to arbitration agreements. The findings of this chapter regarding these follow.

a) A party to an arbitration agreement must have 'the *capacity* to dispose of a right *without consideration* for the submission to arbitration' regarding such right to be valid.'[173] Despite the use of the term 'capacity' this provision is not really aimed at protecting persons who have no capacity under the law to exercise their own rights. The aim is rather ensuring an agent or a person who otherwise acts on behalf of another, does not submit to arbitration without a clear authorisation to that effect. This requirement does not unreasonably impede the conclusion of arbitration agreements.

b) Yet another special requirement is that an arbitration agreement that deals with a future dispute must be specific. Particularly, the dispute must arise from a 'contract or other *specific legal obligation.*'[174] This is a manifestation of the general rule that the object of a contract must be sufficiently defined. It is also consonant with the New York Convention Article II(1), which calls on States Party to recognise an arbitration agreement that aim at submission to arbitration of 'differences ... in respect of a defined legal relationship, whether contractual or not. ...' This is not an unwarranted requirement.

c) An arbitral submission that 'places one of the parties in a privileged position as regards the appointment of the arbitrator' is not valid under Ethiopian law[175] If a party is entitled to appoint the sole arbitrator or all arbitrators without any input from the other party, doubt will be cast on the impartiality and independence of the tribunal so constituted. Without further ado, one may conclude that the prohibition against a party being in a privileged position as regards forming the tribunal is not an unreasonable impediment to arbitration.

d) The arbitration agreement is required to be drawn up in the form required by law for disposing without consideration of the right to which it relates.'[176] That being said, the law presumes freedom of form. It requires written form only with respect to contracts pertaining to immovable property, guarantee, insurance, memoranda and articles of association, statutes of not-for-profits and in regard to contracts with Government or public administration. This rule does not pose particular obstacle to arbitration agreements in the context of international commercial transactions. In fact, it is more liberal than the rules in New York Convention and even the Model Law. Neither of these two recognizes arbitration agreements that are not in 'writing' with respect to any type of transaction.

e) Coming to interpretation, Ethiopian law provides that the provisions of an arbitration agreement pertaining to the jurisdiction of the arbitral tribunal are to be interpreted *restrictively*. The implication of this provision is that any doubt

---

[173]Civil Code of Ethiopia of Ethiopia Proclamation No. 165/1960, Article 3326(1).

[174]*Id.,* Article 3328(3).

[175]*Id.* Article 3335.

[176]*Id.* Article 3326(2).

regarding the scope, existence and validity of an arbitration agreement is to be construed in a way that favours judicial adjudication over arbitration. This rule is ill-suited to the needs of commerce, especially in the context of international transactions. Ethiopia needs to adopt a rule that allows a liberal interpretation of an arbitration clause to the extent the language of the arbitration clause permits.

References

Born G (2001) International commercial arbitration: commentary and materials, 2nd edn. Kluwer Law International

Deakin S, 'Capacitas': contract law and the institutional preconditions of a market economy. Center for Business Research, University of Cambridge Working Paper No. 325. Available at: https:// core.ac.uk/download/pdf/7151443.pdf, last visited on 20 October 2018

Delaney J, Lewis K (2008) The presumptive approach to the construction of arbitration agreements and the principle of separability – English law post Fiona Trust and Australian law contrasted. UNSWLJ 31(1):341

Egert GA (1986) The doctrine of ultravires: recent developments. QLD Inst Technol Law J 73

Fellmeth AX, Horwitz M (2011) Guide to Latin in international law. Oxford University Press

Greenberg S et al (2011) AL international commercial arbitration: an Asia Pacific perspective. Cambridge University Press

Griffin S (1998) The rise and fall of the ultra vires rule in corporate law. MJLS 2(1):5–31

Hesselink M (2005) Capacity and capability in European contract law. Amsterdam Center for Law and Economics, Working Paper No. 2005-09. Available at http://ssrn.com/paper=869246. Accessed 04 Dec 2014

Hosseraye J et al. Arbitration in France, CMS Guide to Arbitration, vol I

Koplowitz E (2012) "I Did Not Agree to Arbitrate That!"- how courts determine if employees' sexual assault and harassment claims fall within the scope of broad mandatory arbitration clauses. CJCR 13:565

Krzeczunowicz G (1996) Formation and effects of contracts in Ethiopian law. Faculty of Law, Addis Ababa University

Mitchel QCG, Richard (2010) English law of contracts, foreign counterparties and ultra vires. BJIB & F Laws 8:464

Park W (2012) Arbitration of international business disputes, 2nd edn. Oxford University Press

Raeschke-Kessler H (2014) Germany in James H Carter (ed)

Redfern A, Hunter M (2004) Law and practice of international commercial arbitration, 4th edn. Sweet and Maxwell, London

Schramm D et al (2010) In: Kronke H et al (eds) Recognition and enforcement of foreign arbitral awards: a global commentary on The New York Convention. Walters Kluver, Austin

Tang Z (2014) Jurisdiction and arbitration agreements in international commercial law. Routledge, Taylor & Francis Group

Uzelac A (2001) The form of arbitration agreement and the fiction of written orality: how far should we go? Croat Arbit Yearb 8:83–107

Vanderlinden J (1969) The law of physical persons. Haile Sellassie I University, Addis Ababa

Weidong Z (2010) Determining the validity of arbitration agreements in China: towards new approach. AIAJ 6

Yadav HR (2012) Doctrine of Ultra Vires Under Companies Act 1956: An Abstract of Doctoral Dissertation Submitted to Maharshi Dayanand University, Rohtak, 10. Available at: http:// shodhganga.inflibnet.ac.in/bitstream/10603/9793/17/17_summary.pdf. Accessed 14 Feb 2015

Chapter 3
Arbitrability

3.1 Arbitrability: Its Various Shades of Meaning

Without going into the nuances, 'arbitrability' concerns whether a dispute may be settled by arbitration.[1] A closer look, however, reveals that the term arbitrability is used in different senses. In some jurisdictions and international instruments it is understood as a '*ratione materiae*' notion, also referred to as 'objective' arbitrability. In other systems, it is a '*ratione personae*' notion, referred to as 'subjective' arbitrability.[2] In yet others, particularly in the United States, the term arbitrability is used in a much wider sense besides the foregoing. It covers the whole set of 'gateway' questions that help answer whether an *arbitrator* or a *court* has the power to decide 'if a given dispute should be submitted to arbitration.'[3] The gateway questions that help determine arbitrability, in this broader United States sense include:[4] (a) whether there is a valid arbitration agreement; (b) whether the dispute in question falls within the scope of the arbitration agreement and (c) whether public policy bars submission of the dispute to arbitration despite the foregoing two questions being answered in favour of arbitration.

Traditionally, at least in the United States, the arbitrators had no power to entertain these gateway questions. The court answered them first. It determined 'arbitrability' in the broader United States sense.[5] This follows from the fact that in the United States, unlike in other pro-arbitration jurisdictions, arbitrators have no competence to decide on the issue of their own jurisdiction if the validity of the *arbitration clause itself* is challenged.[6] Hence, whether the dispute in question is

---

[1]Greenberg et al. (2011), p. 182.

[2]Di Pietro (2009), p. 91.

[3]Shore (2009), p. 70.

[4]*Id.*

[5]*Id.*

[6]*Id.*, at 7.

© The Author(s), under exclusive license to Springer Nature Switzerland AG 2021
S. Y. Tesfay, *International Commercial Arbitration*, European Yearbook of International Economic Law 12, https://doi.org/10.1007/978-3-030-66752-8_3

'arbitrable' or not has to be decided by a court. So, in this broad sense arbitrability is a jurisdictional issue. We will not deal with arbitrability in this broad United States sense of the term in this chapter. That will be discussed in Chap. 5, which dwells on the power of arbitrators to decide on jurisdictional issues.

3.2 Determination of Arbitrability: The Place of Domestic Law

Parties to a contract have no absolute freedom to agree to settle every type of dispute by arbitration.[7] On this much everyone agrees. Opinion is, however, divided as regards the arbitrability of specific issues. Similarly, there is no consensus on whether arbitrability should be determined by reference to domestic law alone or by using a transnational approach, especially by arbitrators.[8]

In the more traditional approach, determination of matters that are arbitrable remains essentially a domestic matter.[9] The argument in support of this viewpoint is that the delimitation of the scope of arbitrable claims entails critical policy decision which involves matters that are beyond purely legal.[10] It is an exercise that requires essential reflection of a pragmatic nature, and calls for legislative or judicial balancing of competing policy considerations.[11] Therefore, lawmakers and even courts reserve the settlement of certain disputes that implicate public interest to community officials, i.e., ordinary courts or special tribunals established by law.[12] These considerations make the determination of arbitrability a national matter, according to the more traditional approach.

Proponents of the traditional approach point in support for their view to the fact that arbitrability remains a subject with regard to which the harmonisation of arbitration rules remains the lowest.[13] The New York Convention does not, for example, attempt to define what subject matters are arbitrable.[14] In fact, it indicates that the court of the jurisdiction in which the recognition and enforcement of an award is sought may refuse to recognise and enforce the award where it determines the subject matter of the dispute is not arbitrable 'under the law of that country.'[15] The UNCITRAL Model Law on International Commercial Arbitration too attempts

---

[7]Reisman et al. (1997), p. 304.

[8]Lehmann (2004), pp. 756 and 761.

[9]Youssef (2009), p. 48.

[10]Id.

[11]Id.

[12]Reisman et al. (1997), p. 304.

[13]Youssef (2009), p. 48.

[14]Di Pietro (2009), pp. 91–92.

[15]United Nations Convention on Recognition and Enforcement of Foreign Arbitral Awards (1958), Article The New York Convention of 1958, V(2)a.

no delimitation of arbitrable matters. On the contrary, Article 1(5) shows that the Model Law is not intended to affect the laws of the state that preclude certain disputes from the domain of arbitration. From this, the proponents of the traditional approach conclude that national legislators and courts are left free to delimit on their own the boundaries of arbitrable matters.[16]

In contrast, the proponents of the transnational approach maintain that arbitrability may be determined, especially by arbitrators, by reference to transnational legal principles. These are, 'general principles of law that have been recognized by a number of legal systems' that we arrive at by distilling the rules on arbitrability in several jurisdictions from different legal traditions.[17] The transnational approach is justified, it is maintained, because in international arbitration 'by definition, more than one law can determine whether arbitration can actually take place or not. Instead of picking one of those laws, the arbitrator can and should explore the content of more than one law . . . .'[18] This comparative analysis of a number of legal systems from across legal traditions will reveal that there are underlying principles by reference to which arbitrability may be determined.[19] Such analysis reveals that there is agreement, at least, on two points according to the proponents of the transnational approach. Firstly, that there exists 'a strong presumption in favour of arbitrability' in international cases is beyond contention.[20] Secondly, and more importantly, 'arbitrability is not excluded by the fact that the dispute is permeated by public policy or the applicability of mandatory law.'[21]

That being said, even the proponents of the transnational approach concede that the question of 'arbitrability cannot be resolved once and for all by one clear-cut rule.'[22] They agree that national laws have a role to play in the determination of arbitrability.[23] It follows, therefore, that those considering arbitration that may potentially come into contact with Ethiopia need to understand how exactly the law in Ethiopia delimits the domain of arbitration. Hence, an attempt will be made in this chapter to explore how arbitrability is understood and the current map of matters that are off-limits for arbitration, if any, in Ethiopia.

---

[16]Mistelis (2009), p. 11.
[17]Lehmann (2004), p. 775.
[18]Id. 770–771.
[19]Id., 764 and 770.
[20]Id., 771.
[21]Id.
[22]Id., 773.
[23]Id.

3.3   Arbitrability as a *'Ratione Materiae'* Notion

National laws do often impose restrictions on the kind of *matters* that can be referred to arbitration. So, in one sense, arbitrability involves the question of whether a 'specific class of disputes' or 'types of issues' can be settled by arbitration.[24] Hence, at the core of arbitrability in this sense is the subject matter of the dispute. Arbitrability understood this way is referred to as 'objective' arbitrability.[25] This is in contradistinction to 'subjective' arbitrability wherein the law focuses on the identity of the parties to a dispute rather than the subject matter of the dispute and limits the involvement of such parties in arbitration. Understood in this latter sense arbitrability is a *'ratione personae'* notion which we will discuss in the section that follows this one.[26]

To come back to 'objective' arbitrability, as recently as a few decades back states and their courts allowed limited scope for arbitration. Particularly, both legislators and courts looked at matters that could be arbitrable through the prism of 'public policy.' In consequence, 'private rights that were entangled with elements of public interest or those that involved public law' were deemed inarbitrable matters.[27]

The limited scope for arbitrability, in particular, its entanglement with public policy was the result of different concerns.'[28] Public policy related concerns that explain the restrictions on the subject matter that can be settled by arbitration may be grouped into three categories.[29]

The first category pertains to the arbitral procedure and its implication on due process. The contention is that arbitration involves less fact finding compared to proceedings in court and hence evidential proceedings in arbitration are not rigorous enough to guarantee a fair and reliable outcome.[30] That the proceedings are private and confidential compounds the problem. Moreover, it is held that arbitral awards are either not reasoned or insufficiently reasoned. That the award made under such situation is generally final and binding exacerbates the matter. It is maintained, therefore, that the arbitral procedure does not guarantee due process and hence matters that involve public policy rules should be inarbitrable.[31]

The second category of reservations on arbitrability stems from the opinion about arbitrators themselves. In some corners, there is doubt regarding the *'ability* of arbitrators to correctly apply public policy rules.'[32] Courts are seen as more

---

[24]Mistelis (2009), p. 4.

[25]*Id.* at 3–4.

[26]Di Pietro (2009), p. 91.

[27]Youssef (2009), p. 50.

[28]Brekoulakis (2009), pp. 21–22.

[29]*Id.*, at 23–30.

[30]*Id.*, at 23.

[31]*Id.*, at 24–25.

[32]*Id.*, at 26.

competent in this regard.[33] Another, but related concern, results from the perception that arbitrators as 'private judges' are by nature in alliance with the interest of private corporations. Since they are in bed with powerful private economic interests, it is maintained, arbitrators are reluctant to take into account, or 'even acknowledge' the legitimate interests of the economically weak, for instance, consumers and employees.[34]

The third concern emanates from the fact that the parties to an arbitration agreement are free to choose the applicable law and the forum in which arbitration takes place. Hence, it is feared that they can make use of the choice-of-law and choice-of-forum rules of arbitration to totally evade the application of the laws of a country including the mandatory provisions of public policy nature that would have otherwise been applicable to the dispute.[35] Therefore, the most valid concern according to Brekloulakis, is that whether arbitrators will *'ever actually apply* the public policy or mandatory provisions of a national law, rather than whether arbitrators *are fit* to apply them.'[36]

Public policy concerns raised above are not the only grounds for limiting the scope of arbitrability. Another theory that underpins the inarbitrability of certain types of disputes stems from the inherent limitation of arbitration as a dispute settlement mechanism. A person must give consent to settle a dispute by arbitration.[37] That arbitration is a consent-based mechanism of dispute settlement has impact on the arbitrability of certain category of disputes.[38] In particular, if an arbitral award concerning a dispute between the parties to arbitration can affect the rights of third parties that did not consent to arbitration, owing to the nature of the subject matter in dispute, then this type of dispute is deemed inarbitrable. For example, in Europe if a dispute between the parties to an arbitration agreement involves the validity and registration of a patent, this is a matter for the exclusive jurisdiction of the court at the place of registration of the patent in dispute.[39] One line of thinking behind this kind of law is that the exclusivity right that results from the registration of a valid patent has *erga omnes* effect, i.e., it is against all people, though some question the validity of this contention.[40]

Owing to the foregoing concerns, and real as well as perceived limitations of arbitration, only few subject matters were arbitrable as recently as few decades ago. Developments on this subject will be raised below in the context of discussing Ethiopian law on objective arbitrability, as the focus of this work is on Ethiopia.

---

[33]*Id.*

[34]*Id.*, at 26–27.

[35]*Id.*, at 30.

[36]*Id.*

[37]Courtney (2009), p. 585.

[38]Brekoulakis (2009), pp. 32–33.

[39]Mistelis (2009), p. 7.

[40]Mantakou (2009), p. 296.

3.3.1 The Scope of 'Objective' Arbitrability in Ethiopia

It is not easy to list down subject matters that are inarbitrable in the Ethiopian context. This is so because the law does not expressly deal with the issue of 'objective' arbitrability. Moreover, one does not come across court cases dealing with 'objective' arbitrability as opposed to subjective arbitrability which will be discussed later. We cannot, however, conclude from this that literally any subject matter is arbitrable in Ethiopia. Certain types of disputes are not amenable to arbitration because arbitration is a consent-based dispute settlement mechanism. The interests of those who have agreed to arbitrate and those that have not may be entangled in a single dispute raising the issue of arbitrability. Moreover, there are certain types of disputes that are so deeply immersed in public policy that they are off-limits for arbitration at least in some jurisdictions. Hence, given the chance courts in Ethiopia are likely to examine whether an award would have impact on the rights of third parties or the dispute implicates core public policy issues making the subject matter inarbitrable.

Besides, the law need not expressly provide in statutes for matters that are not arbitrable. Exclusion from the domain of 'objective' arbitrability may also result from the conferral of exclusive jurisdiction in respect of certain matters on specialised tribunals or national courts.[41] In Ethiopia there are some types of disputes with respect to which the law bestows exclusive jurisdiction on courts. Cases in point are disputes pertaining to family and status. For instance, the Revised Family Code provides that only courts may determine whether a marriage has been concluded, pronounce divorce, and decide on the effects of dissolution of marriage such as the custody of children.[42]

In what follows an attempt will be made to throw some light on subject matters whose arbitrability is uncertain in Ethiopia. In-depth discussion of the objective arbitrability of each and every area of law is clearly beyond the scope of this work. The purpose here is only to alert business people and their legal advisors considering arbitration under Ethiopian law of possible pitfalls and also to hint areas that need legal reform. The focus will be on categories of disputes that are of particular interest to international commercial arbitration.

---

[41]Mistelis (2009), p. 11.

[42]The Revised Family Code Proclamation No. 2013/2000, *Federal Negarit Gazeta*, 6th Year, Extraordinary Issue No. 1, Articles 83(3), 115 and 117. Similarly, 'only a court is competent to decide whether an irregular union has been established between a man and a woman" according to Article 116 of the same Family Code.

3.3.1.1 Bankruptcy and Its Impact on Arbitrability

Bankruptcy and arbitration are two legal procedures with dissimilar objectives and underlying policies.[43] Bankruptcy law is designed to serve the primary purpose of ensuring the highest possible return for creditors *as a group* from the debtor's remaining assets. Besides, it aims at ensuring that no creditor benefits unfairly at the expense of other creditors.[44] Accomplishing the latter of these two objectives requires preventing debtors and creditors alike from engaging in any conduct that would allow a creditor to improve its relative position *vis-à-vis* other creditors such as repossession of the debtor's assets and individual pursuit of legal remedies.[45]

To attain the foregoing core goals, the bankruptcy law of Ethiopia imposes automatic stay on collection efforts by creditors so that their claims are addressed within the bankruptcy process together. To implement this, the law requires the bankrupt debtor to cede control over his business and its assets to the trustee who administers them under the supervision of the commissioner in bankruptcy.[46] Creditors are collectively involved, through the instrumentality of the creditors' committee in the verification of claims against the bankrupt.[47] The declaration of bankruptcy by a court also suspends all individual suits by unsecured creditors. Unsecured creditors will not be able to attach the debtor's property, be that movable or immovable property.[48]

Moreover, to attain the foregoing objectives, the court which declared the debtor bankrupt assumes 'jurisdiction to hear all claims arising in bankruptcy, unless there be claims *in rem* concerning immovable property which remains subject to the ordinary rules relating to jurisdiction.'[49] The Ethiopian court that declared bankruptcy assumes jurisdiction 'notwithstanding that the principal place of business is abroad and a foreign court has exercised bankruptcy jurisdiction.'[50] The Ethiopian court will have no such jurisdiction only if there is an international convention to which Ethiopia is a party that provides otherwise.[51] No convention to which Ethiopia is a party denying jurisdiction to Ethiopian courts in such situation could be found.

---

[43]Liebscher (2009), p. 165.

[44]Kirgis, Arbitration, Bankruptcy, and Public Policy: A Contractarian Analysis at p. 3. Available at: http://pon.harvard.edu/wp-content/uploads/images/posts/kirgis-wip-article-pdf.pdf, Accessed on 20 March 2015.

[45]*Id.*

[46]Commercial Code of the Empire of Ethiopia, Proclamation No. 166/1960, *Negarit Gazeta*, 19th Year, No. 3, Articles 995(1), 1018 and 1023.

[47]*Id.*, Article 1043.

[48]*Id.*, Article 1025(1) and 1026. The claims of all creditors who have no special privilege such as pledge and mortgage fall within what the law calls universality of creditors that is vested by the law with legal personality and represented by the trustee.

[49]*Id.*, Article 990.

[50]*Id.*, Article 974.

[51]*Id.* Article 974(2) *(Com Code)*.

In sum, the basic goal of bankruptcy law is the centralization of disputes concerning the debtor so they are settled by one court in charge of the bankruptcy often by summary procedure rather than adversarial proceedings. In contrast, the objective of arbitration agreements is the removal of issues concerning the debtor from the jurisdiction of the bankruptcy court and the resolution of the disputed matters before a more adversarial arbitral forum.[52] Therefore, the objective of arbitration agreements and bankruptcy law's goal of centralization are on a collision course.[53] Particularly, three main situations provide good examples of the most common conflicts between arbitration and bankruptcy law. In the first type of case, a trustee sues the counterparty to a contract with the bankrupt debtor to recover money, say, for breach of contract or fraud. The counterparty demands the enforcement of an arbitration clause in the contract in order to avoid the jurisdiction of the bankruptcy court.[54]

The second scenario for conflict between arbitration and bankruptcy law comes into play because under Ethiopian law the bankruptcy court can invalidate transactions concluded by a bankrupt debtor during a suspect period, which could go back as much as two years from the date of declaration of bankruptcy. The trustee can demand invalidation of a transaction concluded during the suspect period where it appears that the transaction was motivated to benefit some creditors at the expense of others or to defraud creditors in general by gratuitous transfers to relatives or friends, for example.[55] The trustee can file a preference action, in the parlance of United States bankruptcy lawyers, against one of the debtor's counterparties to invalidate transfers made to the latter prior to the declaration of bankruptcy. In such situation, the counterparty usually moves to enforce the arbitration clause, if any, while the trustee prefers to have the matter decided by the bankruptcy court.[56]

In the third type of cases, the trustee rejects to perform the obligations under a contract. Hence, the counterparty to the contract seeks to enforce an arbitration clause in the contract to determine the damages resulting from the non-performance of the contract. The trustee, on the other hand, prefers the bankruptcy court to arbitration tribunal for the determination of the compensation due.[57] Hence, a conflict between bankruptcy law and arbitration arises.

---

[52]Liebscher (2009), p. 166.

[53]Salzberg and Zinkgraf, *When Two Worlds Collide: The Enforceability of Arbitration Agreements in Bankruptcy*, at 2, available at http://www.foley.com/files/publication/1020c6f0-d08d-4aee-82c7-b282fe0c221a/presentation/publicationattachment/a4edde0a-8a1f-4ea5-bc57-b9a0ccdf4958/salzberg-zinkgraf.pdf, accessed on March 20, 2015.

[54]Kirgis, Arbitration, Bankruptcy, and Public Policy: A Contractarian Analysis, p. 3. Available at: http://pon.harvard.edu/wp-content/uploads/images/posts/kirgis-wip-article-pdf.pdf, Accessed on 20 March 2015.

[55]Commercial Code of Ethiopia, Proclamation No. 166/1960, Articles 977, 978, 1029, 1030, 1031, 1032, 1033 and 1034.

[56]Kirgis, *supra* note 54, p. 14.

[57]*Id.*, p. 15.

In sum, since the parties may in principle agree to arbitrate any contractual dispute, for that matter any other dispute, virtually any relationship can become the subject of a dispute in the context of bankruptcy. Hence, arbitration and bankruptcy can collide in nearly limitless situations.[58] Therefore, the need for determining the domain of arbitration by striking an optimal balance between the objectives behind these two areas of law cannot be overemphasized.

3.3.1.2 The Interplay of Arbitration and Bankruptcy in Ethiopia

Though the bankruptcy law of Ethiopia envisages arbitration as a possibility it does not address the whole spectrum of contexts in which the issue of arbitrability may arise. The only provision of the bankruptcy law that deals with arbitration and compromise reads as follows:

Article 1038 Compromise and arbitration
(1) *After taking the opinion of the creditors' committee and after hearing the bankrupt, whether he presents himself of his own motion or on being summoned by registered letter, the commissioner may authorise the trustees to compromise and arbitrate in respect of any claim concerning the bankrupt estate.*
(2) *Where the value of the subject matter of the compromise or arbitration is not determined or exceeds the jurisdiction of the trustees, the compromise or arbitration shall be ratified by the court.*
(3) *The bankrupt shall be summoned to attend the ratification proceedings and may make an application to set aside the compromise or arbitration.*

This provision envisages the possibility of entering into an agreement to arbitrate after the declaration of bankruptcy as regards *any claim* with the authorisation of the commissioner in bankruptcy. The bankrupt debtor himself has the right to apply for the setting aside of the decision to arbitrate as can be gathered from sub-article 3 of Article 1038. In short, this article seems to grant the option of settling by arbitration or compromise cases where the existence or validity of a claim by an alleged creditor is in dispute. Bankruptcy laws in some other jurisdictions give similar option for the settlement of this kind of disputes. In Austria for instance, such contested claims are arbitrable according to the prevailing opinion.[59]

In what follows we will briefly dwell on how other jurisdictions attempt to reconcile the conflict between arbitration and bankruptcy law. The hope is that familiarity with how other jurisdictions handle the challenge may help Ethiopian courts tackle the problem till a statutory solution is found.

---

[58]*Id.*, p. 13.
[59]Liebscher (2009), p. 169.

3.3.1.3   Arbitration v. Bankruptcy: The US Approach

No statutory solution has been provided for the underlying tension between the Bankruptcy Code and the Federal Arbitration Act (FAA) in the United States. The conflict between the two has, however, been the subject of litigation before courts which have attempted to balance the competing policy considerations behind the two areas of law. Particularly, United States courts up to the level of Circuit Courts have grappled with this matter and attempted to balance the clear public policy in favour of arbitration on which the FFA is premised with the concerns and policies that underlie the Bankruptcy Code.[60] This, they have done by relying on the test that the Supreme Court developed in the *McMahon* case though that case did not involve a conflict between arbitration and bankruptcy. In that case, the Supreme Court held that a party that wants to avoid arbitration of rights arising under a federal statute must established that when passing the particular law Congress *intended to make an exception* to the application of the Federal Arbitration Act as regards disputes that may arise under that statute.[61]

The United States Supreme Court expounded on the foregoing holding in *Shearson/American Express, Inc V. McMahon*. It held that the intention of Congress to make an exception to the FAA can be established from: (a) the statute's text itself, or (b) the statute's legislative history, or (c) demonstration of 'an inherent conflict between arbitration and the statute's underlying history.'[62] The problem is that neither the Bankruptcy Code itself nor its legislative history indicates that Congress intended to make an exception to the application of the Federal Arbitration Act.[63] Therefore, United States courts can rely only on the third segment of the test in Shearson v. *McMahon*. In particular, they may inquire into whether there is an inherent conflict between the Bankruptcy Code and the FAA. Hence, the party objecting to arbitration has to demonstrate to the satisfaction of the court that Congress when passing the Bankruptcy Code intended to preclude a waiver of judicial remedies in respect of the specific right(s) at issue arising from the Bankruptcy Code.[64] Particularly, 'there must be a demonstrated specific conflict between enforcing an arbitration clause and the textual provisions and/or purposes of the Bankruptcy Code to justify the exercise of discretion by a bankruptcy court in refusing to enforce an arbitration clause.'[65]

In applying the 'inherent conflict' test many United States courts have concentrated on whether the claim sought to be arbitrated is 'core' or 'non-core.'[66] Particularly, the substantive right concerned must be grounded or made possible

---

[60]Salzberg and Zinkgraf, *supra* note 53, p. 2.

[61]*Id.*

[62]*Id.*

[63]*Id.*

[64]*Id.*

[65]*Id.*

[66]Kirgis *supra* note 54, p. 16.

because of the Bankruptcy Code or otherwise arise in bankruptcy cases for the claim to be regarded a 'core' claim.[67] That being said, putting one's finger on 'core' matters is not easy. There is no legal provision defining 'core' proceedings. In contrast, the Third Circuit has noted that a non-core proceeding is a proceeding that 'does not involve a substantive right created by the bankruptcy laws and would exist outside of bankruptcy .... .'[68]

This core-noncore dichotomy is exceedingly important. The discretion of the bankruptcy court to deny arbitration hinges on it. It is generally recognised that the bankruptcy court does not have discretion to deny arbitration of noncore proceedings unlike as regards core proceedings.[69] Even as regards core issues some US circuit courts have held that the court has no discretion to deny arbitration automatically. For instance, the Second Circuit in *MBNA America Bank, N.A. v. Hill*, concluded that:[70]

[e]ven as to core proceedings, the bankruptcy court will not have discretion to override an arbitration agreement unless it finds the proceedings are based on provisions of the Bankruptcy Code that 'inherently conflict' with the Arbitration Act or that arbitration of the claims would 'necessarily jeopardize' the objectives of the Bankruptcy Code.

The Second Circuit Court instead held that the bankruptcy court confronted with an arbitration agreement pertaining to a *core* bankruptcy issue has to conduct a 'particularized inquiry into the nature of the claim and the facts of the specific bankruptcy.'[71] It underscored as pertinent for the purpose of this inquiry: (1) the 'centralized resolution of purely bankruptcy issues,' (2) 'the need to protect creditors and debtors from piecemeal litigation,' and (3) 'the undisputed power of a bankruptcy court to enforce its own orders.'[72]

The approach of the United States courts does not give clear guidance as to when exactly an arbitration agreement should be enforced in the context of bankruptcy. The various tests are very vague and malleable.[73] In effect, courts have free hand to do almost anything they want. Anecdotal evidence suggests that bankruptcy judges routinely enforce arbitration agreements, for both noncore and core claims, just to clear cases off the docket. But if so inclined, they also seem to have broad latitude to refuse enforcement of arbitration agreements, at least in respect of core claims.[74]

---

[67] *Id.*

[68] Salzberg and Zinkgraf *supra* note 53, p. 2.

[69] *Id.*

[70] *Id.*, p. 4.

[71] *Id.*

[72] *Id.* (*Salzberg and Zinkgraf at p. 4*).

[73] Kirgis, *supra* note 54, p. 20.

[74] *Id.*

The approach followed in the United States cannot provide a long term solution for reconciling the conflict between bankruptcy and arbitration in Ethiopia. It relies too heavily on the expertise of judges and lawyers. We do not have a sufficient number of judges and lawyers with comprehensive and in-depth knowledge of bankruptcy and arbitration laws in Ethiopia. Not many can claim familiarity with policy considerations that underlie these two areas of law, let alone the interplay between the two areas. In fact, the bankruptcy law has been hardly applied half a century after its issuance, in part, because lawyers and judges are unfamiliar with it.[75]

3.3.1.4   Arbitrability and Bankruptcy: The Approach in Europe

In Europe, there is consensus that 'pure' bankruptcy issues are not arbitrable. This is the case in most jurisdictions as regards issues such as 'the nomination of trustee, the commencement of insolvency proceedings, the reorganisation of the business, orders opening and closing the bankruptcy proceedings, and other measures of conduct and surveillance . . . .'[76] Arbitrators are not allowed to rule on the foregoing matters. Even in the literature these are not issues of contention.[77] However, while everyone agrees that 'core' bankruptcy issues are non-arbitrable, there is no agreement as to which issues are core and which ones noncore. One also gets no uniform answer regarding how exactly the declaration of bankruptcy affects an otherwise arbitrable matter.[78] How some Civil Law jurisdictions address these problems will be briefly discussed below in the hope that this offers some help in the Ethiopian context.

In Austria, section 582 (1) of the Code of Civil Procedure lays down the basic rule as regards arbitrability. It reads in relevant part '[a]ny claim involving an economic interest that lies within the jurisdiction of the courts of law can be subject of an arbitration agreement.'[79] In the context of bankruptcy, in particular, claims by secured creditors for the separation of property over which they have priority from the estate of the bankrupt debtor are arbitrable.[80] The state of the law is not straightforward when it comes to the acknowledgement of contested claims. In such cases, the very existence of the claim being made by the alleged creditor of the bankrupt debtor and its validity is in question. These claims can be settled by arbitration but only if all the persons that will be affected by the claim, i.e. all creditors and the trustee, consent to arbitration.[81]

---

[75]Tadesse (2008), p. 58.

[76]Liebscher (2009), p. 167.

[77]*Id.*

[78]*Id.*

[79]*Id.*, p. 168.

[80]*Id.*, p. 169.

[81]*Id.*

In France, bankruptcy proceedings are dealt with in a centralised manner. The court in charge of the insolvency procedure has jurisdiction to hear and decide on all matters regarding those proceedings.[82] However, the dominant view is that one cannot generalize from this about arbitrability and its scope. The exclusive jurisdiction of the bankruptcy court is limited to matters implicating public policy. If R662-3 of the Code de Commerce that deals with the exclusive jurisdiction of the insolvency court were to be understood as an absolute bar to arbitration, Articles 642-24 of the same Code that expressly authorise the liquidator to conclude arbitration agreements and to compromise with respect to all disputes that concern creditors would have no meaning.[83] The wording of R662-3 of the Code has been interpreted restrictively to limit the powers of the insolvency court in French case law. According to the case law of French courts '. . . the competence of the commercial courts extends only to issues originating from insolvency proceedings or matters which have their source in the application of the provisions of insolvency law, or where the insolvency law affects the resolution of the dispute.'[84]

In Germany, it appears that the arbitration agreement, if any, remains binding despite the declaration of bankruptcy. From literature it seems insolvency neither brings to an end an ongoing arbitration nor prevents initiation of arbitration.[85] According to section 240 of the German Code of Civil Procedure (*'ZPO'*), proceedings before a *state court* are stayed in case of the bankruptcy of one of the parties to the dispute. According to the dominant case law Section 240 of *'ZPO'* is limited in its application to proceedings before *state courts*. It does not cover proceedings before an arbitral tribunal.[86] That being said, an arbitral tribunal will be duty bound to *stay* proceedings before it to enable the trustee to familiarize himself with the case and take appropriate steps to continue with the case.[87] The trustee will be relieved from an arbitration agreement only if the Court is satisfied that the 'arbitration agreement is incapable of being performed.'[88] The Federal Supreme Court has ruled that the arbitration agreement becomes inoperable where the insolvent party has no sufficient funds to ensure its participation in the arbitral proceedings.[89]

In sum, the declaration of bankruptcy does not necessarily end arbitration or prevent initiation of arbitral proceedings in the United States and major European jurisdictions. The courts and laws in these jurisdictions make subtle distinctions between cases based on the underlying policy considerations of the bankruptcy and arbitration laws concerned to determine arbitrability.

---

[82]*Id.*, p. 173.

[83]*Id.*

[84]*Id.*, pp. 173–174.

[85]*Id.*, p. 175.

[86]*Id.*

[87]*Id.*

[88]*Id.*

[89]*Id.*

Coming back to the situation in Ethiopia, it can be said neither the bankruptcy and arbitration laws of the country nor the courts have squarely tackled most of the issues which may involve the interplay of arbitration and bankruptcy laws. Court cases in Ethiopia involving bankruptcy have been few and far in between despite the existence of the law for nearly sixty years now. One may even contend bankruptcy law had simply been dormant till very recently.[90] Given this state of affairs, courts will have a hard time reconciling the objectives of bankruptcy law and arbitration on a case by case basis. Therefore, the need for legal reform to regulate the interplay between arbitration and bankruptcy as clearly and comprehensively as possible cannot be overemphasised.

3.3.2   Competition and Consumer Protection Law and Arbitrability

Competition and consumer protection laws pose the question of arbitrability in many jurisdictions. The concerns and policy reasons underlying the debate regarding the arbitrability of these two fields are different. Yet, Ethiopia has issued a law that lumps together competition and consumer protection law replacing laws that covered the field till recently.[91] Hence, the arbitrability of disputes involving these two fields are dealt with together in this part.

To avoid repetition, we will first have a bird's-eye view of the legal and institutional mechanism the proclamation dealing with both subjects puts in place. The arbitrability of the two fields will then be discussed separately.

3.3.2.1   The Main Features of Ethiopian Competition and Consumer Protection Law

The Proclamation was issued with the objective of creating a competitive and free market that at the same time safeguards the interests of consumers. More particularly, its aim is to 'protect business community from anti-competitive and unfair practices, and consumers from misleading market conduct.'[92] The proclamation

---

[90]Tadesse (2008), pp. 57–59. He speculates multiple factors kept bankruptcy out of the limelight in Ethiopia. According to him, these include: the freeing of the Commercial Code of Ethiopia during the Socialist era (1974–1991), the lack of familiarity of lawyers and even judges with that area of law hence absence of people invoking bankruptcy law and foreclosure laws of the country that allowed banks to directly sell property given as security.

[91]Trade Competition and Consumers Protection Proclamation No. 813/2013, FEDERAL NEGARIT GAZETA, 20th Year, No. 28.

[92]*Id.*, Article 3(1). Under sub article 2 of Article 3 the law spells out its goals with respect to consumer protection as ensuring the goods and services that consumers get are not only safe and suitable to their health but also fair in terms of prices.

applies to 'any commercial activity or transaction in goods or services conducted or *having effect within'* Ethiopia.[93] So, it applies even to commercial activities outside Ethiopia in so far as they hamper competition or adversely affect consumers in Ethiopia.

To achieve the foregoing objectives the law prohibits certain types of conduct and transactions. Among others, it proscribes abuse of dominance that the business person may have in the market. Particularly, it prohibits every business person that may have a dominant position in the market either by himself or acting together with others from, for instance, limiting production, hoarding, selling at prices lower than the cost of production to harm competitors, directly or indirectly imposing unfair prices, and refusing to deal with others unjustifiably.[94] Imposing restrictions on the manufacture or distribution of competing goods or services, and limiting 'where, to whom, or in what conditions, or quantities, or at what prices the goods or services shall be resold or exported' without justifiable economic reason are also deemed abuse of dominance.[95]

Besides, the law prohibits anti-competitive agreements, concerted practices and decisions by business persons and associations in a horizontal relationship such as directly or indirectly fixing prices, 'collusive tendering, dividing markets by allocating customers, suppliers, territories or specific types of goods or services.'[96] Even in vertical relations agreements that have the 'effect of preventing or significantly lessening competition' or 'involve the setting of minimum resale price are prohibited unless they are justified by technological or other pro-competitive gains that outweigh their anti-competitive effect.'[97] The proclamation also outlaws agreements or arrangements of merger that cause or are 'likely to cause significant adverse effect' on competition.[98] To ensure compliance with this rule mergers need approval by the Trade Competition and Consumers Protection Authority.[99] Furthermore, the law prohibits acts of unfair competition. In particular, it requires business persons to refrain from 'any act which is dishonest, misleading, or deceptive and harms or is likely to harm the business interest of a competitor.'[100]

There are several other provisions that aim at the protection of consumers. Among other things, these provisions confer on consumers the right to get 'accurate

---

[93] *Id.*, Article 4(1).

[94] *Id.*, Article 5(2)a to d.

[95] *Id.*, Article 5(2) g and h.

[96] *Id.*, Article 7(1)b.

[97] *Id.*, Article 7(2) and (3).

[98] *Id.*, Article 9(1).

[99] *Id.*, Article 9(2), 10 and 11.

[100] *Id.*, Article 8(1). Under Article 8(2) the law lists some manifestations of unfair competition prohibited by the law. The prohibited acts include possession, disclosure or use of information as regards other person in a manner contrary to honest commercial practice, dissemination of false or equivocal information to consumers and obtaining or attempting to obtain business secrets of competitors through current or former employees of the competitor.

and sufficient information'[101] as regards the goods and services they buy, require affixing labels on goods being sold, prohibit false or misleading advertisements and other conduct that is likely to adversely affect consumers.[102]

The Proclamation has come up with an institutional mechanism to ensure its full implementation. Particularly, it establishes the Trade Competition and Consumers Protection Authority accountable to the Ministry of Trade. It entrusts the Authority with the overall implementation of the Proclamation.[103] The Authority can conduct an investigation where there are sufficient grounds to suspect that an offense sanctionable by administrative or criminal law has been committed.[104] The proclamation also establishes, under the auspices of the same authority, an adjudicative bench with judicial power.[105] This judicial body has jurisdiction on disputes between traders, consumers and traders and even the Authority itself and persons accused of infringing the Proclamation. The judicial body can order administrative measures, impose fine and even award compensation to victims of anti-competitive behaviour and consumers, as the case may be.[106] A person aggrieved by the decision of the judicial bench within the Authority may appeal to the Federal Appellate Tribunal also established by the Proclamation. The decisions of this Appellate Tribunal are final on questions of fact. An appeal lies to the Federal Supreme Court lies on matters of law.[107] Only regular courts have jurisdiction as regards criminal liability that the Proclamation imposes.

3.3.2.2   Competition Law and the Question of Arbitrability

Different bodies that work at the interface of arbitration and competition laws are confronted with the question of arbitrability.[108] For instance, the issue could arise before a court when it is requested to compel a party to arbitrate while the resisting party challenges the validity of the arbitration agreement on grounds of the

---

[101]*Id.*, Article 14(1).

[102]*Id.*, Article 16, 19 and 22.

[103]*Id.*, Article 27 and 30.

[104]*Id.*, Article 36(1)a and b. Breach of some provisions of the proclamation could attract rigorous imprisonment of upto seven years according to Article 43(2). Criminal action is instituted by the prosecutor's of the Authority before an ordinary court. The judicial bench in the authority and the appellate Administrative Tribunal established under the Proclamation have has no jurisdiction as regards criminal liability of offenders according to Article 37(1)b.

[105]*Id.*, Article 28.

[106]*Id.*, Article 32. The administrative measures it can take include the suspension and even revocation of business license of the offender according to Article 32(2) c. The fines that can be imposed can be as high as 10% of the annual turnover of the offender according to Article 42.

[107]*Id.*, Article 39(2).

[108]Brozolo (2010), p. 31. *Arbitration and Competition Law: The Position of the Courts and of Arbitrators*, OECD HEARINGS: Arbitration and Competition, DAF/COMP (2010)40, available at: http://www.oecd.org/competition/abuse/49294392.pdf, accessed on 27 March 2015.

involvement of a competition law issue. Even after an arbitral award has been given the issue of arbitrability can be raised in a proceeding to set aside the award.[109] It could also arise at the stage of recognition and enforcement of awards under the New York Convention.[110] Besides, the arbitrability of issues involving competition law may be raised before arbitral tribunals and administrative bodies entrusted with the enforcement of competition law.[111]

Given the novelty of competition law in Ethiopia and the overall business landscape, no question of arbitrability has come to light as far as this research could uncover, at least.[112] Yet, courts, arbitrators and the judicial organ established under the auspices of the Authority as well as the Authority itself are bound to face the question of arbitrability of disputes involving competition law in the future. Hence, in what follows an attempt will be made to briefly dwell on how the issue of arbitrability has been resolved in other jurisdictions with similar laws. The hope is that Ethiopia can draw some lessons from the approach taken in such jurisdictions.

3.3.2.2.1 The US Approach to Competition Law and Arbitrability

The main competition law in the United States is the Sherman Antitrust Act of 1890. This Act was passed with the aim of 'preserving free and unfettered competition as the rule of trade.'[113] The Sherman Act outlaws agreements 'in restraint of trade' and all forms of monopoly and monopoly behaviour, which it regards as a felony.[114] The Sherman Act has been expanded by the Clayton Act and the Federal Trade Commission Act of 1914.[115]

Under the United States competition law, an innocent party to an agreement that breaches competition law, and for that matter a third party that has been injured by the wrongful competition, is entitled to not only compensatory but also treble (punitive) damages.[116] That means private individuals are given an incentive to participate in the enforcement of competition law especially in light of the award of punitive damages that could be high. In contrast to this, punitive damages are not

---

[109]*Id.*

[110]UN Convention on Recognition and Enforcement of Foreign Arbitral Awards (1958), Article V (1)a. Note that the Convention talks in terms of 'competent authority' but this could be a court in some countries recognition or/and enforcement is sought.

[111]Brozolo (2010), p. 31.

[112]Interview conducted with Aman Assefa, practicing lawyer specializing in competition law who was involved in the drafting of Proclamation 685/2010, the predecessor of the current Proclamation. Interview was conducted on 2 April 2015 at his office.

[113]Lew (2009), p. 248.

[114]*Id.*, pp. 248–249.

[115]*Id.*, p. 294.

[116]*Id.*, pp. 249–250.

awarded in Ethiopia.[117] The competition law of Ethiopia entitles persons who incur damage as a result of 'acts of unfair competition' to payment of compensation in accordance with the 'relevant laws.'[118]

Coming to the specific question of arbitrability, traditionally claims involving anti-trust laws were inarbitrable in the United States. The Second Circuit Court of Appeal had held that 'the pervasive public interest in enforcement of the antitrust laws and the nature of the claims that arise in such case combine to make antitrust claims inappropriate for arbitration.'[119] This position has been abandoned since the landmark decision of the United States Supreme Court in *Mitsubishi Motors Corp. v. Soler Chrysler-Plymouth, Inc.* passed in 1985.[120]

The underlying contract in that case involved, among other things, the distribution of cars manufactured by *Mitsubishi* by *Soler* in Puerto Rico.[121] After *Soler* ordered vehicles, the demand for the cars declined in San Juan, Puerto Rico. Hence, it requested *Mitsubishi* to tranship the ordered cars to other markets in North, South and Central America. *Mitsubishi* would not agree to this purportedly on grounds of suitability of the cars for such markets alleging, for instance, heaters would be needed in some of the proposed new markets.[122] *Soler* disclaimed the order owing to this disagreement. Therefore, *Mitsubishi Motors* moved to enforce the arbitration clause in order to receive liquidated damages for costs in relation to the ordered but not shipped cars.[123] *Soler* came up with a counterclaim alleging a conspiracy to divide markets in breach of the United States Antitrust laws.[124] The arbitration was suspended because the First Circuit Court held that the antitrust counter claim was inarbitrable following the non-arbitrability doctrine enunciated by the Second Circuit in *American Safety Equipment v. J.P. McGuire*, 391 F. 2nd 821 (2nd Cir. 1968).[125] The case eventually reached the Supreme Court of the United States.

The Supreme Court held that disputes involving antitrust claims are arbitrable. The Court reasoned that the mere appearance of an antitrust claim should not alone warrant the invalidation of the selected arbitral forum. It also rejected the contention that antitrust cases are too complex for arbitrators to handle. It reasoned that arbitrators with expertise relevant to the case can be chosen. The Supreme Court emphasised in this regard that the hallmark of arbitration is its adaptability.[126]

---

[117]Civil Code of Ethiopia lays down the basic principle as regards the extent of compensation under Article 2091. The said provision reads: '[t]he damages due by the person legally declared to be liable shall be equal to the damage caused to the victim by the act giving rise to the liability.'

[118]Trade Competition and Consumers Protection Proclamation No. 813/2013, Article 32(1)b.

[119]Lew (2009), p. 251.

[120]Reisman (1997), pp. 313–334.

[121]*Id.*, 313.

[122]*Id.*

[123]*Id.*

[124]*Id.*, at 314.

[125]*Id.*

[126]*Id.*, p. 321.

Further the Supreme Court rejected the core of the American Safety doctrine that the punitive damage makes the plaintiff asserting his right under the Sherman Act like a private attorney-general who protects the interest of the public and therefore such claims should be inarbitrable. The Supreme Court emphasised that no citizen is under an obligation to institute an antitrust claim.[127] But to the extent the private party chooses to institute such claim, the Supreme Court maintained, the claim for treble damages can also be brought before an arbitral tribunal. According to the Court the arbitral tribunal is bound to give effect to the intention of the parties including claims for punitive damages, as in this case, arising from the application of the American Antitrust law.[128] The Court continued:

> [t]he tribunal therefore should be bound to decide that dispute in accord with the national law giving rise to the claim. And so long as the prospective litigant effectively may vindicate its statutory cause of action in the arbitral forum, the statute will continue to serve both its remedial and deterrent function.[129]

The Supreme Court further reasoned that the national courts of the United States can have a second look at the award enforcement stage to ensure the antitrust law has been properly addressed by the arbitrators.[130] It further underscored the central role arbitration plays in the settlement of disputes in international trade. Given this, the Court reasoned 'it will be necessary for national courts to subordinate domestic notions of arbitrability to the international policy favouring commercial arbitration . . . .'[131]

3.3.2.2.2 Competition Law and Arbitrability: The European Union Approach

The European Union attaches very high significance to fair competition in trade. The Treaty of Rome that established the then European Common Market, for example, sought to guarantee the steady expansion of 'balanced trade, and fair competition.'[132] The Lisbon Treaty of 2007 also espouses the establishment of a highly 'competitive market.'[133] Hence, it can be said that ensuring free and fair competition in trade is a major objective of the laws of the European Union.

---

[127] *Id.*, p. 324.

[128] *Id.*

[129] *Id.*, pp. 324–325.

[130] *Id.*, p. 325.

[131] *Id.*, p. 326.

[132] The Treaty of Rome of 25 March 1957 Creating European Economic Community, the preamble of the Treaty. Article 3(f) of The Treaty of Rome further underscores that one of its aims is the 'institution of a system ensuring that competition in the Common Market is not distorted.'

[133] The Treaty of Lisbon Amending the Treaty of European Union and the Treaty Establishing the European Community, 3 December 2007. According to Article 2(3) of the Treaty, its aim is the

To this end, European Union competition law outlaws agreements between undertakings as well as decisions and concerted practices which may appreciably affect trade between member states or 'which have as their object or effect the prevention, restriction, or distortion of competition within the common market.'[134] Article 101 of the Treaty on the Functioning of the European Union provides an illustrative list of prohibited agreements and conducts. These include fixing prices, sharing markets or sources of supply, discriminating by tying dissimilar conditions to equivalent transactions.[135] Furthermore, Article 102 of the Treaty prohibits firms having dominant position in a substantial part of the common market from abusing this position.[136] Among other things, a firm that has a dominant position in the market is required to refrain from imposing, for instance, excessive or exclusionary prices or other trading conditions, discrimination, tying and 'limiting production, markets, or technical development to the prejudice of consumers.'[137]

When it comes to sanctions for breach of competition law the approach in Europe is different from that in the United States. Anti-competitive agreements that violate the provisions of Article 101(1) or arrangements or conducts that constitute abuse of a dominant position under Article 102 of the Treaty are deemed null and void.[138] Moreover, those in breach may be liable to fines imposed by the European Commission. An innocent party to the agreement that transgresses European Union competition law or a third person that has incurred injury in consequence of the breach is not entitled to compensation under European Union law.[139] This is in contrast with the United States competition law, which gives both compensatory and punitive damages to victims of such anticompetitive behaviour.[140]

The implementation of European Union competition law has been decentralised since the issuance of European Council Regulation 1/2003. Under the new system introduced by this Regulation national competition authorities as well as courts can directly apply the substantive rules under Article 101 and 102 of the Treaty on the Functioning of the European Union.[141] The national competition authorities can, for example, impose fines and periodic penalties on those in breach of the Treaty, according to Article 5 of the Regulation.[142] The Regulation also envisages the

---

establishment of a highly competitive internal market within the European Union that will lead to a balanced economic growth and price stability, among other things.

[134]Lew (2009), p. 246.

[135]Dolmans and Grierson (2003), pp. 39–40.

[136]Id., at 39.

[137]Id.

[138]Lew (2009), p. 249.

[139]Id. One needs to note here that European countries may have their own national competition laws. The competition law that applies throughout the Union only provides the minimum requirements agreed upon. So, under national laws compensation may be due to a person who is aggrieved by anticompetitive behavior.

[140]Id.

[141]Müller (2004), p. 726.

[142]Id., at 729.

possibility of cooperation between national courts and the European Union Commission in the enforcement of the competition rules of the European Union. In contrast, there is nothing in the Regulation that provides a legal basis for cooperation between the Commission and arbitrators.[143]

All the same, in Europe it is now accepted that disputes involving European Union competition law can be settled by arbitration as between the parties.[144] The arbitrators decide on the rights *inter se* between the parties while the European Union Commission applies the competition law on behalf of the European Union by investigating breach and imposing fines.[145] So, where an allegation that an agreement or a certain practice violates European Union competition law Articles 101 or 102 is made before arbitrators, they have the authority and duty to rule on this issue.[146] If the arbitrators find that the allegation is well founded, then the agreement concerned will be deemed null and void. In such a case the arbitrators will still have the power to determine the consequence of the nullity of the contract or invalidity of the practice as between the parties and decide on remedies such as damages due as compensation under the applicable national law.[147] The arbitrators cannot go beyond that and impose fines for the violation of the European Union competition law. That is the exclusive jurisdiction of the European Union Commission.[148]

This power of arbitrators to apply European Union competition law was indirectly recognised by the European Court of Justice (ECJ) in *Eco Swiss v. Benetton*.[149] The case dealt with how a national court that has been requested to annul an arbitral award on grounds of violation of EC competition law should deal with the issue where violation of competition law is not regarded a violation of public policy that warrants the annulment of awards under the national laws of the country concerned.[150] The ECJ ruled that the national court must grant the request where it finds that the arbitrators indeed failed to apply or misapplied Article 81 of the EC Treaty (now Article 101 of the Treaty on the Functioning of the European Union). According to the ECJ, a manifest violation of EC competition law results in the annulment of the arbitral award.[151]

---

[143]Zekos (2006), p. 42.

[144]Lew (2009), p. 253. It seems the Mitsubishi decision of the US Supreme Court that arbitrators are capable of applying competition law had impact on actors and institutions that applied the EU Competition Law.

[145]*Id.*

[146]*Id.*

[147]*Id.*, p. 254.

[148]*Id.*

[149]Dolmans and Grierson (2003), p. 43.

[150]*Id.* In the Netherlands where the issue came to the attention of national courts national competition law is not deemed to be a manifestation of fundamental public policy of the state that warrant annulment of an arbitral award or refusal to recognize and enforce the same. That is why the Dutch Supreme Court requested interpretation of the EC competition law pursuant to Article 234 of the EC Treaty to know whether the position is the same under the EC competition law.

[151]Lew (2009), pp. 256–257.

3.3.2.2.3   The US and EU Approach to the Interface Between Competition Law and Arbitration: What Are the Lessons for Ethiopia?

As discussed in the foregoing parts, in the US, EU and many other jurisdictions competition law issues are now arbitrable.[152] Arbitrators are expected to apply the relevant competition law.[153] National courts are also entitled to have the so called 'second look' at whether or not competition law has been applied by arbitrators when the matter comes to their attention either for the annulment of award or recognition and enforcement of the same.[154] Besides, where the relevant competition law provides for fines or other sanctions such as imprisonment to ensure the proper application of competition law, the public authorities entrusted with these tasks retain the power to investigate and impose the said sanctions.[155] Hence, arbitration is only a component of the enforcement of competition law, focussing on the inter-party aspect of the law such as *ex post* allocation of damages to a party that is a victim of the violation of competition law.[156]

Noteworthy at this point is the fact that Ethiopian law imposes as sanctions for the violation of competition law a wider combination of tools than the US and EU law do. They include compensatory damage, fine and even imprisonment.[157] Following the foregoing approach, thus, makes sense in Ethiopia. For one thing, a party to arbitration that feels aggrieved by anticompetitive agreement (conduct) can invoke the law to get the compensation due under the Ethiopian law. Moreover, since Ethiopian law imposes fines and even imprisonment for violation of competition law, the relevant competition authority can ensure compliance with competition law by pursuing these sanctions. That EU competition law to which Ethiopian law bears striking resemblance allows arbitration of competition law matters is noteworthy in this regard. Since Ethiopian law provides imprisonment as a sanction for the implementation of competition law on top of fines provided under EU law, arbitration poses even a lesser risk of underenforcement of competition law of Ethiopia.

Besides, derailing arbitration of an international dispute every time a party alleges competition law issues are involved can seriously limit Ethiopia's ability to benefit from international commerce in goods and services. So, at least when it comes to international commercial arbitration Ethiopia will be better off if domestic notions of arbitrability are subordinated to the needs of international commerce, as the US Supreme Court noted in regard to the US in the *Mitsubishi* case seen already. Ethiopian parties as marginal players, with generally less bargaining position in international commerce, will not benefit from global commerce if Ethiopia insists on

---

[152]OECD Hearings, Arbitration and Competition, DAF/COMP (2010)40, 13 December 2011, at 11, available at http://www.oecd.org/competition/abuse/49294392.pdf, accessed on 20/08/2016.

[153]*Id.*, p. 12.

[154]*Id.*, p. 13.

[155]*Id.*, p. 11.

[156]*Id.*

[157]Trade Competition and Consumers Protection No. 813/2013 Articles 37(2), 42 and 43.

inarbitrability of every claim in which competition law issues are allegedly implicated.

3.3.2.3 Consumer Protection Law and the Question of Arbitrability

Under the Proclamation, a consumer has, without prejudice to warranties or more advantageous contractual terms, the right to demand from the seller in case of defective goods for a replacement or refund of the price paid, and in case of defective service re-delivery of service free of charge or refund of the fee paid.[158] The Proclamation also provides the right to compensation for damage sustained as a result of the use of defective goods or service or for failure to refund or provide replacement for defective goods.[159] Contractual waiver of any rights conferred by the Proclamation on consumers is 'of no effect.'[160] Thus, to the extent a consumer prefers exercise of jurisdiction by the adjudicative bench of the Authority to arbitration, it may be argued that this jurisdiction cannot be ousted by arbitration agreement. That being said, no authoritative statement can be made against arbitration since there is no case law on this subject. Besides, it may be argued that the inadmissible contractual 'waiver' the law refers to is the waiver of a substantive remedy rather than the forum the consumer uses to vindicate his rights.

Another noteworthy point is that Article 30(9) and Article 32(1) (c) of the Proclamation, which deal with jurisdiction of the Adjudicative Branch of the Authority, seem narrow in terms of territorial jurisdiction. For example, the latter limits jurisdiction to 'transactions *conducted*' in Addis Ababa and Dire Dawa, the two territories administered by the Federal Government, rather than transactions having 'effect' in Addis Ababa and Dire Dawa. It is doubtful that many international transactions would meet this condition that triggers the application of the provisions of the Proclamation on consumer protection. We need not, however, go into details regarding the scope of application of this law without digressing too much from the main topic. Suffice it to say that this is yet another area which may raise issues of objective arbitrability.

---

[158]*Id.*, Article 20(2).

[159]*Id.*, 20(3). Other provisions of the Proclamation in, Articles 14 to 26 require access to information, labelling of goods, prohibition against hording and the like in order to protect consumers.
[160]*Id.*, Article 21.

3.3.3   The Erosion of 'Objective' Inarbitrability: The Way Forward for Ethiopia

In many parts of the world, a sea change has taken place dramatically widening the scope of arbitrable subject matters.[161] This change came about owing to many and diverse causes. They ranged from a shift in perceptions regarding arbitral due process and the role of arbitrators to the heightened need to accommodate the requirements of international commerce.[162] In particular, slowly but steadily, many began to assimilate arbitrators to judges resulting in growing trust. According to some authors, arbitrators too began being sensitive in the conduct of arbitration. Particularly, they started being sensitive to due process issues and taking into account other areas of public policy concerns in their decision making process.[163] On top of the foregoing, the growing acceptance of party autonomy arguments, simple faith in freedom of contracts, and the ascendance of the principle of good faith, which prohibits the parties from hiding behind domestic limitations to deny effect to international arbitration agreements, helped arbitrability carry the day.[164]

The erosion of objective inarbitrability was championed by courts especially in the Common Law jurisdictions but also in continental Europe.[165] The US courts, for example, supplied a fundamental policy rationale for the expansion of arbitrability in international matters. They emphasised the importance of predictability of the resolution of disputes in the international commercial system to justify widened scope of arbitrability.[166] They further maintained that avoiding causing damage to the 'fabric of international commerce and trade' necessitates enforcing the parties' agreement to arbitrate, even when the subject matter would be inarbitrable in a domestic context. These explicit references of the US Courts to the jurisdictional needs of international commerce were echoed in other common law jurisdictions . . . such as in New Zealand.[167]

Even in third world countries, the scope of arbitrable matters has expanded significantly.[168] A whole host of factors lead to this gradual, yet deep shift. Cases

---

[161]Youssef (2009), pp. 51–52.

[162]Id.

[163]Brekoulakis (2009), pp. 23–31.

[164]Youssef (2009), pp. 51–52.

[165]Id.

[166]Id., p. 57.

[167]Id.

[168]Greenberg et al. (2011), p. 187. In Sri Lanka, for example, only criminal proceedings are excluded from reference to arbitration. In the Philippines, labor disputes, civil status of persons, validity of marriage and its dissolution, jurisdiction of courts, inheritance expectations, criminal liability and matters that the law precludes from compromises are excluded from the domain of arbitration. The Chinese law too follows a prescriptive approach rather than leaving the matter to courts and arbitrators. It lists down matters that are excluded from settlement by arbitration as those concerning, "marriage, adoption, guardianship, support and succession as well as administrative disputes that must be handled by administrative organs as prescribed by law."

in point are regulatory competition, legal borrowing, and the need to protect foreign investment and commerce.[169] The overall result is that today the domain of arbitration has expanded by leaps and bounds into areas of economic activity involving significant public interest in most parts of the world. In consequence, invocation of public policy to resist arbitrability has significantly diminished, especially, in the sphere of international commercial arbitration.[170]

The expansion of the scope of arbitrable matters has led to newer and simpler drafting techniques for the delimitation of things that are arbitrable and inarbitrable. In earlier times, when arbitrability was mainly determined by reference to public policy considerations, this exercise required complex reflections on conflicting policy goals of various laws to determine arbitrability on a case-by-case basis.[171] The disentanglement of arbitrability from public policy and the liberal pro-arbitration approach in international commerce seen above has led to simplification of decisions on arbitrability. In particular, the public policy test which once required courts and arbitrators to conduct *individual* examination of each subject matter to determine whether or not public policy was involved in regard to each subject matter lost currency.[172]

With the ever increasing trend in favour of the arbitrability of international disputes of economic nature, we are witnessing even newer legal techniques of incorporation of arbitrability into laws [173] Either all matters are considered, *a priori*, arbitrable, unless particular disputes are reserved to exclusive court jurisdiction or arbitrable claims are defined very broadly to cover all disputes pertaining to economic or financial interest.[174] Both approaches are common. The first approach is found in U.S., Canada, and to some extent French law. The second approach characterises Swiss and German law.[175]

Swiss law provides that 'any dispute involving financial interests can be the subject of arbitration'.[176] This is an extremely broad formulation. It allows arbitrability of all rights relating to 'property'—real or personal, tangible or intangible. It totally rejects inarbitrability by reason of the public nature of the applicable rules.[177] German Law combines two approaches in identifying arbitrable claims. It, on the one hand, provides that the parties may arbitrate 'any claim involving an

---

[169]Youssef (2009), p. 61.

[170]*Id.*, pp. 51–52.

[171]*Id.*, p. 56.

[172]*Id.*

[173]*Id.*

[174]*Id.*

[175]*Id.*

[176]*Id.*, p. 60.

[177]*Id.* The Swiss Federal Tribunal envisaged the possibility of a private tribunal applying even public international law rules. It, in a case involving the UN Embargo on Iraq which was effective in Switzerland, declined to consider the UN Embargo on commercial activities with Iraq as a bar to arbitrability of a dispute arising under a contract for the sale of military equipment to the country under sanctions.

economic interest (*vermÖgensrechtlicher anspruch*).'[178] On the other hand, it says arbitrable subject matter also includes 'claims involving no economic interest' so long as they can be the object of settlement by the parties. This classic criterion is given a residual place in the sphere of non-economic rights to bring them into the domain of arbitrability, hence further expanding the scope of arbitrable subject matter.[179]

In light of the foregoing arguments in favour of the expansion of arbitrable matters and the worldwide trend in this regard, it is submitted that Ethiopian courts should not deem any subject matter involving international commercial dispute inarbitrable, unless there is an express statutory provision making the matter inarbitrable.

3.4   Arbitrability as a *'Ratione Personae'* Notion: A Cause for Concern in Ethiopia

In Ethiopia administrative authorities and other entities affiliated with the state object to arbitration on the ground of arbitrability. The foundations of this objection will be discussed in this section. We start by looking at the notion itself.

3.4.1   *'Subjective' Arbitrability: A Misnomer for Limitation on 'Capacity'?*

In some jurisdictions certain entities are not allowed to settle disputes through arbitration. For instance, in some Arab countries recourse by public entities to arbitration was perceived as compromising the interest of the state and its people. In Saudi Arabia, for example, government agencies are not allowed to submit to arbitration except with the consent of the president of the Council of Ministers.[180] This resulted from bad experience with arbitration in relation to government contracts mainly pertaining to the exploitation of natural resources.[181] In some other jurisdictions such restriction is a reflection of similar perception that arbitration

---

[178]*Id.*, pp. 60–61.

[179]*Id. p. 61.*

[180]Kingdom of Saudi Arabia Arbitration Regulations, Royal Decree M/46, Article 3 dated 12-7-1403(25 April 1983, Excerpted in BORN, *supra* note 470, at 162. The Hashemite Kingdom of Jordan introduced a similar amendment to its maritime law. It provided: "(r)egardless of whatever is contained in any other law, any agreement, or stipulation which bars the Jordanian Courts from maintaining disputes relating to bills of lading or carriage of goods is null end void." Amendment Law to the Merchandise Maritime Law, Jordanian Law no. 35 of 1983, Excerpted in BORN *supra* note 470, at 103.

[181]Youssef (2009), p. 62.

generally favours multi-national corporations or other parties from industrialised countries.[182] In yet others, the participation of public authorities or entities affiliated with the state in a dispute settlement the state itself does not control is deemed an affront to the sovereign dignity of the state.[183] Whatever the underlying thinking, certain parties may not submit to arbitration or may do so only after specific pre-conditions are fulfilled in some jurisdictions. This raises the notion of '*ratione personae*' or 'subjective' arbitrability.[184]

The issue raised by such legal restrictions is not strictly speaking that of arbitrability. Such laws do not prohibit submission of certain *issues* or *subject matters* to settlement by arbitration.[185] In other words, the restriction imposed does not pertain to the object of the contract, rather to the 'capacity' to submit to arbitration. Yet, in Ethiopia the misconception on this point is so rampant that courts and authors alike routinely frame the issues raised in this regard as that of arbitrability.[186] Hence, the matter will be dwelt upon briefly below. Since this issue arises in Ethiopia in the context of administrative contracts, the notion of administrative contracts will be briefly introduced first and then the 'arbitrability' of such contracts will be discussed.

3.4.2   Non-Arbitrability of Administrative Contracts

The Civil Procedure Code of Ethiopia says, '[n]o arbitration may take place in relation to *administrative contracts* as defined in Art 3132 of the Civil Code or in any other case where it is prohibited by law.'[187] Interestingly, this provision is found in the Civil Procedure Code rather than the Civil Code which deals with non-procedural aspect of arbitration. The Civil Code says nothing about the arbitrability of administrative contracts, despite dealing with these types of contracts extensively.

Coming to the sanction for inarbitrability in Ethiopia, 'no valid contract' exists unless the 'parties are *capable* of contracting' and the '*object of the contract* is ... *lawful.*'[188] That means both 'subjective' inarbitrability and objective inarbitrability render the contract invalid. In other words, where a contract is concluded by an

---

[182]Mistelis (2009), p. 6.

[183]*Id.*

[184]*Id.*

[185]*Id.*

[186]For example, Zekarias (1994) read generally. Similarly, in an article dealing with arbitration of disputes involving government construction contracts, Tecle Hagos Bahta frames the issue as that of arbitrability rather than capacity of government departments to submit to arbitration. He also cites number of cases in which the courts without any reservation frame this matter as issues of arbitrability. *See* on this, Tecle (2009), pp. 1–32.

[187]Civil Procedure Code Decree No. 52/1965, Article 315(2).

[188]Civil Code of Ethiopia Proclamation 165/1960, Article 1678.

administrative body it is not valid because the administrative authority does not have the *capacity* to engage in arbitration agreements in relation to administrative contracts. Similarly, if the subject matter of the contract is such that it cannot be arbitrated despite the full capacity of the parties the agreement to arbitrate will be invalid because the object of the contract is not 'lawful.'

Entities that are directly or indirectly affiliated with the Ethiopian state routinely raise the defence of inarbitrability. As a result, the discussion of arbitrability in Ethiopia cannot be complete without looking at the meaning and nature of administrative contracts.

3.4.2.1 Administrative Contracts: What Are They?

The Civil Code of Ethiopia distinguishes between contracts between private parties, on the one hand, and what it calls 'administrative contracts', on the other.[189] The latter type of contract is characterized by the provision of public service. Therefore, the party that is deemed an 'administrative' body is given exceptional powers that the law does not confer on private parties to contracts. These powers are known in French law as *'clauses exorbitantes du droit commun'*.[190] One of the powers so conferred is the right to cancel a contract unilaterally.[191] The private party whose contract is cancelled would generally get compensation for loss resulting from the cancellation rather than the right to execute the contract and collect fully the anticipated profits.[192] Ethiopian law also vests in an administrative authority, in principle, the power to unilaterally impose on the other party '... *all the obligations which they think* fit for the proper operation or improvement of the service granted.'[193]

The law defines administrative contract as follows:[194]

> *A contract shall be deemed to be an administrative contract where:*
> a) *it is expressly qualified as such by the law or by the parties; or*
> b) *it is connected with an activity of the public service and implies a permanent*

---

[189]Tecle (2009), p. 6.

[190]*Id.,* p. 7.

[191]*Id.*

[192]*Id.*

[193]Civil Code of Ethiopia Proclamation No. 165/1960, Articles 3216(1). The law also provides for exceptions to this rule specifying the kind of contractual terms that may not be unilaterally modified by administrative authority under 3218–3219 of the Civil Code.

[194]*Id.*

participation of the party contracting with the administrative authorities in the execution of such service; or

c)   *it contains one or more provisions which could only have been inspired by urgent considerations of general interest extraneous to relations between private individuals.*[195]

The first segment of Article 3132(a) is of little value in terms of shedding light on the core nature or essence of this type of contract. It states that a contract is administrative 'if it is expressly qualified as such' by the law. Even if this provision were not included in the Code, one would obviously be obliged to accept the legal characterization of a particular contract as an administrative contract. The first leg of Article 3132(a) thus adds little value to that other law characterising a contract as an administrative contract. In any case, contracts of public works,[196] contracts of supplies[197] and contracts of public service[198] have been identified as administrative contracts by the Civil Code itself.

The second leg of Article 3132(a) states that a contract is to be regarded as an administrative one where 'it is expressly qualified as such . . . by the parties.' Though the law does not make this point expressly, it seems that the mere characterisation of a contract by the parties as an administrative contract is not sufficient. For instance, a contract between a barber and his customer for a weekly haircut against a stipulated annual payment would not be an administrative contract because they chose to characterize it as such in their contract. Reading (b) and (c) of Article 3132, which focus on 'public service' and 'urgent considerations of *general interest extraneous to relations between private individuals'*, clearly suggests that one of the parties must be a public body or an organ of the state or somehow directly affiliated with the state. So, the second leg of Article 3132(a) is useful only to the extent it tells us that a public body or agency may characterise a contract as an administrative one in the agreement itself to preclude confusion about the nature of the agreement.

Of the remaining sub-provisions, Article 3132(c) sheds more light on the essential nature of administrative contracts. Where the contract contains provisions that are 'inspired by urgent considerations of *general interest*, not typical in contracts between private parties, it is an administrative contract. Art. 3132(b) states that a contract will be deemed to be an administrative contract if it fulfils three requirements. First, one of the parties must be an administrative authority. Second, the contract must be connected with an 'activity of public service.' Third, there must be 'permanent participation' by the party contracting with the administrative authorities in the delivery of the 'public service' under the contract.

Ethiopian courts have struggled with the determination of what exactly administrative contracts are. The question of when exactly a contract is to be deemed an

---

[195]*Id.*

[196]*Id.*

[197]*Id.*

[198]*Id.*, Articles 3207–3243.

'administrative' one was taken up by the Cassation Bench of the Federal Supreme Court in *Woira Wood and Metal Works Cooperative Society v. Addis Ababa City Administration Trade and Industry Bureau.*[199] Though the issue did not arise in the context of arbitration, it is of relevance to the determination of arbitrability.

The dispute was about contractual default. Whether the contract in question was an 'administrative contract' became an issue because the law vests jurisdiction in Addis Ababa Municipal Courts instead of the Federal Court when a dispute pertains to administrative contracts relating to the City[200] *Woira Cooperative Society* instituted a legal action against the Addis Ababa Trade and Industry Bureau at the Federal First Instance Court. The Trade and Industry Bureau objected to the jurisdiction of the Federal First Instance Court on the grounds that the dispute arose from an administrative contract. *Woira Cooperative Society* disagreed. It contended, to qualify as an administrative contract under Article 3132(a), which stipulates a contract is administrative '...if it is expressly qualified as such by the law', the contract must pertain to what the law of property calls public domain.[201] The contract did not pertain to this kind of property, according to *Woira*. Moreover, *Woira* argued, the contract in question does not fulfil the requirements under Art 3132(b), which defines a contract as an administrative contract if '... it is connected with an activity of the public service and implies a permanent participation of the *party contracting with administrative authorities in the execution of such service.'*

The Cassation Bench of the Supreme Court held that the contract from which the dispute arose was an administrative contract. Therefore, the Federal First Instance Court did not have the necessary jurisdiction to decide on the matter. According to the Cassation Bench, the determination of whether a contract is administrative is not tied to the provisions of property law or what property constitutes 'public domain' in property law. A contract can be deemed to be 'an administrative contract even when it does not relate to such property. To classify a contract as an administrative contract we have to look at factors like the *type of the contract, subject matter of the contract, the identity of the contracting parties* according to this law [3132].'

---

[199]*Woira Wood and Metal Works Cooperative Society v. Addis Ababa City Administration Trade and Industry Bureau,* Federal Supreme Court, Cassation Bench, File No. 80464 (2012) (*Tahsas 16, 2005 E.C*).

[200]The Addis Ababa City Government Revised Charter Proclamation 361/2003, Federal Negarit Gazeta, 9th Year, No. 86, Article 41(1) confers on City Courts jurisdiction as regards 'suits brought in connections with *administrative contracts* concluded by executive bodies of the City Government.'

[201]Civil Code of Ethiopia Proclamation No. 165/1960, Articles 1444 to 1448 defines state property that form public domain. According to Article 1444(1) property owned by the state is subject to laws applicable to privately owned property. Then the law defines property that forms public domain and hence is treated differently. Article 1445 defines 'public domain' as '*[p]roperty belonging to the State or other administrative bodies ... where: (a) it is directly placed or left at the disposal of the public; or (b) it is destined to a public service and is, by its nature or by reason of adjustments, principally or exclusively adapted to the particular purpose of the public service concerned.'*

Though the Cassation Bench does say, the subject matter of a contract is a factor in the determination of whether a contract is an administrative type, it does not attempt to show why exactly the particular contract in dispute deals with a subject matter that should be deemed administrative. In fact, it does not even mention the subject matter of the contract in the dispute, let alone show why the subject matter of the dispute led it to its finding. One is left with the impression that the fact that one of the parties was an administrative authority was a sufficient condition for the Cassation Bench's characterisation of the contract as an administrative one. Assuming this is true; Article 3132 does not really warrant this conclusion. The Cassation Bench has extended the meaning of administrative contract, it seems.

In *Tana Water Well Drilling and Industry PLC v. Diredawa Administration Water and Sewerage Authority*, the dispute arose from a contract for the drilling of 12 deep wells for the town of Diredawa.[202] Interestingly, the parties had chosen 'adjudication,'[203] a method that is now becoming common in the construction industry, as the dispute settlement mechanism. The Federal Supreme Court reversed the decision of the adjudicator on the ground that this being an administrative contract, the parties could not refer the dispute to an adjudicator. The company sought review on cassation for basic error of law. It argued that Article 315(2) of the Civil Procedure Code prohibiting arbitration of administrative contracts is silent about adjudication. It reasoned that the prohibition does not, therefore, apply to this method of dispute settlement.

The Cassation Bench confirmed the decision of the Supreme Court. It reasoned - adjudication being a binding settlement of disputes by a third party it is not any different from arbitration for the purpose of the prohibition of arbitration of administrative contracts. More pertinently, the Cassation Bench stated the fact that the water wells were meant for use by the public was an important consideration in the characterization of the transaction as an administrative contract.

3.4.2.2   Inarbitrability of Administrative Contracts: The Way Forward

The effectiveness of limitations imposed by domestic laws on the ability of the state, its organs or affiliated bodies to consent to arbitration in matters of relevance to international commerce has declined very significantly.[204] This is due, in part, to a

---

[202]*Tana Water Well Drilling and Industry PLC v. Dire Dawa Administration Water and Sewerage Authority*, Cassation File No. 127459, Unpublished (03 October 2017).

[203]In the context of the construction sector this refers to a form of dispute settlement by a third party that has been appointed by the parties or through a process chosen by the parties. The decision is binding unless and until reversed by a court or an arbitral tribunal, if the contract envisages arbitration after adjudication. Usually this is a much faster process than arbitration. Corbett Haselgrove Spurin, *Adjudication and Claim Settlement for the Construction Industry, available at: http://www.nadr.co.uk/articles/published/Adjudication/Adjudication.pdf,* last visited on 04 October 2018.

[204]Youssef (2009), p. 63.

norm of *international public policy* emanating from an ever increasing number of awards and court decisions that prohibit a state from invoking its own domestic law to rescind an obligation to arbitrate it willingly undertook.[205] In Switzerland, a forum in which many international arbitrations take place, the law explicitly states that a state cannot rely on its own domestic law to restrict the capacity to arbitrate or to derail arbitration by raising the defence of inarbitrability.[206]

This emerging notion of international public policy will seriously impact on the ability of the Ethiopian state and affiliated bodies to raise inarbitrability as a defence in international disputes of commercial nature. In fact, it does seem that there is already recognition of this fact. In a dispute between *Salini Costruttori S.P.A*, an Italian company, and the Addis Ababa Water and Sewerage Authority, inarbitrability was not even raised as a defence by the latter. This is despite the fact that the contract apparently meets the criteria in the definition of an administrative contract under Article 3132 of the Civil Code discussed in Sect. 3.4.2.1 above. It was for the construction of an emergency raw water sewerage reservoir for the city of Addis Ababa. The applicable law was Ethiopian, and the venue of arbitration Addis Ababa.[207] This case will be discussed at length in Chap. 6 that deals with *Kompetenz-Kompetenz,* among others.

Arab countries that had laws prohibiting the arbitration of administrative contracts, like Ethiopia, have now by and large abandoned this stance. Particularly, Algerian, Egyptian, Tunisian and Lebanese laws have changed course on this point.[208] These legal systems no longer exclude subjective arbitrability even in areas that involve very important national interests. They try to address the issue differently. The Egyptian law on transfer of technology has, for example, come up with an innovative approach. It allows arbitration but requires that the venue of arbitration be in Egypt and the applicable substantive law Egyptian.[209] This approach allows arbitration but gives the Egyptian state some control over the outcome of the arbitration. The laws of Egypt govern the substantive aspect of the contract and Egyptian courts wield the power of review at the post award stage.

Ethiopia may use an approach of this sort instead of a blanket rejection of arbitration in matters involving the state and bodies affiliated to it. Relying on a domestic law to reject an arbitration clause which a state organ or entities affiliated with the state willingly signed may not be a valid defence in view of the developments in the area of public policy.

---

[205] *Id.*, pp. 63–64.

[206] Youssef (2009), p. 64.

[207] *Salini Costruttori S.P.A(Italy) vs. The Federal Democratic Republic of Ethiopia, Addis Ababa Water and Sewerage Authority (Ethiopia* (ICC, Case No. 10623/AER/ACS). Case will be discussed in detail in relation to issues it raises. Suffice it say now that the Authority did not raise defence of inarbitrability though that would make a perfect defence by the standard of other cases that were found valid in domestic context.

[208] Youssef (2009), p. 63.

[209] *Id.*

3.5 Conclusion

The protection of the rights of third parties and the interest of the public at large may necessitate imposing restrictions on arbitrability in certain cases. The purpose of this chapter has been to determine subject matters that may not be arbitrated and persons or entities that may not submit to arbitration, if any, under Ethiopian law.

Ethiopian law does not expressly deal with subject matters that are not arbitrable. Besides, there are no court decisions dealing with this issue. That being said, the starting point should be the presumption of arbitrability. That is the approach taken in jurisdictions of significance to arbitration. It makes sense to start with the aim of giving effect to the agreement of the parties to arbitrate, in the absence of a clear legal prohibition against that.

That said, three laws of relevance to international commerce raise the issue of arbitrability in Ethiopia. These are bankruptcy, competition and consumer protection laws. A major goal of bankruptcy law is the maximization of the assets of the bankrupt debtor for the benefit of creditors taken together. It also aims at achieving equitable treatment of creditors. Attaining these goals requires bringing to an end individual suits and centralising proceedings at the bankruptcy court. In contrast, arbitration is a consent based mechanism, which implies decentralisation of proceedings. Nevertheless, the declaration of bankruptcy does not necessarily and automatically exclude arbitrability in many jurisdictions. Courts make individualised assessment of whether the continuation of arbitration is compatible with the core objectives of bankruptcy law. Where arbitration is found incompatible with the core objectives of bankruptcy, then the dispute is deemed non-arbitrable. Following this individualised approach makes sense in Ethiopia.

Coming to competition and consumer protection laws, the concerns and policy reasons that fuel the debate regarding the arbitrability of disputes involving these two fields are different. Yet, in Ethiopia the Trade and Consumer Protection Proclamation No. 813/2013 lumps the two fields together. This Proclamation has come up with an institutional mechanism to ensure its full implementation. Particularly, it establishes the Trade Competition and Consumers' Protection Authority accountable to the Ministry of Trade. It establishes under the auspices of the same authority, adjudicative benches with judicial power. This judicial body has jurisdiction to decide on disputes between traders, consumers and traders and even the authority itself and persons accused of infringing the proclamation. The judicial body can order administrative measures, impose fines and even award compensation to victims of anti-competitive behaviour and consumers, as the case may be. The existence of this institutional mechanism raises the issue of arbitrability of issues involving the competition and consumer protection law. Yet, given the novelty of the mechanism of enforcement of this law and the overall business landscape in Ethiopia, no question of arbitrability has been raised as far as this research could uncover.

That being said, the fact that this law establishes a dispute settlement mechanism should not be understood as proscribing arbitrability of disputes that involve competition and consumer protection law. There is no irreconcilable incompatibility between the mechanism of enforcement that the proclamation envisages and arbitration. Arbitrators can decide on the rights *inter se* giving all the remedies including compensation due under the proclamation to the party that is adversely affected by the infringement of the law. Other sanctions such as fines due for breach of the law and imprisonment can be applied by the judicial bench of the authority, the tribunal that the proclamation establishes and ordinary courts, as appropriate.

Regarding the issue of 'subjective' arbitrability, the Civil Procedure Code of Ethiopia, under Article 315(2) provides: '[n]o arbitration may take place in relation to *administrative contracts* as defined in Art 3132 of the Civil Code or in any other case where it is prohibited by law.' Entities that are directly or indirectly affiliated with the state routinely raise this provision to resist arbitration. Ethiopian courts have struggled with the determination of what exactly constitutes an administrative contract. By and large, the courts tend to find a contract as administrative as long as one of the parties is affiliated with a state. Article 3132 of the Civil Code that defines administrative contracts does not seem to warrant this conclusion.

In any case, the effectiveness of domestic laws imposing limitations on the ability of the state, its organs or affiliated bodies to consent to arbitration in matters of relevance to international commerce has declined very significantly. This is due, in part, to a norm of *international public policy* emanating from an ever increasing number of awards and court decisions that prohibit a state from invoking its own domestic law to rescind an obligation to arbitrate it willingly undertook. Hence, this rule should be abandoned at least, as far as international commercial arbitration is concerned.

References

Brekoulakis SL (2009) On arbitrability: persisting misconceptions and new areas of concern. In: Mistelis, Bekoulakis (eds) Arbitrability international and comparative perspectives. Kluwer Law International, Alphen

Brozolo L, Arbitration and competition law: the position of the courts and of arbitrators. OECD Hearings: Arbitration and Competition, DAF/COMP (2010)40, at p 31. Available at: http://www.oecd.org/competition/abuse/49294392.pdf. Accessed 27 Mar 2015

Courtney T (2009) Binding non-signatories to international arbitration agreements: raising fundamental concerns in the United States and Abroad. RJGLB 8(4):581

Di Pietro D (2009) General remarks on arbitrability under The New York Convention. In: Mistelis, Bekoulakis (eds) Arbitrability: international and comparative perspectives. Kluwer Law International

Dolmans M, Grierson J (2003) Arbitration and the modernization of EC antitrust law: new opportunities and new responsibilities. ICC Int Court Arbitr Bull 14(2)

Greenberg et al (2011) International commercial arbitration: an Asia-Pacific perspective. Cambridge University Press, Port Melbourne

Hearings: Arbitration and Competition, DAF/COMP(2010)40, at p 31. Available at: http://www.oecd.org/competition/abuse/49294392.pdf. Accessed 27 Mar 2015

Kirgis P, Arbitration, bankruptcy, and public policy: a contractarian analysis, p 3. Available at: http://pon.harvard.edu/wp-content/uploads/images/posts/kirgis-wip-article-pdf.pdf. Accessed 20 Mar 2015

Lehmann M (2004) A plea for a transnational approach to arbitrability in arbitral practice. Colum J Transnatl Law 42:753

Lew QCJ (2009) Competition laws: limits to arbitrators' authority. In: Mistelis, Bekoulakis (eds) Arbitrability international and comparative perspectives. Kluwer Law International, Alphen

Liebscher C (2009) Insolvency and arbitrability. In: Mistelis, Bekoulakis (eds) Arbitrability international and comparative perspectives. Kluwer Law International, Alphen

Mantakou AP (2009) Arbitrability of intellectual property disputes. In: Mistelis, Bekoulakis (eds) Kluwer Law International, Alphen

Mistelis L (2009) Arbitrability: international and comparative perspectives. In: Mistelis, Bekoulakis (eds) Arbitrability international and comparative perspectives. Kluwer Law International, Alphen

Müller F (2004) The New Council Regulation (EC) No. 1/2003 on the implementation of the rules on competition. German Law J 5(6):721

OECD Hearings, Arbitration and Competition, DAF/COMP (2010)40, 13 December 2011. Available at http://www.oecd.org/competition/abuse/49294392.pdf. Accessed 20 Aug 2016

Reisman et al (1997) International commercial arbitration: cases, materials and notes on the resolution of international business disputes. The Foundation Press Inc.

Salzberg M, Zinkgraf G, When two worlds collide: the enforceability of arbitration agreements in bankruptcy. Available at http://www.foley.com/files/publication/1020c6f0-d08d-4aee-82c7-b282fe0c221a/presentation/publicationattachment/a4edde0a-8a1f-4ea5-bc57-b9a0ccdf4958/salzberg-zinkgraf.pdf. Accessed 20 Mar 2015

Shore L (2009) The United States' perspective on "Arbitrability". In: Mistelis LA, Brekoulakis SL (eds) Arbitrability: international and comparative perspectives. Kluwer Law International

Spurin CII, Adjudication and claim settlement for the construction industry. Available at· http·//www.nadr.co.uk/articles/published/Adjudication/Adjudication.pdf, last visited on 04 October 2018

Tadesse L (2008) Ethiopian bankruptcy law: a commentary (Part I). J Ethiop Law 22(2)

Tecle HB (2009) Adjudication and arbitrability of government construction disputes. Mizan Law Rev 3(1):1–32

Youssef K (2009) The death of inarbitrability. In: Mistelis, Brekoulakis (eds) Arbitrability international and comparative perspectives. Kluwer Law International, Alphen

Zekarias K (1994) Arbitrability in Ethiopia: posing the problem. J Ethiop Law 17

Zekos G (2006) The European Union's new competition approach and arbitration. HLJ 4(1):36

Chapter 4
The Normative Basis for Decision on the Merits and Procedural Conduct of Arbitration: The Extent of Party Autonomy

4.1 Substantive Resolution Based on 'Principles of Law'

In Ethiopia, the Civil Code and Civil Procedure Code espouse, on the face, different set of norms as the basis for the resolution of the merits of the dispute. According to Article 317(2) of the Civil Procedure Code, the arbitral tribunal is required to '. . . decide *according to law* unless by the submission it has been exempted from doing so.' According to the Civil Code, on the other hand, arbitral submission is 'the *contract* whereby the parties to a dispute entrust its resolution to a third party, the arbitrator, who undertakes to settle the dispute in accordance with the *principles of law*.'[1] (Emphasis added)

A close look at these provisions and the two codes leads us to resolve this conflict in favour of the Civil Code provision. To start with, it is the Civil Code that deals with arbitration and its nature in a meaningful detail.[2] In contrast, the Civil Procedure Code dedicates to arbitration few provisions here and there. Therefore, it is the former that should be deemed the special law as far as the nature of arbitration is concerned. Moreover, it is in the context of listing down what the tribunal should do that Article 317(2) of the Civil Procedure Code provides: '. . . hear the parties and their evidence respectively and decide according to law.' When a statute contains an illustrative list of things, the *ejusdem generis* rule of interpretation is applied to determine whether the statute also applies to particular things that have not been specifically mentioned on the list. According to this rule of statutory interpretation only objects that are similar in nature to those things that have been specifically enumerated may be understood to have been covered by such statute.[3] If we go by that rule 'hearing the parties and their evidence' are procedural matters rather than

---

[1]Civil Code of the Empire of Ethiopia, Proclamation No. 165/1960, *Negarit Gazeta*, 19th Year, No. 2 Article 3325(1).

[2]*Id.* Articles 3325–3346.

[3]Clark and Connolly (2017).

© The Author(s), under exclusive license to Springer Nature Switzerland AG 2021   93
S. Y. Tesfay, *International Commercial Arbitration*, European Yearbook of
International Economic Law 12, https://doi.org/10.1007/978-3-030-66752-8_4

matters of substantive law. Moreover, Article 317 is titled 'procedure before arbitration tribunal.' So, its application is limited to the procedural conduct of arbitration rather than the norms applicable to the substance of the dispute. Besides, Article 315 (4) of the Civil Procedure Code provides that, in case of conflict Articles 3325–3346 of the Civil Code prevail over the provisions of the chapter of the Civil Procedure Code in which Article 315(4) is found. In sum, the Civil Code prevails. Arbitrators are not required to decide 'according to law' only. They may decide based on *principles of law*.[4]

4.1.1 Decision Based on Principles of Law and According to Law: Are They Identical?

Settlement of a dispute based on 'principles of law' is not identical with settlement in accordance with the 'law'. Principles of law consist of objective and abstract notions often developed over the centuries.[5] They may be derived from domestic, foreign or common rules of legal thinking. Some of them find their way into the national laws of countries.[6] Where they are, thus, incorporated into a specific national legal system, they form part of the 'legal norms' in force in the jurisdiction concerned. Some other principles, however, remain unincorporated into a national legal system. In such cases, the principles of law are not really 'legal norms' as regards that particular jurisdiction. They are merely directives of behaviour rather than legal norms as such.[7] In the context of commercial arbitration, it is said that notions like *'pacta sunt servanda, . . . force majeure*, the principle that execution of a contract implies its existence, the principle of interpretation *contra proferentem*, the obligation to mitigate damage, and good faith' are accepted as general principles of law, if they are not already incorporated into the domestic law of a jurisdiction.[8]

 That Ethiopian law allows arbitrators to decide based on principles of law, without the need for specific authorisation by the parties to that effect makes it very liberal compared to jurisdictions that require arbitrators to decide based on law.

---

[4]Civil Code of Ethiopia Proclamation No. 165/1960, Art 3225(1).

[5]Błaszczak and Kolber (2013), p. 190.

[6]*Id.,* at 191 and 198. Polish doctrine, for example, considers: 'freedom of contract in international trade, principle of *rebus sic stantibus, pacta sunt servanda*, the principle of good faith, prohibition of abuse of subjective rights, the principle of cooperation between the creditor and debtor to perform the contract, the principle of liability for breach of contract and damages, prohibition of contradicting the effects of own behavior or prior acts of will (*venire contra factum proprium nemini licet*), the principle that the impossible excludes obligation (*imposibilium nulla obliagatio*), the principle of protection of acquired rights, the principle of protection of trust as transnational general principles of law.'

[7]*Id.,* at 194.

[8]*Id.,* at 192.

4.1.2   Principles of Law and Lex Mercatoria: Are the Two Co-extensive?

Lex mercatoria is understood in many different ways by different authors. Particularly, its substantive content and relationship with national laws are vigorously contested matters.[9] It may be argued that the confusion is owing, partly, to the fact that the concept evolved to acquire different meanings in different times.[10] In any event, the various conceptions of this nebulous concept may be grouped into three headings. According to the first view, *lex mercatoria* is simply a legal order that is created spontaneously by parties engaged in international economic interaction. It exists independently of national legal orders. The second conception is that it is a set of rules, sufficient to resolve a dispute that can be used as an alternative to an otherwise applicable national system of laws, which could be rooted in laws of various nations and trade practice. *Lex mercatoria* is, according to the third conception, a 'gradual consolidation of usages and settled expectations' in international commerce which may supplement the applicable law.[11]

The first conception, *lex mercatoria* as an autonomous legal order, is not tenable. To start with, one cannot demonstrate where such an autonomous legal order derives its normative power from. Secondly, at present, at least, it is not comprehensive enough to deal with all aspects of a commercial dispute.[12] The second understanding of *lex mercatoria* too is not convincing as a matter of current reality. Simply, there are no universal rules of commerce whether grounded on national laws or practice that can sufficiently deal with the intricacies of commercial transactions.[13] It appears that only the third conception of *lex mercatoria* (i.e., international *trade usages* sufficiently established to warrant that parties to international contracts are deemed to have considered as binding) stands the test of a rigorous analysis.

---

[9]Rodriguez (2002).

[10]Michaels (2007), p. 478. It is possible to divide the evolution of this concept into three stages: ancient *lex mercatoria* of the middle ages meaning a 'transnational set of norms and procedural principles that established by and for commerce in (relative) autonomy from states.' The second stage refers to what one may call 'new *lex mercatoria*' as was understood in the twentieth century to mean 'an informal and flexible net of rules and arbitrators establishing a private international commercial law.' The third stage which we may call 'new *lex mercatoria* which moves from an amorphous and flexible soft law to an established system of law with codified legal rules' principally the UNIDROIT Principles of International and Commercial Law and strongly institutionalized court-like international arbitration.

[11]Park (2012), pp. 591 and 596.

[12]*Id.* at 595.

[13]*Id.* at 596–597. Though one may argue, for instance, the *Principles of International Commercial Contracts* published by UNIDROIT in 1994 represent *lex mercatoria* this is not tenable. This can at best be a snapshot of *lex mercatoria* as of 1994, not *lex mercatoria* itself. In fact, this document can turn out to be a competitor to *lex mercatoria* gradually.

No matter how we understand *lex mercatoria,* it and 'principles of law' are not coextensive though some authors mix up the two concepts.[14] Particularly, the sources of *lex mercatoria* are more diverse compared to principles of law. Its sources include '. . . principles of law common to most national legal systems (or at least those relevant to the contract in question), norms set down in widely accepted international treaties, *trade usages of the relevant transnational sectors,* and indeed international arbitral awards'[15] (emphasis added). As can be gathered from this, trade usages and customs form part of *lex mercatoria* but do not constitute principles of law, hence, making *lex mercatoria* wider in its coverage.

When the Civil Code of Ethiopia authorizes arbitrators to settle disputes based on 'principles of law', it allows them to go beyond legal norms embodied in the national laws of a specific country. It authorises them to make use of legal principles that the arbitrators deem appropriate under the specific circumstances. However, it does not authorise arbitrators to apply *lex mercatoria* in its entirety as this notion includes trade usages and customs that do not necessarily qualify as principles of law. In sum, the application of *lex mercatoria,* in its entirety, does not flow from Article 3325 (1) of the Civil Code that recognises principles of law as substantive parameters applicable to the merits of a dispute before arbitrators.

4.2   Foreign Law and 'Rules of Law': Are They on the Menu?

Historically, the conflict of laws rules of the seat of arbitration played a predominant role in the determination of the law applicable to the merits of the dispute. The wishes of the parties to arbitration, in this regard, were given only a secondary consideration. This position was embodied even in the resolution of the Institute of International Law. Article 11 of the 1957 Resolution on the 'Law Applicable to the Substance of the Difference' says, '[t]he rules of choice of law in force in the state of the seat of arbitral tribunal *must be followed* to settle the law applicable to the substance of the difference. *Within the limits of such law,* arbitrators shall apply the law chosen by the parties . . . .'[16] *(Emphasis added).*

This mandatory recourse to the conflict of laws rules of the seat of arbitration in determining the substantive law applicable to the merits of the dispute was severely criticised in the years following the adoption of the above Resolution. Many scholars such as Lazare Kopelmanas in 1964, Philippe Fouchard in 1965 and Pierre Lalive in 1967 contended this position is arbitrary.[17] Lalive, for instance, maintains a country in which an international arbitral tribunal seats has little, if any, interest in having its

---

[14]Błaszczak and Kolber (2013), p. 191.

[15]Reisman et al. (1997), p. 202.

[16]Gaillard (2010), p. 107.

[17]*Id.* p. 109.

choice of law rules determine what rules should apply to the merits of the dispute, as the dispute, in most cases, is totally unconnected to it. He takes the case of Switzerland where numerous international arbitrations take place despite the disputes having nothing to do with Switzerland other than the parties choosing it as a preferred venue. Hence, he muses over what interest Switzerland could have to insist that its choice of law rules should prevail over the choice of parties regarding the applicable substantive law.[18]

Three decades after the adoption of the 1957 Resolution opinion regarding the role of the parties shifted so significantly that even the Institute of International Law itself had to formally reverse its position. Article 6 of its 1989 Resolution reads in relevant part:

> [t]he parties have full autonomy to determine the . . . substantive rules and principles that are to apply to the arbitration. In particular . . . these rules and principles may be derived from different national legal systems as well as from non-national sources such as principles of international law, general principles of law, and the usages of international commerce. To the extent the parties have left such issues open, the tribunal shall supply the necessary rules and principles drawing on the sources indicated in Article 4 . . . .[19]

Article 4, to which the foregoing provision of the 1989 Resolution makes reference, indicates as possible sources: the law the parties to a dispute choose, the law that is indicated by applying the choice of law rules chosen by the parties, general principles of private and public international law, general principles of international arbitration or the law that the courts of the seat of arbitration would apply.[20] We need to underscore, in this connection, that there are no conflict of laws rules in Ethiopia that could tie the hands of the parties and arbitrators as regards the law that must be applied to the substance of the dispute.[21]

Today, most countries have arbitration laws that require arbitrators to respect the choice made by the parties regarding the law applicable to the merits of the dispute. The UNCITRAL Model Law, which has been adopted in many jurisdictions, for example, reads, '[t]he arbitral tribunal shall decide the dispute in accordance with such *rules of law* as are chosen by the parties as applicable to the substance of the dispute.'[22] The Model Law further clarifies this by pointing out that any reference made to the law or legal system of a country is to be construed as directly referring to the substantive law of the jurisdiction concerned to the exclusion of the conflict of laws rules of such state, unless otherwise provided expressly.[23]

It is to be noted further that according to the *Travaux Préparatoires* of the Model Law, the phrase 'rules of law' is broader than the law of a given national jurisdiction.

---

[18]*Id.*

[19]*Id.* p. 110.

[20]*Id.*

[21]Samuel (2000), p. 195.

[22]UNCITRAL Model Law on International Commercial Arbitration 1985 with amendments, G.A. res. 61/33, U.N. Doc. A/40/17, Article 28(1).

[23]*Id.* Article 28(1).

The use of this term in Article 28(1) is aimed at expanding the range of options open to parties. Thus, for example, parties to an arbitration agreement could choose instruments such as the United Nations Convention on Contracts for the International Sale of Goods (Vienna, 1980) as the rules of law applicable to the merits of the dispute.[24] There are only few countries that still do not clearly allow parties to an arbitration agreement the freedom to determine the laws or rules applicable to the merits of the dispute. Such countries tend to be on the fringes of global commerce.[25]

Coming to the state of affairs in Ethiopia, all the indications are that the law leaves the choice of norms to be applied to the merits of the differences between them to the parties to the arbitration agreement. To begin with, according to the very definition of an arbitration agreement under the Civil Code, the arbitrator '. . . undertakes to settle the dispute in accordance with *the principles of law,*' and not the law only.[26] As discussed already 'principles of law' are broader than laws adopted by a specific jurisdiction. Moreover, the arbitrators need not have specific authorisation to decide on the basis of principles of law under Ethiopian law unlike in some other jurisdictions. If arbitral tribunals can go beyond applying laws, and apply principles of law, it may be held that parties are at liberty to determine 'laws' or 'rules of law' to be applied to the merits of the dispute, for a stronger reason. The fact that arbitrators need not be lawyers under Ethiopian law indirectly supports this view point.[27]

Another point that may be raised in support of the freedom of the parties to choose the laws or rules applicable to the merits of the dispute is the fact that Ethiopian law does not prohibit that. The Civil Code of Ethiopia accepts the general principle of contractual freedom according to René David, its drafter.[28] The parties to a contract are, therefore, at liberty to define the object of the contract. David underscores that the law sanctions and 'gives effect to the will of the parties as manifested by their contract' as long as they do not violate any legal prohibitions.[29] The law should, therefore, be understood as presuming freedom rather than prohibition. The contrary view that only matters expressly allowed by the law are lawful would compel society to move at the pace of the lawmaker and hence seriously arrest progress. It is this point that René David makes when he states that contractual freedom is 'fundamental to a society and an economy that wants to leave considerable scope to private initiative.'[30] Article 16 of the Civil Code which vests in every person 'freedom of action' is perhaps a reflection of this, though not dealing precisely with freedom of

---

[24]*Id.* p. 33.

[25]For example, in Uzbekistan the national law applies and in Georgia the law is silent on this issue. In Belarus and Moldova, the parties to dispute are free to choose among the laws of other countries or jurisdictions but not 'rules of law' such as international customs as codified by some organizations etc.. . . European Bank for Reconstruction and Development (2007), p. 10.

[26]Civil Code of Ethiopia Proclamation No. 165/1960, Article 3325(1).

[27]Civil Code of Ethiopia Proclamation No. 165/1960, Article 3339(1). According to this provision, '[a]ny person may be appointed as an arbitrator.'

[28]David (1973), p. 29.

[29]*Id.*

[30]*Id.*

contract.[31] That the Civil Code is silent on this matter other than stating that arbitrators decide based on 'principles of law' implies the parties are free to choose the applicable norms. In other words, laws of any jurisdiction and arguably 'rules of law' embodied in instruments that have not necessarily been adopted in the national laws of any country can be chosen by the parties.[32] There is a recent legal development that gives credence to this view. The Council of Minsters has issued a regulation to implement the Industrial Parks Proclamation. The Proclamation aims at, among other things, carving out a special legal regime for industrial parks. These are 'areas with distinct boundary' designated as industrial parks by the Ethiopian Investment Board.[33] The regulation issued to implement the Industrial Parks Proclamation provides: '[i]ndustrial park end-users that have agreed to resolve their differences by arbitration are at liberty to choose the substantive and procedural law to be applied by the tribunal.'[34] This regulation is meant to apply only to 'areas with distinct boundary' that are designated as industrial parks by the Investment Board. It cannot be directly invoked outside such areas. It may, however, be used as a persuasive authority in favour of the freedom of parties to an arbitration agreement to choose foreign law.

That said, any future revision of Ethiopian law should clearly vest in the parties the right to choose foreign law to govern the merits of the differences between them for disputes that occur outside the context of industrial parks too. That will help obviate unnecessary confusion and limit the room for unwarranted litigation on this subject. Furthermore, any future revision should indicate that the designation of the laws of a specific jurisdiction as applicable refers to the substantive law of that chosen jurisdiction to the exclusion of the conflict of laws rules of that jurisdiction to avoid any confusion. This way, the law can preclude a situation where the substance of the dispute ends up being governed by the laws of a third country that the parties did not envisage owing to the application of conflict of laws rules of the designated country. It is to avoid this kind of scenario that the Model Law states, '[a]ny designation of the law or legal system of a given state shall be construed, unless

---

[31]Civil Code of Ethiopia Proclamation No. 165/1960, Art. 16(1). According to this provision '[e]very person is free to exercise any activity which he deems proper . . . .' Per sub article 2 of the same article '[t]he only restrictions which such freedom admits of are those which are imposed by the respect for the rights of others, morality and the law.'

[32]In this connection, things like the UNIDROIT Principles of International Commercial Contracts and INCOTERMS issued by the International Chamber of Commerce come to mind. It is of course difficult to hold that the entire content of such 'rules' qualify as principles of law that Ethiopian law states should be the normative basis for decision on merits.

[33]Industrial Parks Proclamation 886/2015, Federal *Negarit Gazette*, 21st Year, No. 39. Article 2(1), 25(1), 2(18) and 32(1). The proclamation defines an industrial park as an area with a distinct boundary that is designated as a park by the Ethiopian Investment Board. The proclamation envisages the issuance of implementing regulations and vests in the Council of Ministers the power to issue such regulations under Article 32(1).

[34]Industrial Parks Council of Ministers Regulation No. 417/2017, Articles, 30. Federal *Negarit Gazette*, 23rd Year, No. 93. Article 2(8) of the regulation defines 'industrial park end-user' as 'any industrial park developer, operator, enterprise, employee or resident.'

otherwise expressed, as directly referring to the substantive law of that State and not to its conflict of laws rules.'[35]

4.3 Equity: Its Different Shades of Meaning and Role

The arbitration laws of various jurisdictions differ in the extent to which they allow the parties to an arbitration agreement to authorise the arbitration tribunal to derogate from the strict application of laws and rules of law and decide based on equity. They also seem to attribute different meanings to the term equity.[36] In fact, the term is understood in many different ways even within the context of a specific legal tradition let alone in different jurisdictions and legal traditions.[37] Perhaps, the best way to understand the various shades of meaning of this term is to analyse it in terms of the 'weaker' and 'stronger' understanding of equity following the classification by German legal theoreticians such as Karl Engish and Joseph Esser.[38]

4.3.1 The 'Weaker' Understanding of Equity

According to the 'weaker' understanding of equity, decision based on equity is a 'decision taken *in light of the law* and in accordance with the legal directions which emanate from the strict legal rules in force.'[39] In this understanding, the law may direct a judge to employ equity in order to solve a problem in cases of vagueness of the law or when the law is silent regarding some aspects of the case at hand. So, equity plays a role in decision making within the bounds of the legal system. It is an intra-systematic way of decision making.[40] In this 'weaker' understanding, decision making in equity cannot be at variance with the law. Decisions should always start from the law in force because the law '. . . expresses, in its highest degree of development, what in a given society is considered as just, ethical, adequate and convenient.'[41]

   Analysis of Ethiopian law, particularly the Civil Code, reveals that equity in this 'weaker' sense is fully embraced by Ethiopian laws. For instance, the court may determine the remuneration due to a commission agent on the basis of equity where the remuneration has not been agreed upon and there is no custom regarding this

---

[35]UNCITRAL Model Law as amended in 2006, Article 28(1).
[36]Błaszczak and Kolber (2013), p. 198.
[37]*Id.*
[38]Caramelo (2008), p. 571.
[39]*Id.* p. 572.
[40]*Id.*
[41]*Id.*

matter at the place where the contract was concluded.[42] Similarly, a court may determine wages due to an employee based on equity where this is neither settled by a contract nor by custom of the place where work is performed.[43] In a similar vein, remuneration due to an author is to be fixed by a court based on equity in the absence of agreement regarding the matter between him and the publisher.[44] In some other cases the Civil Code empowers the court to award compensation where equity so requires. For instance, the court is empowered to award compensation on the basis of equity to the owner of land upstream where the exploitation of his land is impaired by prohibition from using water bordering or crossing his land.[45] Likewise, the law authorises a court to award compensation, where equity so requires, to a person whose image has been sold or otherwise used for the enrichment of some other person.[46]

Besides, a number of provisions of the Civil Code direct the court to determine or reduce the *quantum* of compensation due in cases of tortuous acts and omissions having regard to equity. For instance, a court may reduce compensation due where the damage caused by a person 'expands beyond what could reasonably be expected, in consequence of unforeseeable circumstances'[47] or in cases where the person who committed the wrongful act was not in a state to appreciate the wrongful nature of his conduct.[48] Besides, though that is rare, the Civil Code does in some instances authorise total or partial invalidation of a juridical act on grounds of equity. A case in point is Civil Code Article 368(3) that authorises a court to invalidate, in part or in whole, a will made by an interdicted person prior to his interdiction where provisions contained in such will are deemed to be contrary to equity.

We saw in the foregoing paragraphs, that the Civil Code of Ethiopia directs courts to utilize parameters of equity regarding some aspects of situations envisaged by the legal rules the Code itself embodies. These are generally situations the lawmaker has chosen to leave vague or not to set a specific rule about for a variety of reasons. The use of equity envisaged by the Civil Code seems aimed at leaving the work of concretising the rule or principle enunciated by the Code to the courts in certain legally determined situations. The Code does not seem to mandate courts to ignore or disregard the rules embodied in the Code, in a bid to reach what the judge considers equitable despite the law. Hence, it is safe to conclude that the foregoing are instances of use of equity in the 'weaker' sense. Since courts are empowered to

---

[42]Civil Code of Ethiopia Proclamation No. 165/1960, Article 2243.

[43]*Id.*, Article 2535.

[44]*Id.*, Article 2692. In a similar vein, the law authorizes the court to grant compensation to an outgoing farmer tenant in regard of expenses he incurred for cultivation of fruits that are still undetached at the time of the termination of the contract according to Article 3015(1) and (2) of the Civil Code.

[45]*Id.*, Articles 1239 and 1240(1).

[46]*Id.*, Article 29(2).

[47]*Id.*, Article 2101.

[48]*Id.*, Article 2099. *See also* Articles 2100, 2142 and 2160(1) for more on the Courts use of equity.

use parameters of equity in these legally predetermined situations, arbitrators too are empowered to do that as party appointed judges.

4.3.2 The 'Stronger' Sense of Equity

Equity is used in its 'stronger' sense when it is applied in order to resolve disparity that arises when 'the morally accurate, abstract and general norm is in conflict with the moral evaluation of the specific circumstances subject to decision making.'[49] Aristotle, the Greek philosopher, explains this point aptly in *Nichomachean Ethics*. He writes that all laws are 'universal' in that they do not deal with a specific case. Because the lawmaker is compelled to speak universally, and it is not possible to do so correctly about each and every case, the law takes the usual case and addresses that though it is aware of the possibility of errors entailed in this approach.[50] Aristotle says:

> [w]hen the law speaks universally, then, and a case arises on it which is not covered by the universal statement, then it is right, when the legislator fails us and has erred by over-simplicity, to correct the omission - to say what the legislator himself would have said had he been present, and would have put into his law if he had known . . . . And this is the nature of the equitable, a correction of law where it is defective owing to its universality.[51]

Understood in this wider sense, a decision based on equity is an extra-systematic decision. Such decision is not based on the regulatory logic of the legal system and its rules. The decision-maker, in this understanding of equity, is entitled to depart from the rigid legal solutions, which by definition provide rigid decision criteria, and base his decision on the so called justice of the concrete case.[52] So, an arbitrator that has been empowered to decide on the basis of equity understood in this stronger sense wields wider powers than an arbitrator who is empowered to decide based on 'principles of law.'[53]

That said, even when empowered to decide on the basis of equity understood in the 'stronger' sense of the term, an arbitrator cannot disregard the paramount values of the legal order or violate public policy. Conferral of such power only gives the arbitrator a certain leeway to transcend legal norms. Particularly, the tribunal's powers and competence always lie within the boundaries of the parties' own competence. Since the parties to arbitration themselves have no power or right to violate public policy, *a fortiori*, arbitrators too may not do this.[54] If arbitrators violate public policy even where they are authorised by parties to decide based on equity,

---

[49]Błaszczak and Kolber (2013), p. 199.

[50]Quoted in Rubino-Sammartano (1992), p. 7.

[51]*Id.*

[52]Caramelo (2008), p. 573.

[53]Błaszczak and Kolber (2013), p. 190.

[54]*Id.*, p. 204.

understood in the 'stronger' sense, the arbitral award could be annulled or refused enforcement precisely on the ground of violation of public policy. For instance, decision-making on the basis of equity may not justify the violation of the rights of defence. The precise contours and boundaries of this right, however, differ in various legal systems. For that reason, all circumstances must be evaluated *a casu ad casum* in order to determine whether or not public policy has been violated.[55]

In Ethiopian laws, we do not come across instances in which the court could make use of 'equity' in the stronger sense and disregard the law. However, that does not mean that an arbitrator will be similarly confined to the narrower or 'weaker' understanding of equity, despite powers conferred on him by parties to make use of equity in the stronger sense of the term. Though not in relation to Ethiopian Law, Professor René David, the drafter of the Ethiopian Civil Code, contends that an arbitrator has wider powers than a judge in this regard. He maintains that in voluntary arbitration the arbitrator has the powers vested in him by the parties. Hence, the first 'law' he must follow is the private agreement from which arise his powers. The state law does not mean exactly the same to a judge seating in a state court and an arbitrator. For the judge, there is no law beyond what the state prescribes. His powers and duties emanate from the law only. This is not the case with the arbitrator, who neither derives his powers from the state nor decides in its name. The arbitrator must take into account what the parties that empowered him to decide in equity expect of him and thus decide based on 'equity' understood in a stronger sense.[56] Though Ethiopian law indicates the arbitrator undertakes to settle a dispute based on 'principles of law', it does not prohibit parties from authorising the arbitrator to decide based on equity. In the absence of a prohibition against that, interpreting the law in line with what Professor René David, the drafter of the Code, says above makes sense.

Therefore, we may conclude that arbitrators in Ethiopia can go beyond 'principles of law' . . . and decide based on equity understood in both the 'weaker' and 'stronger' sense of the term. Equity in the 'weaker' sense of the word is embraced by the law itself expressly since the law authorises courts to make use of that in a number of situations. As regards, equity understood in the 'stronger' sense there is nothing in the law that prohibits parties from authorising its use by arbitrators. Besides, since the authority of an arbitral tribunal is derived from the agreement to arbitrate and not the law as such, and the tribunal does not decide in the name of the state, parties to an arbitration agreement can validly authorise use of equity in the stronger sense of the term in Ethiopia. This is, of course, subject to compliance with public policy of the state. Hence, it can be said that Ethiopian law is abreast of jurisdictions in the vanguard on this point.[57]

---

[55]*Id.*

[56]Caramelo (2008), p. 574.

[57]Arbitration laws and case law show a number of countries regarded as important centers of international arbitration allow arbitrators to decide based on equity. For example, Article 1051(3) of the German ZPO and Article 822 of the Italian Code of Civil Procedure allow parties to authorize

4.4   Beyond Equity: Mandate to Settle and Modify Contract

At least in theory, it is possible for arbitrators to base their decision on substantive issues on parameters other than rules of law, principles of law and even equity. They may, in some jurisdictions be given a free hand to the extent of modifying the contract between the parties to reach a settlement, if so authorised by the parties to an arbitration agreement. In what follows, we will first explore the trend in this regard in other jurisdictions. We will then examine the state of the law and practice in Ethiopia in the sub-section below.

4.4.1   Overview of the Trend in Other Jurisdictions

Parties to an arbitration agreement sometimes authorise arbitrators to decide as *amiable compositeurs*. There is no consensus as to what this term means though. Particularly, whether it means the same thing as *ex aequo et bono* or something different is contestable. We gather, on the one hand, that the two terms are understood differently at least in some jurisdictions, though that is very seldom sufficiently dealt with in case law and legislations. On the other hand, it does seem that many authors and lawyers treat the two terms as identical in effect and use them interchangeably.

That said, at least historically they seem to be different. The earliest use of the term seems to be in the context of public law. For example, we find it used as early as in 1272, when Bishop Barthélémy and the elders of Cahors appointed *arbitres et amiables compositéurs* to settle their disputes regarding local customs. Similarly, in 1334, we come across the appointment of Philippe de Valois as 'judge, arbitrator, and *amiable compositéur*' to resolve a dispute between the Duke of Brabant and various German princes. In this context of the law of nations it appears that the task of the *amiable compositeur* was finding a landing place that both sides to the dispute would accept as fair rather than decision resulting from strict tenets of international law, if customary international law did exist in that distant era.[58] This notion then found its way into commercial law. By the early nineteenth century it was well established in French law that arbitrators mandated to proceed *comme amiable*

---

arbitrators to decide based on the principles of equity. Similarly, in Switzerland and Poland parties are entitled to authorize the arbitral tribunal to decide on the basis of equity. Interestingly, perhaps in keeping with the English tradition that is less disposed to accept decision based on equity, the English Arbitration Act of 1996 only implicitly allows arbitrators to decide based on equity. Article 46(1)b of the Act provides that the tribunal may decide: "if the parties so agree, in accordance with *such other considerations* as are agreed by them or determined by the tribunal". *See* Błaszczak and Kolber (2013), pp. 199 and 201.

[58]'Honourable Engagement' (2010).

compositeur could 'dispense with observing strict rules of law so that they rule solely by following their conscience and the impulse of natural equity.'[59]

The question of relevance for us, now, is whether a tribunal with such powers may modify or 'rewrite' the contractual terms between the parties to a dispute. It can, if we go by the literal meaning of the term *amiable compositeur*. This is the case because the term means one who effects a settlement.[60] According to Caramelo the Portuguese law of arbitration takes this view. It vests in the *composição amigável* the power to decide 'the dispute by appealing to the composition of the parties, on the basis of the balance of interests at stake.'[61] Mr. Caramelo argues since the Act also allows parties to arbitration agreement to empower the arbitrator to decide according to equity the language of Article 35 must mean something more. He contends we should presume that the legislator uses different words to mean different things. So, settlement of a dispute on the basis of equity in the stronger sense of the term is only part of the powers of the *amiable compositeur*. He can go beyond that.[62]

This should not, however, be understood as giving complete discretion to the extent of empowering the arbitrator to take a sentimental or psychological approach to justice. That would lead to arbitrary decisions. The *amiable compositeur* should, therefore, adhere to certain principles that are widely shared by the members of the relevant business community. These principles are the following:[63]

(a) a presumption that the parties intended to establish an economic equality or balance regarding their contributions agreed in the contract entered into (which balance, if it has been broken, the amiable compositeur, deciding in equity, should try to restore);

(b) a presumption of intended equality of risk, as initially set out in the contract concluded by the parties (which, if it has been later significantly disturbed, the amiable compositeur, deciding in equity, should attempt to rebuild to the extent that is possible, fair and reasonable) and

(c) applying the requirement of good faith in the execution of contracts (employing equity should allow the amiable compositeur to sanction certain behaviours of a party to a contract in bad faith which are not reproachable under the strict rules of law as well as to temper the responsibility of a defaulting party who acted in good faith).

Mr. Caramelo maintains that the dissertation of Professor Eric Loquin embodying the above understanding of *amiable composition* is likely to have been known to the members of the Portuguese Parliament that introduced the wording seen above to

---

[59] *Id.*

[60] *Id.* p. 4.

[61] Caramelo (2008), p. 576. He cites Article 35 of the Portuguese Arbitration Act as conferring such extensive powers in this kind of arbitrator.

[62] *Id.* According to Mr. Caramelo the wording of Article 35 leads one to conclude that the '*composição amigável de litígio*' contemplated therein is not a decision in equity *minus*, but rather a decision in equity *plus*.

[63] *Id.*, p. 577.

Article 35 in the final text of the Arbitration Act.[64] Hence, he argues that an *amiable compositeur* has quasi settlement making power in the Act. He has the power to search for a settlement that has the best prospect of being accepted by both sides. He appeases the parties. For this purpose, he can 'rewrite' the contract to re-establish the initially agreed equilibrium of the contractual *quid pro quo*. This does not, however, go to the extent of rewriting the contract to correct the disequilibrium created by the parties intentionally at the very outset when they signed the contract.[65] In sum, when parties authorise the arbitrator to act as a *compositor amigável* in accordance with Article 35 of the Portuguese Arbitration Act, the arbitrator is empowered to go beyond equity understood in the 'stronger' sense of the term discussed in the foregoing section. He should discharge the 'appeasement function' described above on top of that.[66]

In a 2008 Canadian case,[67] an arbitral tribunal took essentially the same view as that seen above though the trial court and the Court of Appeal in Québec vacated the award on a 'different' ground. The dispute involved a family business. One faction of the family bought the other out of the family's business. The pay out agreed upon was based on a formula that linked the amount to be paid on the profitability of the business at the time of the agreement. The buyout contract contained an arbitration clause authorizing the arbitrator to act as *amiable compositeur*.[68] The business turned out to be extremely profitable. Yet, the family that sold its entitlement to a part of the business received no pay out, on the main, owing to the fact that the formula did not sufficiently integrate future acquisitions into the calculation of 'available funds.' Hence, when the dispute was eventually brought before the *amiable compositeur*, he struck two provisions from the formula in the contract. His determination was that the definition in the formula lead to a result neither of the parties had anticipated. Hence, he reasoned that 'the formula may be amended to ensure that the intention of the parties is fulfilled,' and that the powers of the *amiable compositeur* empower him to do so.[69] He reasoned he was not ignoring the contract. Rather, he was making changes in the contract in order to fulfil the intention of the parties to the contract and concretise the same.[70]

The trial court of Québec, however, vacated the award, and its decision was confirmed by the Court of Appeal. The decision of the Court of Appeal contains a scholarly exegesis of the powers of the *amiable compositeur* that concludes the award would have been above reproach under the law in force in the past. Its

---

[64]*Id.*, p. 578.

[65]*Id.*, pp. 577–578.

[66]*Id.* p. 578. According to some authors in Polish doctrine too an *amiable compositeur* may disregard the rights and obligations 'formulated imperatively' in the contract between the parties. *See also* Błaszczak and Kolber (2013), p. 203.

[67]Bloomberg Law Reports (2010), p. 4, quotes *Coderre* v. *Coderre*, Montreal Court of Appeal, Canada 13 May 2008.

[68]*Id.*

[69]*Id.*

[70]*Id.*

confirmation of the trial court's decision vacating the award was based on Article 944.10 of the Québec Code of Civil Procedure. The said provision which follows the UNCITRAL Model Arbitration Law approach gives effect to *amiable compositeur* designations. However, like the UNCITRAL Model Law, it expressly states that the arbitrators "shall *in all cases* decide according to the stipulations of the contract."[71] (Emphasis added). In other words, even when authorised to act as *amiable compositeurs* the arbitrators under the Model Law cannot depart from the terms of the contract.

Overall, it appears that there is no consensus on the role of *amiable compositeur* in international arbitration doctrine. According to some, arbitrators cannot disregard the contractual terms even when authorised to act as *amiable compositeurs* while others maintain that such arbitrators are allowed to revise the contract, where need be. The former view is popular in Swiss doctrine. The argument in favour of the Swiss view is that allowing arbitrators to revise a contract is irreconcilable with the fundamental principle of *pacta suncta servanda*. There are instances indicating arbitral case law seems to be in line with this viewpoint. Błaszczak and Kolber offer as examples ICC case No. 3267 of 1979 and ICC Case No. 3938 of 1982.[72] In the latter, for instance, the arbitral tribunal reasoned:[73]

> [a]ccording to the dominant doctrine and practice of international commercial arbitration, an arbitrator amiable compositeur remains bound by the contract [ ]. Considerations that may lead the amiable compositeur to mitigate the effects of the application of dispositive provisions of law in specific circumstances are inapplicable in respect of the contract, a special regulation arising out of the parties' own will.

In sum, it must be said that, at least, in arbitration laws drafted following the Model Law approach on this point, arbitrators are not empowered to change the terms of the contract even when empowered to act as *amiable compositeurs* by the parties. Article 28(3) of the Model Law allows the parties to authorise arbitrators to act as *amiable compositéurs* but Article 28(4) makes it clear that '*in all cases*' the arbitral tribunal is to '. . . *decide in accordance with the terms of the contract*' taking into consideration the usages of trade relevant to the transaction in question.[74] (Emphasis added)

---

[71]*Id.*

[72]Błaszczak and Kolber (2013), pp. 207–208.

[73]*Id.*, p. 208.

[74]UNCITRAL Model Law on International Commercial Arbitration with amendments adopted in 2006, Article 28(4). According to the *Travaux Préparatoires* empowering arbitrators to act as amiable compositeurs and for that matter to decide based on equity is not used in all legal systems. So, the model law did not want to regulate this. It only wanted to bring this type of arbitration to the attention of the parties and clarify that the terms of the contract cannot be affected even by arbitrators given such powers. *See* United Nations Commission on International Trade Law (2012), p. 112.

4.4.2 Mandate to Settle: Can Parties Confer This Power on Arbitrators Under Ethiopian Law?

Ethiopian law does not make any reference to *amiable composition*. In fact, all it says regarding substantive basis of arbitral decisions is that arbitrators 'undertake to settle the dispute in accordance with *the principles of law*.' As already discussed, this empowers arbitrators to decide based on 'law', 'rules of law' and even more. The question though is whether this implies that the power of the arbitrator goes so far as to include the possibility of revising the terms of the contract between the parties or disregarding the same to some degree. At least regarding equity, the law says a court may not modify a contract on grounds of equity unless that is expressly provided by law.[75] As already discussed, arbitrators as party appointed judges decide neither in the name nor on behalf of the state. Hence, it may be contended that they have broader powers in this regard where they are authorised to decide based on equity. More specifically, it may be held that where parties authorise arbitrators to act as *amiable compositeurs,* the latter may have even more powers and hence revise the contract subject to limitations imposed by public policy.

However, it must be admitted that there is no much legal authority on this point in Ethiopia. Only one Cassation Court decision may be construed to lend support to such expansive powers of arbitrators though the case does not expressly deal with *amiable composition*.[76] The dispute, in that case involved three members of an extended family. They had been engaged in business together but could not continue as business partners because of serious disagreement. Hence they entrusted settlement of their dispute regarding the winding up of their business to *Sergan Jama* family council, elders from their community.[77] They further undertook to be bound by the decision of these elders though the agreement does not characterise itself as an arbitration agreement. In fact, the agreement indicates that it was the elders who took the initiative and offered to intervene to 'reconcile' the business partners. The latter

---

[75]Civil Code of Ethiopia Proclamation No. 165/1960, Article 1763. In the Civil Code of Ethiopia equity plays a role in determining the content of contracts. Article 1713 provides that parties to a contract are 'bound by the contract and such incidental effects as are attached to the obligations concerned by custom, equity, and good faith having regard to the nature of the contract.' According to Article 1766 of the Civil Code the court may vary a contract where a special relationship such as family relationship exists between the parties and such relationship compels them to deal with each other in accordance with equity.

[76]*Mukemil Mohammed v. Miftah Kedir*, Federal Supreme Court of Ethiopia, Cassation File Number 38794, (24 Megabit 2001 EC, Reported in Cassation Decisions of the Federal Supreme Court Volume 9, pp 173–175).

[77]Agreement between Miftah Kedir, Mukemil Mohammed and a third partner also signed by seven traditional elders dated 3 November 1997 (23 Tikimt 1990 E.C). The file was obtained from the attorney of one of the parties and a copy is retained.

only accepted efforts at 'reconciliation' and undertook to be bound by the decision of the *Sergan Jama* family council.[78]

On 18 November 1997, just 15 days after the signing of the agreement above the *Segan Jama* elders made known their findings reached after conducting inquiry and 'convincing' the parties to the dispute. After partial compliance with the decision of the elders, Mr. Miftah Kedir discontinued effecting payments. Hence, Mr. Mukemil Mohammed applied to the Federal First Instance Court for the execution of the decision of the elders.[79]

Mr. Miftah Kedir contended that there was no agreement to arbitrate, and therefore, the 'findings' of the elders do not amount to an arbitral award. According to him, there was no award that could be 'executed' by a court. The Federal First Instance Court heard the testimony of the persons involved in 'resolving' the dispute. From that testimony it gathered that they were engaged in reconciling and convincing the parties. The Court concluded that the elders were not acting as arbitrators. The exercise was 'conciliation' rather than arbitration.[80] In consequence, the First Instance Court decided that there was no award to execute. The exercise being 'conciliation', the parties are not bound by the findings of the conciliators unless they 'expressly agree in writing to confirm them' per the requirement of the Civil Code.[81] In the case at hand, there was no written agreement between the parties confirming acceptance of the terms of the compromise drawn by the conciliators, the First Instance Court noted.[82] Mr. Mukemil Mohammed appealed to the Federal High Court. The High Court confirmed the decision of the First Instance Court.[83]

Aggrieved by this decision of the two courts, Mr. Mukemil Mohammed sought review on cassation for 'basic error of law.' For the Cassation Bench, the fact that the parties to the dispute had agreed to be bound by the decision of the elders was sufficient to characterize the exercise as arbitration. The Cassation Bench reasoned the agreement indicates that 'the tribunal' was established to 'reconcile the misunderstanding' concerning property and money between the named parties and that the

---

[78]*Id.* The agreement contains a penalty clause. It stipulates the person who fails to abide by the decision of the Sergan Jema family council will have to pay by way of penalty 50,000 Birr to the State, 40,000 Birr to the other party and 10,000 Birr to the Sergan Jema elders. The agreement was signed by the three people in dispute and seven *Sergan Jema* elders.

[79]Application for execution of 'arbitral award' lodged by Mr. Mukemil Mohammed dated 12 December 2001(03 Tahsas 1994 EC). The outstanding amount for which execution was lodged was Birr 170,122.75 (One hundred seventy thousand one hundred twenty two and seventy five cents).

[80]*Mukemil Mohammed v. Miftah Kedir*, Federal First Instance Court, Case No. 00136, decision rendered on 26 September 2007.

[81]Civil Code of Ethiopia Proclamation No. 165/1960, Article 3322(2) provides '[t]he parties shall not be bound by the terms of the compromise drawn up by the conciliator unless they have expressly undertaken in writing to confirm them.'

[82]*Mukemil Mohammed vs Miftah Kedir*, Federal First Instance Court, File No. 00136, 26 September 2007.

[83]Mukemil Mohammed v. Miftah Kedir, Federal High Court, Case No. 60530, Decision dated 17 April 2008 (Miazia 9, 2000 EC).

said parties 'undertook to accept the findings and decisions' of the tribunal.[84] This agreement shows that the parties vested in the *shimaglies* power to pass decisions and 'agreed to accept the decisions' passed by them, according to the Cassation Bench. The Cassation Bench, therefore, reversed the decision of the lower courts that characterised the exercise as conciliation rather than arbitration and ordered that the 'award' be executed.[85]

Noteworthy is the fact that the Cassation Bench of the Federal Supreme Court characterises the *Sergan Jama* council as an arbitral tribunal despite noting that they aimed at '*reconciling*' the misunderstanding between the relatives. The touchstone on which this characterisation depended was the fact that the parties to the dispute had 'undertaken to accept the findings and decisions' of the Council. The Cassation Bench disregarded the testimony given in the First Instance Court by the elders themselves as regards how they proceeded from which the First Instance Court concluded the exercise was conciliation rather than arbitration. Though an arbitration agreement need not necessarily designate itself as such[86] the intention to arbitrate must be there, in our view.

In any case, coming to the issue at hand, the normative basis for decision of arbitrators, the Cassation Bench did not even inquire into the substantive basis of the decision of the elders. As traditional elders, effectively what they did was reach a decision that they deemed fair in view of, among other things, the blood relationship between the parties to the dispute, and the need to close the chapter and move forward as relatives.[87] Yet, the Cassation Bench accepted their decision as an arbitral award.

Leaving aside whether the Cassation Bench got the facts of the case and the intention of the parties right, in this particular case, there is no doubt that for the Cassation Bench, the undertaking to be bound by the outcome of the decision of a third party is the critical factor. There is no need to even consider the normative basis of the decision by the third party, if we go by this decision.

In contrast to its finding in *Mukemil Mohammed v. Miftah Kedir*, in a *dictum* in a later case, the Cassation Bench emphasises the duty of arbitrators to stick to the agreement of the parties and arguments raised before the tribunal in deciding matters

---

[84]*Mukemil Mohammed v. Miftah Kedir*, Federal Cassation File No. 38794. My own free translation of the Cassation Court decision reported in Cassation Court Decisions Volume 9, pp. 173–175.

[85]*Id.*

[86] Haris et al. (2007), p. 52. In David Wilson Homes Ltd v. Survey Services Limited, a clause in an insurance policy that read as 'any dispute or difference arising hereunder . . . shall be referred to a Queen's Counsel of the English Bar to be mutually agreed . . . or in the event of disagreement by the Chairman of the Bar Council' was deemed to constitute an arbitration agreement despite no mention of arbitration at all in the clause. That the dispute was referred to a third party that would render a binding decision and that the matter related to an insurance policy rendered any construction of this clause to mean something different from arbitration lead to this conclusion.

[87]Telephone interview, with Mr. Miftah Kedir, conducted on 21 February 2015. Unfortunately, I could not get the views of Mr. Mukemil Mohammed, who reportedly, has passed away.

before them.[88] In *Ethio-Telecom v. PTE International Incorporated*, the latter had undertaken to carry out various tasks aimed at improving the performance of the personnel of *Ethio-Telecom*. As per the contract, *Ethio-Telecom* was expected to pay US$4 million in three instalments. 12% of each instalment was to be withheld as guarantee for performance of the contract. The amount so withheld was to be released to *PTE International* within 15 days from completion of the project if implementation of the project was found to be satisfactory.[89]

PTE International could not complete the tasks per the agreement. The evaluation carried out by *Ethio-Telecom* revealed that only 71% of the tasks envisaged in the contract had been successfully carried out. *PTE International* did not contest this finding.[90] Yet, *Ethio-Telecom* did not seek performance of the balance of the contract. *PTE International* demanded that Ethio-Telecom release, from the amount withheld by the latter as guarantee of good performance, a sum that represents work successfully completed (i.e. 71% of the amount withheld).[91] The Arbitral Tribunal, formed per the arbitration clause, granted the claim of *PTE International* on the theory that the internal review undertaken by *Ethio-Telecom* amounts to novation, a new contract, and payment of a percentage of the guarantee can be implied from that.[92] The Cassation Bench did not find this tenable. It disagreed on grounds of form requirements for modification of contract which are of no interest to us since we are not concerned with substantive legal issues. More pertinently, the Cassation Bench remarked that 'an arbitral tribunal should decide based on valid undertakings agreed upon by contracting parties.'[93] Though clearly the Cassation Bench was not addressing the issue of *amiable composition* in this particular case, its emphasis on the importance of arbitrators sticking to the terms of contract does not augur well for the notion. The Cassation Bench sounds, in this case, predisposed to reject modification of contract by arbitrators, even where the latter are given mandate to settle.

That said, *Ethio-Telecom v. PTE International* does not really stand for a rejection of *amiable composition*. The Cassation Bench only made a remark about a doctrine that was not dispositive in the particular case without even mentioning it by name. *Mukemil Mohammed v. Miftah Kedir* appears to be a more pertinent authority. Hence, we may conclude that an arbitral tribunal may revise the contract between

---

[88]*Ethio-Telecom v. PTE International Incorporated*, Cassation Case No. 63063, Cassation Bench of the Federal Supreme Court, 03 *Hidar* 2005 EC. Reported in Cassation Bench Decisions Vol. 14 (2013). The central issues the Cassation Bench addressed are whether review on Cassation is possible despite a finality clause in the arbitration agreement and the substantive issue of whether the facts of the case indicate there was *novation* of contract. So, the case is not really authority on the issue of amiable composition. It is only an *obiter dictum*.

[89]*Id.*

[90]*Id.*

[91]*Id.*

[92]*Id.*

[93]*Id.* Incidentally the Cassation Bench underscored that arbitral tribunals should also decide based on arguments raised in the proceedings implying arbitral proceedings are adversarial.

the parties to a dispute, at least so long as the parties have authorised it to do so, and undertaken to be bound by the resultant decision.

4.5   Procedural Conduct of Arbitration: Flexibilities Allowed

In procedural matters, arbitration broadly resembles commercial litigation in a domestic court. Just like in a national court it 'will in many cases involve, for instance, the submission of written pleadings, and legal arguments (often by lawyers), the presentation of documentary evidence, oral testimony . . . , and the rendition of a reasoned award. . . .'[94] That being said, the arbitration agreement may in many jurisdictions affect the procedure to be followed to varying degrees.

In so far as the procedural conduct of commercial arbitration with foreign element is concerned, the earliest view with strong following was that which drew analogy between the arbitrator and the judge in the seat of arbitration. This view point was first crystallised in the Geneva Protocol on Arbitration Clauses of 1923. Article 2 of this instrument provided that the arbitral procedure was subject to the law of the country in which the arbitration takes place.[95] This position found its clearest expression in the 1957 Resolution of the Institute of International Law in its Amsterdam Session. Article 9 of the Amsterdam Resolution reads in relevant part: 'the law of the place of the seat of the arbitral tribunal shall determine whether the procedure to be followed by the arbitrators may be freely established by the parties . . .'[96]

The above position was severely criticised in the years that followed on grounds of the very tenuous relationship that exists between the procedural law at the seat of arbitration and the international arbitration taking place there. The contention was that it is more consistent with the nature of arbitration to give precedence to the choice of the parties. Hence, the position started to be eroded quickly. The New York Convention of 1958 departed from the tenet of the Amsterdam Resolution in this regard by giving precedence to the intent of the parties over the procedural law of the seat of arbitration.[97] The Convention takes the focus away from the seat of arbitration to the jurisdiction in which recognition and enforcement is sought and gives the latter jurisdiction discretion to deny recognition and enforcement on grounds of procedure followed by arbitrators. Particularly, it provides that recognition and enforcement may be refused if ' . . . the composition of the arbitral authority or the arbitral procedure was not in accordance with the agreement of the parties, *or, failing*

---

[94]Born (2001), p. 2.
[95]Gaillard (2010), p. 94.
[96]*Id.*
[97]*Id.*, pp. 95–96.

such agreement, was not in accordance with the law of the country where the arbitration took place.'[98] (Emphasis added)

Owing to the foregoing developments one observes that many jurisdictions permit parties to the arbitration agreement to choose the procedure that will govern the conduct of arbitration or even tailor-make procedural rules for their specific dispute. As a result, one may observe, dramatic differences in the procedural dimension of arbitration across industrial sectors, institutional rules of arbitration, types of dispute and even parts of the world in which the arbitrations took place.[99] In what follows we will look at the procedural conduct of arbitration in Ethiopia and the level of flexibility the law gives to the parties and arbitrators.

The Civil Code of Ethiopia makes reference to the Civil Procedure Code as regards procedural conduct of arbitration. It provides: '[t]he procedure to be followed by arbitration tribunal shall be as prescribed by the Code of Civil Procedure.'[100] The relevant provision of the Civil Procedure Code of Ethiopia provides that the procedure before an arbitral tribunal must 'as near as may be, be the same as in a civil court.'[101] More particularly, it reads 'the arbitral tribunal . . . shall hear the parties and their evidence respectively and decide according to law unless by the submission it has been exempted from doing so.'[102] The last phrase of this provision gives the parties to an arbitration agreement the right to exempt the tribunal from having to follow the procedural laws in force.

Even going beyond this, parties may choose that the arbitrators follow the rules of procedure of an arbitral institution. This is what the Civil Code envisages when it provides that the term 'arbitral submission' has to be understood as inclusive of 'the provisions of the arbitral code to which the parties may have referred.'[103] If parties may by agreement incorporate arbitral codes, which can only mean rules of arbitration institutions, which for the most part are procedural rules, one may contend the parties to an arbitration agreement can also tailor-make the rules of procedure they want to be applied to their dispute. At least there is no prohibition against that in Ethiopian law.

In sum, one can gather from the cumulative reading of the provisions of the Civil Procedure Code and the Civil Code that arbitrators are not bound to follow each and every single provision of the Procedure Code. In this regard Professor Sedler maintains that the 'provisions of the Procedure Code should be employed as a guide but should not be used where they would disrupt the informality of arbitral proceedings resulting in increased costs and delay in the disposition of the case.'[104]

---

[98]UN Convention on Recognition and Enforcement of Foreign Arbitral Award of 1958, Article V (1)d.

[99]Born (2001), p. 2.

[100]Civil Code of Ethiopia Proclamation No. 1965/1960, Article 3345(1).

[101]Civil Procedure Code Decree No. 52/1965, Art 317(1).

[102]*Id.,* Article 317(2).

[103]Civil Code of Ethiopia Proclamation No. 165/1960, Article 3346.

[104]Sedler (1968), p. 388.

According to him, one of the very aims of submitting a dispute to arbitration is avoiding the expenses and time involved in court proceedings. This purpose would be defeated if pleadings and the like required by the Code of Civil Procedure were to be complied with scrupulously.[105] Sedler does, however, emphasise that the arbitral procedure must adhere to the basic principles and values embodied in the procedural laws. For instance, the proceedings must be fair to all the parties. Particularly, the provisions of the Civil Procedure Code of Ethiopia that are designed to ensure every party gets opportunity to present his side of the case must be complied with.[106]

The Highest Court in Ethiopia seems prepared to accept procedural flexibility subject to few exceptions. In *Mukemil Mohammed v. Miftah Kedir*, cited already the Federal First Instance court had concluded what the *Sergam Jama* council conducted was conciliation rather than arbitration because, among other things, 'there was no indication that the procedure they followed was the same as that followed by courts' in adjudicating cases.[107] The Cassation Bench of the Federal Supreme Court found this reasoning invalid. It reiterated the provisions of Article 317(2) of the Procedure Code that require arbitrators to 'hear the parties and their evidence.' In addition to this, the Cassation Bench emphasised that the arbitral tribunals must respect the right of parties to arbitration '*to ask questions*'.[108] Presumably, by the right to ask questions the Cassation Bench meant the right to cross examine witnesses or otherwise challenge evidence. Other than this, the Cassation Bench did not expressly say anything about the extent to which an arbitral tribunal may possibly deviate from the procedure that a court follows. However, the fact that it accepted as a valid award a decision by traditional elders without any evidence of the procedure followed says a lot.[109] It seems the Cassation Bench is prepared to accept any procedure as valid so long as the parties are 'heard', each party is given chance to 'adduce his evidence' and 'ask questions'—probably meaning cross examine witnesses and question evidence.

---

[105] *Id.*

[106] *Id.*

[107] *Mukemil Mohammed v. Miftah Kedir*, Federal First Instance Court, File No. 00136.

[108] *Mukemil Mohammed v. Miftah Kedir*, Federal Supreme Court of Ethiopia, Cassation File No. 38794.

[109] In *Mukemil Mohammed v. Miftah Kedir* the seven persons that gave the decision the legal significance of which was in dispute were members of Sergan Jama family council, traditional elders of the clan to which the parties in dispute belonged. There were no written pleadings. One can see the procedure was not really adversarial as the elders were making attempt to reconcile the parties by persuasion as the Cassation Court itself notes and presumably they were exerting psychological pressure to effect settlement. Yet the Cassation Bench accepted a decision reached in this manner as a valid arbitral award that can be enforced.

4.6 Conclusions

In this chapter, the extent of autonomy that Ethiopian law vests in parties to an arbitration agreement to determine the substantive and procedural rules to be applied to arbitration between them was considered. We find that Ethiopian law is uncharacteristically liberal on these subjects. To start with, the law defines arbitration as the settlement of a dispute by reference to principles of law—a notion that is much wider than law or even rules of law. As a consequence, unlike in some other jurisdictions,[110] in Ethiopia, the arbitration agreement need not expressly authorize the application of principles of law to the merits of a dispute for that to apply. This demonstrates that Ethiopian law is more liberal than many arbitration friendly laws such as those that follow the UNCITRAL Model Law approach on this subject[111] and arguably German law.[112]

Moreover, Ethiopian law does not prohibit parties to an arbitration agreement from choosing foreign law or even rules of law as applying to the substance of a dispute between them. Given the absence of proscription, we may hold that parties are at liberty to choose foreign law and rules of law. In the same vein, we can conclude that parties are free to authorise a tribunal to apply equity both in the

---

[110]Błaszczak and Kolber (2013), pp. 191–192. In Poland, for example, express authorization by the parties is required for the tribunal to apply principles of law. In contrast, the Swiss and French laws as well as legal doctrine developed in the two countries provide that the basis of decision should be '*règles du droit*', thus implicitly allowing the use of general principles of law as the basis for decision, so long as at least the general principles are part of the legal system. *See also*, Hosseraye et al. 2012, p. 352. The 2011 French Law leaves to the parties the choice of law applicable to the substance of the dispute but, where the parties have not made choice, the arbitrators are free to apply the 'rules of law' That they consider appropriate. In other words, the arbitrators do not need an express authorization by parties to apply 'rules of law' instead of limiting themselves to the law of a specific country. The use of the words 'rules of law' instead of 'law' is deliberate. They aim at enabling the arbitrators to apply principles of law rather than being bound to the laws of a specific country.

[111]UNCITRAL Model Law on International Commercial Arbitration with Amendments as Adopted in 2006, Articles 28(1) and (2) of the Model Law indicate disputes are to be resolved based on '*rules of law*' chosen by the parties to the arbitration agreement. In case parties to arbitration agreement fail to choose the applicable law, arbitrators are to apply '*the law*' determined by the conflict of laws rules they consider are applicable. So, where parties have not chosen 'rules of law', what will apply is a specific law reached through the application of conflict of laws rules. So where the 'law' of the specific state reached at by application of conflict of laws rules does not mandate the application 'principles of law', only the laws of the specific state will apply to the substance of the dispute.

[112]German Code of Civil Procedure (*ZPO*) of 1998, Section 1051(1) provides that arbitrators are to decide disputes in accordance with such '*rules of law*' as are chosen by the parties. 'Rules of law' are generally construed to be broader than 'the law' as seen in relation to French Law. So, the use of this term suggests parties can, according to German law, validly choose the application of principles of law. But providing for cases where parties to dispute have not chosen substantive law applicable to the dispute, sub 2 of Section 1051 says '*the law*' of the state, with which the subject matter of the proceeding is most closely related applies. Here the change in language indicates use of 'principles of law' is not the default option unlike in Ethiopia. *See* German Arbitration Law of 1998, tenth Book of the Code of Civil Procedure, available in English at: http://www.dis-arb.de/en/51/materials/german-arbitration-law-98-id3, accessed on 13/09/2011.

weaker and stronger or extra-systematic sense to the substance of a dispute between them. Somehow less settled is the issue of whether parties to an arbitration agreement can confer on a tribunal a mandate to settle—vesting in it the power to re-write some contractual obligations of the parties, in order to re-establish the balance of interest at stake short of violating public policy. The decision of the Cassation Bench in *Mukemil Mohammed v. Miftah Kedir* suggests even that is a possibility.

Coming to autonomy regarding procedural matters, parties to an arbitration agreement do have maximum flexibility, to the extent of tailor-making the procedure the tribunal should follow. The only limit is that the procedure so devised should not unfairly favour one party over another. Particularly, every side must be afforded the opportunity to be heard and present its evidence.

References

Błaszczak L, Kolber J (2013) General principles of law and equity as a basis for decision making in arbitration. CLR: 189

Born G (2001) International Commercial Arbitration: commentary and materials, 2nd edn. Kluwer Law International

Caramelo AS (2008) Arbitration in equity and amiable composition under Portuguese law. J Int Arbitr 25

Clark K, Connolly M (2017) A guide to reading, interpreting and applying statutes. https://www.law.georgetown.edu/academics/academic-programs/legal-writing-scholarship/writing-center/upload/statutoryinterpretation.pdf. Accessed 14 May 2017

David R (1973) Commentary on contracts in Ethiopia (trans: Kindred M). Haile Selassie I University

Gaillard E (2010) Legal theory of international arbitration. Martinus Nijhoff

Haris B et al (2007) The Arbitration ACT 1996: a commentary, 4th edn. Blackwell Publishing Inc

'Honourable Engagement' (2010) Bloomberg law reports, insurance law, vol 4(8). https://www.cahill.com/publications/published-articles/000092/_res/id=File1/Honorable_Engagement.pdf. Accessed 22 Jan 2015

Hosseraye J et al (2012) Arbitration in France, CMS Guide to Arbitration, vol I

Michaels R (2007) The True Lex Mercatoria: law beyond the state. Ind J Global Leg Stud 14(2):447

Park W (2012) Arbitration of international business disputes, 2nd edn. Oxford University Press

Reisman et al (1997) International commercial arbitration: cases, materials and notes on the resolution of international business disputes. The Foundation Press Inc

Rodriguez A (2002) Lex Mercatoria. www.law.au.dk/fileadmin/site_files/filer_jura/documenter/forskning/rettid/artikler/20020046.pdf. Accessed 20 July 2016

Rubino-Sammartano M (1992) Amiable Compositeur (joint mandate to settle) and Ex Bono Et Aequo (discretional authority to mitigate strict law) - apparent synonyms revisited. J Int Arbitr

Samuel T (2000) Toward generalizing judicial jurisdiction in Ethiopia. TFLR-Private Int Law 8:195

Sedler RA (1968) Ethiopian civil procedure. Haile Selassie I University in Association with Oxford University Press, Addis Ababa

Chapter 5
Kompetenz-Kompetenz and Separability

5.1 *Kompetenz-Kompetenz* of the Arbitral Tribunal: The Contest Between the Legitimacy and Efficacy of Arbitration

Two potentially conflicting goals permeate international commercial arbitration. On the one hand, there is a need to ensure the use of arbitration is based on the consent of the parties and hence the resulting award is seen as legitimate. On the other hand, there is a desire to make arbitration an effective and therefore an attractive alternative to litigation.[1] In other words, since international commercial arbitration is consent-based if a party is compelled to arbitrate in the absence of an agreement to arbitrate the legitimacy of the arbitration and the resultant award is compromised. Conversely, arbitration becomes a costly and non-expeditious mechanism if a party has an option to go to court, before the arbitration is over, to prevent the arbitration from going forward.[2]

Legal jurisdictions differ in the extent to which they appreciate the challenge of striking the right balance between the competing goals of efficacy and legitimacy of arbitration. They also vary in how they attempt to articulate a workable framework of analysis to address the problem.[3] That said, in many jurisdictions, the doctrines of *Kompetenz-Kompetenz* and separability are deemed to hold the keys to unlock the mysteries associated with striking the right balance between the two competing goals.[4] The two doctrines, which speak to the same question of who determines the jurisdiction of the arbitral tribunal, are thus embodied in the laws of many

---

[1]Bermann (2012), pp. 1–2.

[2]*Id.,* p. 5.

[3]*Id.,* p. 3.

[4]*Id.,* p. 13.

S. Y. Tesfay, *International Commercial Arbitration*, European Yearbook of International Economic Law 12, https://doi.org/10.1007/978-3-030-66752-8_5

jurisdictions in some form. They are among the most widely recognised concepts in international commercial arbitration.[5]

In this part of this chapter we will use the doctrine of *Kompetenz-Kompetenz* as the basis for the analysis of Ethiopian law. Our aim is assessing the extent to which Ethiopia law balances concerns of legitimacy and efficacy of arbitration. To this end, we will attempt to throw some light on whether or not arbitral tribunals have the power to decide on their own jurisdiction under Ethiopian law. In particular, we will dwell on the basis and scope of such powers. We will examine whether Ethiopian courts are by law prohibited from entertaining the issue of arbitral jurisdiction till the arbitral tribunal decides on this matter. Moreover, we will evaluate whether or not Ethiopian law governing these issues is compatible with the law and practice of international commercial arbitration. Besides, we will examine Ethiopian law on this topic in view of public international law rules of relevance to this matter as pronounced by international arbitral tribunals. We reserve the doctrine of separability for the next part. We start by shedding some light on the doctrine of *Kompetenz-Kompetenz*.

5.1.1 Kompetenz-Kompetenz: *A Chameleon-like Notion*

Kompetenz-Kompetenz, which literally means 'jurisdiction on jurisdiction', is a much more vexed principle than it appears at first. It has 'a chameleon-like quality that changes colour according to the national and institutional background of its application.'[6] The general understanding is that this doctrine 'permits an arbitral tribunal to determine its own jurisdiction' where that is challenged.[7] This is referred to as 'positive' *Kompetenz-Kompentenz* by some authors, and in this piece. In its most basic form, this doctrine is an anti-sabotage mechanism.[8] It reduces the possibility of derailment of arbitration by a simple allegation that the arbitration agreement is unenforceable owing to any number of contract law defences. It enables the arbitral tribunal to decide on such defences and proceed with the arbitration, where it finds it has jurisdiction.[9]

This basic rule, however, tells only a part of the story.[10] First, there are issues, at least in some jurisdictions, as to whether the doctrine covers cases where the very existence, validity and scope of the arbitration clause itself are at issue.[11] Second, the basic rule also says nothing about the flip side of this rule, which imposes restrictions

---

[5]Susler (2009), pp. 119-20-20.
[6]Park (2012), p. 232.
[7]Bermann (2012), p. 14.
[8]Park (2012), p. 233.
[9]*Id.*
[10]*Id.*
[11]Tang (2014), p. 75.

on the intervention by courts so the arbitral tribunal has the first opportunity to determine its own jurisdiction.[12] It does not specify the exact stage at which courts may or may not intervene. Third, the doctrine remains silent about the standard of review the courts should employ where they do intervene in the process to access the arbitration agreement and its consequence.[13] For instance, in some jurisdictions the standard of review employed by courts will be *prima facie* or full depending on whether the review is conducted before or after the arbitral tribunal has been constituted or rendered its award. The rules on intervention by courts in this regard may also vary depending on whether the arbitration is domestic or international.[14] Fourth, in jurisdictions where parallel proceedings before a court and an arbitral tribunal are possible, there is an issue as to the effect of such proceedings.[15] Fifth, where the law provides that the arbitral tribunal has the first word on its own jurisdiction, there are differences as to whether such word is final or subject to review by courts.[16]

Overall, *Kompetenz-Kompetenz*, in and of itself, says not much about the course of action a court or an arbitral tribunal confronted with the foregoing type of issues should take. As a result, there is diversity on the timing, extent and impact of intervention by courts in jurisdictional matters in the context of arbitration giving *Kompetenz-Kompetenz* different shades of meaning in different jurisdictions.[17] The consequence is that the doctrine is understood in some jurisdictions in ways that favour efficacy of arbitration over its legitimacy. In some others the reverse is the case. Many other jurisdictions provide hybrid solutions lying somewhere in the spectrum between the two extremes.[18]

Our aim in this part is, therefore, to evaluate the extent to which Ethiopian law balances concerns of legitimacy and efficacy of arbitration. To this end, we will attempt to explain whether or not arbitral tribunals have the power to decide on their own jurisdiction under Ethiopian law, positive *Kompetenz-Kompetenz*. Particularly, we will discuss the basis and scope of such powers. We will also examine whether or not Ethiopian courts are by law prohibited from entertaining the issue of arbitral jurisdiction till the arbitral tribunal decides on this matter. Furthermore, we will assess whether or not Ethiopian law on these issues is compatible with the law and practice of international commercial arbitration. Finally, we will examine whether or not Ethiopian law governing this subject matter is trumped by the rules of public international law and international public policy.

---

[12]Susler (2009), p. 125.

[13]*Id.*, at, 120.

[14]Park (2012), p. 238.

[15]Tang (2014), p. 75.

[16]*Id.*, p. 76.

[17]Park (2012), pp. 234–237.

[18]*Id.*, p. 248–249.

5.1.2   Kompetenz-Kompetenz *in Jurisdictions of Significance: A Snapshot*

A good starting point to answer the foregoing questions is to look at how the notion of *Kompetenz-Kompetenz* is understood and applied in jurisdictions of significance to international commercial arbitration. This comparative approach will help us locate where in the spectrum of the different understandings, the notion as understood in Ethiopia lies. Hence, in what follows, we will have a bird's-eye view of how this notion is understood in different jurisdictions first. We will do this by starting with the French law which emphasizes efficiency of arbitration, perhaps more than any other. We will then proceed down the spectrum towards jurisdictions that relatively emphasize legitimacy. Towards the middle of the spectrum the question of which law is more pro-efficiency than the other becomes murky. The aim here is not really to conclusively rank the laws of different countries on this subject. Rather, our purpose is limited to giving a background for an easier understanding of Ethiopian law on *Kompetenz-Kompetenz*, and drawing lessons, if any. We need to bear this in mind from the outset.

5.1.2.1   *Kompetenz-Kompetenz* in French Law

The French arbitration law, which must have informed the arbitration rules of the 1960 Civil Code of Ethiopia,[19] was fully overhauled for domestic and international arbitration in 1980 and 1981 respectively.[20] These rules have further been amended by the Decree No. 2011-48 of January 13, 2011 which introduces Articles 1442 to 1527 to the Code of the Civil Procedure.[21] This new French law aims at consolidating France's appeal as a venue for international arbitration. Hence, it embodies the distinctively pro-efficiency stance taken by the French courts as regards *Kompetenz-Kompetenz*.[22]

The new French arbitration law empowers an arbitral tribunal to decide on its own jurisdiction, when that is challenged before the tribunal.[23] This is a feature of many

---

[19]David (1963), p. 192. Unfortunately, we do not find documented preparatory works dealing with this part of the Civil Code of Ethiopia. But René David, the drafter of the Code himself tells us that by choosing continental jurists, Ethiopian authorities indirectly choose the Code to be modelled after continental civil codes, when it comes to concepts. From this, and the fact that René David was a French Jurist one may gather that the French arbitration laws of the time informed the drafting of the Ethiopian law on arbitration.

[20]Castellane (2011), p. 371.

[21]*Id.*

[22]Bermann (2012), pp. 15–16.

[23]Castellane (2011), p. 373. Article 1465 which vests in the arbitral tribunal power to decide on objections against its jurisdiction is found in the part of the Code that deals with domestic arbitration. All the same, it applies automatically to international arbitration too owing to Article

other modern arbitration laws.[24] What distinguishes the French law from such other laws is the prohibition it imposes on courts from entertaining challenges to the jurisdiction of arbitral tribunals save in exceptional circumstances. Article 1448 of the new law reads, '. . . a court *shall refuse* to hear a dispute which is covered by an arbitration agreement unless an arbitration tribunal has not been seized of the dispute . . . and the arbitration agreement is *manifestly void or inapplicable.*'[25] (Emphasis added) So, according to the French approach, *Kompetenz-Kompetenz* has not only a positive dimension of empowering an arbitration tribunal to decide on its own jurisdiction, whether the challenge is directed at the arbitration clause itself or the container contract, but also a negative dimension of barring courts from entertaining jurisdictional issues at the outset of arbitration.[26] In other words, French law embodies both positive *Kompetenz-Kompetenz* and negative *Kompetenz-Kompetenz*.

The obligation imposed by French law on a court to refer disputes to arbitration is broader than that under the New York Convention. According to the Convention,

[t]he court of a Contracting State, when seized of an action in a matter in respect of which the parties have made an agreement within the meaning of this article, shall, at the request of one of the parties, refer the parties to arbitration, unless it finds that the said agreement is null and void, inoperative or incapable of being performed.[27]

Once an arbitral tribunal has been constituted, the French judge has no option but to sit on his or her own hands and wait until the arbitral tribunal renders an award. Put differently, once constituted the arbitral tribunal must always have the first opportunity to decide on its own jurisdiction under the French law.[28] In contrast, the Convention does not draw a line after which courts should not entertain challenge to the jurisdiction of the arbitral tribunal. It follows that a challenge to the

---

1506 that indicates Article 1465 applies unless the parties have reached agreement excluding the application of the latter.

[24]For instance, the 2006 UNCITRAL Model Law on International Commercial Arbitration provides under Article 16(1) '[t]he arbitral tribunal may rule on its own jurisdiction, including any objections with respect to the existence or validity of the arbitration agreement.' The 1985 version of the UNCITRAL Model law uses identical language under Article 16(1) of the same. So, in countries that follow the Model Law on this point, arbitrators have positive *Kompetenz-Kompetenz*.

[25]Castellane (2011), p. 372. For this purpose when arbitrators accept their mandate and hence the tribunal is constituted the arbitral tribunal is deemed to have been seized of the dispute pursuant to Article 1456 of the new law. From that date on wards, the courts are prohibited to entertain issues regarding jurisdiction of arbitral tribunal until the tribunal returns its own award. This new rule embodies the 2006 decision of *Cour de Cassation* in *American Bureau of shipping v. Copropriété Jules Verne*.

[26]Bermann (2012), pp. 16 and 18. Note that some jurisdictions like the US do not allow arbitrators to decide on their own jurisdiction if the validity of the arbitration clause itself is directly attacked rather than the general validity of the main contract. We need not dwell on this at length here as that issue will be discussed at a more pertinent stage.

[27]UN Convention on the Recognition and Enforcement of Foreign Arbitral Awards (1958), Article II(3).

[28]Park (2012), p. 239.

jurisdiction of the arbitral tribunal may be entertained under the Convention at any time so long as the grounds listed under Article II(3) of the Convention are fulfilled as a close reading of the said provision shows.

Yet another way in which the French law ties the hands of a judge is by limiting the grounds on which the judge may refuse to refer disputes to arbitration only to cases where the arbitration agreement is *manifestly void or inapplicable*. This allows the French judge to conduct only the most superficial review of the arbitration agreement such as whether the agreement is *clearly void* for lack of any signature.[29] He is not allowed to pose more complex questions regarding the validity of the arbitration agreement such as its scope of coverage at the pre-award stage.[30] By analogy from this, French Courts have declined to refer disputes to arbitration where an arbitration agreement 'manifestly does not exist, manifestly does not bind the party sought to be bound, manifestly does not cover the dispute at hand, or is otherwise manifestly unenforceable.'[31]

In contrast to the French law, under the New York Convention an arbitration agreement need not be '*manifestly*' null and void for the judge to be able to entertain the dispute on jurisdiction. Under the Convention, the judge may not refer the dispute to arbitration where he finds the arbitration agreement is '*null and void, inoperative or incapable of being performed.*'[32] In other words, the judge under the Convention may conduct a relatively more intrusive review of the arbitration agreement compared to what is possible under the French law before referring the matter to arbitration.

In sum, under Article 1448 of the New French Civil Procedure Code, the court is allowed to question the jurisdiction of an arbitral tribunal at the pre-award stage only if two cumulative conditions are fulfilled. Specifically, if 'no arbitral tribunal has yet been constituted *and* the agreement to arbitrate is, for one reason or another, manifestly ineffective or unenforceable.'[33] The French courts are allowed to make full inquiry into arbitral jurisdiction once the arbitral tribunal has returned its award.[34] So, what the French law does is give the first word, on its own jurisdiction to the arbitral tribunal subject to intrusive examination after the award.[35] The overall

---

[29]*Id.*

[30]*Id.*

[31]Bermann (2012), p. 17.

[32]UN Convention on Recognition and Enforcement of Foreign Arbitral Awards of 1958, Article II (3). Note here that even under the New York Convention the court is under no obligation to examine the validity of arbitration agreement at pre-award stage even on grounds listed down under Article II (3) of the Convention. What the Convention says is the Court *must refer the dispute to arbitration* unless the arbitration agreement suffers the defects listed in the same article. Yet some authors understand have an opposite understanding. Castellane, for example, contends under Article II(3) of the New York Convention the 'courts *must examine* the validity of the arbitration agreement, if challenged, before referring the parties to arbitration.' *See* Castellane (2011), p. 372.

[33]Bermann (2012), p. 17.

[34]*Id.*, at 19.

[35]Park (2012), p. 242.

outcome is that the French approach gives primacy to the efficiency of arbitration over its legitimacy.[36]

The French position which gives across-the-board deference to arbitrators or alleged arbitrators, as the situation may turn out to be, has not gained widespread acceptance.[37] Many other jurisdictions of significance to international arbitration follow a more flexible and nuanced approach to the role of courts in the determination of arbitral jurisdiction.[38] In what follows we will briefly look at these approaches beginning with the position taken by German law.

5.1.2.2 *Kompetenz-Kompetenz* in German Law

The German arbitration law is based on the UNCITRAL Model Law of 1985.[39] The arbitral tribunal may, therefore, rule on its own jurisdiction under the German law.[40] The power of the tribunal in this regard goes to the extent of ruling on whether an arbitration agreement exists and its validity according to the Civil Procedure Code ('ZPO') Section 1040(1).[41] So, German law clearly posits positive *Kompetenz-Kompetenz*, or the power of the arbitral tribunal to decide on its own jurisdiction as does the French law.[42] It is also similar to the French law to the extent the German 'ZPO' Section 1032(2) provides that a court may decide on the jurisdiction of arbitrators only if request is made to the court before an arbitral tribunal is constituted.[43] Incidentally, Section 1032(2) of the 'ZPO' is a deliberate deviation from the Model Law which does not preclude application to a court for the determination of arbitral jurisdiction even after an arbitral tribunal has been constituted.[44]

The similarity between the French and the German approaches ends here. Particularly, the German law does not embrace the French approach to negative

---

[36]Bermann (2012), p. 18.

[37]Park (2012), p. 242.

[38]*Id.*

[39]*Id.*, at 244. *See* for more details the English translation of the tenth book of the Civil Procedure Code of Germany, ZPO, issued in 1998 available at: www.disarb.org/en/51/materials/german-arbitration-law-98-id3, accessed on 12 February 2016.

[40]Civil Procedure Code of Germany (*ZPO*) 1998, Article 1040(1).

[41]According to the German Civil Procedure Code, ZPO, amended in 1998, Section 1040(1) 'the arbitral tribunal may rule on its own jurisdiction, and in this connection, on the existence or validity of the arbitration agreement.' *See also* Lörcher, *Arbitration in Germany*, 1 CMS Guide to Arbitration, pp. 372–373.

[42]Bermann (2012), p. 20.

[43]Barceló III (2003), p. 1131.

[44]Bermann (2012), p. 20. See Section 1032(2) of the ZPO that reads, '*prior to the composition of the arbitral tribunal* an application may be made to the court to declare whether or not arbitration is admissible. Emphasis added. The 1985 UNCITRAL Model Law, Article 8, has no counterpart for this provision.

Kompetenz-Kompetenz.[45] Though cognizant of the fact that arbitration would proceed more smoothly if courts were denied any room for intervention in matters of arbitral jurisdiction until after the arbitral award is given, the German law does not go down that route. It recognizes that following that approach would create inefficiency of its own in the longer run as awards may have to be vacated for lack of arbitral jurisdiction after full-fledged arbitration with all the attendant costs, including time lost.[46] Hence, the ZPO provides, so long as the arbitral tribunal has not been constituted, the possibility of lodging an application to the court seeking its determination on whether or not the dispute is subject to arbitration.[47] In consequence, the arbitral and judicial proceedings may have to go forward side by side.[48] In fact, even in cases where the dispute lands in a court first the party that disputes judicial jurisdiction and wants arbitration may initiate arbitration. There will be parallel proceedings in such a case too.[49]

Interestingly, German law expressly states its preference for arbitrators to decide on their own jurisdiction at the earliest possible time 'by means of a preliminary ruling.'[50] Such an award is subject to an immediate judicial recourse to set it aside.[51] In contrast, under the UNCITRAL Model law, arbitrators at their own discretion, decide on their own jurisdiction as an interim award or at the very end with the award on the substance of the dispute.[52]

Coming back to the French approach, another point of distinction between it and the German approach on negative *Kompetenz-Kompetenz* is the standard of review that a court uses in assessing arbitral jurisdiction. Unlike a French court, a German court will not restrict itself to a *prima facie* review of the arbitration agreement.[53] Rather, it will fully examine the agreement and deny arbitral jurisdiction if it finds

---

[45]*Id.*

[46]*Id.*

[47]German Civil Procedure Code, *ZPO* (1998), Section 1032(2).

[48]Bermann (2012), p. 21.

[49]German Civil Procedure Code, ZPO (1998), Section 1032(3) states clearly that arbitration may be commenced or continued despite a pending litigation before a court on the issue of arbitral jurisdiction.

[50]*Id.*, Section 1040(3).

[51]Barceló (2003), p. 1131. According to Section 1040(3) of the ZPO, any party that feels aggrieved by the finding of the arbitral tribunal on its own jurisdiction may request the court, within a 'month after having received a written notice of that ruling' to decide on the question of arbitral jurisdiction. This again could result in a possibility of parallel proceedings as the foregoing application to the court does not have the effect of halting arbitration where the finding of the arbitral tribunal had been in favor of its own jurisdiction.

[52]UNCITRAL Model Law on International Commercial Arbitration as amended in 2006 Article 16 (3). According to this provision, if the arbitral tribunal chooses to rule on its own jurisdiction as a preliminary question and the decision is that it has jurisdiction any party may within a month from having come to know of the decision appeal to a court with jurisdiction. The decision of such court is not appealable.

[53]Bermann (2012), p. 19.

the arbitration agreement is 'null and void, inoperative or incapable of being performed' according to ZPO Section 1032(1).[54]

Thus, overall, we see that though German approach to *Kompetenz-Kompetenz* is close to the arbitral efficiency end of the spectrum; it is more nuanced and calibrated than the French approach. It reflects a deeper commitment to ensuring arbitration is consent-based and seeks more the legitimacy that such consent fosters.[55]

5.1.2.3 *Kompetenz-Kompetenz* Under the *UNCITRAL Model Law*

The *UNITRAL Model Law* which was used as the basis for the arbitration laws of over 60 countries in all the six inhabited continents within just 25 years from its adoption in 1985 is a good comparator for assessing Ethiopian law on this subject.[56] Hopefully, Ethiopia will consider this law, at least, as a starting point in any future law revision. Thus, the need for dwelling on the position of the *Model Law* on the subject of *Kompetenz-Kompetenz* cannot be overstated.

Under the *Model Law*, '[t]he arbitral tribunal may rule on its own jurisdiction, including any objections with respect to the existence or validity of the arbitration agreement.'[57] In other words, the tribunal can rule on the 'foundation, content and extent of its mandate and power.'[58] So, the *Model Law* embodies positive *Kompetenz-Kompetenz* in the widest sense of the term.[59]

As regards the timing of the decision, the *Model Law* vests in the arbitral tribunal discretion to decide on any objection to its jurisdiction either as a preliminary question or together with the award on the merits.[60] In case the tribunal decides it has jurisdiction as a preliminary matter, recourse to a court is possible subject to three procedural safeguards aimed at protecting the efficacy of arbitration.[61] First, recourse to a court is possible only within a short period of time, thirty days from receipt of notice of the ruling. Second, the decision of the court confirming arbitral jurisdiction is not appealable. Third, the arbitral tribunal is at liberty to continue with

---

[54]*Id.*

[55]*Id.*, p. 21.

[56]Walsh (2010), p. 215.

[57]UNCITRAL Model Law on International Commercial Arbitration as amended in 2006, Article 16 (1).

[58]Explanatory Note by the UNCITRAL Secretariat on the 1985 Model Law on International Commercial Arbitration as amended in 2006, p. 30.

[59]In some jurisdictions, arbitral tribunals have power to decide on their own jurisdiction regarding the scope of their powers etc... but not on the very existence and validity of the arbitration agreement hence embodying *Kompetenz-Kompetenz* in relatively narrower sense. See, for example, the discussion below on the law of the United States of America, on this subject.

[60]UNCITRAL Model Law on International Commercial Arbitration as amended in 2006, Article 16 (3).

[61]*Id.*

the arbitral proceeding and make an award on the merits while the recourse from its jurisdictional determination is pending before the court.[62]

Incidentally, a report of the UN Commission on International Trade Law on an earlier draft of the *Model Law* indicates that a finding by an arbitral tribunal that it lacks jurisdiction does not preclude recourse to the court. The aggrieved party can apply to the court to obtain a ruling on whether a valid arbitration agreement exists.[63] That said, the arbitral tribunal that had ruled it lacked jurisdiction should not be compelled to proceed with the arbitration if its finding on jurisdiction is reversed by the court.[64]

Coming to the role of the court, modelled after the *New York Convention*, the *Model Law* imposes on the court the obligation to refer to arbitration, any dispute that is subject to an arbitration agreement. This obligation does not apply if the court 'finds that the agreement is null and void, inoperative or incapable of being performed.'[65] That said, scrutiny of the *Model Law* reveals that it takes the middle road when it comes to permitting courts to intervene in the determination of arbitral jurisdiction.[66] For instance, it leaves more room for intervention by courts in the determination of arbitral jurisdiction compared to the French and even the German law. Under the French law, a court is allowed to make only a *prima facie* evaluation of the arbitration agreement even where a court is seized of the jurisdictional dispute before the constitution of the arbitral tribunal.[67] The court is required to refer the dispute to arbitration unless the arbitration agreement is manifestly null (*manifestement nulle*).[68] The Working Group on the *Model Law* had considered including the word 'manifestly' in Article 8(1) in front of 'null and void' . . . to produce similar effect as the French law.[69] It, however, dropped that idea in the end.[70] Hence, the *Model Law* now simply reads: '[a] court before which an action is brought in a matter which is the subject of an arbitration agreement shall . . . refer the parties to arbitration unless it finds that the agreement is *null and void, inoperative or incapable of being performed.*'[71] (Emphasis added)

---

[62] *Id.*

[63] The United Nations Commission on International Trade Law (1985), para. 163.

[64] *Id.*

[65] *See* UNCITRAL Model Law on International Commercial Arbitration as amended in 2006, Article 8(1). The New York Convention in a similar language imposes on courts of Contracting States the duty to refer to arbitration, an action . . . in respect which parties have made agreement to arbitrate, within the meaning of the Convention, unless the court 'finds that the said agreement is null and void, inoperative or incapable of being performed.'

[66] Susler (2009), p. 128.

[67] Park (2012), p. 242.

[68] *Id.*

[69] Susler (2009), p. 129.

[70] *Id.*

[71] UNCITRAL Model Law on International Commercial Arbitration as amended in 2006, Article 8 (1).

Arbitration may be commenced or continued, under the *Model Law*, despite an ongoing challenge to arbitral jurisdiction before a court of law on any of the foregoing grounds.[72] In consequence, there is a real possibility of simultaneous proceedings on jurisdictional dispute before a court and an arbitral tribunal.[73] Such parallel proceedings may cause unnecessary expenses to the parties, for instance, when the court finds that the arbitral tribunal lacked jurisdiction after the arbitration had run its full course. The UN Commission on International Trade Law commented in relation to the 1985 draft that the *Model Law* provides ways of minimising the chances of this from happening.[74] First, it allows the arbitral tribunal the possibility of deciding on the question of its jurisdiction as a preliminary matter.[75] Second, it vests in the arbitral tribunal the discretion of waiting for the decision of the court on jurisdiction when it has serious doubt as regards its own jurisdiction.[76]

The drafting history of the *Model Law* sheds very little light on the meaning of the grounds on which the court declines arbitral jurisdiction under Article 8(1).[77] In New Zealand, a country which has based its law on the *Model Law*, the Law Commission indicated in its 1991 report entitled 'Arbitration' that 'null and void' covers disputes that are not arbitrable or with respect to which relief can be obtained only from a court.[78] It further explained that the arbitration agreement would be 'null and void' if it is 'discharged, frustrated, suspended, or practically ineffective.'[79] 'Inoperative' refers, according to the Law Commission, to a situation where the arbitration agreement has ceased to have effect while 'incapable of being performed' refers to a situation in which the arbitration agreement is ineffective right from the beginning, for instance, because the arbitration clause was too vaguely worded.[80]

In sum, scrutiny of the *Model Law* reveals that it takes the middle road when it comes to permitting courts to intervene in the determination of arbitral jurisdiction. For instance, it leaves more room for intervention by courts in the determination of arbitral jurisdiction compared to the French and even the German law we saw already. In spite of this, the approach of the *Model Law* is characterized as the middle-of-the-road because there are other jurisdictions that vest in courts even more expansive role in the determination of arbitral jurisdiction, as will be discussed shortly.

---

[72]UNCITRAL Model Law, Article 8(2) provides arbitral proceedings may be commenced or continued, as the case may be, despite an ongoing challenge to arbitral jurisdiction before a court of law.

[73]Park (2012), pp. 252–253.

[74]The United Nations Commission on International Trade Law (1985), par. 92.

[75]*Id.*, par. 92. See also, UNCITRAL Model Law on International Commercial Arbitration as amended in 2006, Article 16(3).

[76]*Id.*, para. 92. *See also* UNCITRAL Model Law, as amended in 2006, Article 8(2).

[77]Kawharu (2008), p. 253.

[78]*Id.*

[79]*Id.*

[80]*Id.*

5.1.2.4 *Kompetenz-Kompetenz* Under English Law

The Arbitration Act 1996 confers on the arbitral tribunal the power to rule on its own jurisdiction. Section 30 reads as follows.[81]

(1) *Unless otherwise agreed by the parties, the arbitral tribunal may rule on its own substantive jurisdiction, that is, as to-*

    (a) *Whether there is a valid arbitration agreement,*
    (b) *Whether the tribunal is properly constituted, and*
    (c) *What matters have been submitted to arbitration in accordance with the arbitration agreement.*

In contrast to Article 16 of the *Model Law*, the positive rule of *Kompetenz-Kompetenz* embodied under Section 30(1) of the Arbitration Act is non-mandatory. The parties to an arbitration agreement can in writing limit the jurisdiction of the arbitral tribunal to rule on its own substantive jurisdiction.[82] Furthermore, the tribunal's decision regarding its own jurisdiction is not final though in practice that may well be the case in certain circumstances.[83]

Regarding the timing of decision on jurisdiction, ordinarily, the arbitral tribunal has the option of deciding as a preliminary award or in the final award under the Arbitration Act.[84] However, the Act affords the parties to arbitration the possibility of, by agreement, compelling the arbitral tribunal to decide on its jurisdiction in a preliminary award.[85] The purpose of giving this right to the parties to arbitration is to minimize the possibility of arbitral tribunals abusing the discretion vested in them, and delaying decision on the tribunal's jurisdiction to the detriment of the interest of the parties.[86]

As regards the role of courts, the Act entitles a party to an arbitration agreement against which legal proceedings are brought in a court to apply to the court in which such proceedings have been brought for a stay of the judicial proceedings.[87] Upon such application, the court has the obligation to grant a stay unless satisfied that 'the

---

[81] Arbitration Act of England and Wales of 1996 (of England), Section 30(1). Incidentally, despite its name, the Act applies where the seat of arbitration is in England, Wales and Northern Ireland according to Section 2(1) of the Act.

[82] Haris et al. (2007), pp. 151 and 154. Note that Model Law does not indicate any possibility for parties to limit the arbitral tribunal's power to decide on its own jurisdiction. Article 16(1) of the Model Law, simply and only reads: '[t]he Arbitral tribunal may rule on its own jurisdiction, including any objections with respect to the existence or validity of the arbitration agreement.'

[83] *Id.* at 151–152.

[84] Barceló (2003), p. 1130.

[85] *Id.*

[86] *Id.* The party opposing arbitration naturally prefers an early decision on arbitral jurisdiction. Even the party favoring arbitration may want early ruling on this. That party may worry that a belated decision might result in a waste of time and resource if a court reverses the finding by the arbitral tribunal in favor of arbitration.

[87] The Arbitration Act of England and Wales of 1996, Section 9(1).

arbitration agreement is null and void, inoperative, or incapable of being performed.'[88] The Act uses identical language with that used in the New York Convention and the Model Law.[89]

However, English courts believe they have roles in the determination of arbitral jurisdiction that do not necessarily correspond with the *Model Law* rule.[90] In one case, faced with an application for a stay, an English court has held that various procedural options are open to the court.[91] The first is conducting a full review and finding that there is an arbitration agreement. Second is conducting a full review and finding there is no arbitration agreement and dismissing the application for a stay. The third avenue is simply staying the judicial proceeding pending determination on arbitral jurisdiction by the arbitral tribunal. The fourth option is for the court to refrain from making an immediate decision, and ordering the trial of the issue.[92] In going for one or the other of these routes, English courts weigh, among other things, 'the interest of the parties and avoidance of unnecessary delay or expense.'[93]

In a 2011 case, the English High Court declined to stay the judicial proceeding before it in a matter that was at the same time pending under ICC arbitration in New York. In fact, in *Excalibur Ventures LLC v. Texas Keystone Inc & Ors,* the court went to the extent of issuing an anti-arbitration injunction despite not even having a supervisory role on the foreign arbitration.[94] In that case, 'the Gulf Defendants' claimed that they were not actually parties to the arbitration agreement. The English Court was convinced that indeed the 'Gulf Defendants' were not parties to the arbitration agreement and had objected to the jurisdiction of the arbitrators in a timely manner though the objection was rejected.[95] Given this state of affairs, the High Court felt continuation of the arbitration would be 'unconscionable,' 'oppressive' and 'vexatious' and hence issued injunction against the arbitration relying on Section 37 of the 1981 Senior Courts Act, a law that precedes the 1996 Arbitration Act.[96] Similarly, in *Albon v. Naza Motor Trading,* the English Court took

---

[88]*Id.*, Section 9(4).

[89]UN Convention on Recognition and Enforcement of Foreign Arbitral Awards of 1958, Article II (3) and UNCITRAL Model Law on International Commercial Arbitration of 2006, Article 8(1).

[90]Haris et al. (2007), pp. 64–65.

[91]*Id.*, pp. 63–64 cites *Birse Construction Ltd v. St. David Ltd,* where the issue was whether a contract incorporating arbitration was entered into.

[92]*Id.*

[93]*Id.*, p. 64.

[94]Gaffney (2012), pp. 113–114.

[95]*Id.*

[96]*Id.*, at 111 and 115. Gaffney contends though this decision infringes upon competence-competence, too much should not be read into it. Rather he maintains the case should be understood in its context and the unique situation under which it arose. From the facts of the case one gathers that the party that started arbitration in New York, *Excalibur* started the court proceeding in England in order to get some technical advantage which it could not get in New York. Once it failed to get the tactical benefits it sought in UK it applied for the discontinuation of the court case it started. The author says the court found this behavior of Excalibur 'unconscionable' 'oppressive' and

jurisdiction to decide on the competence of an arbitral tribunal seating in Malaysia because the claimant convincingly argued that the signature on the arbitration agreement was forged.[97] In yet another case, *Claxton Engineering v. TXM*, the English Court took jurisdiction where the applicant disputed the very existence of the arbitration agreement that allegedly mandated arbitration abroad.[98]

In *Excalibur Ventures*, Globster J said that section 30 of the English Arbitration Act does not require the arbitral tribunal to decide on its own jurisdiction. It only allows it to determine its own jurisdiction.[99] Besides, he maintained that the Act does not impose an obligation on a person who contends it is not a party to an arbitration agreement to have this question determined by the arbitral tribunal whose authority is being disputed.[100] Hence, a person who disputes the arbitral jurisdiction can apply to a court to determine whether the arbitral tribunal has jurisdiction, so long as that person has not participated in the arbitration itself. Such court can give injunction against the other party from starting the arbitration or to discontinue the same.[101]

Another noteworthy feature of the English law is that once both sides have commenced participation in the arbitration, the arbitral tribunal itself may request the court to determine the arbitral jurisdiction. The court will accept the request if it is satisfied that the taking of jurisdiction by the court is likely to save the cost of adjudication and the application is made promptly enough.[102]

The foregoing shows that the English Courts are inclined to intervene in matters of arbitral jurisdiction despite the 1996 Arbitration Act embodying the *Kompetenz-Kompetenz* rule both in the positive and negative sense of the rule. Hence, we can conclude, compared to the French, German and even the *Model Law* jurisdictions there is more emphasis on the legitimacy of arbitration under English law.

5.1.2.5 *Kompetenz-Kompetenz* Under the US Law

The development of the *Kompetenz-Kompetenz* doctrine has been a very slow process in the United States. In fact, we do not come across this term as such.[103] The Federal Arbitration Act (FAA) that governs international commercial arbitration

---

'vexatious'. So, Gaffney holds this decision of the English Court should be seen in this special context. Secondly, the English court was relying on 'Senior Court's Act' rather than the 1996 Act for its conclusion according to him. I do not think the latter argument of Gaffney carries much water. The court did what it did despite the 1996 Arbitration Act which as a latter law should have prevailed over the Senor Courts Act in case of inconsistency between the two. It rather seems that this is how English courts understand the 'negative effect of Kompetenz-*Kompetenz*.'

[97]Tang (2014), p. 86.

[98]*Id.*

[99]*Id.*, pp. 84–85.

[100]*Id.*, p. 84.

[101]*Id.*

[102]*Id.*

[103]Graves and Davydan (2011), p. 158.

does not embody this doctrine.[104] On the contrary, Section 4 of the FAA assigns to courts the determination of whether parties agreed to arbitrate.[105] So, this doctrine owes its existence to the jurisprudence of the courts of the United States.

In *First Options, Inc. v. Kaplan*, the US Supreme Court held that the right starting point is a presumption that a court must decide 'arbitrability', which in the parlance of the US courts includes the determination of the 'existence, validity and scope of any arbitration agreement.'[106] However, in a *dicta* of this same case, the Court said that the presumption that courts, and not arbitral tribunals, decide 'arbitrability' can be overcome by adducing 'clear and unmistakable' evidence that shows the parties wished to delegate to the arbitral tribunal the power to decide on its own jurisdiction.[107] What was raised as a hypothetical situation in *First Options* was presented before the Court as a real situation in *Rent-A-Center, West, Inc. v. Jackson*. In *Rent-A-Center*, the arbitration agreement contained an actual 'delegation' of the jurisdictional issue to arbitrators. Hence, faced with the choice between confirming its *dicta* from *First Options* and explaining it away, the Supreme Court by a majority vote confirmed the possibility of contractually empowering arbitrators to decide on their own jurisdiction.[108] The Supreme Court reasoned that subjecting a jurisdictional dispute to arbitration is not any different from subjecting any other contractual dispute to arbitration, grounding its conclusion on FAA Section 2.[109]

That means in contrast to what we saw above regarding other countries, positive *kompetenz-kompetenz*, emanates from a contract rather than the law itself in the USA.[110] As a result, arbitrators in the US have no jurisdiction to decide on a challenge directed at the very existence of the agreement giving them such powers. In such a case, a court and sometimes a jury will have to decide whether the agreement exists at all.[111]

An interesting question that raises its head at this point is whether the arbitral tribunal's decision on its own jurisdiction is subject to review by courts. Reading together *Rent-A-Center* and *Hall Street Assoc. v. Mattel, Inc.*, we gather that the judicial review of an arbitral decision is limited to the narrow grounds under

---

[104]Rosen (1993), p. 599.

[105]United States Arbitration Act, Pub. L. 68-401, 43 Stat. 883, Feb. 1925. Section 4 reads in relevant part '(a) party aggrieved by the alleged failure, neglect or refusal of another to arbitrate under a written agreement for arbitration may petition any United States district Court which, save for such agreement, would have jurisdiction . . . .'

[106]Graves and Davydan (2011), p. 161.

[107]*Id.* While the US Supreme Court has not yet dwelt on what exactly constitutes 'clear and unmistakable' evidence for the purpose the vast majority of lower courts have found, for instance, incorporation of arbitration rules that provide for *Kompetenz Kompetenz* is sufficient. See page 162 of the same.

[108]*Id.*, p. 165.

[109]*Id.*, pp. 161–162.

[110]*Id.*, p. 162.

[111]Park (2012), p. 246.

Section 10 of the FAA.[112] In other words, once contractually accorded *Kompetenz-Kompetenz*, the decision of the arbitral tribunal on its own jurisdiction is assimilated to a decision on the merits of the dispute. Hence, it is not subject to review by courts as the review of such decision does not figure in Section 10 of the FAA.[113] The consequence of all this is that the US law, as it stands now, is similar to what German law was prior to the adoption of the 1998 Arbitration Law, when the *Bundesgerichthof* had decided that a *Komptenz-Kompetenz-klausel* was valid and decision reached on its basis binding.[114]

As regards the negative effect of *Kompetenz-Kompetenz* the Federal Arbitration Act Section 201 incorporates the New York Convention Article II (3)[115] when the arbitration in question is deemed to be international.[116] According to this provision, the court of a contracting state that is seized of a matter covered by an arbitration agreement is under obligation to 'refer the parties to arbitration unless it finds that the said agreement is null and void, inoperative, or incapable of being performed.'[117] The review at this stage is not *prima facie* in the US though some have contended that the language of Article II (3) of the Convention calls for a superficial review at this stage.[118]

Overall, the foregoing shows that the US law emphasises the legitimacy of arbitration much more than the laws of any of the major jurisdictions of significance to international commercial arbitration. It is almost on the legitimacy end of the spectrum.

---

[112]Graves and Davydan (2011), p. 166.

[113]United States Arbitration Act of 1925, Section 10 of the Act lists the grounds for vacating an award. They include cases where, 'the award is procured by corruption, fraud or untrue means', cases where there was evident partiality on the part of arbitrators, cases of misconduct on the part of arbitrators such as refusal to hear evidence that is pertinent and material to the controversy and cases where arbitrators exceed their powers.

[114]Park (2012), p. 244.

[115]Barceló (2003), p. 1135. Section 208 of the Federal Arbitration Act (FAA) of 1925 clearly stipulates that chapter 1 of the FAA applies in so far as it does not contravene with the New York Convention.

[116]*Id.* For this purpose arbitration is international if the arbitration agreement contemplates the issuance of an award in a country, other than the United States, that is a party to the New York Convention or though the seat of arbitration is the US, if the US does not all the same consider the arbitration as domestic arbitration. The latter of these possibilities raises complex questions which we need not dwell on for our purpose.

[117]UN Convention on Recognition and Enforcement of Foreign Arbitral Awards, Article II(3).

[118]Susler (2009), p. 138. Note that it makes sense for the judicial review at the outset to be rigorous given that the review of arbitral tribunal on its own jurisdiction is not subject to review by courts as a result of the Supreme Court's decision in *Hall Street*. As seen already post award review is limited to the grounds under section 10 of the FAA under which review of the arbitrators' decision on their own jurisdiction does not appear.

5.1.2.6   The Chinese Law and *Kompetenz-Kompetenz*

China is one of the very few countries in the world that does not recognise the doctrine of *Kompetenz-Kompetenz* according to some authors,[119] although others seem to dispute that claim.[120] The arbitral tribunal has no legal authority to determine its own jurisdiction.[121] Such power is reserved to the arbitral institution administering the arbitration, usually translated into English as 'arbitration commission' and the People's Court. Article 20 of the Chinese law reads as follows.

> If a party challenges the validity of the arbitration agreement, he may request the arbitration commission to make a decision or the People's Court to give a ruling. If one party requests the arbitration commission to make a decision and the other party requests the People's Court for a ruling, the People's Court shall rule.[122]

Similarly, the People's Court decides if a dispute arises as to which arbitration commission was agreed upon by the parities to an arbitration agreement.[123] In other words, if ambiguity arises as to the identity of the arbitral institution under auspices of which the arbitration was agreed to be conducted, the People's Court decides on the identity of the agreed upon institution.

There is, however, a movement towards the recognition of the *Kompetenz-Kompetenz* rule. Article 6(1) of the 2005 CIETAC Rules, for instance, provides that if the parties have agreed to arbitrate under the rules of the CIETAC, it 'shall have the power to determine the existence and validity of an arbitration agreement and its jurisdiction over an arbitration case. The CIETAC may, if necessary delegate such power to the arbitral tribunal.'[124] That said, Chinese law still clearly emphasises legitimacy of arbitration over its efficiency.

---

[119]Greenberg et al. (2011), p. 225. Among Asia pacific nations Fiji, Papua New Guinea, and Solomon Islands are said to not recognize the doctrine of *Kompetenz-Kompetenz* while Vanatu has no law at all on arbitration.

[120]Tang (2014), p. 85. According to Tang 'challenges to the validity of arbitration clause can be brought either to chosen tribunal or the people's court.' It seems Tang is confusing 'arbitration commission' with arbitral tribunal. Of course, as seen above, now there is a possibility of the arbitration commission delegating this to the arbitral tribunal itself. But that is a possibility that applies only where a particular arbitration commission, CIETAC, has been chosen.

[121]Greenberg et al. (2011), p. 226.

[122]*Id.*

[123]*Id.*

[124]*Id.*, p. 227.

5.1.3 Kompetenz-Kompetenz *Under Ethiopian Law: Legitimacy at any Cost*

Now that we have had a bird's-eye view of *Kompetenz-Kompetenz* in jurisdictions of significance to international commercial arbitration we will look at its status under Ethiopian law. We will start with the power of the arbitral tribunal to determine its own jurisdiction, positive *Kompetenz-Kompetenz,* and then proceed to the role of court in the determination of arbitral jurisdiction.

5.1.3.1 Positive *Kompetenz-Kompetenz*: Its Basis and Scope in Ethiopia

The provisions of relevance to positive *Kompetenz-Kompetenz* in Ethiopia are Civil Code Articles 3330 and 3329. The former is titled 'scope of jurisdiction' and reads as follows.[125]

(1) *The arbitral submission may authorize the arbitrator to decide difficulties arising out of the interpretation of the submission itself.*

(2) *It may in particular authorize the arbitrator to decide disputes relating to his own jurisdiction.*

(3) *The arbitrator may in no case be required to decide whether the arbitral submission is or is not valid.*

Particularly, reading Article 3330(2) and (1) of the Civil Code together we understand that the arbitrator will have the authority to decide on 'disputes relating to his own jurisdiction' or 'difficulties arising out of the interpretation of the submission itself' only where the arbitral submission authorises him to do so. We gather from these provisions that positive *Kompetenz-Kompetenz,* to the extent it does exist under Ethiopian law, emanates from a contract rather than the law itself. Hence, where the contract is silent on the subject the arbitral tribunal will have no power at all to decide on any type of challenge directed at its own jurisdiction. So, the law in Ethiopia is similar with the US law on this point.[126] In contrast, the power of an arbitral tribunal to decide on its own jurisdiction emanates from the law itself, rather than contract in the more arbitration friendly jurisdictions like England, Germany and *Model Law* based jurisdictions.[127]

Another noteworthy point is that under Ethiopian law even the parties themselves cannot vest in the arbitral tribunal the power to decide on the very existence or

---

[125]Civil Code of Ethiopia Proclamation No. 165/1960, Article 3330.

[126]Graves and Davydan (2011), p. 165. In Rent-A-Centre, West, Inc. v. Jackson, the Supreme Court confirmed by a majority vote the possibility of contractually empowering arbitrators to decide on their own jurisdiction.

[127]The Arbitration Act of England and Wales of 1996, Section 30, German Civil Procedure Code (ZPO) of 1998, Section 1040(1), UNCITRAL Model Law on International Commercial Arbitration as amended in 2006, Article 16(1).

validity of the contract giving it jurisdiction.[128] The law provides, particularly, that the 'arbitrator may in no case be required to decide whether the arbitral submission is or is not valid.'[129] The maximum that the parties can do is authorising the arbitrator to decide on the 'scope' of his own 'jurisdiction.'

This is a logical consequence of positive *Kompetenz-Kompetenz* grounded on a contract rather than the law itself. If the jurisdiction of an arbitral tribunal to determine its own jurisdiction emanates from a contract, then, allowing arbitrators to rule on challenges directed at the very existence or validity of the same contract becomes a contradiction in terms. Therefore, the inclusion of the prohibition under Article 3330(3) in the Civil Code gives internal logical coherence to the law.

Its logical consistency aside, this rule makes obstructing arbitration a walk in a park. All the party that wants to impede arbitration has to do is just make an allegation, even a patently false one, challenging the validity or existence of the arbitration agreement. Since, an arbitral tribunal cannot decide on such a challenge, the arbitration will have to stop until a court finds that the allegation is unfounded and orders the resumption of the arbitration. We recall that in the US, where *Kompetenz-Kompetenz* is similarly grounded on contract, challenges to the very existence or validity of the arbitration clause itself are decided on by the courts or even by a jury in certain cases rather than by the arbitrators themselves.[130] So, Ethiopian and the US law on international arbitration are once more similar though impeding arbitration is much more difficult in the US, among others, because US courts are much more arbitration friendly and knowledgeable in comparison to Ethiopian courts.

Yet another noteworthy point about Ethiopian law is that even in cases where the arbitration agreement confers on the arbitrator authority to decide disputes regarding the 'scope' of his own jurisdiction the arbitrator is required to interpret powers vested in him 'restrictively.' The Civil Code states, '[t]he provisions of the arbitral submission relating to the jurisdiction of the arbitrators shall be interpreted restrictively.'[131] We do not come across a similar rule of interpretation in other jurisdictions of significance discussed already.

---

[128]This is in contrast with French law according to which the parties cannot even by explicit agreement deny arbitrators to decide on their own jurisdiction by ruling on challenges to the validity of the arbitration agreement, if that is questioned. The principle of *Kompetenz-Kompetenz* cannot be overridden by the parties even if they so wish according to Castellane. *See* Castellane (2011), p. 373.

[129]Civil Code of Ethiopia Proclamation No. 165/1960, Article 3330(3).

[130]The United States Arbitration Act of 1925, provides in relevant part of Section 4 '(i)f the making of the arbitration agreement or . . . be in issue, the court shall proceed summarily to the trial thereof.' The party alleged to be in default of the arbitration agreement may within a legally specified period also demand a jury trial of the issue.

[131]Civil Code of Ethiopia Proclamation 1965/1960, Article 3329. Incidentally, this provision applies to courts too. Hence, whoever is called upon to interpret arbitral submission regarding the jurisdiction of arbitrators is required to interpret the agreement restrictively. This provision is underscoring the fact that the law presumes judicial jurisdiction. In other words, the law is not pro-arbitral jurisdiction.

5.1.3.2 Negative *Kompetenz-Kompetenz* and Judicial Intervention in Ethiopia

The laws of jurisdictions that are known to be significant players in the field of international arbitration explicitly embody the negative *Kompetenz-Kompetenz* rule, tying the hands of courts to prevent intervention in matters of arbitral jurisdiction once an arbitral tribunal is constituted, save on narrowly defined grounds.[132] Ethiopian law imposes no comparable restriction on courts. What follows demonstrates this.

5.1.3.2.1 Judicial Intervention Possible at Any Stage of Arbitration

Ethiopian law does not prohibit courts from entertaining challenges to arbitral jurisdiction at any stage of the arbitral proceeding so long as the objections had been made to the arbitral tribunal itself in a timely manner. An objection to a court's jurisdiction must be raised in the statement of defence.[133] Since the procedural aspect of arbitration must '. . . as near as may be, be the same as in a civil court,' a jurisdictional objection to arbitration too must be made in the statement of defence, in principle.[134] The outcome of delay, in our view, should be refusal by courts to entertain the belated objection to arbitration. Unfortunately, we could not find any court case that either affirms or negates this viewpoint.

Interestingly, an arbitral tribunal was confronted with a belated challenge to its jurisdiction in *Chanyalew Yilma v. Flora Eco Power (Ethiopia) PLC*.[135] After the parties exchanged statements of claim and defence, the Respondent applied to the Tribunal seeking leave to amend its statement of defence. The petition was granted. The Respondent introduced preliminary objections in the amended statement of defence. These included an allegation that there was no valid arbitration agreement,

---

[132]Park (2012), pp. 235, 239, 242. French courts will entertain disputes on the validity of arbitration agreement only so long as arbitral tribunal has not been constituted and even then in the most superficial manner such as when the clause is clearly void for lack of the requisite signatures of parties. In England, the situation is slightly different from France. Litigants have right to seek declaratory decision by court on arbitral jurisdiction only if they did not start taking part in the arbitration. In Switzerland, even a court asked to appoint arbitrators cannot engage in full examination of arbitral agreement. Full review of the agreement has to wait till after arbitration has taken its course.

[133]Civil Procedure Code of Ethiopia Proclamation No. 165/1960, Article 234(1)(C). As a matter of exception objections that pertain to substantive jurisdiction of a court may be raised at any time according to Article 9(2) of the Same Code. We will discuss that at a more appropriate point below.

[134]*Id.*, Article 317(1).

[135]*Chanyalew Yilma v. Flora Eco Power (Ethiopia) PLC*, an arbitration conducted under the auspices of the Arbitration Institute of Addis Ababa Chamber of Commerce and Sectorial Associations, in 2013.

and hence the Tribunal lacked jurisdiction.[136] It seems, the Sole Arbitrator, Mr. Yazachew Belew, was of the view that this was a calculated move to stall the arbitration by relying on the Civil Code rule denying arbitrators jurisdiction to even consider challenges directed at the validity of an arbitration agreement.[137] To avert this, the Tribunal first established that leave to plead preliminary objections was neither requested by the Respondent nor granted by the Tribunal when it permitted amendment of the statement of defence. Then it ruled the challenge to the Tribunal's jurisdiction was inadmissible. It reasoned:[138]

> The law (Article 244(3) of the Civil Procedure Code) on the consequence of failure to plead preliminary objections, if any, at the 'earliest possible opportunity' is crystal clear: such objections are deemed waived and hence cannot be raised at any later stages of a proceeding. The party who benefits from these objections simply loses the benefits if it fails to invoke the objections at the earliest possible opportunity. And that 'earliest possible opportunity' is at the time of filing a statement of defence (Article 234(1) (c)). Thus, the defence of preliminary objection is time-bounded and stage-precluded. Belated preliminary objections are simply inadmissible and shall not be considered. This is the principle under Ethiopian law.

Under arbitration laws of jurisdictions like Germany, England and many other jurisdictions that follow the *UNCITRAL Model Law*, jurisdictional objections are deemed waived unless raised at an appropriate time.[139] The conclusion reached by the sole arbitrator in *Chanyalew Yilma v. Flora Eco Power (Ethiopia) PLC* is of similar effect though the arbitrator had to rely on general rules for making preliminary objections for lack of provisions specifically dealing with arbitral proceedings in such context.

The outcome would have been totally different had the objection to the jurisdiction of the tribunal been made in a timely manner. A party that has made a timely objection to the jurisdiction of an arbitral tribunal reserves its right of recourse to the judiciary at any stage of the arbitral proceedings. For instance, the Federal First Instance Court of Ethiopia did entertain jurisdictional objections while arbitration was going on before an ICC Tribunal in *Addis Ababa Water and Sewerage Authority*

---

[136]The Respondent invoked, in the amended statement of defense, various grounds to call into question the validity and existence of the arbitration agreement. Among others, it alleged that the contract was not signed by Mr. François Achour, the General Manager of Flora Eco Power (Ethiopia) PLC, that the General Manager had no special power of attorney necessary to consent to arbitrate, and no attempt to solve the dispute amicably was made though that is a precondition to arbitration in the agreement.

[137]Civil Code of Ethiopia of Ethiopia Proclamation No. 165/1960, Article 3330(3) provides arbitral tribunals may not decide on challenges directed at the validity of the arbitral submission, even if parties to arbitration agreement expressly authorize them to do so.

[138]Chanyalew Yilma v. *Flora Eco Power (Ethiopia) PLC.*

[139]German Civil Procedure Code (*ZPO*), Section 1040(2), English Arbitration Act of 1996, Section 31(1) and UNCITRAL Model Law of 2006, Article 16(2). The Model Law allows the arbitral tribunal to as a matter of exception admit a delayed objection to its jurisdiction where the tribunal finds the delay is justified according to Article 16(3).

v. SALINI Costruttori.[140] We will discuss this case in detail later on. Suffice it, for now, to note that Ethiopian courts will entertain recourse to them made by a party to arbitration where such party had objected to the jurisdiction of the arbitral tribunal in a timely manner.

As a matter of exception, in Ethiopia, recourse to courts is also possible even where the objection to the jurisdiction of an arbitral tribunal had not been made in a timely manner, if the ground for the objection pertains to the subject matter jurisdiction of the arbitral tribunal. The defence of lack of subject-matter jurisdiction is never waived.[141] This is because this limit to the jurisdiction of the arbitral tribunal arises from the law itself. Parties to arbitration cannot by their consent or failure to object in a timely manner confer jurisdiction on an arbitral tribunal where the subject matter of the dispute is not arbitrable under the law. A party can raise this kind of objection at any time and stage of the arbitration arguably without the need for even amending its statement of defence, for example.[142]

So, if a party to arbitration makes a belated objection alleging the dispute is not arbitrable, for instance, the arbitral tribunal in Ethiopia will be compelled to stop the arbitration pending decision on this issue by a competent court. This is the case, because unlike in most other jurisdictions, in Ethiopia an arbitral tribunal has no jurisdiction to decide on any challenge directed at the validity or existence of the arbitration agreement.[143] The law denies effect to even an express agreement conferring on an arbitral tribunal the jurisdiction to decide disputes affecting the validity of the arbitration agreement.[144] Hence, a party that feels the case is beginning to go against it can so easily stall an ongoing arbitration at any stage of the proceeding by just alleging that the dispute is not arbitrable.

Under the US law, which comes closest to the Ethiopian law in this respect, courts may at any stage of arbitration order a full examination of the validity of the arbitration clause to determine whether the parties did in fact agree to arbitrate.[145] That said, even in the US one comes across pale hints of negative *Kompetenz-Kompetenz*. For instance, in *Pacificare v. Book*, the US Supreme Court takes a 'wait and see' approach with respect to public policy questions relating to the arbitration of a treble damages claim.[146]

---

[140]*Addis Ababa Water and Sewerage Authority v. SALINI Costruttori S.P.A*, Federal First Instance Court of Ethiopia, Case No. 1510/93, ruling rendered on May 14, 2001.

[141]Civil Procedure Code Decree No. 52/1965, Article 9(2) provides that '[w]hen and as soon as a court is aware that it has no material jurisdiction to try a suit, it shall proceed in accordance with Art. 245, notwithstanding that no objection is taken under Art. 244 to its material jurisdiction.' That means even where the parties do not raise objection to the jurisdiction of a court pursuant to Article 244 the court is required to strike out the suit where it lacks material jurisdiction under Article 245.

[142]A court may allow amendment of pleading by either party under Ethiopian law '. . . at any time before judgment' according to Article 91(1) of the Civil Procedure Code.

[143]Civil Code of Ethiopia Proclamation No. 165/1960, Article 3330(3).

[144]*Id.*

[145]Park (2012), p. 235.

[146]*Id.*, p. 242.

5.1.3.2.2   Parallel Proceedings Not Guaranteed

Ethiopian law does not guarantee the possibility of even parallel proceedings before an arbitral tribunal and a court on the issue of arbitral jurisdiction, unlike German law, for example.[147] In Germany, once initiated, arbitration is allowed to run its course even where a party has sought judicial declaration on the issue of arbitral jurisdiction pursuant to Section 1032(2) of the ZPO. In fact, even where a court has first started considering the issue of arbitral jurisdiction, the party seeking arbitration is at liberty to initiate arbitral proceedings.[148] In other words, even though the German law does not embody negative *Kompetenz-Kompetenz* in the manner the French law does, it does not lend a free hand to a party that wants to disrupt arbitral proceedings.[149] The two proceedings are allowed to go ahead concurrently.

Similarly, the *UNCITRAL Model Law* envisages the possibility of simultaneous proceedings on arbitral jurisdiction before a court and an arbitral tribunal. It does not give the court the right to issue an injunction against the arbitration going forward pending its own decision on the issue of arbitral jurisdiction.[150] Ethiopian law does not embody a similar prohibition against the court. So, the court can issue an injunctive order against the arbitral proceeding pending the settlement of the dispute on jurisdiction before it.[151] This is yet another testament to the primacy accorded to the legitimacy of arbitration over its efficacy in Ethiopia.

5.1.3.2.3   Appeal to a Higher Court: Another Avenue to Prolong
the Disruption of Arbitration

Under Ethiopian law the plaintiff or the defendant may 'appeal against *any final judgment* of a civil court.'[152] As an exception to this rule, the law provides that no appeal may be lodged, even when an appeal lies from a judgment or order, if under the Civil Procedure Code 'a remedy is available in the court which gave such judgment or made such order' without first exhausting the available remedy.[153] The decision of a court finding that a dispute is subject to arbitration and declining to

---

[147]Bermann (2012), p. 21. *See also* UNCITRAL Model Law of 2006, Article 8(2).

[148]German Civil Procedure Code, ZPO as amended in 1998, Section 1032(3) provides arbitral proceeding may 'be commenced or continued' even where the issue of arbitral jurisdiction is already pending before a court either because that was raised by a party that wants the dispute to be referred to arbitration or just because an application was lodged to a court to determine whether or not arbitration is admissible.

[149]Bermann (2012), p. 20.

[150]Park (2012), pp. 252–253.

[151]Civil Procedure Code of Ethiopia Decree No. 52/1965, Article 155 and Civil Code of Ethiopia, *supra* note 168 Article 2121. These provisions will be reproduced and discussed in relation to the SALINI case below.

[152]Civil Procedure Code of Ethiopia Decree No. 52/1965, Article 320(1).

[153]*Id.*, Article 320(2).

entertain the dispute any further is a 'final judgment' within the meaning of Article 320(1) of the Civil Procedure Code. This is so because no remedy is available in the same court from this decision. Therefore, appeal is not barred on the ground of availability of a remedy within the same court from a decision finding arbitral jurisdiction.

Another rule in the Civil Procedure Code of Ethiopia that precludes appeal from a court decision is that which deals with decisions on 'interlocutory matters.'[154] By way of exemplification, the Civil Procedure Code lists as interlocutory matters, '. . . decision or order on adjournments, preliminary objections, the admissibility or inadmissibility of oral or documentary evidence and permission to sue as a pauper.'[155] A decision on an interlocutory matter may be raised as a ground for an appeal when ultimately the court makes a final judgment and when an appeal is lodged against the latter.[156] As we can gather from the examples, interlocutory decisions or orders are decisions made by a court pending the final disposition of the dispute. In other words, a party against whom an interlocutory order or decision is given still has the chance of winning the case in the same court. In contrast, there is no possibility of ultimately winning before the same court, if a court makes a determination that it has no jurisdiction because the dispute is subject to arbitration. That means the law prohibiting appeal from a court decision on interlocutory matters does not cover a court decision finding in favour of arbitral jurisdiction.

In sum, there is no prohibition, express or otherwise, in the Civil Procedure Code against lodging an appeal from a court decision finding a dispute is subject to arbitration. On the contrary, a court ruling in favour of arbitral jurisdiction can be regarded as a 'final decision' from which appeal can be lodged within the meaning of Article 320(1) of the Civil Procedure Code. As a result, arbitration can be stalled for years, owing to this, till the parties exhaust all 'remedies' in appellate courts. This is in sharp contrast with, for example, the *Model Law* rule which prohibits appeal from a court's finding in favour of arbitral jurisdiction.[157]

5.1.4   Jurisdictional Battle Between an Ethiopian Court and Arbitral Tribunal: Lessons from the SALINI Case

The fact that Ethiopian law is so lopsided in favour of the legitimacy of arbitration does not necessarily preclude the possibility for jurisdictional battles between Ethiopian courts and arbitral tribunals. In fact, that Ethiopian law does not contain provisions aimed at limiting the involvement of courts in jurisdictional disputes to

---

[154]*Id.*, Article 320(3).

[155]*Id.*

[156]*Id.*

[157]UNCITRAL Model Law on International Commercial Arbitration as amended in 2006, Article 16(3).

ensure the efficacy of arbitration creates a fertile ground for jurisdictional disputes. For example, Ethiopian courts have felt at liberty to interfere in arbitration even where what is disputed is neither the validity of the arbitration agreement nor its scope. The jurisdictional battle between an ICC tribunal and Ethiopian courts in the dispute between *Addis Ababa Water and Sewerage Authority (AAWSA) and SALINI Costruttori S.P.A*, an Italian Company illustrates this point. We will, thus, dwell on this case below.

In *Addis Ababa Water and Sewerage Authority (AAWSA) v. SALINI Costruttori S. P.A.*[158] the parties were in disagreement as to whether what was agreed upon was an institutional arbitration under the auspices of the International Chamber of Commerce, ICC or an *ad hoc* arbitration under the arbitration rules of the Civil Code of Ethiopia, Articles 3325 to 3346. Yet, the Federal First Instance Court of Ethiopia felt compelled to give a temporary injunction against the ICC arbitral proceeding pending a ruling by the First Instance Court on the type of arbitration agreed upon by the parties.[159]

The contract that gave rise to this dispute had two parts. Part I contained 'general conditions of contract' while part II contained 'special conditions of particular application.' Article 67.3 in the general conditions of contract (Part I), on the one hand provided, '[a]ny dispute . . . shall be finally settled, unless otherwise specified in the Contract, under the Rules of Conciliation and Arbitration of the International Chamber of Commerce by one or more arbitrator/s appointed under such rules . . . .'[160]

On the other hand, the Special Conditions of Particular Application, in Part II of the Contract, state in relevant part:[161]

Clause 67- Settlement of Dispute-Arbitration

Add the following new sub clauses to Clause 67.3 of Part I.

67.3.1 The place of arbitration shall be Addis Ababa, Ethiopia

67.3.2 The language of arbitration shall be English

67.3.3 The substantive law(s) applicable shall be the Ethiopian law

67.3.4 The rules for arbitration shall be the Civil Code of Ethiopia under Articles 3325.

On the basis of certain alleged breaches, SALINI, the Italian Company, made a request for arbitration pursuant to Article 4 of the ICC Rules. AAWSA objected to the ICC arbitration alleging that the parties had rather agreed to an *ad hoc* arbitration under Articles 3325 *et seq* of the Civil Code of Ethiopia. SALINI's position was that the Civil Code provisions on arbitral submission were 'added' to supplement, if need

---

[158]*Addis Ababa Water and Sewerage Authority v. SALINI Construttori S.P.A.*, Federal First Instance Court of Ethiopia, File No. 1510/93 (2001).

[159]*Id.*

[160]Contract quoted in *SALINI Costruttori S.P.A v. The Federal Democratic Republic of Ethiopia, Addis Ababa Water and Sewerage Authority*, ICC case No. 10623/AER/ACS, Para. 11.

[161]*Id.*, at Para. 12.

be, the ICC Rules already referred to in the Arbitration clause in Part I of the Contract.

The ICC Tribunal was established despite this disagreement on jurisdiction. AAWSA did not, however, drop its objection. In fact, it insisted that the question of jurisdiction be settled as a preliminary matter. However, AAWSA's request for early decision on jurisdiction was denied by the ICC Tribunal. Yet, AAWSA continued participation in the ICC Arbitration.[162] In yet another procedural order, Procedural Order II, the ICC Tribunal rejected the request by AAWSA that the venue for the first hearing be Addis Ababa, the place of arbitration. The Tribunal decided it would be more convenient for the Tribunal and even the parties if the first hearing took place in Paris without prejudice to Addis Ababa being the place of arbitration.[163] This triggered a challenge to the arbitrators by AAWSA under the ICC rules. The ICC Court rejected the challenge.[164]

When the challenge to the arbitrators before the ICC Court failed, AAWSA initiated an action in the Federal First Instance Court of Ethiopia. It sought a declaration that the ICC Arbitral Tribunal lacked jurisdiction in this matter and that what was agreed upon was an *ad hoc* arbitration.[165] Moreover, AAWSA submitted an affidavit seeking an order against SALINI, to stop breach of the arbitration clause and to desist from participation in the arbitration before the ICC Tribunal. The injunction sought under Articles 155 and 165 of the Civil Procedure Code was temporary pending the final determination of the issue before the First Instance Court.[166]

The Civil Procedure Code provision on which *AAWSA* relied to request issuance of injunction by the Ethiopian court is titled '[i]njunction to [r]estrain [r]epetition or [c]ontinuance of [b]reach' and reads as follows.[167]

(1) *In any suit for restraining the defendant from committing a breach of contract or other act prejudicial to the plaintiff, whether compensation is claimed in the suit or not, the plaintiff, may at any time after the institution of the suit, and either before or after judgment, apply to the court for a temporary injunction to restrain the defendant from committing the breach of contract or act complained of, or any breach of contract or act of like kind arising out of the same contract or relating to the same property or right.*

(2) *The court may by order grant such injunction, on such terms as to the duration of the injunction, keeping an account, giving security, or otherwise, as it thinks fit.*

---

[162]*Id.* Contract quoted in Salini Construttori V. FDRE, AA water and swerege authority, para. 12.

[163]*Id.*, at Para. 60.

[164]*Id.*, at para. 74.

[165]*Addis Ababa Water and Sewerage Authority v. SALINI Construttori S.P.A.*, Federal First Instance Court, File No. 1510/93.

[166]*Id.*

[167]Civil Procedure Code of Ethiopia Decree 52/1965, Article 155.

(3) *Nothing in this Article shall affect the provisions of Article 2121of the Civil Code.*

The Civil Code provision to which sub-article 3 above makes cross-reference lays down the basic considerations for granting injunctive order. It first states that a court may issue an injunctive order to restrain a defendant from committing acts that are prejudicial to the plaintiff. It then goes on to qualify that under sub-article 2 by providing:[168]

> [a]n injunction shall be granted only where there are good reasons to believe that the act prejudicial to the plaintiff is likely to be carried out and where the injury with which he is threatened is such that it cannot be redressed by an award of damages.

The Federal First Instance Court considered the request for a temporary injunction against SALINI's participation in the ICC arbitration in Paris. The Court issued a cease and desist order against SALINI pending its final decision on the type of arbitration Clause 67 of the Contract provided for. The Court also indicated that it might issue a different order reversing the temporary injunction even before finally deciding on the jurisdictional dispute. It reasoned as follows.[169]

> Clause 67 of the Contract between the parties submitted as evidence by the current petitioner clearly indicates that in the event of dispute between the parties the venue of arbitration is to be Addis Ababa and the applicable laws Articles 3325 et seq of the Civil Code of Ethiopia (arbitral submission). This being the case, the Court is satisfied that the continued conduct of arbitration in Paris exposes the current petitioner to the kind of damage ... that cannot be made good by monetary compensation. Therefore, pending the final resolution of the matter before this Court or issuance of an order reversing the current one, the court orders the Respondent (SALINI), pursuant to Article 155 of the Civil Procedure Code, to cease and desist from breach of obligations it assumed under Clause 67 of the Contract between the parties. (Translation Mine)

The logical effect of this order was halting the arbitration before the ICC tribunal as no party would participate, given this order. The ICC Arbitral Tribunal rightly understood the effect of the injunction that way.[170] Further the ICC Tribunal observed the injunction by the Federal First Instance Court of Ethiopia was rendered on the ground that the Court had power to decide on the issue of the Arbitral Tribunal's competence to the exclusion of the Arbitral Tribunal itself.[171]

---

[168]Civil Code of Ethiopia Proclamation No. 165/1960, Article 2121(2).

[169]*Addis Ababa Water and Sewerage Authority v. SALINI Costruttori S.P.A*, Federal First Instance Court, File No. 1510/93.

[170]*SALINI Costruttori S.P.A v. The Federal Democratic Republic of Ethiopia, Addis Ababa Water and Sewerage Authority*, ICC Case No. 10623/AER/ACS, Para. 121-4.

[171]*Id.*, at Para. 151.

5.1.4.1 Injunctive Order Issued by the Ethiopian Court Rejected

Confronted with the injunction order issued by the Federal First Instance Court, the ICC Tribunal felt the need to consider whether or not it was under legal obligation to defer to the judicial order and halt the arbitral proceedings. Serious consideration of this issue was deemed necessary given the fact that the order was issued by a court of the country where the arbitration had its legal seat.[172] The ICC Tribunal held, after a thorough consideration, that an arbitral tribunal that faces such an order has discretion to comply or not to comply with it.[173] The Tribunal put forward three major arguments, which it developed to varying degrees, to justify its decision to disregard the injunctive order by the Ethiopian court. They focus on: (1) the tribunal's duty to give effect to the agreement of the parties to 'arbitrate', (2) the duty of state courts under the New York Convention and (3) international public policy against a state entity frustrating an agreement to arbitrate.

In what follows, attempt will be made to briefly dwell on the merits of each of the foregoing arguments of the ICC Tribunal. From the outset, we need to emphasize that our primary goal here is not really making an authoritative assessment of whether the ICC Tribunal was right or wrong in this particular case. Our aim is rather limited to demonstrating that anything short of legal reform, including all sorts of arguments by arbitral tribunals, is unlikely to prevent obstruction of arbitration in the Ethiopian context.

5.1.4.1.1 Upholding the Agreement of the Parties 'to Arbitrate' as a Ground for Disregarding the Injunctive Order of the Court

The Tribunal found compliance with the injunctive order issued by the Federal First Instance Court of Ethiopia would result in denial of justice and convert the agreement to arbitrate into a 'dead letter.'[174] That being the case, the Tribunal continued, it is not bound by the injunctive order of the court of the seat of arbitration.[175] It reasoned:[176]

> ... [a]n international arbitral tribunal is not an organ of the state in which it has its seat in the same way as the court of the seat would be. The primary source of the Tribunal's powers is the parties' agreement to arbitrate. An important consequence of this is that the Tribunal has a duty vis-à-vis the parties to ensure that their arbitration agreement is not frustrated. In certain circumstances, it may be necessary to decline to comply with an order issued by a court of the seat, in the fulfilment of the Tribunal's larger duty to parties.

---

[172] *Id.*, Para. 126.

[173] *Id.*, Para. 127.

[174] *Id.*, Para. 140 and 142.

[175] *Id.,* Para. 128.

[176] *Id.*

The Tribunal underscored that it was within its power to go beyond the domestic legal system of Ethiopia to lend efficacy to the agreement of the parties to arbitrate. It reasoned, though one cannot maintain a contract is binding in and of itself without support from any legal system, nor can it be contended that a contract to submit a dispute to arbitration derives its validity exclusively from the legal system of the seat of arbitration.[177]

This finding of the ICC Tribunal has garnered support from some authorities in the field of arbitration. Professor Bachand, for example, finds the Tribunal's position as tenable.[178] He sets out by acknowledging that there is diversity of views regarding the effect of injunction orders issued by courts of the seat of arbitration on the jurisdiction of the arbitral tribunal. He then argues in support of the viewpoint which treats an international commercial arbitration agreement like any other contract containing a foreign element.[179] The implication of this perspective is that the efficacy of the agreement does not necessarily depend on the rules of a specific legal order. Rather the effects of the international agreement should be assessed like any contract that raises conflict of laws issues.[180] That being the case '. . . the effects of an international commercial arbitral agreement depend on the rules in force in each legal order to which it is connected as well as on the treatment afforded under these rules to the parties' desire to resort to arbitration.'[181] Therefore, he concludes, the legal order that gives effect to the agreement to arbitrate should be chosen over the laws of the seat that frustrate the agreement to arbitrate.[182]

The implication of this point of view is that the international arbitral tribunal is not bound by injunctive order of the seat of arbitration, even where such order is perfectly legal under the laws of the seat of arbitration, if the court order frustrates the agreement of the parties to arbitrate.[183] According to this view, the application of a rule that frustrates the agreement to arbitrate can be deemed appropriate only where the arbitral tribunal finds that the said rule is in force in each and every legal system to which the agreement to arbitrate has connection.[184] Even then, Prof. Bachand opines, the better approach may be for the arbitrators to 'carry on and make an award, because there will always exist the possibility that the tribunal's assessment of the law in force in those legal orders was mistaken.'[185]

The foregoing suggests that Prof. Bachand subscribes to the delocalisation by contract theory. According to this strand of delocalisation of arbitration the validity or regularity of an award is tested when enforcement is sought; and since

---

[177] *Id.*, at 129.
[178] Bachand (2005), p. 2.
[179] *Id.*
[180] *Id.*
[181] *Id.*
[182] *Id.*
[183] *Id.*
[184] *Id.*, p. 3.
[185] *Id.*

enforcement may be sought in a number of countries there should never be a single state with power to determine the validity of an award once and for all.[186] The proponents of this view challenge the importance of the seat of arbitration on various grounds. They hold that the choice of the seat is a matter of convenience and in some other cases motivated only by the desire for neutrality. Further, they maintain that the seat is not determined by the parties very often. It is rather determined by the arbitration institution chosen by the parties. Besides, they contend, since the arbitration tribunal is only transitory, the seat of the arbitration has no connection with the dispute. Hence, they conclude, the seat of arbitration has no particular significance to international arbitration.[187] In sum, the gist of the contention of the proponents of this view is that the validity of an international arbitration is derived from a legal system from which recognition is sought, also called *jurisdiction de réception,* rather than the court of the seat of arbitration.[188]

This approach would, however, have an undesirable, and yet inevitable effect of 'multi-localization' of arbitral awards.[189] In other words, it would oblige the award creditor to defend recognition and enforcement potentially all over the world as the award debtor would be able to challenge the award in every jurisdiction where recognition and enforcement is sought. Even from the perspective of the award debtor there would be unwelcome consequences. The aggrieved party would have to follow the award creditor since it will have no right to initiate the process of challenging the award.[190] In some other scenarios, such as when an arbitral tribunal rejects a case alleging it has no jurisdiction, this approach would result in an outright denial of justice, if the court of the seat of arbitration has no say in the matter. The proponents of delocalisation do not seem to fully envisage such adverse consequences of their views on arbitration itself.[191]

That said, it must be admitted that the question of the relationship between the laws of the seat, *lex arbitri,* and arbitration is one of the most debated issues in international commercial arbitration.[192] However, it should be underscored that the debate between 'territorialists' and 'transnationalists' has been, by and large, settled by the arbitration laws and conventions over the years. The prevailing reality is that 'delocalisation' of arbitration is possible only when and to the extent the *lex arbitri* allows it.[193] Widely adopted laws such as the UNCITRAL Model Law and the New York Convention have a strong territorialist tendency. Hence, the prevailing opinion today is that, except in rare cases where laws other than that of the seat have been validly chosen by the parties, international arbitral proceedings must be

---

[186]Petrochilos (2004), p. 39.

[187]Lew et al. (2003), p. 64.

[188]Petrochilos (2004), para 249.

[189]*Id.*

[190]*Id.*

[191]*Id.*

[192]Schwartz (2005), p. 795.

[193]*Id.*

conducted in compliance with the mandatory rules in force at the seat of arbitration.[194] Hence, the arbitration laws of the seat, Ethiopian laws in this case, cannot be disregarded. Therefore, theories such as the delocalisation theory should not in any manner diminish the significance of creating a legal framework that is conducive to arbitration with a foreign element.

Another failing of the *SALINI* Tribunal in disregarding the injunctive order of the Ethiopian court is that the Tribunal was somehow 'selective' in its focus of what was really agreed upon by the parties.[195] Party autonomy, on which the Tribunal relies to justify its decision to disregard the injunction by the Ethiopian Court, requires that the Tribunal gives effect to the agreement of the parties in its entirety. This, of course, includes the *lex- arbitri* as chosen by the parties.[196] By choosing to arbitrate in Ethiopia, it can be contended that the parties agreed to make the arbitration subject to the supervisory jurisdiction of the Ethiopian courts to the extent that is permissible under Ethiopian law.[197] The ICC Tribunal did not find that as a matter of Ethiopian law the Ethiopian court had no power to give injunctive order. In fact, the Tribunal did not at all attempt to consider Ethiopian law on the subject.[198] By failing to even consider the rules of the *lex arbitri,* the Tribunal denied effect to the agreement of the parties to arbitrate in Ethiopia, thus, itself frustrating the legitimate expectation of the parties.[199]

Even Professor Bachand concedes that adherence to the theory that a tribunal's authority ultimately emanates from the agreement of the parties is not sufficient to conclude that an arbitral tribunal can disregard an injunctive order of a court of the seat. He maintains such a conclusion is tenable only where the injunction is contrary to the intention of the parties.[200] He concludes the decision of the ICC Tribunal disregarding the injunctive order in the *SALINI* case meets this requirement too.[201]

The reality, however, is that Clause 67 of the contract makes mention of both ICC rules and Civil Code provisions on *ad hoc* arbitration. As a result, whether the parties

---

[194]*Id.*, p. 796.

[195]Mohtashami (2005), p. 4.

[196]*Id.*

[197]*Id.*

[198]*Id.*

[199]*Id.*

[200]Bachand (2005), pp. 3–4.

[201]*Id.*, at 4. Prof. Bachand contends the injunctive order in the Salini case frustrates the agreement of the parties to arbitrate because once parties agree to arbitrate under the ICC rules, the Tribunal has *Kompetenz-Kompetenz* per Article 6(2) of the ICC rules in force at the time. This, according to him excludes the possibility of injunctive order by a court that frustrates the ICC tribunal's power to determine its own jurisdiction. The problem with Prof. Bachand's reasoning is that he assumes the parties agreed to arbitrate under ICC rules when this was in fact at the heart of the dispute. The first instance court gave the injunctive order because it was clearly faced with an ambiguous arbitration clause that indicates both ICC and ad hoc arbitration. Two reasonable people could disagree as to what was agreed upon. Hence, the court gave an injunctive order pending its ruling on this matter or earlier reversal of the injunction.

agreed to an institutional or *ad hoc* arbitration is a matter over which reasonable persons with no self interest in the dispute could disagree.[202] It is very difficult to conclude that the parties contemplated the possibility of issuance of an injunctive order by an Ethiopian court and agreed that such order be denied effect. Professor Bachand does not proffer the reason why he reached this conclusion about the intention of the parties.

Given the ambiguity regarding the type of arbitration agreed upon and the fact that *Kompetenz-Kompetenz* can only result from a contract under the Civil Code of Ethiopia, the court was within its powers to give temporary injunction pending the determination of the type of arbitral procedure agreed on.[203] We need to emphasise here that *Kompetenz-Kompetenz* does not flow from the law itself in Ethiopia. It is only the ICC Tribunal's own determination that what was agreed upon was ICC arbitration as supplemented by the Civil Code provisions under Article 3324 *et seq.* that 'entitled' the Tribunal to *Kompetenz-Kompetenz*.

Overall, arguments based on party autonomy are no guarantee for the effective conduct of international commercial arbitration in Ethiopia. Particularly, the 'battle' between the Ethiopian court and the ICC tribunal in the *SALINI* case demonstrates that the failure of Ethiopian law to embody the *Kompetenz-Kompetenz* rule can result in the derailment of international arbitration even where the arbitration is conducted under the auspices of an eminent international institution like the ICC.

5.1.4.1.2 'Duty' of Ethiopian Court Under the New York Convention to Refer Disputes on Jurisdiction of Arbitral Tribunal to the ICC Tribunal

Another argument that the ICC Tribunal relied on is the duty of courts under the New York Convention. Contracts to arbitrate international disputes are, according to the ICC tribunal, 'validated by a range of international sources and norms extending

---

[202]*SALINI Costruttori S.P.A v. The Federal Democratic Republic of Ethiopia, Addis Ababa Water and Sewerage Authority*, ICC Case No. 10623/AER/ACS, Para. 211 to 213. Even the ICC Tribunal acknowledged that there was an ambiguity that required interpretation. The Tribunal, thus, employed various techniques of interpretation. It relied on everything ranging from the text of the agreement to the negotiating history and exchange of documents immediately preceding the signing of the contract. It concluded, on the basis of such analysis, that what was agreed upon was ICC arbitration as supplemented by the Civil Code of Ethiopia provisions providing for *ad hoc* arbitration. The conclusion was a compromise at face value, as both apply. In essence, however, the tribunal ruled in favour of ICC arbitration as it found ICC rules prevail in case of conflict with Civil Code of Ethiopia rules on arbitration.

[203]Civil Procedure Code Decree No. 52/1965 and Civil Code Proclamation Code No. 165/1960. Under Article 155 of the Civil Procedure Code and Article 2121 of the Civil Code of Ethiopia, a court may give temporary injunction where it has good reason to believe that damage that cannot be redressed by award of compensation is likely to result unless it issues an injunctive order.

beyond the domestic seat itself.'[204] In particular, the Tribunal maintained that the New York Convention is relevant in this case, although Ethiopia is not a party to it. Specifically, it relied on Article II (1) of the Convention that obligates each contracting state to 'recognize an agreement in writing under which the parties undertake to submit to arbitration all or any differences . . . .' The Tribunal found Article II (3) of the New York Convention particularly relevant. The Tribunal cited the said provision which reads:[205]

[t]he court of a Contracting State, when seized of an action in a matter in respect of which the parties have made an agreement within the meaning of this article, shall, at the request of one of the parties, refer the parties to arbitration, unless it finds that the said agreement is null and void, inoperative or incapable of being performed.

The Tribunal then underscored that an overwhelming majority of states have ratified or acceded to the New York Convention. Hence, it concluded, it 'is clear *the duty of the Arbitral Tribunal* in this respect is not founded exclusively in the Ethiopian Legal order.'[206] The Convention addresses the courts of contracting states, and not arbitral tribunals. Given this fact, we are left wondering why the Tribunal felt legally obliged to place itself in the shoes of the courts of the contracting states. In any event, the gist of the Tribunal's line of reasoning is that the New York Convention confers on it authority even though Ethiopia is not a party to the Convention.

The Tribunal seems to be implying that the New York Convention has been so widely accepted that it has now acquired the status of customary international law binding even non-signatories. This is a very interesting argument though, unfortunately, the Tribunal did not fully and clearly develop it. Indeed, 'rules set forth in a treaty' may sometimes attain the status of customary international law, and thus become binding on third-states.[207] Not to be bound, a non-signatory state will have to show that it persistently objected to the crystallization of the norms embodied in the treaty. In other words, the state will have to show that it 'protested loud and often' to avoid being bound by an emerging global custom.[208]

That said, the Tribunal's position that the New York Convention vests in it immunity from injunctive orders by the courts of the seat is less than convincing. First, the basic rule as embodied in the Vienna Convention on the Law of Treaties is that '[a] treaty does not create either obligations or rights for a third State without its consent.'[209] This principle was underscored by the International Law Commission during its deliberations prior to the adoption of the Vienna Convention on the Law of Treaties.[210] Given this basic rule and the fact that Ethiopia by a clear statute has

---

[204] *SALINI Costruttori S.P.A v. The Federal Democratic Republic of Ethiopia, Addis Ababa Water and Sewerage Authority*, ICC Case No.10623/AER/ACS, para. 129.

[205] *Id.*, at para. 130 to 131.

[206] *Id.*, at para. 134.

[207] Aust (2000), p. 210.

[208] Bederman (2002), p. 37.

[209] Vienna Convention on the Law of Treaties, concluded on 23 May 1969, Vienna, Article 34.

[210] Shaw (2003), p. 835.

expressly prohibited *Kompetenz-Kompetenz* unless embodied in an arbitration agreement itself since 1960, the Tribunal did not discharge its burden of proof to show Ethiopian courts are bound by the New York Convention.[211]

Second, as noted, the provisions of Article II(3) of the New York Convention are addressed at the courts of States Party to the Convention while the Arbitral Tribunal takes them as if they were addressed to itself when it says the tribunal's 'duty' is not exclusively based on the Ethiopian legal order.[212] It did not establish why it is under legal obligation to place itself in the shoes of the courts of the Contracting States.

Third, even assuming the New York Convention has attained customary international law status thus binding Ethiopia, and that obligations imposed on courts by the Convention bind arbitral tribunals, it does not necessarily follow that the ICC Tribunal is free from injunctive orders by the courts of the seat. Nothing in the Convention would really prohibit the Ethiopian courts from doing what the First Instance Court did. The Convention only requires the courts of contracting states to enforce agreements to 'arbitrate.' The Ethiopian party was not resisting arbitration. Nor was the Ethiopian court refusing to refer the matter to arbitration. The court was rather faced with an arbitration agreement that raises a *bona fide* issue of contract interpretation. Particularly, whether what was agreed upon was an *ad hoc* or ICC arbitration was not clear given that reference was made to both in the arbitration clause.

Given the foregoing and the fact that *Kompetenz-Kompetenz* does not arise from the law itself in Ethiopia, the Ethiopian Court had no legal basis to deny a day in court to the party that disputed the jurisdiction of the ICC Tribunal.

5.1.4.1.3   Use of Domestic Courts to Frustrate Arbitration Contrary to International Public Policy

The ICC Tribunal also made an international public policy based argument to justify its disregard of the injunction issued by the Ethiopian court. It developed this argument as follows.

---

[211]Note that the provisions of the Civil Code that limit the competence of arbitral tribunal to decide on its jurisdiction, and Civil Code Article 2121 that allows courts to give injunctive order on which the Ethiopian court relied was issued in 1960, just two years after the adoption of the New York Convention on Recognition and Enforcement of Arbitral Awards which the Tribunal seems to imply has attained the status of customary international law. So, arguably, Ethiopia's adoption of those laws shows it did not acquiesce into the development of customary international law in the matter covered by these provisions of Ethiopian law. In other words, it may be held that Ethiopia has 'objected' to the elevation of norms embodied in the New York Convention to the status of customary international law binding on it. Without further ado, we believe at least, the Tribunal did not sufficiently show that Ethiopia is bound by the norms of the New York Convention despite being a non-party.

[212]*SALINI v. Federal Democratic Republic of Ethiopia, Addis Ababa Water and Sewerage Authority*, ICC Case No. 10623/AER/ACS, para. 134.

The Tribunal started out by noting that the essence of what *AAWSA* sought from the First Instance Court of Ethiopia was a ruling on the ICC Tribunal's jurisdiction. It further underlined that the Ethiopian Court issued the injunctive order pending its decision on the jurisdiction of the ICC Tribunal.[213] This was, according to the Tribunal, a clear breach of the principle of *Kompetenz-Kompetenz*. The Tribunal reasoned, the parties may in the arbitration agreement 'authorize the arbitrator to decide the disputes relating to his jurisdiction' pursuant to Article 3330(2) of the Civil Code of Ethiopia. It then stated its conclusion that what the parties had agreed to was arbitration under the ICC Rules. That being the case, it continued, the parties had by agreement conferred on the Tribunal the power to decide on its own jurisdiction because Article 6(2) of the ICC Rules embody the principle of *Kompetenz-Kompetenz*.[214] Therefore, the Tribunal underscored, the right time for the Ethiopian Court to consider whether or not the Arbitral Tribunal had jurisdiction would be in the context of an action to set aside the award, after the Arbitral Tribunal has had the chance to decide on its own jurisdiction. The Court, the ICC Tribunal underlined 'has no power to pre-empt the Arbitral Tribunal from deciding on its own jurisdiction.'[215] Hence, it concluded making its own determination on the issue of its jurisdiction was perfectly legal.[216]

Since the Tribunal could lawfully decide on its own jurisdiction, the injunction by the Ethiopian court was contrary to international public policy, according to the ICC Tribunal. Particularly, the Arbitral Tribunal stated, 'a state or state entity cannot resort to the state's courts to frustrate an arbitration agreement.'[217] This, it said, is a principle of international law which the Respondent, a state entity, is attempting to defy by making use of its own courts.[218]

The Arbitral Tribunal cited, in support of this position, various authorities. Interestingly, one of the authorities relied upon was a previous ICC case between *SALINI* (Claimant) and the Predecessor of *AAWSA*, the Respondent. The Arbitral Tribunal quoted the previous tribunal's ruling as follows:[219]

L'ordre public international s'opposerait avec force à ce qu'un organe étatique, traitant avec des personnes étrangères au pays puisse passer ouvertement, le sachant et le voulant, une clause d'arbitrage qui met en confiance le cocontractant et puisse ensuite, que ce soit dans la procédure arbitrale ou dans la procédure d'exécution, se prévaloir de la nullité de sa propre parole.

---

[213]*Id.*, para. 152.

[214]*Id.*

[215]*Id.*, para. 153.

[216]*Id.*

[217]*Id.* para. 156.

[218]*Id.*

[219]*Id.*, para. 161. The previous ICC Case that the Tribunal cites from *Le Statut des usages du commerce international devant les jurisdictions arbitrales*, 1973 Rev. Arb. 122, 145 and 109 J.D.I 971, 977 (1982) is ICC 1939 with commentary by Yves Derains.

According to the Tribunal's own translation this means:[220]

> international public policy would be strongly opposed to the idea that a public entity, when dealing with foreign parties, could openly, knowingly, and willingly, enter into an arbitration agreement, on which its contractor would rely, only to claim subsequently, whether during the arbitration proceedings or on enforcement of the award, that its own undertaking was void.

Besides, the Tribunal quotes rulings in other arbitral cases to make the point that a state cannot rely on its own laws to deny effect to an international arbitration agreement.[221]

The Tribunal draws analogy between the foregoing and a situation in which a state makes use of its own courts rather than its own laws to deny effect to an international arbitration agreement. It noted first that the question of whether a state can resort to its own courts, as opposed to its own law, to renege on an arbitration agreement had not given rise to a similarly well-established body of case law. Yet, it concluded, there is no significant difference between a state changing its law to deny effect to an international agreement to arbitrate on the one hand, and making use of its courts 'to have the arbitral agreement suspended or terminated' be that on the grounds of alleged nullity of the agreement or some other ground on the other hand.[222] Both amount to nothing but reneging on its own agreement to submit to an international arbitration.[223] In the present case, the Tribunal concluded, *AAWSA*, a state entity, was resorting to the State's own courts to renege upon the arbitration agreement. This, according to the Tribunal, was illegitimate.[224]

This international public policy based arguments by the ICC Tribunal against temporary injunction issued by the Ethiopian Court pending determination of whether the agreed upon arbitration was *ad hoc* or ICC arbitration is misplaced, it seems. The First Instance Court was faced with an arbitration clause that was clearly ambiguous and hence required interpretation.[225] It gave injunctive order only

---

[220]*Id*. Note that here the Ethiopian entity seems not to be resorting to domestic court but rather contending the agreement to arbitrate is not valid. Most probably the Ethiopian entity is relying on Civil Procedure Code Article 315(2) which states '(n)o arbitration may take place in relation to administrative contracts as defined in Article 3132 of the Civil Code or in any other case where it is prohibited by law.' We have discussed this provision and numerous court cases arising under it in chapter four dealing with arbitrability in Ethiopia.

[221]*Id*. para. 162 and 163. One of the cases the Tribunal quoted to this end is *Framatome v. Atomic Energy Organization of Iran* in which Iran had maintained the relevant arbitration agreement was void because the approval by the Council of Ministers required by Article 139 of the Iranian Constitution was not complied with, which made the submission to arbitration of disputes concerning state property conditional upon the approval the Council of Ministers and notification to Parliament was not complied with. It similarly quoted award in the 1982 case between Elf Aquataine Iran v. NIOC.

[222]*Id*., para. 166.

[223]*Id*.

[224]*Id*., para. 176.

[225]It should be noted that the predecessor of the Ethiopian party (AAWSA) and SALINI had been involved in a dispute that ended in an ICC arbitration in 1970s. This fact is indicated in this very

pending the determination of what exactly was agreed on, an *ad hoc* or ICC arbitration. We need to underscore here that it is only the ICC Tribunal's own finding that what was agreed on was ICC arbitration.[226] The First Instance Court had not resolved the problem resulting from the ambiguity of the arbitration clause at the time it issued the injunctive order.

Though the First Instance Court could not make a final determination on this issue because it was overtaken by developments at the ICC Tribunal and appeal to the Supreme Court, it could, in theory, have decided that what was agreed upon was ICC arbitration. In that event, the ICC Tribunal would have jurisdiction to decide on its own jurisdiction since the validity of the arbitration agreement was not at issue in this case.[227] That said, one could not rule out a contrary finding by the Ethiopian Court given the ambiguity of the arbitration clause of the contract. In other words, the possibility of the court finding that what was agreed on was an *ad hoc* arbitration under the Civil Code of Ethiopia was still open at the time it issued the injunctive order. The effect of this latter finding would be absence of *Kompetenz-Kompetenz* since under Ethiopian law such power of an arbitral tribunal arises only from a contract. So, pending the determination of the type of arbitration agreed on, the Court had no basis, under Ethiopian law, to leave the issue of jurisdiction for decision by the ICC Tribunal. In any case, dictates of international public policy on which the Tribunal relies are highly subjective and cannot be beyond contention.

It should be underlined here that we are not contending a state entity can lawfully frustrate an agreement to arbitrate by resorting to its own national courts. Whether or not this international public policy based argument of the ICC Tribunal is valid, is beyond our contention.[228] All we are saying is that the factual basis for the

---

arbitration. So, both sides must have thought there was a distinct possibility of dispute at the time of the conclusion of the arbitration clause. Clearly, the Ethiopian party did not want an ICC Arbitration. SALINI on the other hand insisted on ICC arbitration. The outcome of the negotiation on this point was an arbitration clause that mentioned both ICC arbitration and the rules of the Ethiopian Civil Code that provide for *ad hoc* arbitration. May be each side hoped the resultant ambiguity would be resolved in its favour. In any case, both the ICC Tribunal and the Ethiopian courts were confronted with the ambiguity resulting from this bad compromise. And the problem was exacerbated by the fact that under Ethiopian law *Kompetenz-Kompetenz* results only from contract, rather than the law itself. It is in this light that the SALINI-AAWSA saga and the battle between the ICC Tribunal and Ethiopian courts should be seen.

[226]The contract between the parties under Sub-Clause 67.3 mentions ICC arbitration while Under Sub-Clause 67.3.4 it indicates Civil Code of Ethiopia rules on arbitration that provide for *ad hoc* arbitration. Given this apparent contradiction in the agreement itself the ICC Tribunal had to engage in extensive interpretation to reach the conclusion that what was agreed on was ICC arbitration as complemented by the Civil Code of Ethiopia provisions, if need be. *See*, the ICC Award in *Salini Costruttori S.P.A (Italy) v. The Federal Democratic Republic of Ethiopia Addis Ababa Water and Sewerage Authority*, Para. 211.

[227]Pursuant to Civil Code of Ethiopia, Article 3330(3), parties cannot even by an express agreement authorize the arbitral tribunal to decide 'whether the arbitral submission is or is not valid.'

[228]Applying public international law rules to a dispute in a commercial arbitration raises a number of interesting issues. At least traditionally that is not the sphere of public international law. Hence, a number of challenges could be raised against the approach of the Tribunal. Questions that may be

application of this rule was not met at the time the First Instance Court issued the injunctive order. The court order was beyond reproach at the time because, unlike in most other jurisdictions, *Kompetenz-Kompetenz* arises only from contract under Ethiopian law. And whether the parties had agreed to confer this power on arbitrators was in issue before the First Instance Court. That is why it seems the Court felt compelled to issue the temporary injunction. In short, it is the state of Ethiopian law that resulted in the denial of *Kompetenz-Kompetenz* to the ICC Tribunal. The First Instance Court is not to blame.

In sum, under Ethiopian law an arbitral tribunal has no competence to decide on whether what was agreed upon was an *ad hoc* or institutional arbitration let alone decide on challenges directed at the very existence or validity of arbitration agreement or even scope of the powers of the tribunal. Ethiopian law compels arbitral tribunals to sit on their hands and wait for courts to determine almost any type of challenge directed at the jurisdiction of the tribunal.[229] This can effectively defeat the whole purpose of the agreement to arbitrate as it did ultimately happen in the *SALINI* case. *SALINI* had no option but to withdraw the arbitral claim and settle for a third of its global claims besides covering all its costs of the arbitration and foregoing any interest for delayed payments.[230]

---

raised include: Are companies that are parties to business transactions subjects of international law entitled to rights directly under international law? Does international law create rights for such entities as such or only as between states? Even if it does create rights for private entities how are such rights vindicated, through a system of espousal in which the relevant states become parties or in an arbitration to which a private entity is a party? Is there a wide and representative practice accompanied by *opinio juris* that supports the position of the arbitral tribunal on this point? That said, these and similar public international law questions are beyond the scope of this work.

[229] At the risk of speculating, one could conclude from the Salini case that Ethiopian courts would intervene whenever arbitral jurisdiction is disputed no matter what the ground for that. If, for example, the arbitration clause provides for good faith attempt at amicable settlement prior to employing arbitration and one of the parties contests arbitral jurisdiction alleging that such attempt was not made, it seems Ethiopian courts would intervene. This is a likely result because the law simply does not give arbitrators jurisdiction to decide on their own jurisdiction no matter the ground on which that is called into question. Would the courts also intervene into other contentions targeting the arbitration agreement such as the agreed language of arbitration and the place of arbitration? We do not have authoritative answer since but ruling out court intervention even in such cases is not possible. That the law itself does not vest in an arbitral tribunal jurisdiction to decide on their own jurisdiction invites a party that wants to obstruct arbitration to resort to courts.

[230] Compromise Agreement between Addis *Ababa Water and Sewerage Authority and SALINI Costruttori S.P.A*, dated 17 July 2002, Articles 1, 4 and 5. Though the global compensation sought by *SALINI* was US $26,700,000 it had to settle for US $9,510,000 payable in several instalments without interest. It had to also shoulder its costs of litigation.

5.2   Separability of the Arbitration Agreement from the Underlying Contract

This section dwells on the separability of an arbitration agreement from the main contract, a conceptual cornerstone of commercial arbitration. Particularly, the meaning and implications of the doctrine is discussed first. Then, the theoretical and practical justifications for the doctrine are explored. Finally, the status of the doctrine under Ethiopian law is examined.

5.2.1   The Doctrine of Separability: Its Meaning and Implications

The term 'separability of arbitration agreement' stands for the notion that the arbitration clause in a contract is severable and autonomous from the main contract of which it is a part.[231] This doctrine is also referred to as autonomy of the arbitration agreement and severability of the arbitration agreement in different literatures.[232]

The doctrine of separability has profound implications in arbitration law. One consequence of paramount significance to arbitration is that it makes obstruction of arbitration difficult. Particularly, the invalidity of the underlying contract does not affect the validity of the arbitration clause because these two are deemed different contracts.[233] When parties enter into a contract containing an arbitration cause, Justice Schwebel maintains, they conclude effectively two contracts, the 'arbitral twin of which survives any birth defects or acquired disability of the principal agreement.'[234] As a result, challenges directed at the validity of the main contract do not impact on the jurisdiction of the arbitral tribunal.[235] In particular, the invalidity of the main or the 'container' contract does not necessarily undermine an arbitral award of a tribunal established on the basis of the arbitration clause in the main contract.[236] The jurisdiction of the arbitral tribunal will be affected by the invalidity of the underlying contract only if 'the defect causing the invalidity of the main contract necessarily extends, by its very nature to the arbitration clause.'[237]

---

[231]Redfern et al. (2009), p. 117.

[232]Samuel, 'Separability of Arbitration Clauses – Some Awkward Questions About the Law of Contracts, Conflict of Laws and the Administration of Justice', at 1, available at: https://www.biicl.org/files/4160_separabi.pdf. According to Samuel separability and severability are the more common words used to refer to the concept in the English speaking world while the French refer to the same as the *autonomie de la clause compromissoire.*

[233]Smit (2003), p. 2.

[234]Leboulanger (2007), p. 4.

[235]*Id.*

[236]Smit (2003), p. 2.

[237]United Nations Commission on International Trade Law (2012), p. 76.

Another, yet similar implication is that, the arbitration clause survives the termination or expiration of the main contract hence preserving the jurisdiction of the arbitral tribunal to entertain claims arising from the main contract when the said contract was still in force.[238] Owing to its foregoing implications, among others, the separability doctrine is regarded as a 'conceptual cornerstone of international arbitration.'[239]

Another ramification of the separability doctrine is the converse of the above. Specifically, the invalidity, expiry or termination of the arbitration clause does not necessarily affect the underlying contract.[240] Yet another consequence of the separability doctrine is that the law governing the arbitration agreement and the *lex contractus*, law governing the main contract, may be different.[241] In fact, potentially the law governing the formation and validity of the arbitration agreement, the law applicable to the substance of the contract and the law that governs the arbitral proceedings could all be different.[242] In the absence of choice made by the parties themselves, the determination of the law which applies to each of the foregoing three rests on the application of the choice of law rules according the prevalent view.[243]

5.2.2 Justifications for the Doctrine of Separability

Different authors, international tribunals and courts have put forward theoretical and practical justifications for the doctrine of separability. To start with the theoretical justification, one explanation is that the agreement of the parties to arbitrate is distinct and independent from the underlying contract because 'the mutual promises to arbitrate [generally] form the *quid pro quo* of one another and constitute a separable and enforceable part of the [underlying] agreement.'[244] Others justify the doctrine of separability on the ground that the main contract and the arbitration agreement are 'different kinds of agreements.'[245] The former contract concerns itself with the 'substantive rights and obligations' of the parties to the contract as opposed to the arbitration clause which deals with 'procedural' issue of dispute resolution.[246] The arbitration agreement defines the process of dispute resolution which will apply

---

[238]Smit (2003), p. 2.

[239]Born (2001), p. 56.

[240]Smit (2003), p. 2.

[241]Leboulanger (2007), p. 7.

[242]*Id.*

[243]*Id*, at 7–8. Possibly laws of four different jurisdictions could be relevant to the three aspects above. These are the law chosen by parties either expressly or impliedly to govern the arbitration agreement itself, the law of the venue of arbitration, the law governing the main contract and the law of the forum in which judicial enforcement is sought.

[244]Born (2001), p. 56.

[245]Leboulanger (2007), p. 6.

[246]*Id.*

only if need be and is only 'ancillary' to the substantive agreement of the parties.[247] Some others hold 'the arbitration agreement is *accessory* to the right of action which goes together with the substantive provisions of the contract.'[248]

Practical justifications are, however, equally or even more compelling than theoretical explanations of this doctrine. The doctrine of separability is necessitated by the need to prevent parties from reneging on their obligation to arbitrate by the simple expedient of alleging the contract is void, for instance.[249] If a mere claim, that the underlying contract is invalid, breached or performed and hence not any more in force were to deny effect to the arbitration clause the whole purpose of the arbitration agreement would be defeated.[250] It is precisely for resolving such disputes that the parties enter into arbitration agreement.[251] In sum, in the absence of the doctrine of separability, any claim, even a patently false one, that the underlying contract is invalid on any number of grounds would force arbitrators to sit on their hands till this issue is settled by a national court. This would seriously impact on the existence of arbitration as an alternative to litigation in court.

Minimizing the involvement of courts in arbitration is particularly important in the context of international transactions. Efficiency of international business depends on the fulfilment of the expectations of the parties in regard to the dispute settlement mechanism. Particularly, the expectation of parties from different legal traditions is met if any dispute is resolved in a neutral, non-national arbitral forum, regardless of any challenges to the validity of their underlying contract.[252] So, recognition of the doctrine of separability is, in part, dictated by the practical reality of the need to foster international commerce.

5.2.3 The Doctrine of Separability in Ethiopia

The law in Ethiopia is completely silent about the separability of the arbitration clause from the underlying contract. What is more, no court case that deals with this doctrine could be found, despite research into the issue. Definitely, there is no Cassation Court decision to date with a power of precedent regarding this matter.

Given the complete silence of the law establishment of this doctrine by the judiciary is not ruled out. Particularly, the courts may rely on theoretical and practical justifications of the kind discussed in the section immediately preceding this. Specifically, in the context of international commerce, the role that the doctrine plays in meeting the expectations of the parties to settle disputes in a neutral,

---

[247]*Id.*

[248]*Id.*

[249]*Id.*

[250]Redfern et al. (2009), Par. 2.89.

[251]*Id.*

[252]Leboulanger (2007), p. 6.

non-national arbitral forum irrespective of challenges to the underlying contract comes to mind.

Besides, the very reason the parties include an arbitration clause in a contract is so arbitrators decide on any dispute as to whether the underlying contract is valid, performed or breached. Non-recognition of the separability doctrine frustrates the very intention of the parties to arbitrate disputes regarding these issues. Not accepting this doctrine also flies in the face of the principle of interpretation that requires interpretation in accordance with 'the common intention of the parties.'[253]

Besides, given the near universal recognition of the doctrine of separability, contracting parties most likely do not expect challenges to the underlying contract, not directly targeting the arbitration clause itself, result in the denial of the arbitral jurisdiction. Hence, interpretation that gives effect to the doctrine of separability would be in line with the rule that requires contracts be 'interpreted in accordance with good faith having regard to the loyalty and confidence which should exist between the parties according to business practice.'[254] Professor Krzeczunowicz maintains this general rule of interpretation, which is not dealing with separability as such, should be understood as requiring incorporation of usage into a contract when interpreting the same.[255] So, given the near universal recognition of the doctrine of separability acceptance of the doctrine as a usage forming part and parcel of the contract between the parties would be tenable. At least, it may be argued that such interpretation would not violate Ethiopian law because all that the law denies arbitrators is the power to decide on 'whether the *arbitral submission* is or is not valid,' and not on the validity of the underlying contract.[256] If anything, interpretation in favour of separability would give effect to the purpose of the agreement to arbitrate.

The recognition of the doctrine of separability by the judiciary in the face of the silence of the law is not really a novelty. In fact, it is the courts that first recognised the doctrine in leading commercial jurisdictions. Legislations only codified the case law. For instance, in France, a country to which Ethiopian law has perhaps the closest affinity, it is the *Cour de Cassation* that first established the separability doctrine in 1963, just three years after the adoption of the Civil Code of Ethiopia. In *Ets. Raymond Gosset v. Maison Freres Carapelli* it held that the arbitration agreement has full legal autonomy and is not affected by the invalidity of the main contract in which it is included.[257] This case law has now been made part of Decree No. 2011-48 of January 13, 2011. Article 1447 states that the arbitration clause

---

[253]Civil Code of Ethiopia Proclamation No. 165/1960, Article 1734(1).

[254]*Id.*, Article 1732. See also Article 1713 of the Civil Code, which provides parties are bound not only by the terms of the contract but also by such 'incidental effects as are attached to the obligations concerned by custom, equity and good faith having regard to the nature of the contract.' (Civil Code).

[255]Krzeczunowicz (1996), p. 83.

[256]Civil Code of Ethiopia Proclamation No. 165/1960, Article 3330(3).

[257]Leboulanger (2007), p. 5.

remains valid even when the underlying contract is found to be 'void due to avoidance, invalidity, or termination.'[258]

Similarly, in England it is the courts that first recognised this doctrine. English judges expressly recognised the separability doctrine as part of the English law in the well-publicized *Harbour Assurance Co. (UK) Ltd. v. Kansa General International Insurance Co. Ltd. Others.*[259] Now, the doctrine is enshrined in the English Arbitration Act of 1996. The Act states, '[u]nless otherwise agreed by the parties, an arbitration agreement which forms or was intended to form part of another agreement . . . shall not be regarded as invalid, non-existent or ineffective because that other agreement is invalid, or did not come into existence or has become ineffective, and it shall for that purpose be treated as a distinct agreement.'[260]

In the same vein, the Federal Arbitration Act of the United States makes no mention of the separability doctrine. It is a series of Supreme Court decisions that have entrenched the separability doctrine in the US federal law. In *Prima Paint Co. v. Flood and Conklin Manufacturing Co.* the US Supreme court held that allegations of fraud and misrepresentation inducing the underlying contract, not specifically targeting the arbitration clause are matters to be decided by arbitrators, and not the courts, in the absence of evidence that the parties intended to exclude this from arbitral jurisdiction.[261] This position has been refined and cemented in *Buckeye Check Cashing Inc. v. Cardegna* in which the Supreme Court held the fact that the underlying contract is void or otherwise illegal under state law does not affect the arbitration clause.[262]

That being said, in Ethiopia the best way is for the lawmaker to expressly recognise the doctrine of separability. It is unlikely that Ethiopian courts will any time soon establish the doctrine. There are two rules in the Civil Code which could adversely affect the establishment of this doctrine by courts. The first is the rule that requires restrictive interpretation of 'the provisions of the arbitral submission.'[263] This provision is not really dealing with the separability of the arbitration clause from the rest of the contract in which it is found. All that it requires is that the scope or coverage of 'the provisions' of the arbitration clause be understood restrictively. It calls for a restrictive understanding of the content of the clause rather than the relationship of the clause with the rest of the contract in which it is contained. Yet, it is possible that many judges and practitioners alike will understand the provision as restricting the powers of arbitrators to decide on challenges directed at the validity

---

[258]Castellane (2011), p. 372.

[259]Leboulanger (2007), p. 5. This was not the first time that English Courts recognized this doctrine. A series of contradictory decisions were actually made by the English courts prior to this. As far back as 1942, the House of Lords had confirmed the separability doctrine.

[260]Arbitration Act of England and Wales of 1996, Section 7.

[261]Martinez-Fraga (2009), pp. 131–132.

[262]*Id.*, at 143–144.

[263]Civil Code of Ethiopia Proclamation No. 165/1960, Article 3329 titled interpretation provides 'the provisions of the arbitral submission relating to the jurisdiction of the arbitrators shall be interpreted restrictively.'

of the container contract, even when the validity and scope of the arbitration clause itself is not directly called into question.

The other challenge to the establishment of the separability doctrine by courts could emanate from a general rule in Ethiopian law pertaining to the severability of contractual terms. Ethiopian law recognizes the doctrine of severability of contractual terms, though the term itself is not used in the law.[264] That the Ethiopian law of contracts embodies the notion of severability of contractual terms leaves the window open for the judicial establishment of the doctrine of separability of arbitration clause. The possible challenge though is that the law also says the entire contact may be affected by a contractual provision that is invalid, breached or otherwise unenforceable if the provision concerned is so important that it affects the essence of the contract.[265] A breach is regarded as a fundamental breach or as affecting the essence of a contract if 'the very basis of the contract is affected by the non-performance and, because of it, it is reasonable to hold that the claimant would not have concluded a contract so affected.'[266] It is possible, therefore, that judges and practitioners may rely on this rule and conclude that it is reasonable to assume that a party would not have entered into an agreement to arbitrate without the terms of the underlying contract the validity of which is called into question or breached. However, this kind of logic should not apply to the arbitration clause. Parties include arbitration clauses in a contract precisely so the arbitrators decide on any dispute regarding the validity, breach, and the like of the underlying contract irrespective of the importance of that provision of the contract.

In sum, though there seems to be no cogent legal argument against the establishment of the separability doctrine by Ethiopian courts it is unlikely that they will enunciate this doctrine any time soon. The fact that we do not come across court cases even discussing the doctrine nearly seven decades after the adoption of the Civil Code is not a good sign. Therefore, amendment of the arbitration law to include something along the lines of the UNCITRAL Model Law provision which embodies the doctrine[267] that has gotten near universal acceptance[268] would go a long way in

---

[264]Civil Code of Ethiopia Proclamation No. 165/1960, Article 1813. This provision titled 'partial invalidation' reads, '[w]here part only of a contract is vitiated, only that part shall be validated [sic] unless such invalidation affects the essence of the contract.' As we can gather from the very title of the provision which is partial 'invalidation' the word 'validated' should be read as 'invalidated.' The controlling Amharic version also makes this clear. Similarly, Article 1788 which deals with unilateral cancellation of contract by a party provides, '[a] party may cancel the contract . . . where the performance by the other party of his obligations has become impossible or is hindered so that the essence of the contract is affected.' This implies where the impossibility of performance of an obligation does not affect the essence of the contract the rest of the provisions of contract will apply with necessary adjustments to the performance of the contract.

[265]*Id.*, Articles 1785, 1788 and 1813 quoted above read together.

[266]*Id.*, Article 1785(3).

[267]UNCITRAL Model Law on International Commercial Arbitration with amendments in 2006. Article 16(1) of the 1985 Model Law provides '. . . an arbitration clause which forms part of a contract shall be treated as an agreement independent of the other terms of the contract.'

[268]Leboulanger (2007), p. 6.

minimizing obstruction of arbitration and making Ethiopia a venue of choice for arbitration. Ethiopia fails to recognise this doctrine, which is a conceptual cornerstone of international commercial arbitration, at its own peril.

5.3   Conclusions

In this chapter, the role of an arbitral tribunal and a court in the determination of arbitral jurisdiction was explored. Analysis of the issue in this chapter demonstrated that the legitimacy of arbitration trounces its efficacy completely under Ethiopian law. Particularly, any allegation, even a patently false one, that the arbitration agreement is invalid or non-existent has to be settled by a court. The parties to an arbitration agreement cannot even by an express term authorise the arbitral tribunal to decide on such challenge. Moreover, the tribunal does not have jurisdiction to decide on challenges directed even only at the scope of its powers unless the parties have vested in it such powers. This is a rarity given an arbitration clause is mostly a midnight clause drafted at the end of the contract negotiation with minimal deliberation.

Since Ethiopian law does not itself vest in an arbitral tribunal the jurisdiction to decide on its own jurisdiction an Ethiopian court may, if it so wishes, intervene whenever arbitral jurisdiction is disputed no matter what the ground for that. The way Ethiopian courts handled the *SALINI* case gives credence to this conclusion as neither the validity and existence of the arbitration agreement nor the scope of powers it conferred on arbitrators was at issue in that case.

As if a readily available recourse to court from arbitration were not bad enough, the law does not guarantee even parallel proceedings before a court and an arbitral tribunal. An Ethiopian court may issue injunctive order to halt the arbitral proceeding pending decision on the issue of arbitral jurisdiction. In fact, Ethiopian courts do issue such orders as seen in the *SALINI* case. Moreover, even where a court finds there is an obligation to arbitrate, nothing in Ethiopian law prevents the party that lost the case from lodging an appeal against that jurisdictional finding. The appellate court may in turn issue an injunctive order against the resumption of the arbitration pending its decision on the appeal. What makes things even worse is that a party that wants to obstruct arbitration can, even after exhausting appellate remedies, seek review on cassation on grounds of basic error of law before the Cassation Bench of the Federal Supreme Court.[269] The Cassation Bench too can issue injunction against the continuation of the arbitration pending its decision on the application for review on Cassation.

That Ethiopian law and the jurisprudence of Ethiopian courts are completely silent regarding the doctrine of separability may further exacerbate the foregoing

---

[269]Federal Courts Proclamation No 25/1996, Federal *Negarit Gazeta*, 2nd Year, No. 13, Article 10 (1) & (3).

problem. Courts will likely intervene in the manner above even when a challenge on grounds of invalidity or breach is directed at the underlying contract rather than the arbitration clause itself.

In sum, the 'legitimacy' of arbitration is ensured at an unacceptably high cost to its efficacy under Ethiopian law. In fact, it is hard to maintain that arbitration exists as a real alternative to litigation in courts in Ethiopia.

The analysis in this chapter demonstrates a number of steps that may right this imbalance between the legitimacy and efficacy of arbitration. The most arbitration friendly step is to confer on an arbitration tribunal full powers to decide on its own jurisdiction even when the very existence and validity of the arbitration agreement is disputed. This is the approach taken in many jurisdictions of significance to international commerce. In countries that take this approach the courts can review questions of arbitral jurisdiction at the post award stage. In other words, arbitral tribunals are allowed to have the first word while the courts of the seat of arbitration have the last word. This approach ensures the efficiency of arbitration. Hence, adopting this approach will make it easier for Ethiopian parties to international business transactions to convince their foreign counterparts to agree to arbitration in Ethiopia.

If the above approach is found to be too lopsided in favour of the efficacy of arbitration, limiting recourse to court available to a party resisting arbitration to a period before the commencement of arbitration is an option to consider. Under this approach if the party that resists arbitration had not already commenced legal action before a court of law it would be entitled to invoke a court's jurisdiction anytime between receipt of the notice of arbitration and the constitution of the arbitral tribunal. If the party resisting arbitration fails to seek judicial intervention within this window of time, it will still have the chance of raising its objections to the arbitral tribunal. Moreover, the possibility of challenging arbitral jurisdiction at the post award stage is still open.

At the very least, Ethiopia should adopt a number of streamlined mechanisms to create a semblance of balance between the legitimacy and efficacy of arbitration. First and foremost, Ethiopian law should confer on an arbitral tribunal jurisdiction to decide on any question of relevance to arbitral jurisdiction subject to parallel proceedings before a court on the same issue. That means a court should not have the power to issue an injunctive order against the continued conduct of arbitration. Second, the right to appeal from a determination by a court in favour of arbitral jurisdiction should be abolished. Third, review on cassation should be barred on issues of arbitral jurisdiction. These measures will be disincentives to an unscrupulous party contemplating to seek judicial intervention with obstructionist intent.

References

Aust A (2000) Modern treaty law and practice. Cambridge University Press

Bachand F (2005) 'Must an ICC tribunal comply with an anti-suit injunction issued by The Courts of the Seat of Arbitration?' (Comment on Salini Costruttori S.p.a. v. Ethiopia, December 7, 2001). Mealey's International Arbitration Report 20(3)

Barceló J III (2003) Who decides the arbitrators' jurisdiction? Separability and competence-competence in transnational perspective. Vand J Transnatl Law 36:115

Bederman DJ (2002) The spirit of international law. University of Georgia Press

Bermann G (2012) The "Gateway" problem in international commercial arbitration. Yale J Int Law 37(1):1

Born G (2001) International commercial arbitration: commentary and materials, 2nd edn. International, Kluwer Law

Castellane B (2011) The new French law on international arbitration. J Int Arb 28(4):371

David R (1963) Civil code for Ethiopia, considerations on the codification of the civil law in African countries. Tulsa Law Rev 37:200

Gaffney J (2012) Non-party autonomy: displacing the negative effect of the principle of 'competence-competence' in England? A comment on Excalibur ventures LLC v. Texas Keystone Inc & Ors. J Int Arb 29(1):107

Graves JM, Davydan Y (2011) Competence-competence and separability American style. In: Kröll S et al (eds) International arbitration and international commercial law: synergy, convergence and evolution. Kluwer Law International

Greenberg S et al (2011) International commercial arbitration: an Asia pacific perspective. Cambridge University Press, New York

Haris B et al (2007) The arbitration Act 1996: a commentary, 4th edn. Blackwell Publishing

Kawharu A (2008) Arbitral jurisdiction. NZULR 23:238

Krzeczunowicz G (1996) Formation and effects of contracts in Ethiopian law. Faculty of Law, Addis Ababa University, Addis Ababa

Leboulanger P (2007) The arbitration agreement: still autonomous? In: Berg (ed) International Arbitration 2006: back to basics? Kluwer Law International

Lew JDM et al (2003) Comparative international commercial arbitration. Kluwer Law International, The Hague

Lörcher T. Arbitration in Germany, CMS Guide to Arbitration 1

Martinez-Fraga PJ (2009) The American influence on international commercial arbitration: doctrinal developments and discovery methods. Cambridge University Press

Mohtashami R (2005) In defense of injunctions issued by the courts of the place of arbitration: a brief reply to Professor Bachand's commentary on Salini Costruttori S.P.A v. Ethiopia. Mealey's Int Arbitr 20(5) Report 4

Park W (2012) Arbitration of international business disputes, 2nd edn. Oxford University Press

Petrochilos G (2004) Procedural law in international arbitration. Oxford University Press, New York

Redfern A et al (2009) Redfern and hunter on international arbitration, 5th edn. Oxford University Press

Rosen JA (1993) Arbitration under private international law: the doctrines of separability and Compétence de la Compétence. Fordham Int Law J 17(3):619

Samuel A, 'Separability of Arbitration Clauses – Some Awkward Questions About the Law of Contracts, Conflict of Laws and the Administration of Justice', Available at: https://www.biicl.org/files/4160_separabi.pdf

Schwartz EA (2005) Do international arbitrators have a duty to obey the orders of courts at the place of arbitration? Reflections on the role of the Lex Loci Arbitri in the light of a recent ICC award. In: Asken G et al (eds) Global Reflection on International Law, Commerce and Dispute Resolution, International Chamber of Commerce

Shaw M (2003) International law, 5th edn. Cambridge University Press

Smit R (2003) Separability and competence-competence in international arbitration: Ex Nihilo
    Nihil Fit? Or can something indeed come from nothing? American Bar Association, Section of
    International Law and Practice, Spring Meeting
Susler O (2009) The jurisdiction of the arbitral tribunal: a transnational analysis of the negative
    effect of competence. Macquarie J Bus Law 6:119
Tang Z (2014) Jurisdiction and arbitration agreements in international commercial law. Routledge
    Taylor & Francis Group
United Nations Commission on International Trade Law (1985) Yearbook, Volume XVI: 1985,
    Report on the work of the Commission's eighteenth session (Vienna 3-21 June) (A/40/17)
United Nations Commission on International Trade Law (2012) UNCITRAL 2012 Digest of Case
    Law on The Model Law on International Commercial Arbitration. 76 United Nations
    Publication
Walsh TW (2010) 2006 UNCITRAL model law: are states adopting the law in letter and spirit?
    Arbitration and ADR Review

Chapter 6
Judicial Review of Arbitral Awards

6.1 The Judicial Scrutiny of Arbitral Awards: A Snapshot of the Approach Taken in Different Jurisdictions

There is no international convention that regulates the judicial scrutiny of awards, other than by the courts of the enforcement jurisdiction. Hence, different positions have been taken on this subject.[1] At one end of the spectrum is the position that an arbitral award, especially one that does not have connection to the seat of arbitration, should be free from any judicial review.[2] At the opposite end of the spectrum is the position that assimilates arbitral awards to domestic judgments. Of course, there are intermediate positions that dot the spectrum.[3] These include national laws that mandate intervention, mainly to set aside or vacate awards which do not meet certain legally prescribed requirements. There are also few jurisdictions that are closer to one end of the spectrum that allow appeal on the merits of the award, mostly for error of law that the parties may agree to waive.[4]

The difference in positions taken reflects how different jurisdictions attempt to balance the 'rival goals of finality and fairness' of awards.[5] Freeing awards from judicial scrutiny promotes finality while fairness may require some measure of judicial supervision.[6]

---

[1]Abedian (2011), pp. 556–557.

[2]Id., p. 554.

[3]Id.

[4]Blackaby et al. (2009), p. 607.

[5]Abedian (2011), p. 555.

[6]Park (2012), p. 316.

© The Author(s), under exclusive license to Springer Nature Switzerland AG 2021
S. Y. Tesfay, *International Commercial Arbitration*, European Yearbook of International Economic Law 12, https://doi.org/10.1007/978-3-030-66752-8_6

6.1.1 Jurisdictions at the Pro-finality End of the Spectrum

Belgium is a country at the pro-finality end of the spectrum. In fact, Belgium had completely 'delocalized' international commercial arbitration by eliminating the possibility of having an award set aside by courts, by its law issued in 1985.[7] Article 1717(4) of the Judicial Code of Belgium required Belgian courts to take cognizance of an application to set aside an award only if at least one of the parties had connection to Belgium. Specifically, Belgian nationality, residence, and as regards legal persons, place of incorporation, branch or operation in Belgium were deemed sufficient connections to Belgium to warrant taking cognizance of an application to set aside.[8] The idea was to make Belgium an attractive venue for international commercial arbitration by eliminating the possibility of interference in awards by Belgian courts altogether.[9] That law apparently had the opposite effect. The assessment that the law had failed led to the May 1998 amendment to the Judicial Code which allows for setting aside unless waived by the parties themselves in the agreement providing for arbitration or a contract concluded thereafter.[10]

In France, another country on the finality end of the range, no appeal to courts is possible on substantive merits of the award.[11] The only permissible recourse to courts is an application to set aside the award. The grounds for this action are such things as the nullity, absence or expiration of the agreement to arbitrate, irregularity in the appointment of the arbitrators, arbitrators exceeding their powers, failure to comply with due process and situation where the enforcement of the award would be contrary to international public policy.[12] The grounds for setting aside are exhaustive and errors of judgment by arbitrators, be that on points of fact or law, are not in and of themselves grounds for the setting aside of an award.[13] On the whole the grounds

---

[7]Abedian (2011), p. 563.

[8]*Id.*

[9]*Id.*

[10]Code Judiciaire 19 May 1998 Amending the Belgian Legislation Relation to Arbitration, Article 1717 para. 4, free translation available at http://www.jus.uio.no/sisu, accessed on August 21, 2012.

[11]Gaillard and Savage (1999), p. 923.

[12]*Id.*, at 924. It is to be noted that the only difference resulting from the dichotomy between domestic and international arbitration is as regards the grounds for setting aside the award. Only an international award may be set aside on the ground that it is at variance with international public policy.

[13]*Id.*, at 923. Contrary view is held by Kovacs. According to him, the ground for setting aside an award for non-compliance with 'international public policy' has been interpreted to mean the "French conception of international public policy", and not a truly "international public policy". That is understood as an entirety of rules and other matters of fundamental significance that the French legal system upholds. So, an award may be set aside because of how the arbitrators handled the merits of the dispute in the award where that is deemed to be in breach of French international public policy. Principles that have been held by courts as constituting French international policy, for this purpose, include that contracts whose object is to corrupt are void, that contracts must be performed in good faith and contractual obligations cannot be of an indefinite duration. Also awards giving effect to illegal deals or criminal activity, discrimination, either religious, racial or sexual,

for setting aside an award in France are inspired by the philosophy behind Art V of the 1958 New York Convention, but have even more pro arbitration bias than the Convention.[14] Hence, even regarding this action, the permissible grounds are more limited than those provided for in the UNCITRAL Model Law that we shall see in the next sub-section.[15]

Another point that puts the French law at the pro-finality end of the spectrum is the fact that it gives effect to prospectively made agreements to exclude even an application for setting aside. The new law of France that came into effect on 1 May 2011 allows the parties to agree to exclude this recourse for scrutiny of awards at any time.[16] Exclusion agreements are valid even where one or more of the parties to the arbitration agreement have domicile, habitual residence or place of business in France.[17]

Switzerland is yet another country at the pro-finality end of the spectrum. Inspired by the Belgian law, Swiss law allows the parties to agree to exclude application to set aside an award. To be enforceable, the exclusion agreement must be in writing.[18] It must also expressly state that what is being waived is proceeding to *set aside*. The requirement of an express waiver is not met just because parties agreed to finality of the award or made reference to arbitration rules that provide for finality.[19] Unlike under French law, for the exclusion agreement to be valid none of the parties should have its domicile, habitual residence or place of business in Switzerland.[20]

Peru, Russia, Sweden and Tunisia are other countries that enforce agreements excluding setting aside proceedings.[21] However, specific conditions in which the waiver agreement is possible and enforceable as well as its exact ramifications vary from jurisdiction to jurisdiction.[22] Suffice it to say, for our purpose, that an

---

and any violation of human rights may be set aside as contrary to 'international public policy. Kovacs (2008), pp. 430–431. It is interesting to note that though the action that lies is an action to set aside or annul rather than to change the contents of the award, the court will have to examine the merits of the award hence bordering an appellate review proper.

[14]Gaillard and Savage et al. (1999), pp. 983, 996–997.

[15]*Id. See also* the French Code of Civil Procedure 14 May 1981 read Art 1504 and 1502 together, available at http://www.jus.uio.no/lm/france.arbitration.code.of.civil.procedure.1981/sisu_mani fest.html, accessed on August 20, 2011.

[16]Kirby (2012), p. 127.

[17]*Id.* Interestingly, even where parties have waived application to set aside validly, French law allows the party who thus could not have applied to have the award set aside, resist recognition and enforcement of the same award in France, on the New York Convention Grounds which are essentially the same as the grounds for setting aside that had been waived.

[18]*Id.*, at 126.

[19]*Id.*, 126–127.

[20]*Id.*, at 127.

[21]Scherer (2016), made available for advance access at: http://arbitration.oxfordjournals.org, accessed on 15 July 2016.

[22]*Id.*

increasing number of countries are allowing the parties the freedom to in advance conclude agreements excluding the setting-aside of awards.[23]

6.1.2   The Middle-of-the-Road Approach

Perhaps in the middle of the continuum is the *UNCITRAL Model Law* approach which resulted from a deliberate exercise to harmonise the law with respect to international arbitration. It embodies the most popular approach for striking a balance between the finality and fairness of awards.[24] The Model Law allows only one type of recourse against an award, setting aside.[25] The grounds for setting aside, which mirror the grounds for non-recognition of a foreign arbitral award under Article V of the New York Convention, are also exhaustively listed.[26] They are divided into two categories. The first category, listed under Article 34(2)(a) as grounds to be proven by the party, consists of (i) incapacity on the part of the parties to conclude an arbitration agreement, or invalidity of the arbitration agreement under the relevant applicable law; (ii) violation of due process resulting in the inability of a party to present his case; (iii) excess of authority of the tribunal and (iv) the composition of the tribunal or the arbitral procedure being at variance with the agreement of the parties.[27] The second category, grounds that can be raised by a court on its own initiative per Article 34(2)(b), are: (i) the subject matter of the dispute not being capable of settlement by arbitration and (ii) violation of the public policy of the state in which the tribunal sits.[28]

The laws of many jurisdictions of significance to international trade follow the Model Law approach. Chinese law, for instance, follows an essentially similar approach as that followed by the Model Law when it comes to 'foreign-related arbitration awards'.[29] There is no appeal and grounds for setting aside such awards are exhaustively listed.[30] Similarly, the German law follows the Model Law approach when it comes to recourse to court from arbitral awards. It provides that recourse to court against an arbitral award is made only by means of an application to set aside.[31] It also lists exhaustively the grounds on which this application may be

---

[23]*Id.*, at 3.

[24]Abedian (2011), p. 558.

[25]UNCITRAL Model Law on International Commercial Arbitration with amendments as adopted in 2006, Art 34.

[26]Greenberg et al. (2011), p. 419.

[27]UNCITRAL Model Law on International Commercial Arbitration as amended in 2006, Article 34 (2)(a).

[28]*Id.*, Article 34(2)(b).

[29]Jingzhou (2008), p. 85.

[30]*Id.*

[31]German Code of Civil Procedure (1998), ss 1059(1)(2) and 1026.

lodged to court. In fact, from the very outset the Code makes it clear that courts are not to intervene in arbitration procedure at all unless expressly authorized by the law.[32]

In contrast to what we discussed in relation to the countries in the finality end of the spectrum, an agreement reached beforehand purporting to fully exclude an application to set aside is not valid in many countries in this group. Full advance waiver is, for example, not possible in Brazil, Egypt, Germany, and India.[33] In Germany, for instance, Section 1059(2) no 1 of the Civil Procedure Code lists down four grounds that mirror the grounds under the Model Law Art. 34(2) and Article V (1) of the New York Convention. Parties may waive the right to apply for the setting aside of the award on the grounds which pertain to things like the validity and scope of the arbitration agreement, the constitution of the tribunal and the right of the parties to be heard.[34] Waiver is, however, valid only if the parties are aware of the potential defect of the award, and hence effect of the waiver. That means waiver is always possible after the award is rendered, but not necessarily in advance.[35] The parties cannot under any condition waive their right to appeal on the grounds under section 1059(2) no 2, non-arbitrability and violation of public policy. These are grounds for setting aside awards meant to safeguard the interest of the public at large.[36]

6.1.3   Jurisdictions at a Relative Pro-Fairness End of the Spectrum

The laws governing international commercial arbitration in the United States and in England and Wales may be deemed to be at a relative pro-fairness end of the continuum. Compared to other major trading nations they put emphasis on fairness. In what follows, we briefly dwell on the features of the laws of these jurisdictions on recourse from arbitral awards.

6.1.3.1   The Law in the United States of America

A mix of state and federal laws govern international commercial arbitration in the United States. Though the Federal Arbitration Act (FAA) of 1925 pre-empts state laws in cases of conflict, it has not been held to fully 'occupy the field' and hence

---

[32]*Id.*

[33]Scherer (2016), p. 6.

[34]*Id.*, p. 8.

[35]*Id.*

[36]*Id.*

preclude all state law on the subject.[37] So, state laws on arbitration, which in the overwhelming majority of cases are adopted from the Uniform Arbitration Act (UAA) of 1955 or the Revised Uniform Arbitration Act (RUAA), are still important.[38]

The FAA, UAA and RUAA do not allow appeal on the substantive merit of an arbitral award.[39] More specifically, the Federal Arbitration Act which pre-empts the other laws allows a US court in and for the district in which the award was made to vacate an award upon the application of a party in any of the following cases:[40]

(1) *Where the award was procured by corruption, fraud, or undue means.*
(2) *Where there was evident partiality or corruption in the arbitrators, or either of them.*
(3) *Where the arbitrators were guilty of misconduct in refusing to postpone the hearing, upon sufficient cause shown, or in refusing to hear evidence pertinent and material to the controversy; or of any other misbehaviour by which the rights of any party have been prejudiced.*
(4) *Where the arbitrators exceeded their powers, or so imperfectly executed them that a mutual, final, and definite award upon the subject matter submitted was not made.*

These are not focused on substantive review of the merits of the award on questions of law or fact. The parties may not by an agreement prescribe grounds for vacatur adding to the foregoing statutory grounds. The US Supreme Court has found that this is unacceptable.[41] So, as far as the statutory grounds for the judicial review of awards are concerned the US is pretty much in the middle of the spectrum.

What pushes the US slightly towards the fairness end of the spectrum is a common law ground. On top of the FAA based grounds, the Federal Supreme Court remarked in *Wilko v. Swan*, awards can be vacated in cases of 'manifest disregard of the law.'[42] Though *Wilko v. Swan* was reversed on a different ground, the dictum regarding manifest disregard of the law and its effect continues to be

---

[37]Bermann (2009), p. 1335.

[38]*Id.*

[39]Uniform Arbitration Act of 1955, ss 12, Uniform Arbitration Act (Last Revised in 2000) ss 23 available at: http://www.jus.uio.no/lm/usa.uniform.arbitration.act/sisu_manifest.html, accessed on August 26, 2011. The Federal Arbitration Act does not make distinction among arbitrators when it comes to their duty to be impartial. All are expected to be impartial while that is an option left for parties to decide in the UAA. Compare with Federal Arbitration Act ss 10 available at: http://www.law.cornell.edu/uscode/9/usc_sec_09_00000010%2D%2D%2D000-.html, accessed on Sep 30, 2012.

[40]The United States Arbitration Act, Pub. L. 68-401, 43 Stat. 883, Feb. 1925 Section 10(a).

[41]Tyler and Parasharami (2008), p. 613.

[42]Helm (2007), p. 5.

invoked to vacate awards.[43] All Federal Circuit Courts recognise it as a valid ground for vacatur.[44]

Manifest disregard of the law is not, however, understood in identical ways.[45] Because the Supreme Court did not define the boundaries of this ground in *Wilko,* different Circuit Courts have come up with different formulations.[46] In one construction 'misapplication of a law' is not enough. There has to be 'disregard' of the law for an award to be vacated on this ground.[47] In another construction, the 'manifest disregard of the law' standard requires a party seeking review to show the arbitrator knew and understood the law but disregarded it on purpose. This standard can be met very seldom.[48] Following this narrowing trend, the 5th Circuit Court ruled in *Sapic v. Government of Turkmenistan* that the award should be upheld even where it is manifest that the arbitrators acted contrary to the applicable law unless this would result in a 'significant injustice.'[49]

However understood, this ground for review of awards allows, at least, a limited reinvestigation of the merits of the award on points of law. We do not find a comparable ground for the setting aside of awards under the Model Law. So, we may conclude, the US position is, relatively speaking, a bit on the pro-fairness side of the spectrum.

6.1.3.2   English Law

The Arbitration Act of 1996 is even further tilted towards the fairness end of the spectrum, at least, as compared to other jurisdictions that are considered significant players in international commercial arbitration. It allows review of the substantive merit of the award on question of law. Section 69(1) of the Act allows a party to an arbitration proceeding to appeal on a point of law from an arbitral award unless the parties have by an agreement waived this right.[50] The question of 'law' is not as wide as it appears at first sight though. By virtue of Section 82(1) of the Act that gives minor definitions, 'question of law' means only issues arising in relation to the laws of England and Wales or Northern Ireland as appropriate. Questions pertaining to any other law are regarded as questions of fact.[51]

Besides, agreements purporting to exclude the right to appeal have been construed broadly. For instance, an agreement allowing an arbitral tribunal to dispense

---

[43] *Id.*

[44] *Id.*

[45] National Conference of Commissioners on Uniform State Laws (2000), pp. 83–84.

[46] Helm (2007), p. 5.

[47] *Id.*

[48] Moses (2008), p. 197.

[49] Helm (2007), p. 6.

[50] Arbitration Act of England and Wales of 1996, ss 69(1).

[51] Haris et al. (2007), p. 334.

with the tribunal's reasons for its award has been found to constitute a valid exclusion of the right to appeal under s.69(1).[52] Moreover, it has been found that exclusion agreements can be incorporated by cross reference to arbitration rules that do not actually spell out the right to appeal under s. 69(1). For instance, in a case where parties had agreed to arbitration under ICC Rules, Art 24 of which read 'by submitting the dispute to arbitration [by the ICC], the parties shall be deemed to have waived their right to any form of appeal in so far as such waiver can validly be made', this was found to constitute a valid exclusion of the right to appeal under s.69 (1).[53]

This right to appeal is subject to several restrictions which we will discuss in comparison to appeal from award in Ethiopia. We need not dwell on it any further, for our current purpose of providing a comparative backdrop for the discussion of Ethiopian law. So, let us now proceed to looking at the grounds for the judicial review of awards in Ethiopia.

6.2   Setting Aside of Awards

We saw in Sect. 6.1.2 above that in most jurisdictions the only recourse available to a party that is aggrieved by an arbitral award is an action to set aside or annul the award. Grounds for setting aside arbitral awards are almost exclusively matters of local law. Neither the New York Convention nor any other leading international treaty imposes express limits on the grounds for the setting aside of awards.[54] Therefore, every country has discretion to determine, through legislation or otherwise, the level of control it wishes to exercise over the arbitral process. Particularly, each country has the option to differentiate, in this regard, between 'international' and 'domestic' arbitrations.[55] Ethiopian law does not distinguish between awards that have significant connection to Ethiopia and those that may be deemed purely 'international'.

The law in Ethiopia deals with the setting aside of arbitral awards under Articles 355 to 357 of the Civil Procedure Code. Article 355(1) reads, '[n]otwithstanding any agreement to the contrary, the parties to arbitration proceeding may, on conditions laid down in Art. 356, apply for an order that an award be set aside.' So, the recourse to have an award set aside is not subject to waiver. In contrast, as discussed under Sect. 6.1 above the laws of countries like Belgium, France, Switzerland, and the 1996 Arbitration Act of England and Wales allow waiver of this recourse, at least as regards arbitrations in which none of the parties has significant ties to the jurisdiction concerned. It is to be noted further that Article 355(1) does not distinguish between

---

[52]*Id.*, p. 335.
[53]*Id.*
[54]Born (2009), p. 2552.
[55]Redfern and Hunter (2004), pp. 9–16.

waiver made before and after the award is rendered. This is in contrast to, for example, the position in Germany where an agreement concluded to exclude an application to set aside an award is valid where that is made after the award has been rendered as seen under Sect. 6.1.2 above.

The provision of the Civil Procedure Code of Ethiopia that deals with the grounds for the setting aside of awards reads as follows.

Art. 356 Grounds for application
No application under Art. 355 shall be made except where:

(a) *the arbitrator decided matters not referred to him or made his award pursuant to a submission which was invalid or had lapsed;*
(b) *the reference being to two or more arbitrators, they did not act together; or*
(c) *the arbitrator delegated any part of his authority, whether to a stranger, to one of the parties or to a co-arbitrator.*

So, in Ethiopia an application to set aside an award must be based on one or more of the above grounds. It cannot be based on any other ground as we can gather from the restrictive language of the *chapeau* of Art. 356. This is in line with the approach in many jurisdictions including those that follow the Model Law approach as seen in Sect. 6.1 above.

Coming to the specific grounds, despite its formulation that appears to encompass only few cases, the law in Ethiopia can be construed to cover many of the grounds recognised for the setting aside of awards in other jurisdictions. Below, we attempt to show how much of the Model Law grounds for the setting aside of awards can be read into Article 356.

6.2.1   Jurisdictional Grounds

Some of the grounds for the setting aside of awards under Article 34(2) of the Model Law are jurisdictional in nature. For instance, an award will be set aside if the 'agreement to arbitrate' is not 'valid' because the parties to the agreement were under some kind of incapacity. Similarly, an award can be set aside if the agreement to arbitrate is not valid under the law the parties have subjected it to, or in the absence of choice of law by the parties, where the agreement is not valid under the law of the country where the award was made.[56] Moreover, an award can be validly set aside where the award deals with a dispute not contemplated by the parties or not falling within the terms of the submission. Likewise, an award can be set aside when it contains decisions on matters that go beyond the scope of the arbitral submission and

---

[56]UNCITRAL Model Law on International Commercial Arbitration as amended in 2006, Art 34(2) (a)i and UN Convention on the Recognition and Enforcement of Foreign Arbitral Awards, Art V(1) a.

when the decisions on matters that fall within the scope of the submission and those that do not cannot be separated.[57]

The corresponding provision of the Ethiopian law states that an application to set aside an award may be made where 'the arbitrator decided matters not referred to him or made his award pursuant to a *submission which was invalid* or had lapsed.'[58] (Emphasis added). Though this provision is very concise compared to the jurisdictional grounds for the setting aside of awards under the Model Law seen above, it can, if broadly construed, cover all the ones mentioned therein. For instance, the incapacity of one of the parties to the 'agreement to arbitrate', a ground under the Model Law for the setting aside of an award, can be covered by interpreting 'award pursuant to a submission which was invalid' as inclusive of this ground. This is so because under Ethiopian law any contract, including an agreement to arbitrate, can be declared invalid if the party to it was under incapacity.[59]

Even where a valid agreement to arbitrate exists, it may well be the case that the dispute in question does not fall within its scope or may not have been contemplated. As seen already, the Model Law makes this a ground for the setting aside of the award concerned. This ground too can be deemed covered by the Ethiopian law, which provides for the setting aside of an award where the arbitrator has decided 'matters not referred to him'. The problem with this wording is that it does not indicate the course a judge should follow where the arbitrator has decided on matters referred to him and others that were not, within a single award. The Model Law gives a solution to this problem. It provides that the entire award will be set aside only if the decisions that fall within the scope of the submission and those that go beyond it cannot be separated. It can be argued that a similar conclusion may be validly reached by an Ethiopian judge without violating the provisions of Art 356 of the Civil Procedure Code. It is to be noted that this provision aims at restricting the grounds for setting aside, not the grounds for upholding an award. So, it may be maintained that Ethiopian law is consistent and coextensive with the Model Law standards when it comes to the jurisdictional grounds for the setting aside of arbitral awards.

---

[57]UNCITRAL Model Law on International Commercial Arbitration as amended in 2006, Art 34(2) (a)iii. *See also* Art V(1)C of the New York Convention of 1958.

[58]Civil Procedure Code Decree 52/1965, Articles 355(1) and 356(a) read together.

[59]Civil Code of Ethiopia Proclamation No. 165/1960, Art. 1678. Incapacities are divided into two broad categories: general and special. The former relate to the age or mental condition of a person or sentence passed against him while the latter is prescribed by reason of nationality of the person or functions discharged by him. The grounds are general civil law grounds into which we do not need to delve here.

6.2.2 Procedural Grounds

The second category of the grounds for the setting aside of arbitral awards under the Model Law consists of grounds which one may crudely call procedural grounds. The basis for challenge in this category is that the tribunal flouted proper rules of procedure or acted in a manner not envisaged by the parties. The Model Law mirrors the New York Convention on this subject. It provides that an award will be set aside if a party was unable to present its case owing to lack of proper notice as regards the appointment of arbitrators or the proceedings or otherwise.[60] Likewise, an award may be set aside if either the composition of the arbitral authority or the arbitral procedure is shown to have been at variance with the agreement of the parties, or in the absence of an agreement in this regard, not in compliance with the laws of the country in which the arbitration is conducted.[61]

The Ethiopian law on the setting aside of awards does not really provide coextensive counter parts for the above procedural grounds. It provides two grounds which fall under this category. The first is that provided for under Art. 356(b), according to which an award may be set aside when the arbitrators, where they happen to be two or more, did not act together. The second ground is that provided for under Art. 356(c): an award may be set aside where the arbitrator did not exercise his authority personally, particularly where he delegated it to a stranger, a party or even co-arbitrators according to this provision.[62] A reasonable interpretation of these two grounds arguably covers the Model Law grounds for the setting aside of an award, according to which an award may be set aside if the composition of the arbitral authority or procedure is at variance with the agreement of the parties or the applicable law.

It seems we cannot stretch the foregoing grounds under Ethiopian law to cover other procedural grounds provided for under the Model Law. Particularly, a party may not seek, under Ethiopian law, the setting aside of an award, on the ground that it could not present its case owing to lack of proper notice of appointment of arbitrators, the proceeding and the like, unlike under the Model Law.[63] In Ethiopia, some of these are rather grounds for appeal, as we shall see in Sect. 6.3.1 below.

Yet another ground for the setting aside of awards found under the Model Law which Ethiopian law does not cover is a situation where the award is in 'conflict with the public policy of the state.'[64] So, overall, Ethiopian law is more restrictive than the

---

[60]UNCITRAL Model Law on International Commercial Arbitration as amended in 2006, Article 34 (2)(a),ii. Compare with UN Convention on the Recognition and Enforcement of Foreign Arbitral Awards, Art V (1)b.

[61]*Id.*, UNCITRAL Model Law, Art 34(2)a)iv, Compare with UN Convention on the Recognition and Enforcement of Foreign Arbitral Awards, Art V(1)d.

[62]Civil Procedure Code Decree No. 52/1965, Articles 355(1) and 356(b) and (c).

[63]UNCITRAL Model Law on International Commercial Arbitration as amended 2006, Article 34 (2)(a)(ii).

[64]*Id.*, Article 34(2)(b)(ii).

laws of most jurisdictions of significance when it comes to the grounds for the setting aside of awards. Hence, if setting aside were the only kind of judicial scrutiny of awards recognised under Ethiopian law, the law in Ethiopia would have been more on the finality side of the spectrum. That is not the case, however, as we shall see in the next section.

The party that seeks to have an award set aside will have to apply to the court that would have had appellate jurisdiction if the dispute were litigated in a court rather than before an arbitral tribunal.[65] Where such court finds that none of the grounds under Article 356 has been met, the application is dismissed and the award remains valid and enforceable. On the contrary, if the court is satisfied that the application fulfils one of the exhaustively listed grounds for the setting aside of awards, then the award is deemed 'null and void'.[66]

Ethiopian Law does not deal with what happens to the arbitration agreement where the award is set aside. Particularly, it is silent on whether the arbitration agreement survives, and under what circumstance, if at all, a different tribunal is established. Under German law that addresses this issue, the agreement to arbitrate becomes operative again when an award is set aside, in the absence of a contrary indication.[67] A comparable provision would make sense under Ethiopian law as well, especially as regards some of the grounds for the setting aside of awards. For instance, if the ground for the setting aside of an award is a failure of the arbitrators to 'act together', Article 356(b), or delegation of an arbitrator's authority to a 'co-arbitrator' under Article 356(c), the better approach is establishing a different tribunal, unless the arbitrators have been named in the arbitration agreement itself. Especially in an international transaction, the chosen mechanism of dispute settlement, arbitration, should not be easily abandoned because of the dereliction of duty on the part of individual arbitrators. Abandoning arbitration results in the loss of an effective remedy, given the much higher chance of global enforcement of arbitral awards.

6.3 Appeals from Award

Ethiopian law does not limit recourse to court from an arbitral award to setting aside, unlike the Model Law and the laws of the jurisdictions that follow its approach. It provides for the right to appeal on grounds that in other jurisdictions constitute grounds for the setting aside of the award. Moreover, appeal is possible from an award on the substantive merit of the award.[68] We will, under Sect. 6.3.1 below, discuss the grounds for appeal that are deemed as grounds for the setting aside of

---

[65]Civil Procedure Code Decree No. 52/1965, Articles 355(2) and 352.

[66]*Id.,* at Article 357.

[67]German Code of Civil Procedure of 1998, ss 1059(5).

[68]Civil Procedure Code Decree No. 52/1965, Article 351.

awards in other jurisdictions. In Sect. 6.3.2, we will dwell on the right to appeal from an award on the substantive merit of the same, a recourse that is rarely available in the rest of the world, as can be gathered from the discussion under Sect. 6.1 above.

6.3.1 Appeal from an Award on Non-Substantive Grounds

Ethiopian law vests in the parties to arbitration the right to appeal from an award where irregularities or misconduct have occurred, like a failure to inform the parties to arbitration or one of them of the time or place of hearing; or arbitrators took evidence in the absence of a party; or heard one of the parties but not the other.[69] These are only examples of irregularities and misconduct giving rise to the right to appeal, as we can gather from the use of the word 'in particular'. So, the due process grounds for the setting aside of awards under Model Law Article 34(2)(a)(ii) either fall within the express words of Article 351 or otherwise come under it. Put differently, a party who had been denied an opportunity to present his case, owing to lack of proper notice of the arbitral proceedings, can *appeal* from the award in Ethiopia, instead of applying to have the award set aside.

Since the available recourse is appeal, the court may confirm, vary or reverse the award appealed from. This is unlike in the case of an application to set aside where the court's only options are either confirming or vacating the award. A court entertaining an appeal also has, in principle, the discretion to remit to arbitrators an award for their reconsideration in cases of appeal on grounds other than the ones at hand.[70]

Besides appeal based on procedural irregularities seen above, Ethiopian law states under Art 351 the possibility of appeal from an award on the grounds that follow:[71]

(a) *the award is inconsistent, uncertain or ambiguous...,*

(b) *the arbitrator omitted to decide matters referred to him,*

(c) *irregularities have occurred in the proceedings, in particular where the arbitrator*

   (i) *failed ....to comply with the terms of the submission regarding the admissibility of evidence, or*

   (ii) *refused to hear the evidence of material witness or took evidence in the absence of the parties or one of them, or*

(d) *the arbitrator has been guilty of misconduct in particular where:*

   (i) *he heard one of the parties and not the other*

   (ii) *he was unduly influenced by one party, whether by bribe or otherwise, or*

   (iii) *he acquired an interest in the subject matter of dispute referred to him.*

---

[69] *Id.*, Article 351(c)1,ii and d(i).

[70] *Id.*, Read together Art 353, 354(1) and 351(c)I, ii and d(i).

[71] *Id.*, Article 351.

As can be gathered from the *chapeau* of Art 351 which reads, '[n]o appeal shall lie from an award except where:' the above is an exhaustive list of the grounds for appeal, apart from the grounds for appeal based on procedural irregularity already discussed, and hence omitted from the list. That being said, 'appeal' to a court is a remedy which does not exist in most trading nations[72] and countries that have based their arbitration legislations on the Model Law.[73] Hence, that Ethiopian law provides for an appeal from an award will be a reason for concern, at least, to foreign parties considering arbitration in Ethiopia.

That being said, some of the above grounds for appeal are deemed legitimate grounds for recourse to court in other jurisdictions, *albeit* under some other formulation. This may be done under what may be called a rubric of 'public policy' grounds. This ground for the setting aside of arbitral awards mirrors the ground for non-enforcement of foreign arbitral awards in the New York Convention[74] and is also found in the Model Law[75] as a possible ground for annulling an award in the country in which it is made.

Public policy as a ground for annulling awards is a fluid concept with many nuances and hence we cannot define it here. For the moment, suffice it to say that courts have, for example, set aside and declined the enforcement of awards obtained by fraud or bribery. For instance, French courts have set aside awards obtained through bribe.[76] Similarly, German courts have held that the enforcement of an award leads to evident abuse of public policy where the award 'enforces an agreement contrary to *bonos mores*, or breaches a rule which is part of the very basis of the social or economic order of a country, or in case the award is obtained by fraud.'[77]

The recourse to court under Article 351 of the Civil Procedure of Ethiopia, however, differs from that in other jurisdictions in two respects. First, the remedy available under this provision is an appeal rather than an application to set aside. Second, there are some grounds for 'appeal', under Article 351, which do not seem to fulfil the 'violation of public policy' requirement as understood in the jurisdictions that provide this as a ground for the setting aside of awards. For instance, one is hard pressed to show why failure of the arbitrators to 'comply with the terms of the

---

[72]*See* generally Berger (1998), p. 606.

[73]European Bank for Reconstruction and Development, International Commercial Arbitration Assessment, Report On the Assessment in the CIS(Armenia, Azerbaijan, Georgia, Kazakhstan, Kyrgyz Republic, Moldova, Russia, Tajikistan, Turkmenistan, Ukrain, Uzbekistan and Mongolia (2007), Available at: www.ebrd.com/downloads/legal/judicial/arbitration.pdf, accessed on September 8, 2012.

[74]UN Convention on the Recognition and Enforcement of Foreign Arbitral Awards (1958), Art. V (2)b.

[75]UNCITRAL Model Law on International Commercial Arbitration as revised in 2006, Art 34(2) (b)(ii).

[76]Born (2009), p. 2627.

[77]*Id.*, at 2628.

submission regarding the admissibility of evidence'[78] would necessarily amount to a violation of public policy. In fact, one can imagine situations where honouring such an agreement could violate public policy.

Where an appeal lies, the law in principle leaves the remedies the appellant gets to the discretion of the court. The court can 'confirm, vary or reverse' the award appealed from. Moreover, it can, where it thinks fit, remit the award for reconsideration by the *arbitrators who made it.*[79] It is to be noted that the court does not always have the discretion to remit the award appealed from for reconsideration by arbitrators. It can remit the award back to arbitrators when it finds the award to be inconsistent, uncertain or ambiguous or when it believes that the arbitrators have failed to decide on a matter referred to them.[80] The court may not remit the award for reconsideration by the arbitrators if the ground for appeal has to do with 'irregularities' such as 'failure to inform the parties or one of them of the time or place of the hearing.'[81] The same holds true where the ground for appeal is failure, on the part of the tribunal, to comply with the terms of the submission regarding the admissibility of evidence.[82] Similarly, the case cannot be remitted for reconsideration by the tribunal where the arbitrator has been guilty of misconduct such as taking bribes or acquiring interest in the subject matter of the dispute.[83] Remitting cases back to the same arbitrators, in such cases, would result either in miscarriage of justice or, at least, the appearance of that.

6.3.2 Appeal to Court on the Substantive Merit of the Award

In this section, attempt will be made to highlight the arguments for and against appeal on the substantive merit of arbitral awards first. We will then discuss the position of Ethiopian law. In particular, attempt will be made to show the pre-conditions for appeal on the merits in Ethiopia and how that compares with English law, the only jurisdiction of significance that allows such review.

---

[78]Civil Procedure Code Decree No. 52/1965 of Ethiopia, Article 351(c)i.

[79]*Id.*, Art 353. This Article reads: '[w]ithout prejudice to its power to confirm, vary or reverse the award appealed from, the Appellate Court may, where it thinks fit, remit such award or a portion thereof to the reconsideration of the arbitrator.'

[80]*Id.*, Art. 354(1) and 351(a) and (b). It is to be noted from these provisions that an award may also be remitted for reconsideration of the arbitrators who made it when the ground for appeal is that the award is 'on its face wrong in a matter of law or fact'. But this has been discussed in relation to appeal on substantive merit of awards and need not be dwelt upon here.

[81]*Id.*, Article 351(c)(i).

[82]*Id.*

[83]*Id.*, Art. 351(d).

6.3.2.1 The Pros and Cons of Review on the Merit

Opinion is divided on the desirability of the judicial scrutiny of the substantive merit of arbitral awards. The first viewpoint, which is less prevalent, is that awards should be subject to some form of judicial scrutiny on merits. The proponents of this position put forward several justifications. To start with, they maintain that leaving awards free from review by courts would increase the possibility of arbitral tribunals rendering inconsistent decisions on the same or similar points of law. Even worse, knowing that their awards are not subject to scrutiny, arbitrators may be tempted to be lax in the discharge their duties, they contend.[84] Thus, it is maintained, 'finality' of awards is desirable only when the stakes are low, and the risk of error is outweighed by the need for speed and continuation of business relationship. On the other hand, when the amount is very high, as is mostly the case in international commercial arbitration, and continued business relationship is not necessarily a top priority of the parties; review of a rogue award on the merits is desirable. Proponents of this view even allege that there is empirical evidence, though limited, showing more and more cases being litigated in courts in jurisdictions that do not allow review on merits, to avoid awards nothing can be done about when they go unacceptably wrong on the merits.[85]

Besides the foregoing, other justifications are raised in support of review of awards on the merit. For instance, various points were raised to justify the passage of the 1996 English Arbitration Act allowing for a limited appeal on point of law. It was held that the parties to arbitration should not be assumed to have agreed that the tribunal would obviously misapply the pertinent laws. So, it was argued, where the parties have not agreed otherwise, the assumption should be that the parties want the courts to reverse obvious misapplication of the law by arbitrators.[86] Yet another reason for the passage of this rule was the belief that in cases of major significance, public interest requires review of decisions of arbitrators when they are extremely questionable.[87] Allowing for such appellate review under exceptional circumstances was deemed necessary by the lawmakers given the tradition of arbitration by non-lawyers in certain commercial sectors such as construction and trading in commodities.[88] It was also believed that appellate review of such cases would contribute to the further development of English law.[89]

The foregoing is not, however, the dominant view, as can be gathered from the more general discussion on the finality and fairness of awards in Sect. 6.1 above. The more prevalent position is that appeal on the merits, for that matter any review focused on the substance of the award, does more bad than good, especially in the

---

[84] Redfern and Hunter (2004), p. 501.

[85] Knull and Rubins (2000), pp. 534–536.

[86] Haris et al. (2007), p. 335.

[87] *Id.*

[88] Blackaby et al. (2009), p. 609.

[89] Colman (2007).

context of international commercial arbitration. One argument that is raised against review on the merits is that it opens the door to courts effectively substituting the award by their own decision under the guise of a limited review.[90] Secondly, confidentiality which is an important consideration in business relationships is lost when the dispute is brought to court on appeal.[91] Thirdly, the appeal process may be used for tactical purposes such as to delay the enforcement of an award, thus defeating a key purpose of commercial arbitration.[92] Owing to such reasons, the prevailing view favours prohibition of judicial scrutiny of awards for substantive merit.

6.3.2.2 Grounds for Appeal on the Merits in Ethiopia

We saw in Sect. 6.3.1 above that in Ethiopia appeal lies from arbitral awards on a variety of grounds. To focus on appeal on the substantive merit of awards, the subject of discussion in this sub-section, Articles 350 and 351 of the Civil Procedure Code read together provide for it. Article 350(1) reads, '[a]ny party to arbitration proceedings may, *in the terms of the arbitral submission* and *on the conditions laid down in Art. 351*, appeal from any arbitral award.' Art. 351 that lists down the grounds for appeal reads in the pertinent part '[n]o appeal shall lie from an award *except* where the award is . . . *on its face wrong* in matter of *law or fact.*'[93] In short, the parties to arbitration have the right to lodge an appeal to the court with jurisdiction, where the award is '. . .*on its face wrong in a matter of law or fact.*'[94]

The qualifying phrase, 'on its face wrong', seems to imply that the award is wrong in law or fact should be easily discernible from a quick reading or investigation. It should be apparently wrong. The Amharic version of the provision uses a word that more appropriately translates as 'directly' wrong. Either way, the essence of the provision seems to be that the award is wrong in a matter of law or fact should be very easy to see. Unfortunately, no court decision affirming or contradicting this line of interpretation could be found.

The best way to understand where Ethiopian law stands on appeal on the merits is to compare it with English law, which we saw stands at the pro-judicial scrutiny end of the spectrum as compared to other jurisdictions of significance to international commercial arbitration. Under English law, for an appeal to lie, either all the parties

---

[90]Redfern and Hunter (2004), p.

[91]*Id.*

[92]*Id.*

[93]Civil Procedure Code Decree No. 52/1965. The rest of Article 351 deals with grounds for appeal that do not pertain to the merits of the award such as irregularity in arbitral proceeding, misconduct on the part of arbitrators and the like we discussed in the previous sub-section.

[94]*Id.*, Art 351(1). *See also National Mining Corporation PLC v. Dani Drilling PLC*, Cassation Division of the Federal Supreme Court, File No. 42239, (November 2010) and *National Motors Corporation v. General Business Development,* Cassation Division of Federal Supreme Court, File No. 21849, (November 2007).

must agree to that or leave to bring appeal must be granted by the court. The court is not allowed to grant the leave unless it is satisfied that:[95]

a)   the determination of the question concerned will substantially affect the right of at least one of the parties to arbitration;
b)   the question was one that was put before the arbitrator(s) for determination;
c)   the review should be based on the findings of fact in the award (not an attempt to review the findings on facts by the arbitrators under the guise of question of law[96])
d)   the decision is 'obviously wrong' or of 'general public importance' and the arbitrator(s) decision is at least open to 'serious doubt' and
e)   it is 'just and proper' for the court to decide on the question given the totality of the circumstances.

Ethiopian law allows much more intervention than the Arbitration Act of 1996, which we said is at the pro-fairness end of the spectrum. To start with, under Ethiopian law the right to appeal is not restricted to legal issues. It is available so long as the award is 'on its face wrong in matter of law or *fact*.' Obvious factual errors in the award are subject to judicial review on appeal. In contrast, under English law the available appeal is limited to 'questions of law'.[97] Even as regards appeal on questions of law, Ethiopian law provides no carefully crafted conditions, such as the ones under (a) to (e) above that the English law puts in place as preconditions for appeal. Only the requirement that the decision be 'obviously wrong', a part of the English standard indicated under (d) above, is sufficient in Ethiopia.

In short, Ethiopian law allows lots of room for the judicial review of awards on their substantive merit. No jurisdiction of significance to international commercial arbitration allows a comparable level of judicial scrutiny on the merits.

6.3.3   Waiver of Appeal from Award

The right to appeal from an award on non-substantive grounds (Sect. 6.3.1) and substantive grounds (Sect. 6.3.2) above is subject to waiver by the parties.[98] To be

---

[95]Arbitration Act of England and Wales of 1996, at ss 69(2)&(3), ss 70(2) and(3). It is to be noted that the question of law that can be reviewed is only that concerning English Law. So, where the applicable law is non-English law though international commercial arbitration taking place in England the award will not be subject to review under this section. See Blackaby et al. (2009), p. 609.

[96]Haris et al. (2007), p. 338. The aim is to decline leave where questions of fact are dressed up as questions of law to get permission to appeal and courts have resisted such attempts.

[97]Arbitration Act of England and Wales of 1996, Section 69(1) reads, '[u]nless otherwise agreed by the parties, a party to arbitral proceedings may (upon notice to the other parties and to the tribunal) appeal to the court on a question of law arising out of an award made in the proceedings.

[98]Civil Procedure Code Decree No. 52/1965, Art 350(2).

valid, the waiver must, however, be made with 'full knowledge of the circumstances.'[99] In *Dragados J. and P. Joint Venture vs. Saba Construction Private Limited Company* the Cassation Bench of the Federal Supreme Court interpreted 'full knowledge of the circumstances' in ways that restrict making valid waivers.[100]

Dragados had signed a contract with the Ethiopian Roads Authority for the rehabilitation and upgrading of the Addis Ababa-Jimma road. It sub-contracted part of the work to *Saba Construction PLC*. Under Article 17 of the sub-contract, it was agreed that disputes between the parties would be settled by arbitration under the auspices of the Addis Ababa Chamber of Commerce and Sectoral Associations Arbitration Center. Article 20(2) of the 'Rules of Procedure' of the Center indicated that awards given under the auspices of the Center are non-appealable.[101]

Eventually, a dispute arose between the parties to the sub-contract and arbitration commenced. The arbitrators gave an award in favour of *Saba Construction PLC*. *Dragados* appealed against the award to the Federal Supreme Court. The Court dismissed the 'appeal.' It reasoned, a choice of an arbitration centre implies that the parties have agreed to be bound by the Rules of Arbitration of the Centre concerned. The Rules of Arbitration of the Center preclude appeal from awards rendered under the auspices of the Center.

Dragados then sought review on Cassation by the Cassation Bench of the Federal Supreme Court. The Cassation Bench framed the issue as: 'does an arbitration clause by which the parties to a contract agree to arbitrate disputes under the auspices of an arbitration centre, preclude appeal from an award, where the Rules of the Center concerned happen to provide for finality of awards?'[102] The Cassation Bench found the agreement did not amount to a waiver of the right to appeal. It ruled that the decision of the Federal Supreme Court dismissing the appeal involved a fundamental error of law.

The Cassation Bench in Dragados reasoned that the right to appeal is a basic right. Waiver of this right is valid only when made with 'full knowledge of the circumstances' according to the Civil Procedure Code. The Code states that '[t]he parties may waive their right of appeal but any such waiver shall be of no effect unless made with full knowledge of the circumstances.'[103] At the 'stage of submission' to arbitration, it cannot be said that the parties have full knowledge of the circumstances, the Cassation Bench reasoned.[104] The Cassation Bench indicated that the commentary on the Civil Procedure Code by Allen Sedler supports this line of

---

[99]*Id.*, Article 350(2).

[100]*Dragados J and P Joint Venture v. Saba Construction Private Limited Company*, Federal Supreme Court, Case No. 37678 (28 Nov. 2008).

[101]*Id.*

[102]*Id.*

[103]Civil Procedure Code Decree No. 52/1965 of Ethiopia, Article 350(2).

[104]*Dragados J and P Joint Venture v. Saba Construction Private Limited Company*, Federal Supreme Court, Case No. 37678(2008).

reasoning. Indeed, a look at Sedler's book supports that. He writes, almost in passing:

> [t]he appeal may be subject to the terms of the arbitral submission, and the parties may waive their right of appeal, provided that the waiver is made with full knowledge of the circumstances. This would indicate that the parties may not waive their right to appeal in the arbitral submission, since at the time the submission was prepared they could not have had full knowledge of the circumstances.[105]

Sedler, on whose authority the Cassation Bench relies says absolutely nothing other than the above. He gives neither reasons that lead him to take this position nor the practical implications of this interpretation on arbitration as an alternative dispute settlement mechanism.

In this connection, it is to be noted that the Cassation Bench is not really using the term 'submission stage' in a technical sense, to refer to an agreement to arbitrate concluded after a dispute has arisen. The Court does not seem to be distinguishing between an arbitration clause included in the main contract and a 'submission agreement' concluded after a dispute arises. It simply states 'at the stage of submission' to arbitration it cannot be said that the parties have full knowledge of the circumstances. In any case, if waiver of the right to appeal is not valid at the 'stage of submission,' for lack of 'full knowledge of the circumstances,' for a stronger reason, waiver made in an arbitration clause in the original contract is also not valid. The parties do not even know whether there will be a dispute when signing a contract with an 'arbitration clause.' The facts of the case at hand show that the arbitration was based on an arbitration clause in the sub-contract between *Dragandos* and *Saba*. No submission agreement was signed after the dispute arose.

One may, however, contend that this decision should be restricted to the facts of the particular case. In other words, since the case arose from an arbitration clause, despite the use of the term 'submission' by the Cassation Court, it may be argued that the rule should apply only to cases where waiver is made in arbitration clauses, and not a submission agreement. This interpretation would allow waiver of appeal made in a submission agreement to stand. This would make sense because at this stage the parties know more about the 'circumstances' of the case. Since a dispute has already arisen, they make the waiver of appeal with more knowledge of the consequences.

Unfortunately, this line of interpretation is unlikely to carry much weight in Ethiopia. The Civil Code of Ethiopia uses the term 'arbitral submission' in a broad sense to refer to any type of arbitration agreement. In fact, Chapter 2 of Title XX of the Code dealing with arbitration agreements in general is titled 'arbitral submission.' Moreover, none of the provisions in the said Chapter uses the term arbitral submission in a way that shows this term exclusively refers to an arbitration agreement dealing with an existing dispute. In fact, we come across provisions indicating the opposite usage. For instance, one provision of the code reads; '[a]n *arbitral submission relating to future disputes* shall not be valid unless it concerns

---

[105]Sedler (1968), p. 389.

disputes which flow from a contract or other specific legal obligation.'[106] (Emphasis added). Evidently, the term 'arbitral submission' has been used broadly, in this provision, to cover what is referred to as an 'arbitration clause' in arbitration literature. See Sect. 2.1 in Chap. 2 for more on this point.

Coming back to the decision of the Cassation Bench in *Dragados v. Saba*, it has a very far reaching consequence. The interpretation of the Cassation Bench simply makes every award subject to appeal unless the parties mutually agree to waive the right to appeal after the award is disclosed to them. The possibility of the parties to an arbitration concluding an agreement to waive the 'right to appeal', after an award has been rendered and made known to them is very slim.

Interestingly, nearly two years after *Dragados*, the Cassation Bench in *National Mining Corporation PLC v. Dani Drilling PLC* uses language that suggests waiver of appeal can be made before knowing the award. The Cassation bench remarks in a general discussion about alternative dispute resolution, the Civil Procedure Code of 1965, 'particularly, Article 350(2) vests in the parties to a dispute the right to agree that the arbitral award will be final. In such cases, the award may be set aside on grounds listed under Article 356 but no appeal lies . . . .'[107]

These remarks do not really reverse the ruling in *Dragados JP v. Saba Construction PLC* though. For one thing, waiver of the right to appeal was not at issue in *National Mining PLC v. Dani Drilling PLC*. The issue was whether the parties can by agreement preclude review on Cassation. So, what the Cassation Bench said should be rather regarded as *obiter dictum*. Besides, if it wanted to reverse *Dragados JP v. Saba Construction PLC*, the Cassation Bench would have clearly indicated that. It did not even mention the case.

In sum, that arbitral awards are subject to appeal to court on various grounds and that waiver of appeal can be validly made only after the award is known to the parties is an extremely serious challenge to the success of arbitration in Ethiopia. This effectively reduces arbitration to a prelude to litigation in court.

6.3.4 Freedom to Opt in a Court

Opinion is divided on whether the parties to an arbitration agreement should have the freedom to opt in courts and provide for a more expanded review of an award than stipulated in the law. For instance, an agreement expanding the grounds for the setting aside of an award is valid in Germany since 2007. Referring to the contractual nature of international arbitration, the German Supreme Court held, '[b]ecause the binding nature of the awards is based on the parties consent, the parties are also free

---

[106]Civil Code of Ethiopia Proclamation No. 165/1960, Article 3328(3).

[107]*National Mining Corporation PLC v. Dani Drilling PLC*, Federal Supreme Court, File No. 42239, (November 2010).

to restrict the award's binding nature and tie it to certain conditions.'[108] One of these conditions can be an expanded judicial review of the award.[109] William Park contends freedom in this regard makes sense, especially in international transactions.[110]

Unlike in Germany, the freedom to opt in courts is not recognized as valid in many jurisdictions of significance to international commercial arbitration. In France, for instance, though the parties are allowed to waive by agreement the right to lodge an application to set aside an award, as discussed in Sect. 6.1 already, they cannot by an agreement expand the grounds for the judicial review of awards.[111] The case law of the United States has taken a similar approach. In *Hall Street Associates, L.L.C. v. Mattel, Inc* the US Supreme Court ruled that the parties cannot in their agreement to arbitrate expand the grounds on which a court may review an arbitral award. The implication is that the finality of awards trumps party autonomy in matters of international commercial arbitration.[112]

The question of whether to allow the parties to arbitration agreements to opt in judicial review of arbitral awards for errors of law or fact was hotly debated during the revision of the Uniform Arbitration Act between 1996 and 2000 in the US. One of the arguments raised in support of giving the parties to arbitration agreements the right to 'opt-in' court review on merits was that allowing this safety net would assuage the fears of those who are hesitant to accept arbitration as a conflict resolution mechanism.[113] Opponents contended that allowing the parties to have a 'second bite at the apple' on the merits would reduce arbitration to a prelude to litigation in court rather than an alternative to it. Allowing such an option would, it was maintained, lead to a routine inclusion of such a possibility in arbitration agreements, robbing awards of finality, thus making arbitration more time consuming and expensive. Hence, that possibility was not included in the Revised Uniform Arbitration Act.[114]

English law seems to be taking a similar position. In *Guangzhou Dockyards Co. v ENE Aegiali I*, Blair J opined, though in an obiter dictum, that 'under English law . . . it is very doubtful that the court has jurisdiction to hear an appeal from arbitrators on questions of fact, even if parties were to agree to such an appeal.'[115]

Coming to Ethiopian law the parties to an arbitration agreement can opt-in courts into their dispute and provide for grounds for appeal. In other words, if the

---

[108]Scherer (2016), p. 10.

[109]*Id.*

[110]Park (2012), p. 323.

[111]Scherer (2016), p. 10.

[112]Tyler and Parasharami (2008), pp. 617–618. *See also* United States Arbitration Act of Feb. 1925, Sections 8, 9 and 10.

[113]Uniform Arbitration Act of 1955 (Last Revised in 2000), with Preparatory Note and Comments, 78.

[114]*Id.*

[115]Scherer (2016), p. 10.

arbitration clause provides for a possibility to 'appeal' from an arbitral award, that provision will be valid even where none of the grounds for appeal listed down under Art 351 is fulfilled. Article 350(1) of the English version of the Civil Procedure, which is less than clear on this point, reads '[a]ny party to arbitration proceedings *may, in the terms of the arbitral submission* and conditions laid down in art 351 appeal from any arbitral award.'[116] The use of the word 'and' appears to make these two cumulative requirements. In this reading of Article 350(1), not only an agreement of the parties *but also* the fulfilment of at least one of the conditions listed down under Art 351 would be necessary for an appeal to lie.

However, three reasons can be put forward against the cumulative reading of Article 350(1). The first is that it is possible to argue in favour of a non-cumulative reading despite the use of the word 'and', particularly, in the absence of solid jurisprudence in support of that reading. The use of the word 'and' does not necessarily imply a cumulative reading of things listed. The word could as well be read to mean 'or' since it is used to show a list of options in some cases.

Secondly, sticking to a cumulative reading of the two requirements under Art 350 (1) would result in untenable conclusions. For example, a party to arbitration will not be able to appeal to a court, under the cumulative reading of the provision, even where the arbitrator has been guilty of misconduct or taken bribes or acquired personal interest in the matter in dispute, which are grounds for appeal under Art. 351(d). The failure of the parties to provide for the right to appeal in their submission would preclude the right to appeal.[117] In other words, a cumulative reading of Article 350(1) would allow an award which is an outcome of corruption to stand. It is very unlikely that the lawmaker intended the provision to have this effect.

A third reason for holding that these are not cumulative requirements is that the controlling Amharic version of 350(1) does not use the word 'and.' Instead, it uses the term 'or', thus, making appeal from an award available alternatively in cases where the arbitral submission provides for the possibility of appeal and when the conditions laid down under Art 351 are fulfilled. Hence, the parties to an arbitration agreement have all the freedom to agree, if they so wish, that the award will be subject to review on appeal and provide the possible grounds for such appeal in Ethiopia.

One cannot reach a similar conclusion when it comes to an agreement of the parties to expand the grounds for the setting aside of awards. Article 355(1) reads, '*[n]otwithstanding any agreement to the contrary*, the parties to arbitration proceedings may, on the conditions laid down in Art. 356 apply for an order that an award be set aside.'[118] Then Article 356 lists the grounds for the setting aside of

---

[116] Civil Procedure Code Decree No. 52/1965, Article 350(1).

[117] *Id.*, 351(4). Note that this article provides a party may appeal from an award where the arbitrator takes bribe or acquires interest in the subject matter of the dispute or is otherwise found to have engaged in misconduct. In other jurisdiction these kinds of things constitute rather grounds for setting aside, and not appeal.

[118] *Id.* Article 355(1).

awards in a language that does not suggest the parties are free to expand the list. The *chapeau* of 356 reads, '[n]o application under Art. 355 *shall be made except where'* and the grounds are listed exhaustively below it.[119] No word or phrase that indicates the list is only illustrative is used. For more on the grounds for the setting aside of awards in Ethiopia, one is referred to Sect. 6.2 above.

In sum, under Ethiopian law, the parties to an arbitration agreement can opt in courts to review the award on appeal. The right to appeal from an award is an extremely rare remedy in other jurisdictions as seen under Sect. 6.3.2.1. Yet, Ethiopian law does not only provide for this right but also allows the parties to arbitration agreement to expand the grounds for appeal available under the law. In an odd pro-arbitration twist, the law does not allow the parties to expand the grounds for the setting aside of awards.

6.4   Review of Award on Cassation

In this section, we will dwell on review on cassation in Ethiopia and its impact on the success of arbitration. We will introduce the nature of this recourse and its distinction from the allied recourse of appeal first, in Sect. 6.4.1. Then, we will discuss Ethiopian case law which deals with review on cassation under Sect. 6.4.2. Finally, we deal with the implication of the case law on arbitration in Sect. 6.4.3.

6.4.1   Cassation: Its Nature and Distinction from Appeal

Besides appeal, many developed legal systems recognise a category of recourse against judicial and other adjudicatory decisions. The recourse is known by different names in different jurisdictions such as *cassation, cassazione, casaciòn and revision,* for example.[120] The English language is a notable exception in that it has no distinct word for it. This does not, however, mean that a procedure which is a counterpart for cassation rather than appeal in the eyes of a comparative lawyer never existed or does not exist in the Common-Law system.[121]

In the post-revolutionary France, which provided the model for the legal systems which use the two terms 'appeal' and 'cassation', the distinction between these two recourses was very clear. On 'appeal,' the appellate court 'considered afresh the questions at issue on their facts as well as at law.' It could affirm the decision appealed from or replace it with its own decision, for all purposes.[122]

---

[119]*Id.*, Article 356.
[120]Jolowicz (1988), p. 2045.
[121]*Id.*
[122]*Id.*, p. 2046.

In contrast, the role of the jurisdiction of cassation was limited to an examination of the 'legality' of the decision under attack. The facts would be taken as already found and no proof would be admitted. The cassation court had the alternative of affirming or annulling the decision under review on cassation. The cassation court would not come up with its own decision to resolve issues that remain outstanding between the parties because of an annulment.[123] The old English 'writ of error' was similar in essence to the above pre 1837 French notion of cassation.[124]

Today, neither form of recourse exists in a pristine form. Even where there are separate 'courts of appeal' and 'courts of cassation,' it is no longer possible to distinguish between their respective roles and functions.[125] The blurring of the boundary between appeal and cassation manifests itself, among others, in the increasing trend of power to replace defective decisions that cassation courts are given. In France for example, every Chamber of Court of Cassation is vested with power to 'decide finally, on purely legal grounds', on a first cassation.[126]

Review on cassation is one of the most enduring features of the Ethiopian legal system. It was known and practiced in some form or another in the different stages of the development of the country's legal system.[127] For example, the Civil Procedure Code that was issued during the time of the last emperor lists courts having appellate jurisdiction under Article 321. It then states under Article 322 that 'nothing in Article 321 shall prevent an appellant who has *exhausted his rights of appeal* from making a petition to His Imperial Majesty's *Chilot* for a review of the case under Art. 361 to 370.'[128] During the era of the Military Government cassation proper was heralded by Proclamation No. 9/1987. A final decision of the Supreme Court or other courts containing a fundamental error of law was made subject to review by a division of the Supreme Court constituted temporarily.[129]

The constitution that is currently in force states that the Federal Supreme Court 'has a power of cassation over any final court decision containing a basic error of law'.[130] It leaves particulars of the review to determination by subsidiary laws.[131] Members of the Constitutional Assembly discussed when an error of law should be deemed 'basic'. The minutes of the discussions by the Assembly show that an error should be deemed basic when there is a 'glaring' and 'grave' error in the case.[132] No

---

[123]*Id.*, at 2046–2047.

[124]*Id.*, at 2047.

[125]*Id.*, 2048.

[126]*Id.*, 2054.

[127]Mehari Redae, 'Basic Error of Law', (Unpublished Material, Available on File, p. 1.

[128]Civil Procedure Code Decree No. 52/1965, Article 321 and 322.

[129]Mehari, *supra* note 127, p. 1.

[130]Constitution of the Federal Democratic Republic of Ethiopia, Proclamation No. 1/1995, Federal *Negarit Gazeta*, 1st year, No. 1, Article 80(3)a.

[131]*Id.*

[132]The Minutes of the Constitutional Assembly of the Federal Democratic Republic of Ethiopia No. 26-29 (Addis Ababa, 1993, Unpublished) at 134–140. The current practice is that a panel of

clue beyond that was given especially regarding civil cases. The subsidiary law that was supposed to provide particulars about the power of cassation does no more than reiterate the power of Cassation of the Federal Supreme Court and list down decisions over which the Court has such power.[133] A more recent law ascribes the power of precedent to the interpretation of laws by the Cassation Bench of the Federal Supreme Court.[134] Legislations in force in Ethiopia do not directly address the question of whether arbitral awards are subject to review on cassation. Only case law does that. We discuss the case law in the part that follows.

6.4.2   The Review of Awards on Cassation and Waiver of the Review

In *National Mineral Corporation PLC v Dani Drilling PLC*,[135] the Cassation Division of the Federal Supreme Court followed a purposive interpretation of the law providing for cassation and essentially ruled that arbitral awards are subject to review on cassation. It further ruled that review on cassation cannot be waived by an agreement. There are many turns and twists in the reasoning and statements of fact in this case. Most pertinently for our purpose, the application for review on cassation and the Cassation Bench decision keep on mentioning the award itself and at times the Supreme Court decision that confirmed it. This creates confusion as to whether the decision the review of which was sought is that of the arbitral tribunal or the Supreme Court. Besides, the application for review on cassation in this case was filed on 27 December 2008. This is just a month after the *Dragados J and P v. Saba Construction PLC* decision, in which the Cassation Bench had ruled that a finality agreement made at the 'submission stage' does not preclude 'appeal' because the parties do not have 'full knowledge of the circumstances' at that stage. So, we need to distinguish between these two cases. This is why we dwell on the case at length.

To start with the facts of the case, *Dani Drilling PLC* had undertaken to conduct drilling work for *National Mining Corporation*. The contract provided for arbitration and contained a finality clause. A dispute arose in relation to the termination of the contract and arbitration was conducted. The arbitrators awarded *Dani Drilling PLC* damages for a wrongful termination of the contract.[136]

---

three judges of the Federal Supreme Court decide whether or not a 'basic error' of law exists in a given case. Where they find one exists, the case will be reviewed by the Cassation Division of the Supreme Court consisting of five judges.

[133]Federal Courts Proclamation No. 25/1996, Federal *Negarit Gazeta*, 2nd Year, No. 13, Article 10.

[134]Federal Courts Reamendment Proclamation, Proc. No. 454/2005, Federal *Negarit Gazeta*, 11th Year, No. 42, Article 2(1).

[135]*National Mining Corporation v. Dani Drilling PLC*, Federal Supreme Court, Cassation File No. 42239 (2010).

[136]*Id.*

National Mining Corporation appealed from this award to the Federal Supreme Court. It alleged that the arbitrators did not follow Article 317(1) of the Civil Procedure Code, which provides that the procedure before an arbitration tribunal 'shall as near as may be, be the same as in a civil court.' Particularly, it alleged that the arbitrators 'did not frame the issue properly', 'did not *weigh* the evidence appropriately' and 'did not follow correctly the rules of interpretation.'[137] The Supreme Court dismissed the appeal per Article 337 of the Civil Procedure Code.[138] This is a provision according to which an appellate court can dismiss an appeal without even calling on the respondent '[w]here the appellant states in his memorandum of appeal that he bases his appeal entirely on the record of the original hearing and does not apply for permission to call additional evidence . . .' and the appellate court 'thinks fit and *agrees with the judgment appealed from.*'[139]

National Mining Corporation, therefore, sought review on cassation. The grounds on which it sought review on cassation were incorrect 'framing of the issue,' 'weighing of the evidence' and 'interpretation of the laws' by the arbitral tribunal and the confirmation of the award by the Supreme Court.[140] It did not allege any procedural irregularity on the part of the Federal Supreme Court. It is to be noted, at this point, that the rejection of an appeal under Article 337 does not imply that no 'appeal' lies in theory. A court rejects an appeal under this provision because the appellant has stated he relies 'entirely on the record of the original hearing' and the appellate court on a review of the documents and after an oral hearing of the appellant sees no reason to call on the respondent because it '*agrees with the judgment appealed from.*' So, essentially, what *National Mining Corporation* sought from the Cassation Bench was a review of the arbitral award for 'basic error' of law.

Owing to the foregoing and because the Respondent contended that the finality clause precludes review on cassation, the Cassation Bench framed the issue as 'whether or not the finality clause in the agreement between the parties precludes a review on cassation?'

The Cassation Bench held that review on Cassation for 'basic error of law' is possible despite an arbitration agreement providing for the finality of award.[141] The Cassation Bench did not however rely on its reasoning in *Dragados J and P v. Saba Construction PLC*, discussed in relation to the waiver of appeal in Sect. 6.3.3 above. In that case, it had held that a waiver of 'appeal' made at the 'stage of submission' to arbitration does not preclude the 'right to appeal' because a waiver made at that stage cannot be deemed to have been made 'with full knowledge of the circumstances'

---

[137]*Id.*

[138]*Id.*

[139]Civil Procedure Code of Ethiopia Decree No. 52/1965, Article 377.

[140]*National Mining Corporation v. Dani Drilling PLC,* Federal Supreme Court, Cassation File No. 42239 (2010).

[141]*Id.*

within the meaning of Article 350(2) of the Civil Procedure Code.[142] The Cassation Bench could not rely on that case because the issues in the two cases are different. In *Dragados* the issue was whether a finality clause results in waiver of the right to 'appeal.' In *National Mineral Corporation PLC v Dani Drilling PLC*, the current case, what was at issue is 'review on cassation', about which the Civil Procedure Code is silent. Besides, the Cassation Bench believed that the *rationale* for the two remedies is so different that a waiver agreement made at any point in time cannot preclude review of an award on cassation. It reasoned as follows.[143]

> It is believed that a system of review on cassation has as one of its essential purposes ensuring a uniform interpretation and application of laws in a country. For this reason, one can consider that the system of cassation is a mechanism for ensuring rule of law. It is clear that rule of law will be ensured if bodies entrusted with rendering quality judgments are subject to judicial control. On top of this, dispensing justice requires that similar matters are treated similarly. In other words, the very basis of justice is entertaining similar matters in a like manner. This can happen when proclamations, regulations, directives as well as policies are interpreted correctly and uniformly. It is the institution of cassation, at the apex of the judicial body that sees to it that laws are interpreted and implemented correctly and uniformly.

> Moreover, a uniform interpretation and application of laws ensures the equality of citizens before the law. The FDRE Constitution under Articles 13(1), 25 and 85(1) imposes on the Judiciary the obligation to respect and ensure respect for the equality of citizens before the law. The system of cassation is a mechanism for ensuring that judicial bodies discharge their obligations in this regard. Another point that is beyond debate at the conceptual level is that a decision that involves an error of law should not remain in force. When such a decision remains in force, the society loses faith in the judicial bodies. The system of cassation is instituted to deny force to decisions that entail error of law and thus garner credence and respect for the judicial bodies. From all this, one can gather that the system of cassation is instituted for the benefit of the legal system, judicial bodies and with a view to ensuring rule of law.' (Translation is mine)

The reasoning of the Cassation Bench consists of five explicitly and implicitly made prepositions that build on one another. These are:

a) that review on cassation was instituted long after the 1960 Civil Code and 1965 Civil Procedure Code which provide for arbitration and deal with the grounds for appeal from the same;

b) that according to this new system *any final decision* is subject to review on cassation for basic error of law;

c) that the system of cassation has been instituted to guarantee 'equality before the law', 'rule of law' and uniform interpretation and application of laws, and hence as much in the interest of all citizens as in that of the specific parties to a dispute;

---

[142]*Dragados J and P Joint Venture v. Saba Construction PLC*, Federal Supreme Court, File No. 37678 (Nov. 2008).

[143]*National Mining Corporation v. Dani Drilling PLC*, Federal Supreme Court, Cassation File No. 42239((Nov. 2010).

d) that, on the contrary, arbitration results from an arbitration agreement, and creates rights and obligations for the parties concerned and those who claim under them, and not third parties and

e) that, in consequence, an arbitration agreement cannot preclude review on cassation that has been instituted to benefit the public at large, because of the privity of contracts.

It is submitted that the reasoning of the Cassation Bench is less than convincing on two accounts. Particularly, preposition 'b' and 'c' do not seem to be valid. At least, they have not been supported by sufficiently detailed reasoning that demonstrates their validity.

To start with preposition 'b', the Cassation Bench reads into the laws that institute review on cassation a term that is not used by them. Particularly, the law does not state the Cassation Bench is vested with power to review *all final decisions*. The pertinent provision of the FDRE Constitution, reads, '[t]he Federal Supreme Court has a power (of) cassation over any final *court decision* containing a basic error of law. Particulars shall be determined by law.'[144] (Emphasis added)

The Proclamation that gives effect to the above constitutional provision lists, only court decisions as subject to review on cassation. It reads as follows.[145]

In cases where they contain fundamental error of law, the Federal Supreme Court, shall have the power of cassation over:

1) *Final decisions of the Federal High Court, rendered in its appellate jurisdiction;*
2) *Final decisions of the regular division of the Federal Supreme Court and*
3) *Final decisions of the Regional Supreme Court rendered as a regular division or in its appellate jurisdiction.*

There is no word or phrase, in the above article, indicating the list is meant to be illustrative, thus, encompassing other decisions such as arbitral awards. Moreover, the list is consistent with Article 80(3) of the FDRE Constitution which institutes review on cassation of any final *court decision*. All the decisions listed by the Proclamation are decisions of courts, and the list is exhaustive.

Given that the laws that institute review on cassation indicate as subject to review on cassation only 'final court decisions,' and not arbitral awards, one would expect that the Cassation Bench would at least attempt to give reasons for assimilating arbitral awards to final court decisions. It did not do that. Particularly, the Cassation Bench did not account for the dissimilarity between arbitration and litigation in court. For example, a judge decides in the name and on behalf of the state, while an

---

[144]Constitution of the Federal Democratic Republic of Ethiopia, Proclamation No. 1/1995, Federal *Negarit Gazeta*, 1st Year, No. 1, Article 80(3).

[145]Federal Courts Proclamation No. 25/1996, Federal *Negarit Gazeta*, 2nd Year, No. 13, Article 10.

arbitrator does not. Moreover, the jurisdiction of a court over a dispute emanates from the law. In contrast, the jurisdiction of an arbitral tribunal results from the consent of the parties. At this juncture, it is instructive to compare how the Czech Constitutional Court distinguished between an arbitral award and an act of a public authority such as a court judgment. The case under consideration arose from an application for a 'constitutional review,' a mechanism modelled after the German individual constitutional complaints, *Verfassungsbeschwerde*.[146] The Czech Court denied the application for a constitutional review of the award. It reasoned, among others, that:

> [t]he arbitral tribunal is not a public authority. . . . [A]rbitrators do not construe law, but they 'only' create obligations between the parties. Their authority is not derived from the sovereign power of the state, but from the contractual autonomy of parties. Therefore, an arbitral award is not an act of a public authority and a review of the same by way of a constitutional complaint is inadmissible.[147]

The Cassation Bench did not account for these dissimilarities when it implicitly drew analogy between awards and court decisions in *National Mineral Corporation PLC v Dani Drilling PLC*.

Besides, the Cassation Bench did not take into account confidentiality, one of the main motives for choosing arbitration as a dispute settlement mechanism. Third parties will know little, if anything, about the exact legal reasons that lead to a particular award, let alone whether a 'basic error of law' was committed. In contrast, court proceedings are public and judgments remain in the public domain. As a consequence, it is relatively much easier to spot whether a judgment resulted from a basic error of law. All these differences make the analogy, for purposes of review on cassation, between a final court decision and an arbitral award difficult.

In sum, the Cassation Bench did not, in the opinion of the author, show that the values and policy reasons behind arbitration and litigation are so similar that review on cassation that the law provides for in relation to final court decisions should by analogy apply to arbitral awards too.

Coming to the other leg of the reasoning of the Cassation Bench in *National Mineral Corporation PLC v Dani Drilling PLC*, (i.e., proposition 'c' above) the Cassation Bench states that ensuring 'rule of law' and 'equality before the law' are the goals of review on cassation. It does not, however, attempt to demonstrate how reviewing an arbitral award on cassation results in the attainment of these goals. Arbitration is 'an essentially horizontal private-law relationship' resulting from an agreement to arbitrate.[148] The arbitral tribunal is only a contractual construct voluntarily established by the parties to a dispute. The tribunal is not vested with public authority.[149] Given this, question as to how 'rule of law' and 'equality before the

---

[146]Gyarfas (2012), p. 394. Under this Constitutional Model, individuals can directly apply to the Constitutional Court if their fundamental rights are infringed by public authority.

[147]*Id.*, at 395–396.

[148]*Id.*, at 394.

[149]*Id.*, at 401.

law' are implicated in an arbitral proceeding naturally arises. This question is all the more relevant because in Ethiopia a party aggrieved by an arbitral award has already other opportunities for judicial review. It can apply to a court with jurisdiction to have the award set aside, lodge an appeal on non-substantive grounds and even question the substantive merit of the award as discussed under Sects. 6.2, 6.3.1 and 6.3.2 above respectively. Moreover, the final decisions of courts in any of the foregoing recourses are subject to review on cassation. The Cassation Bench should have, at least, attempted to show why bypassing all these remedies to review the decision of an arbitral tribunal, a body that does not act on behalf of the state, contributes to the attainment of the 'rule of law' and 'equality before the law'.[150] The answer to this question is not self-evident.

Review on cassation of an arbitral award despite a finality clause was raised as an issue before the Cassation Bench of the Federal Supreme Court in yet another case, *Ethio-Telecom Corporation vs. PTE International Incorporated*.[151] The Cassation Bench simply confirmed its decision in *National Mining Corporation v. Dani Drilling PLC* above. It remarked that this issue had already been addressed in Cassation Case No, 42239. It did not go beyond that.

In fact, as recently as 24 May 2018 the Cassation Bench has reversed an international arbitral award.[152] On 26 May 2016, *Ethio-Djibouti Railway Enterprise*, the award debtor, filed a petition to have an award in favour of *Consta Joint Venture*, an Italian firm, reviewed. The arbitration was carried out in The Hague under the auspices of the Permanent Court of Arbitration though the formal seat of the Arbitration was Addis Ababa. The Procedural Rules on Conciliation and Arbitration of Contracts Financed by the European Development Fund applied to the arbitration.[153] These rules state that '[t]he award shall be made in writing and shall be *final and binding* on the parties.'[154]

Despite this rule, agreed upon by the parties to arbitration, the Cassation Bench reiterated its decision in *National Minerals Corporation v, Dani Drilling PLC* discussed above and found it is within its right to review the award. The arbitral tribunal had decided by a majority vote in favour of Consta Joint Venture. It had awarded twenty million Euros to Consta JV as compensation for the delay in the performance of the contract that the tribunal attributed to the Ethio-Djibouti Railway Enterprise. The Cassation Bench annulled the award in its totality. It ruled that Consta had committed fraud to secure the contract for the rehabilitation of the

---

[150]Given this blanket justification for review on cassation, an interesting question that has not yet been tested is whether the Cassation Bench would find it appropriate to review an arbitral award where the applicable law is foreign law.

[151]*Ethio-Telecom Corporation v. PTE International Incorporated*, Federal Supreme Court, Cassation File No. 63063, (No. 2013).

[152]*Ethio-Djibouti Railways Enterprise v. Consta Joint Venture*, Cassation File No. 128086, Cassation Bench of the Federal Supreme Court.

[153]Procedural Rules on Conciliation and Arbitration of Contracts Financed By the European Development Fund, Decision No. 3/1990 of the ACP-EEC Council of Ministers of 29 March 1990.

[154]*Id.*, Article 33.3.

railway. Therefore, the Cassation Bench ruled that the very contract is invalid. The Cassation Bench could not however decide on the consequences of invalidation. It mused that it is not possible to remand the matter to the arbitral tribunal to decide on the consequences of invalidation given that the arbitral tribunal had a totally different view. Neither could the Cassation Bench decide on the consequences of the invalidation in the same file, according to it. So, it simply stated that 'a party, if any that believes it has rights in relation to the consequence of the invalidation of the contract may seek legal remedies.'[155]

In sum, clearly, review on Cassation has now started to affect international awards. If the Cassation Bench follows a similar approach even where the seat of arbitration is outside Ethiopia, unlike in this case, then, that will be the final nail in the coffin of arbitration as an alternative to litigation in courts as far as Ethiopia is concerned.

6.4.3   The Implications of the Case Law on the Success of Arbitration

That arbitral awards are subject to review on cassation despite finality clauses poses a serious threat to the success of arbitration in Ethiopia. Particularly, the fluidity of the fact-law dichotomy and the absence of guidelines for the determination of whether an error of law is a 'basic' error or not are serious concerns.

6.4.3.1   The Fact-Law Dichotomy

Though the Cassation Bench may review awards only for 'error of law', and not error of fact, this dichotomy is much less precise than it appears at first glance. The Cassation Bench can easily review questions of fact without openly transgressing the boundaries between error of law and error of fact. This is possible because of the notorious imprecision of the 'fact' 'law' dichotomy.[156] Jolowicz identifies the three possibilities below.[157]

> First, it is widely held that the qualification of the facts is a question of law. Secondly, the traditional idea that the interpretation of private documents such as a contract or a will is a question of intention and thus of fact is overcome by the concept of 'distortion.' Thirdly, as a jurisprudential development or by actual legislation a decision may be quashed on cassation if its findings of fact are inadequately motivated: based upon the idea that a court of cassation cannot perform its function, especially that of considering the qualification of the facts, if the facts are not adequately stated, the door is open for it to consider almost any point of fact.

---

[155] *Ethio-Djibouti Railways Enterprise v. Consta Joint Venture*, Federal Supreme Court, Cassation File No. 128086.

[156] Jolowicz (1988), p. 2051.

[157] *Id.*

Owing to the genuine difficulty that the Cassation Bench faces in drawing the distinction between questions of fact and law and the foregoing possibilities one can imagine it can review on cassation pretty much any case that comes before it. In this relation, one notes the observation made about much more advanced judiciaries like that of France and Germany years back. About review on cassation in France, it was said that 'of the elements of the dossier produced in the lower courts the court of cassation can do with them what it likes, and for Germany, that, contrary to the intention of the legislature, Revision before the *Bundesgerichtshof* has become a '*Tatsacheninstanz*'.[158]

Without going into the merits of the foregoing observations about the past situation in France and Germany it may be concluded that a similar blurring of the boundaries between 'fact' and 'law' by the Cassation Bench could well happen in Ethiopia. Informal discussion with practicing colleagues confirms that this is at least what many lawyers feel about review on cassation in Ethiopia. They say practicing lawyers apply for review on cassation almost as a matter of routine to try their luck.

6.4.3.2   Nonessential Error of Law or 'Basic' Error of Law: No Easy Way to Tell One from the Other

Even where the Cassation Bench passes the hurdle of distinguishing between questions of 'law' and 'fact', it is confronted with yet another question of whether the 'error of law' is 'basic' or otherwise. Unfortunately, the law instituting cassation provides no yardstick that helps answer this question. What is more, the Cassation Bench has not come up with any guidelines for the determination of this matter. All it does is assign three judges to make a *prima-facie* determination of the issue. These screening judges appear to work on the theory that 'one knows a *basic* error of law when he sees it.'[159] So, all they do is go through the file of the lower court, and 'look' for 'basic' error of law.

From the foregoing one can tell that review of awards on cassation, which is not even subject to waiver, is one of the biggest obstacles to the success of international commercial arbitration in Ethiopia. No comparable review exists in any jurisdiction that can be considered a significant player in the field of international arbitration. If arbitration is to have any chance of success in Ethiopia, review of awards on cassation must be abolished. At the very least, it should be subject to waiver by the parties in the arbitration agreement.

---

[158]*Id.*

[159]Mehari Redae, "Basic Error of Law" unpublished material, available on file, p. 3.

6.5   Correction, Clarification and Supplementation of Awards: The Role of Courts

Arbitral awards may have errors, ambiguities and omissions of many types. These range from minor typographical errors to inaccurate reference to evidence, miscalculation of amounts, failure to address particular claims, evidence or arguments and even outright confusion of the parties.[160] Such risks do occur, among other things, because arbitrators do not necessarily master precise legal terminology, do not always master the language in which they draft awards and the disputed mater could be highly complex and technical.[161] When the mistake, omission or error is of such magnitude and consequence that the party affected cannot live with it, the question of who should rectify this arises. Particularly, who among the arbitral tribunal that gave the award, the court of the seat of arbitration or authority requested to enforce the award entertains this matter becomes an issue.[162] Since this chapter is concerned only with the judicial review of awards at the seat of arbitration we do not dwell on the role of the enforcement court. Our treatment of the role of the arbitral tribunal too will be limited to what is necessary to the exposition of the role of the court.

Opinion is divided as to whether the arbitral tribunal or the court of the seat of arbitration is better placed to supplement, correct and interpret an award. Those who think the court of the seat of arbitration should be mandated with these tasks contend that allowing arbitrators to play these roles could drag on the process for a long time. Besides, the process may be used by the tribunal potentially as a cover for making an essentially new award, thus, compromising the *res judicata* effect of awards.[163] Going beyond these practical concerns, some hold that once an arbitral tribunal has rendered its final award, it loses its capacity to act, including the power to interpret, correct or supplement the award. This, in the parlance of the common-law jurisdictions, is called *functus officio*, Latin for 'office performed.'[164] The implication of this doctrine is that the arbitrators will be able to consider the case only if a new agreement allowing this is reached by the parties concerned, a rule to this effect exists in the applicable arbitration rules or when there is a clear statutory basis for this.[165]

Others maintain that the arbitral tribunal, and not the court of the seat, should be allowed to clarify, interpret, rectify and supplement an award, if need be. The contention is that the arbitral tribunal, as the author of the award, is better placed to discharge these tasks. Besides, they argue, in many jurisdictions the remedy a

---

[160]Born (2009), p. 2511.

[161]*Id.*

[162]Poudret and Besson (2007), p. 760.

[163]Born (2009), p. 2512.

[164]*Id.*, p. 2513.

[165]Poudret and Besson (2007), p. 760.

court can give is limited to setting aside, an extreme measure that will frustrate the agreement to arbitrate.[166]

The leading international conventions on international arbitration do not really address the *functus officio* doctrine. The New York Convention, for example, comes closest to acknowledging this doctrine when it provides that awards may be recognized when they are 'binding' which implies when there is no possibility for a subsequent alteration of the award. It does not however address whether the arbitrator has the power to correct, interpret, supplement or otherwise make changes to an award. These matters are left almost entirely to national laws.[167]

Though historically the *functus officio* doctrine was enshrined in many national laws, this has changed. Thus, the Model Law in its most recent revision envisages the possibility of the tribunal interpreting,[168] correcting[169] and making additional awards[170] within a limited time period following the making of the award. Many countries have, while accepting the principle that the arbitral tribunal becomes *functus officio*, mandated the tribunal to have 'specified, carefully-delineated residuary statutory authority.' Such is the approach taken, for instance, by countries like Germany, Belgium, France, the Netherlands, and Japan.[171] Let alone minor corrections, clarifications and supplementations of awards, putting in place the possibility of review of awards on merits within the arbitral system itself is not unheard of. That is common in maritime and commodity arbitrations.[172] Similarly, the arbitration rules under the 1965 Convention on the Settlement of Investment Disputes, commonly referred to as the ICSID, have carefully crafted internal review mechanism.[173]

The approach taken by Ethiopian law on the *functus officio* doctrine is not that clear. There is no provision in the law that expressly authorises an arbitral tribunal to correct, clarify or supplement the award it made. The absence of an express authorization does not necessarily amount to a prohibition though. Particularly, it may be argued that the arbitral tribunal has all the powers a court that rendered a judgment has in respect of these matters. One may rely, in support of this view, on

---

[166]*Id.*

[167]Born (2009), p. 2514.

[168]UNCITRAL Arbitration Rules (as revised in 2010), Ga. Res. 65/22, Article 37, available at: www.uncitral.org/pdf/english/texts/arbitration/arb-rules-revised-2010-e.pdf, accessed on September 10, 2012.

[169]*Id.*, Art 38(1) and (2). The arbitrators can even of their own initiative correct awards that contain computational, clerical, typographic or 'any error or omission of similar nature'. (UNCITRAL Arbitration R).

[170]*Id.*, Art 39. Additional award can be made on claims presented in the arbitral proceedings but not decided upon by the arbitrators. The request for additional award is to be filed within 30 days from the receipt of the award.

[171]Born (2009), pp. 2515–2516.

[172]Redfern and Hunter (2004), para 9-09. Arbitration rules that provide review of awards include the Rules of Chambre Arbitrale Maritime de Paris, which deals with most of maritime arbitrations in France.

[173]*Id.*

the Civil Procedure Code article that reads,'[t]he procedure before an arbitration tribunal …shall as near as may be, be the same as in a civil court.'[174] The Civil Procedure Code vests in a court the power to correct clerical, arithmetical mistakes, accidental slip or omission in its judgment, decree or orders either on the application of a party concerned or of its own motion.[175] From this it may be contended that an arbitral tribunal should be allowed to make similar changes.

On the other hand, it may be held that while the arbitrators can correct, clarify or even supplement the award they made, they can do this only if a court mandates them to. This follows from a cumulative reading of three provisions, namely, Articles 351(a) and (b), 353 and 354(1). Article 351(a) provides for appeal from an award where the award is 'inconsistent, uncertain or ambiguous'[176] and 351 (b) when the 'arbitrator omitted to decide matters referred to him.'[177] Article 353 that deals with the powers of the Appellate Court in general terms vests in such court the power to remit the 'award or a portion thereof to the reconsideration of the arbitrator' where it thinks fit. Finally, Article 354(1) limits the power of the Appellate Court to remit the award to arbitrators to situations provided for under Article 351(a) and (b).[178] The latter deals with an award that is 'inconsistent, uncertain, or ambiguous or is on its face wrong in matter of law or fact' and a situation where the arbitrator omitted to decide matters referred to him. Therefore, that an arbitral tribunal can correct, clarify or supplement an award when instructed by a court to do so is beyond dispute. In contrast, one cannot make a similarly categorical statement about an arbitral tribunal's power to engage in this exercise without a court order to that effect.

That Ethiopian law allows recourse to court to seek correction, clarification or supplementation of awards can potentially be a serious obstacle to the success of arbitration. This opens yet another door to take the dispute to courts consigning arbitration to the starting phase for litigation in court rather than an alternative to the latter. Moreover, the arbitrators who made the award are in a far better position to correct, interpret, and supplement an award than a court. Besides, correction or modification of an award by arbitrators would also pose lesser risk of non-recognition and enforcement abroad. We deal with this practical concern in the section below.

---

[174]Civil Procedure Code of Ethiopia Decree No. 52/1965, Art 317(1).

[175]*Id.*, Art. 208. According to this Article, 'the court may at any time of its own motion or on the application of either party correct, any clerical or arithmetical mistakes in any … judgment, decree or order, or any errors arising therein from any accidental slip or omission …'

[176]*Id.*, Art 351(a).

[177]*Id.*, Art 351(b).

[178]Article 351(a) of the Civil Procedure Code deals with cases where the award is 'inconsistent, uncertain or ambiguous or is on its face wrong in a matter of law or fact.' Art. 351(b) adds to this a scenario in which the arbitrator 'omitted to decide matters referred to him.'

6.6   Modification of Award by Court: Impact on Enforceability

We saw under Sects. 6.2–6.5 above that Ethiopian law allows recourse to court from an arbitral award on various grounds. Particularly, we saw that appeal from an award on non-substantive or substantive merits of the award, review on cassation and even seeking correction, additions and interpretation of awards by courts is possible. The court has the power to vary the award in all these cases. The question, then, arises: is the end product an award or a judgment? And this brings us to the issue enforceability abroad.

The classification of a decision as an 'arbitral award' can be of critical importance as particular consequences follow from that determination. Despite the concept being a touchstone, on the understanding of which, legal consequences depend, with few exceptions, national legislations and international conventions do not expressly define an 'arbitral award.'[179] Nevertheless, one can derive from national arbitration legislations and judicial authorities under the various international conventions a reasonably good definition.[180] As can be gathered from these, an award is the decision that an arbitrator makes as between 'opposing contentions, having weighed the evidence and submissions.'[181] It aims at making and recording the binding decision of the arbitrator on the contested matter.[182] Particularly, an award is an instrument the arbitrators 'intend to be the final expression of their decision on a substantive matter.'[183]

It is unlikely that an 'award' that has been substantially varied or modified by a court, say, either on appeal, or review on cassation will be regarded as an award. Even 'correction', 'interpretation' or 'supplementation' by a court may discolour an award so much so that it looks more like a judgement than an award. In the more extreme case where an Ethiopian court reverses an award and gives its own decision, instead, as it can, the decision is not an award at all. It is a judgement, pure and simple. The court intervention in such cases may have adverse consequences. To start with, the agreement of the parties to arbitrate may be practically defeated. Moreover, enforceability abroad of the end result of the whole exercise diminishes significantly.

It is submitted that Ethiopian laws allowing courts to tamper with awards should be revised if the country is to make the most of its accession to the New York Convention and enhance its chances of becoming a seat of international arbitration. Pending that, it is recommended that Ethiopian courts exercise their discretion to revise, modify, correct awards with caution, especially, as regards awards whose

---

[179]Born (2009), pp. 2347–2350.

[180]*Id.* at 2349.

[181]Turner (2005), p. 3.

[182]*Id.*, at 4.

[183]Born (2009), p. 2353.

enforcement is likely to be sought outside Ethiopia. The safer course of action for the court, in such cases, is to use its discretion under Article 353 and 354 of the Civil Procedure Code, and remit the award for reconsideration by the arbitral tribunal. If remission of the case back to the arbitral tribunal is not possible under the law, such as in cases of corruption, appointment of a different tribunal should be considered, whenever that is compatible with the terms of the arbitration agreement.

6.7   Conclusions

This chapter explored whether and how Ethiopian law balances the rival goals of finality and fairness of arbitral awards. It found that Ethiopian law provides for judicial review of arbitral awards in four ways with far-reaching consequences.

Firstly, Ethiopian law allows 'appeal' against an award on grounds which are addressed differently in most other jurisdictions. Some of the grounds for appeal also constitute grounds for the setting aside of an award in most other jurisdictions owing to the adoption of the UNCITRAL Model Law and the indirect effect of Article V of New York Convention. This calls for the amendment of the law to make it compatible with the law and practice in the rest of the world on this subject. Yet others are grounds that do not entitle a party to any recourse to court in other jurisdictions. For instance, an appeal lies under Ethiopian law from an award on grounds of inconsistency, ambiguity, uncertainty, or failure to address all the matters referred to arbitration. These are matters which an arbitral tribunal is best placed to handle. Hence, many jurisdictions, including those that follow the Model Law approach, entrust the rectification of such deficiency of an award to an arbitral tribunal within a specified window of time.

Secondly, under Ethiopian law, an appeal lies against an award on the substantive merit of the award, where the award is 'on its face wrong in a matter of law or fact.' As if this were not lopsided enough in favour of the fairness of awards, the law permits contractually expanding the grounds for appeal. To make things even worse, the Cassation Bench of the Federal Supreme Court has held that parties to an arbitration agreement may not at the 'submission stage' exclude appeal to court against an award.

Thirdly, arbitral awards are also subject to review on cassation for 'basic error of law.' The fact-law dichotomy is notoriously imprecise. Hence, the possibility of a successful spinning of an error of fact into an error of law to seek review on cassation cannot be ruled out. Moreover, there are neither legal nor judicial guidelines for the determination of whether an error of law is a 'basic' error. This imprecise standard of review on cassation means an award under review could be varied or overturned in reality owing to a factual error or minor legal error under the guise of a 'basic error of law'. To make matters worse, the Cassation Bench of the Federal Supreme Court has held that review on cassation is instituted as much in the interest of all citizens as in that of the specific parties to arbitration, and therefore, cannot be waived by agreement. This means potentially every award can end up before the Cassation Bench. This effectively reduces arbitration to a prelude to litigation in courts.

Where a review on appeal or cassation lies, the pertinent court can confirm, vary or reverse the award. In consequence, the outcome of a process that started out as arbitration could be essentially a judgment rather than an arbitral award. This may defeat the very goal of the agreement to arbitrate. Particularly, it could significantly diminish the ability of the winner to have the 'award' enforced outside Ethiopia.

All of the foregoing recourses to court except the setting aside of awards are uncommon in other jurisdictions. Cumulatively, they limit award finality in favour of fairness to an extent that is unparalleled in any jurisdiction of significance to international commercial arbitration. They relegate arbitration to a preparation for litigation before courts. Introducing the following changes should be considered in order to make arbitration a meaningful alternative to litigation.

1. Broaden the grounds for the setting aside of awards along the lines of the Model Law, and the grounds for resisting the recognition and enforcement of foreign awards under Article V (1) (a) to (d) of the New York Convention. To this end, particularly, change the grounds for appeal under Ethiopian law like failure to inform the parties to arbitration or one of them, of the time or place of hearing; or arbitrators taking evidence in the absence of a party; or hearing one of the parties but not the other to grounds for setting aside, instead. Similarly, change grounds for appeal that pertain to the misconduct of arbitrators such as taking bribe, and acquiring interest in the subject matter of a dispute to grounds for setting aside. In the same vein, change grounds for appeal that pertain to non-compliance with the terms of an arbitration agreement to grounds for the setting aside of an award. Then make setting aside the only recourse to court from an arbitral award.

2. If the recommendation under 1 above is found to be too lopsided in favour of award finality, abolish, at the very least, judicial review of awards on questions of fact and come up with carefully crafted legal standards which must be met for appeal to lie on questions of law. In any case, grant the parties to an arbitration agreement the right to waive the right to appeal on any ground at any stage of arbitration, including in the arbitration agreement itself.

3. Grant an arbitration tribunal carefully crafted powers to make corrections, clarifications and supplemental awards within a narrow window of time after the award is made known to the parties. Abolish any possibility of a court making clarifications, corrections and additions to an arbitral award.

4. Abolish review of awards on cassation for 'basic error of law.' This is not only a type of review that does not exist in any other jurisdiction of significance to arbitration but also very open to abuse.

References

Abedian H (2011) Judicial review of arbitral awards in international arbitration: a case for an efficient system of judicial review. J Int Arbitr 28(6):553

Blackaby et al (2009) Redfern and hunter on international arbitration, 5th edn. Oxford University Press

Berger K (1998) The modern trend towards exclusion of recourse against transnational arbitral awards: a European perspective. Fordham Int Law 12

Bermann G et al (2009) Restating the U.S. law of international commercial arbitration. PSLR 113 (4):1333

Born G (2009) International commercial arbitration, vol 2. Kluwer Law International

Colman A (2007) The question of appeals in international arbitration 2 (Modern Law for Global Commerce). Available at: http://www.uncitral.org/pdf/english/congress/colman.pdf. Accessed 27 July 2011

European Bank for Reconstruction and Development, International Commercial Arbitration Assessment (2007) Report On the Assessment in the CIS (Armenia, Azerbaijan, Georgia, Kazakhstan, Kyrgyz Republic, Moldova, Russia, Tajikistan, Turkmenistan, Ukrain, Uzbekistan and Mongolia). Available at: www.ebrd.com/downloads/legal/judicial/arbitration.pdf. Accessed 8 Sep 2012

Gaillard E, Savage J (eds) (1999) Fouchard, Gaillard, Goldman on international commercial arbitration. Kluwer Law International

Greenberg S et al (2011) International commercial arbitration: an Asia Pacific perspective. Cambridge University Press

Gyarfas J (2012) Constitutional scrutiny of arbitral awards: odd precedents in Central Europe. J Int Arbitr 29(4):391

Haris et al (2007) The Arbitration ACT 1996: a commentary, 4th edn. Blackwell Publishing Inc.

Helm K (2007) The expanding scope of judicial review of arbitration awards: where does the buck stop? DRJ 61(4)

Jingzhou T (2008) One award-two obstacles: double trouble when enforcing arbitral awards in China. AIAJ 4(1):83

Jolowicz JA (1988) Appeal, Cassation, Amparo and all that: what and why? In: Estudios en homenaje al Zamudio H. Available at: bibliohistorico.juridicas.unam.mx/libros/2/643/26.pdf, last visited on 14 October 2016

Kirby J (2012) Finality and arbitral rules: saying an award is final does not necessarily make it so. J Int Arbitr 29(1):119

Knull W, Rubins N (2000) Betting the farm on international arbitration: is it time to offer an appeal option? Am Rev Int Arbitr 2(11):531

Kovacs R (2008) Challenge to international arbitral awards: the French approach. J Int Arbitr 25 (4):421

Moses M (2008) The principle and practice of international commercial arbitration. Cambridge University Press

National Conference of Commissioners on Uniform State Laws, Comments to the Uniform Arbitration Act (Last Revised in 2000) at 83–4

Park W (2012) Arbitration of international business disputes, 2nd edn. Oxford University Press

Poudret J, Besson S (2007) Comparative law of international commercial arbitration. Sweet and Maxwell

Redfern A, Hunter M (2004) Law and practice of international commercial arbitration, 4th edn. Sweet and Maxwell, London

Scherer M (2016) The fate of parties' agreement on judicial review of awards: a comparative and normative analysis of party-autonomy at the post-award stage. Arbitr Int 4

Sedler A (1968) Ethiopian Civil Procedure. Haile Sellassie I University in Association with Oxford University Press

Turner R (2005) Arbitration awards: a practical approach. Blackwell Publishing Ltd

Tyler T, Parasharami A (2008) Finality over choice: Hall Street Associates L.L.C. v. Mattel, Inc. (U.S. Supreme Court). J Int Arbitr 25(5)

Chapter 7
Recognition and Enforcement of Foreign Arbitral Awards

7.1 Parallel Legal Regimes for Recognition and Enforcement

In principle, no state is under any obligation to recognise or enforce foreign awards. Each state is at liberty to determine the conditions under which it recognises or enforces foreign awards.[1] Attempts to change this state of affairs were made by the 1923 Geneva Protocol on Arbitration Clauses and the 1927 Geneva Convention on the Execution of Foreign Arbitral Awards.[2] These instruments were not successful. The most salient shortcoming of the Geneva Convention was that it required obtaining confirmation of an award in its country of origin to have the award enforced in other countries under the Convention.[3] Hence, major improvements were sought.

The International Chamber of Commerce, ICC, came up with a proposal aimed at having a convention that requires the enforcement of 'international' arbitral awards. The proposal was taken up and enriched by an *ad hoc* committee of the United Nations Economic and Social Council (ECOSOC).[4] At this stage, scepticism about the feasibility and even desirability of genuinely 'international' awards as proposed by the ICC became prevalent. Hence, a more conservative approach providing for the enforcement of 'foreign' rather than 'international' awards prevailed when the final text of the New York Convention was adopted on 10 June 1958.[5]

The New York Convention does not fully harmonise all aspects of international arbitration. All it does is just provide cornerstones for arbitration. In particular, it imposes on States Party two major obligations. First, it requires them to recognise

---

[1]Balthasar (2016), p. 50.

[2]*Id.*, p. 51.

[3]*Id.*

[4]*Id.*

[5]*Id.*

© The Author(s), under exclusive license to Springer Nature Switzerland AG 2021   205
S. Y. Tesfay, *International Commercial Arbitration*, European Yearbook of
International Economic Law 12, https://doi.org/10.1007/978-3-030-66752-8_7

arbitration agreement made in writing and their courts to refer the parties to such an agreement to arbitration, whenever they are seized of a dispute involving a matter covered by such agreement.[6] We have already discussed this in Chap. 5 when dealing with negative *Kompetenz-Kompetenz*. The second obligation the Convention imposes is the duty to recognise and enforce foreign arbitral awards.[7]

With 165 States Party as at 23 September 2020, the New York Convention is one of the most widely ratified treaties in the world.[8] Ethiopia ratified the Convention in March 2020 subject to declarations and reservation.[9] Ethiopia has pursuant to Article I(3) of the Convention declared that it will apply the Convention for the recognition and enforcement of arbitral awards made only in the territory of another contracting state.[10] That means Ethiopia assumes no obligation under the Convention to recognize and enforce arbitral awards made in countries that have not ratified the Convention. Some of the countries so excluded are Ethiopia's own neighbors with whom it has significant economic relationships such as Eritrea, Somalia and South Sudan.[11]

Ethiopia has, on the basis of Article I(3) of the Convention, also declared that it will apply the convention to 'differences arising out of legal relationships, whether contractual or not, which are considered commercial under the national law of Ethiopia.'[12] There is no Ethiopian law that classifies 'legal relationships' as 'commercial' and 'non-commercial.' The closest that the law comes to this is when it defines persons to be regarded as traders for the purposes of the Commercial Code of Ethiopia. Article 5 of the Code states that traders are persons 'who professionally and for gain carry on' some 21 economic activities which it lists exhaustively.[13] Another provision of the Commercial Code states that '[b]usiness organizations shall be deemed to be of *commercial* nature where their objects under the memorandum of association or in fact are to carry on any of the activities specified under Art. 5' of the Commercial Code.[14] One may, reading these two provisions together, contend that the 21 economic activities listed under Article 5 are 'commercial' activities. It may, therefore, further be argued that legal relationships involving these activities are

---

[6]UN Convention on Recognition and Enforcement of Foreign Arbitral Awards of 1958, Article II (1) & (3).

[7]Balthasar (2016), p. 50.

[8]UN Convention on the Recognition and Enforcement of Foreign Arbitral Awards, Ratification Status, available at: http://www.newyorkconvention.org/countries, last visited on 23 September 2020.

[9]The Convention on the Recognition and Enforcement of Foreign Arbitral Awards Ratification Proclamation No. 1184/2020, Articles 2 and 3, *Federal Negarit Gazeta*, 26th Year No. 21 (2020).

[10]*Id.* Article 2(1).

[11]UN Convention Ratification status, *supra* no. 8.

[12]The Convention on the Recognition and Enforcement of Foreign Arbitral Awards Ratification Proclamation No. 1184/2020, Federal Negarit Gazeta 26th year, No. 21, Article 2(2).

[13]Commercial Code of the Empire of Ethiopia Proclamation No. 166/1960, Article 5, *Negarit Gazeta*, 3rd Year No. 3 (1960).

[14]*Id.*, Art. 10.

'commercial relationships.' It is hard to tell whether this argument would carry the day in a court of law especially where a non-trader is a party to the transaction. The author could not find any court decision on this specific issue. It seems there is none.

In any case, since the list of economic activities under Article 5 of the Commercial Code is exhaustive there would be many economic activities that would not be regarded as 'commercial' even by the standard of this criteria.[15] That means, even if engaging in activities under article 5 were to be deemed establishing a 'commercial relationship' triggering the application of the New York Convention despite Ethiopia's 'commercial' declaration, there would be many economic relationships that would be excluded from the application of the Convention.

The ratification proclamation goes beyond making the two declarations above that are permissible under the New York Convention. Ethiopia has crafted in the proclamation its own reservation to further limit the number of foreign awards in respect of which recognition and enforcement may be sought based on the Convention. The proclamation states, '[t]he Convention only applies in the Federal Democratic Republic of Ethiopia with respect to [a]rbitration [a]greements concluded and arbitral awards rendered after the date of its accession to the Convention.'[16]

A cumulative reading of the two requirements restricts the application of the Convention to arbitral awards resulting from arbitration agreements signed after Ethiopia's accession to the Convention. The author had the opportunity to attend a consultation organized by the Office of the Attorney General that was spearheading the ratification of the Convention. The experts from the office indicated that they were proposing this provision to safeguard the state and parastatals from liability that may result from numerous arbitration clauses that had been almost habitually included in contracts. Though the legality of this reservation and even its language is not beyond contestation, a couple of countries like Malta, Serbia, Montenegro and Slovenia have made similar reservations.[17]

Ethiopia deposited its instrument of accession to the New York Convention on 24 August 2020.[18] So, if we take a cumulative reading of the requirements under Article 3 of the Proclamation, the Convention may be invoked in support of the recognition and enforcement of arbitral awards resulting from arbitration agreements entered into after 24 August 2020. However, it may be contended that only arbitral awards resulting from arbitration agreements concluded after 22 Nov. 2020 can be enforced on the basis of the Convention. The latter view is supported by the fact that

---

[15]For instance, providing communication services using satellite and internet, providing health care service, providing organized educational service, operating security services and the like have not been included in the exhaustive list under Article 5.

[16]The Convention on Recognition and Enforcement of Foreign Arbitral Awards Proclamation No. 1184/2020, Article 3.

[17]The New York Arbitration Convention ratification status, *supra* note 8.

[18]*Id.*

the Convention itself states it comes into force on the 19th day after the deposit of the instrument of accession by the acceding state.[19]

No matter which interpretation we take, few foreign awards will be recognized and enforced in Ethiopia on the basis of the Convention in the coming three or so years. Generally, it takes a couple of years for a contract with an arbitration clause to result in a dispute, for the arbitration to be finalized, and recognition and enforcement of the award sought. On top of this, there will be awards that are not covered by the Convention because Ethiopia has made the "reciprocity" and "commercial" declarations. Therefore, there will be two parallel legal regimes governing the recognition and enforcement of foreign arbitral awards in Ethiopia. Hence, we discuss in this chapter the legal regimes that apply to non-convention awards and convention awards. We will first discuss the rules that apply to the recognition and enforcement of non-convention awards. Then we will deal with the recognition and enforcement of convention awards.

7.2   Recognition and Enforcement of Non-convention Awards

Ethiopian law is simply silent about the recognition of non-convention awards. But the Cassation Court has given decisions that are peculiar to recognition though in the context of foreign judgments. These decisions are relevant to the recognition of non-convention arbitral awards. Hence, in Sect. 7.2.1 below we will deal with issues that are unique to the recognition of non-convention awards. We will then deal with the enforcement of non-convention awards under Sect. 7.2.2.

7.2.1   Recognition of Awards Not Covered by the New York Convention

The recognition of foreign arbitral awards receives no much attention. Mostly, we find it mentioned almost in passing when dealing with enforcement. Nevertheless, recognition is of significant implications in its own right. To start with, the enforcement of a foreign award cannot take place without recognition though the latter is often simply implied without much discussion.[20] Moreover, in some cases an award creditor may seek recognition of the award without seeking its enforcement. The need for recognition alone may arise where a court action is filed involving the same parties to arbitration as regards the subject matter that was already settled by

---

[19]UN Convention on the Recognition and Enforcement of Foreign Arbitral Awards (1958), Article XII(2).

[20] Greenberg et al. (2011), p. 427.

arbitration.[21] The party that relies on the award will, in such a case, object to the judicial proceeding and seek recognition of the arbitral award as binding.[22] Similarly, an award creditor may seek recognition of a foreign award to invoke it as a ground for set-off or counterclaim.[23]

The Civil Procedure Code, which applies to non-convention awards is simply silent about the recognition of foreign arbitral awards. It deals with foreign arbitral awards in a chapter titled '[e]xecution [o]f [f]oreign [j]udgments.'[24] Article 461 that is specifically dedicated to 'enforcement' of foreign awards is found in that chapter. This Article, which will be discussed in due course, lays down the rules that apply to the 'enforcement' of foreign awards without mentioning recognition. It also states that the rules of the Code dealing with the enforcement of foreign judgments apply by analogy to the enforcement of foreign awards. That is of little help though. The law is silent as regards the recognition of foreign judgments too.

Unfortunately, no actual case in which the 'recognition' of a foreign award was sought in Ethiopia could be found. There are no reported cases, at least. However, the Cassation Bench of the Federal Supreme Court has reached a relevant decision in *Rawda Mumie v. Abdella Abdulrahman,* though the case arose from a foreign judgment.[25] Particularly, this case may be invoked when an award creditor wants to use a foreign award to object to a suit regarding a dispute settled by arbitration or as a ground for set off or counterclaim in Ethiopia. The case may be applied by analogy to foreign awards. This is so because, the rules that apply to foreign judgments do apply to foreign awards by analogy under the Civil Procedure Code of Ethiopia.[26] Hence, we briefly discuss it now.

Ms. Rawda Mumie and Mr. Abdella Abdulrahman were divorced in Ethiopia. While the Ethiopian court that decided to dissolve the marriage was considering the pecuniary effect of the divorce, Ms. Rawda Mumie produced a decision of a Canadian Court giving a condominium in Toronto and a house in Ethiopia to her.[27] At the High Court, she argued that the matter in dispute has been settled already by a decision of a court, *albeit* Canadian. Hence, she contended that the

---

[21]*Id.*

[22]*Id.*

[23]*Id.*

[24]Civil Procedure Code of Ethiopia Decree No. 52/1965, Articles 456–461.

[25]*Rawda Mumie v. Abdella Abdulrahman,* CASSATION BENCH OF THE FEDERAL SUPREME COURT, Case No. 54632, Decision Rendered on 7 June 2011, Reported in Cassation Bench Decisions Vol. 12.

[26]Civil Procedure Code of Ethiopia Decree No. 52/1965, Article 461(2) provides '[t]he provisions of the proceeding Articles shall apply by analogy when the enforcement of a foreign award is sought.'

[27]The liquidation of pecuniary effect of the marriage was being considered by the Federal First Instance Court in File No. 64296 in when Ms Rawda Mumie introduced the decision of the Canadian court, rendered on 1 July 2006. In consequence, the case was transferred to the High Court because the First Instance Court had no jurisdiction to entertain matters involving a foreign judgment.

matter is *res judicata*. She also prayed the court to recognise her right to enforce the decision of the Canadian Court.[28] The High Court rejected the prayer. It reasoned: the effects of a divorce should be regulated based on the laws of the country in which marriage was concluded. Besides, the decision of the Canadian court which gives the matrimonial property to one party violates, according to the High Court, Article 34 of the Ethiopian Constitution that guarantees the equality of spouses at the time of the dissolution of their marriage.[29] The Federal Supreme Court confirmed the decision of the High Court.[30] Hence, Ms. Rawda Mumie applied for review on cassation for 'basic error of law.' The essence of her petition was that the lower courts committed basic error of law by disregarding the decision of a Canadian court on the matter in dispute.

The Cassation Bench confirmed the decisions of the High Court and the Supreme Court, *albeit* for a different reason.[31] It did not challenge the fairness or constitutionality of the decision of the Canadian Court. Instead, interestingly the Cassation Bench relied on the fact that Ms. Rawda Mumie had not applied for the execution of the Canadian judgment but rather raised it in defence to put an end to the liquidation proceedings in Ethiopia.[32] According to the Cassation Bench, one can assess whether a foreign court decision meets the requirements for recognition 'when the party that benefits from that decision applies for its enforcement' pursuant Articles 456–461 of the Civil Procedure Code, 'and not when adduced in defence against a suit brought against it.'[33] Hence, where the petitioner, Ms. Rawda Mumie, has not applied for enforcement, 'her contention that this decision has *res judicata* effect per Article 5 of the Civil Procedure Code has not been found to be convincing.'[34] In essence, the Cassation Bench ruled that the recognition of a foreign judgment can be sought only within the context of an application for enforcement. According to it, recognition is simply an inseparable implication of an action for enforcement rather than a stand-alone petition.

Though Articles 456–461 of Civil Procedure Code deal with the 'execution' of foreign judgments and awards, and do not mention recognition at all, it would be more logical to apply the same provisions and recognise judgments and awards, if need be, even where execution is not sought. Recognition is implied in every execution, anyway. The Cassation Bench sent a wrong message, it seems. Particularly, a party resisting the recognition of a foreign award or fending off a claim for set-off will now be able to raise the decision of the Cassation Bench in his defence. There seems to be no legitimate purpose for allowing that.

---

[28] *Abdella Abdulrhaman v. Rawda Mumie*, Federal High Court of Ethiopia, Case No. 71195.

[29] *Id.*

[30] *Rawda Mumie v. Abdella Abdulrahman*, Federal Supreme Court of Ethiopia, Case No. 51738.

[31] *Rawda Mumie v. Abdella Abdulrahman*, decision by the Cassation Bench of the Federal Supreme Court in Case No. 54632.

[32] *Id.*

[33] *Id.*

[34] *Id.*

In *Alemnesh Abebe v. Tesfaye Gessese*,[35] another case decided just days after its decision in *Rawda Mumie*, the Cassation Bench similarly rejected a foreign judgment that was raised in support of a *res judicata* defence, though it did not stick to the same line of reasoning. The parties to that case were married in Ethiopia, where they had a house. After leaving for the US and living there for years, they divorced in Maryland, USA. Years after the divorce, Ms Alemnesh Abebe filed a suit at the Federal First Instance Court alleging that Mr. Tesfaye Gessese had been collecting rent from their common house in Addis for years and demanding her half of the rent already collected and division of the property between the two. Mr. Tesfaye Gessese made a preliminary objection on the ground that the Montgomery County Family court of Maryland, USA had settled the effects of the divorce. Hence, the matter is *res judicata* based on Article 5 and 244(2) b of the Civil Procedure Code of Ethiopia, he contended. The Federal First Instance Court found this defence acceptable and declined to entertain the suit. The Federal High Court confirmed that decision. Hence, Ms Alemnesh Abebe sought review on cassation. The Cassation Bench quashed the decision of the lower courts. It held the decision of the US court has no *res judicata* effect. It reasoned:[36]

> In the matter under consideration it was not demonstrated that the parties had obtained a judgment abroad regarding the property located in Ethiopia. *Nor was it demonstrated that the decision of the foreign court clearly meets the requirements under Articles 456 to 461 of the Civil Procedure Code for recognition by Ethiopian courts.* Therefore, the rejection of the claims by the plaintiff on the ground of *res judicata* by the lower courts entails basic error of law. (Emphasis added)

Though it reached a similar decision the Cassation Bench did not, however, stick to its reasoning in *Rawda Mumie*—not explicitly at least. To stick to the reasoning in the previous case, the Cassation Bench would have simply stated that the enforcement of the decision of the Montgomery County Family Court, Maryland, USA was not sought in Ethiopia, and therefore, it cannot be *recognised* and raised in defence against another action. Instead, it called into question whether the US Court decision covered the house in Ethiopia. And more pertinently, for our current purpose, it reasoned that the US Court decision 'clearly meets the requirements under Article 456–461 of the Civil Procedure Code for recognition by Ethiopian courts' had not been demonstrated.

It is to be noted that the Cassation Bench is less than precise in the way it cites authority. For example, Article 461 that it cites deals with the enforcement of a foreign arbitral award, rather than a foreign judgment. Nonetheless, the Cassation Bench makes reference to this provision too. It seems what the Cassation Bench had in mind was Article 458(a) that requires reciprocity. Whatever the reasoning, the Cassation Bench in the end denied the possibility of raising as defence foreign judgments.

---

[35] *Alemnesh Abebe v. Tesfaye Gessese*, The Cassation Bench of the Federal Supreme Court, Case No. 59953, Decision Rendered on 10 June 2011, Reported in Cassation Court Decisions Vol. 12.
[36] *Id.*

7.2.2 The Enforcement of Non-convention Awards

The Civil Procedure Code of Ethiopia provides the conditions under which foreign arbitral awards may be enforced in Ethiopia. It reads as follows.[37]

Art. 461 Enforcement of foreign awards

(1) Foreign arbitral awards may not be enforced in Ethiopia unless:

(a) reciprocity is ensured as provided for by Art. 458 (a);

(b) the award has been made following a regular arbitration agreement or other legal act in the country where it was made;

(c) the parties have had equal rights in appointing the arbitrators and they have been summoned to attend the proceedings;

(d) the arbitration tribunal was regularly constituted;

(e) the award does not relate to matters which under the provisions of Ethiopian laws could not be submitted to arbitration or is not contrary to public order or morals and

(f) the award is of such nature as to be enforceable on the condition laid down in Ethiopian laws.

(2) The provisions of the preceding Articles shall apply by analogy when the enforcement of a foreign award is sought.

We will examine the foregoing provisions in two parts. We will first dwell on Article 461(1) (a) which requires the establishment of 'reciprocity' as the precondition for the enforcement of foreign awards. We then look at the rest of the provisions of Article 461 dealing with the exceptional circumstances in which a foreign award may not be enforced despite the establishment of reciprocity.

7.2.2.1 Establishment of Reciprocity: A Precondition for Enforcement

A non-convention foreign arbitral award 'may not be enforced in Ethiopia unless ... reciprocity is ensured as provided for by Art. 458(a).'[38] The provision to which the cross reference is made states that foreign judgments are not to be enforced in Ethiopia unless 'the execution of Ethiopian judgments is allowed *in the country in which the judgment to be executed was given*'.[39] (Emphasis added) The value the cross reference adds is, therefore, its explanation of reciprocity. Particularly, in

---

[37]Civil Procedure Code of Ethiopia Decree No. 52/1965, Article 461.

[38]*Id.*, Article 461(1)a.

[39]*Id.*, Article 458(a).

establishing reciprocity the reference should be 'to the *country* in which the foreign award *was made.*' Other factors such as the nationality, domicile, or place of incorporation of the award creditor seeking enforcement in Ethiopia are immaterial.

Since reciprocity is a precondition for the enforcement of foreign awards in Ethiopia, the question as to how exactly it is understood by Ethiopian courts raises its head. Particularly, questions that may be raised include the following.

(a) Is the existence of a bilateral or multilateral treaty requiring the enforcement of Ethiopian awards in the country in which the award was made sufficient when whether that state discharges its treaty obligation has not been tested in practice?
(b) Is reciprocity established if the country in which the award was made is a party to a multilateral convention that requires it to enforce foreign awards irrespective of their country of origin?
(c) Is reciprocity fulfilled if the country in which the award was made has domestic laws that require the enforcement of foreign awards irrespective of their country of origin?
(d) Is reciprocity established if in practice the courts of the country in which the award was made enforce foreign awards despite the absence of any treaty or statutory obligation to that effect? And
(e) Should reciprocity be presumed in the absence of proof that the country in which the award was made does not enforce Ethiopian awards?

Unfortunately, no Ethiopian court cases in which the foregoing questions were involved could be found in relation to foreign arbitral awards. There are, however, cases involving foreign judgments which raise the same question of reciprocity. Since reciprocity is required for the enforcement of both foreign judgments and awards, the cases are equally relevant to the enforcement of foreign awards in Ethiopia. We look at some of the cases below.

Ethiopian courts have been inconsistent in their understanding and application of the principle of reciprocity.[40] *In the matters of Paulos Papassinous*, for example, Mr. Papassinous sought to enforce a Greek judgment declaring him a testamentary successor to the property of his deceased mother located in Ethiopia.[41] To determine whether Greece enforces Ethiopian judgments, the High Court instructed the Ministry of Foreign Affairs to provide information. The latter responded by just stating that the two countries have signed 'no treaty of judicial assistance.'[42] The High Court emphasized that the applicant had not adduced any other evidence to show Greece enforces Ethiopian judgments. It then declined to enforce the Greek judgment reasoning 'since there is no treaty that enables Ethiopian courts to execute judgments rendered in Greece, we hereby reject the application of the judgment-creditor.'[43] On appeal to the Supreme Court Mr. Papassinous stressed that

---

[40]Tecle (2011), p. 123.

[41]Samuel (2000), p. 569.

[42]*Id.*, p. 570.

[43]*Id.*

Article 458(a) of the Civil Procedure Code does not require the existence of a treaty between the two countries. All it requires is proof that judgments rendered in Ethiopia are enforced in Greece. Interestingly, Greece freely enforces foreign judgments in so far as they do not violate natural justice, *res judicata* and public order.[44] Yet, the Supreme Court rejected the appeal. It reasoned 'Ethiopian judgments can be executed in a foreign state if there is a treaty of judicial assistance between Ethiopia and that state.'[45] And it was ascertained by the lower court that there is none between Ethiopia and Greece, the Supreme Court underscored.[46]

According to the High Court, for a foreign judgment to be enforced on the basis of Article 458(a), the person seeking enforcement must show that Ethiopian judgments are, as a matter of fact, enforced in the country in which the judgment was given. Alternatively, there must be a treaty of judicial assistance between Ethiopia and the foreign country concerned. Showing a liberal foreign law that generally allows the enforcement of foreign judgments without requiring reciprocity is not sufficient, though the court did not state that expressly. The Supreme Court chose an even more restrictive interpretation, focussing on the existence of a treaty of judicial assistance. Taking the existence of a treaty of judicial assistance as the only proof to establish that a foreign country enforces Ethiopian judgments can have extremely bad consequences.[47]

In *Goh-Tsibah Menkreselassie v. Bereket Habte-selassie*, the Federal High Court looked at the reciprocity issue from the vantage point of giving a fair treatment to the party seeking enforcement.[48] It held that the absence of a treaty of judicial assistance should not limit the rights of private citizens. Hence, enforcement should be refused only when there is an agreement to that effect, it held.[49] This is an extreme position though very pro judgment creditors. It is hard to imagine states concluding treaties providing for non-enforcement of their respective judgments.[50] This position also denies any effect to the principle of reciprocity embodied in Article 458(a). It is nevertheless to be welcomed that it underlines the adverse effect of the principle of reciprocity on private individuals. Decisions in other cases do not focus on this aspect of the principle much.

In *Michael Kohler v. Derlexia Kenyat,* the enforcement of the judgment of a US court was sought. According to the Federal High Court's ruling, proof that the United States enforces Ethiopian judgments should be adduced given the absence of a treaty of judicial assistance between the US and Ethiopia.[51] It, thus, required the applicant to prove that. The applicant claimed two Ethiopian judgments had been

---

[44]*Id.,* p. 571.
[45]*Id.,* p. 570.
[46]*Id.*
[47]Tecle (2011), p. 123.
[48]*Id.,* p. 124.
[49]*Id.*
[50]*Id.*
[51]*Id.,* pp. 124–125.

enforced in the US.[52] The Court then instructed the Ministry of Foreign Affairs to confirm the claim. The Ministry indicated that it was unable to trace the alleged cases.[53] The applicant, then, contended that the Uniform Child Custody Jurisdiction Act of the US requires the courts of the United States to recognise and enforce foreign judgments regarding child custody.[54] The High Court, thus, held child custody decisions of US Courts should be enforced in Ethiopia as the US courts are legally required to enforce foreign awards on this subject.[55] So, the existence of a liberal foreign law that provides for the enforcement of foreign judgments was a sufficient proof that Ethiopian judgments would be enforced in the US in matters of child custody for the High Court.

Incidentally, the United States has 'no federal law governing the recognition and enforcement of foreign judgments . . . .'[56] The 50 states have their own set of laws providing for conditions under which foreign judgments may be recognised and enforced.[57] It appears that the Uniform Child Custody Jurisdiction Act on which the High Court relied actually applies to inter-state child custody decisions.[58] In any case, the right approach to check reciprocity is investigating how an Ethiopian judgment fares in the particular US state in which the US judgment was made, rather than generally inquiring whether the United States enforces Ethiopian judgments. It seems the Ethiopian Court erred in framing the issue. That being said, whether the Federal High Court was right in its understanding of the US law is not that important for our purpose. The major import of this ruling is that reciprocity can be proven by showing a liberal foreign law that provides for the enforcement of foreign judgments though not specifically dealing with how the judgment of Ethiopian courts are to be treated. This is a pro justice interpretation that violates neither the letter nor the spirit of Article 458(a) of the Civil Procedure Code.

Unfortunately, in *Ms. Yusra Abdulmuein and others v. Mr. Abdulkeni Abdulmuein*[59] the Federal Supreme Court and the Cassation Bench took a more restrictive interpretation. They ruled that a party seeking enforcement has to either show that Ethiopia has a treaty obligation to enforce the foreign judgment or the foreign country in which judgment was given, in point of fact, enforces Ethiopian judgments. In that case, involving members of a family, Ms. Yusra Abdulmuein and others sought the enforcement of a Yemeni judgment in Ethiopia. Mr. Abdulkeni Abdulmuein resisted the enforcement alleging, among other things, that there is no evidence showing Yemen enforces Ethiopian judgments. The Supreme Court denied

---

[52]*Id.*, p. 125.

[53]*Id.*

[54]*Id.*

[55]*Id.*

[56]Zeynalova (2013), p. 156.

[57]*Id.*, p. 157.

[58]Tecle (2011), p. 125.

[59]*Yusra Abdulmuein, Hussein Abdulmuein and Ahmed Abdulmuein v. Abdulkeni Abdulmuein*, Federal Supreme Court, Cassation File No. 78206.

enforcement on the ground that the parties seeking enforcement had neither proven that Yemen enforces Ethiopian judgments nor the existence of a treaty between the two countries requiring Ethiopia to enforce Yemeni judgments. The Cassation Bench reversed this decision but only to require the Supreme Court to give the parties seeking enforcement sufficient time to prove either of the two. So, we now have a binding precedent about how the reciprocity requirement of Article 458(a) of the Civil Procedure Code is met. Proof has to be adduced showing that Ethiopian judgments are, as a matter of fact, enforced in the foreign jurisdiction concerned or there must be a treaty obligation requiring Ethiopia to enforce the judgments of the country concerned. Since the reciprocity rule applies to both foreign judgements and arbitral awards, the interpretation applies to foreign awards too.

The position taken by the Supreme Court and its Cassation Bench regarding reciprocity is unhelpful, it appears. Reciprocity should be understood and applied in view of the objective of Article 458(a). Generally, reciprocity is a measure of self-help aimed at persuading other countries to enter into conventions providing for the enforcement for foreign judgments.[60] Reciprocity is also aimed at incentivising states to take the initiative in showing respect and deference to the judgment of the state that applies the principle of reciprocity, short of entering into conventions.[61] This may happen in the hope that the latter state will reciprocate by applying the reciprocity rule it has.

That being said, applying the reciprocity rule to the desired effect is not easy. It is, for example, very difficult to apply this rule because courts are ill-suited to determine foreign state practice in respect of enforcement. The daunting judicial fact-finding challenge the application of this rule entails has lead some authors to conclude that the rule is almost unworkable.[62] We recall here the wrong approach the Federal High Court took in *Michael Kohler v. Derlexia Kenyat* in its attempt to determine whether Ethiopian judgments are enforced in the US. We also remember that the Ministry of Foreign Affairs that was instructed by the High Court to verify the claim that the United States enforces Ethiopian awards, responded it was unable to verify the claim. In some jurisdictions, such as in the United States, expert testimony is used to minimise challenges of this sort, thought that too has its own drawbacks.[63] Another way of alleviating the burden on courts is to task a branch of the executive to determine the practice of other countries in regard to the recognition and enforcement of foreign judgments or awards, as the case may be, and keep a list that is periodically updated.[64] Perhaps this would be more feasible and in line with the trend in Ethiopia. Ethiopian courts often instruct the Ministry of Foreign Affairs to

---

[60]Michaels (2009), p. 2.

[61]Samuel (2000), p. 571.

[62]Coyle (2014), p. 1121.

[63]*Id.* Some of the negative impacts of use of expert testimony in the determination of foreign state practice include, exposing the claimant to additional costs and possibility of inconsistent outcomes because the experts used could give opposing testimony.

[64]*Id.*, p. 1122.

determine the foreign practice in regard to the enforcement of Ethiopian judgments. Unfortunately, the Ministry does not keep a periodically updated list. Besides, there is neither a consistent practice nor any institutional memory regarding the handling of such requests from the Ethiopian courts on the part of the Ministry.[65]

Even worse, though fair enough in the abstract, the reciprocity rule does lots of injustice to the judgment creditor, sometimes to no apparent proportional legitimate purpose. This is the case, especially, when it is applied to international commercial arbitral awards. It victimizes an innocent award creditor in an effort to retaliate against the state in which the award was made.[66] This is particularly unfair because the award creditor seeking enforcement may have no significant connection with the country in which the award was made. The country may have been chosen as the seat of arbitration purely to ensure neutrality, for example. Where the award creditor has neither business presence in the country nor citizenship, he has little leverage, if any, on the country in which the award was made. So, insisting on reciprocity will not necessarily yield the desired result of changing the behaviour of that state regarding the treatment of foreign awards.

Coming back to the interpretation of reciprocity given by the Cassation Bench in *Ms. Yusra Abdulmuein and others v. Mr. Abdulkeni Abdulmuein*, it does not, in certain situations, serve the purpose of reciprocity. At times, it can even defeat the very purpose of the reciprocity rule. We recall, at this point, that the Cassation Bench ruled that reciprocity can be proven by either producing proof that there is a treaty-based obligation for Ethiopia to enforce foreign judgment or evidence showing that the country, in which the judgment was made, as a matter of fact, enforces Ethiopian judgments. This means a judgment or award rendered in a country with a liberal pro enforcement domestic law will not meet the requirement of reciprocity in Ethiopia even when no attempt to enforce Ethiopian judgment or award in that country had been made. This brings to mind the holding of the High Court in relation to a Greek judgment in the *Paulos Papassinous* case. In such cases, the judgment/award creditor is penalised for no purpose as the country of the award has already pro enforcement law. Given the opportunity, Ethiopian judgments or awards would have been enforced in such country. At least, that is how the existence of a pro-enforcement law should be understood. In case where a jurisdiction has a reciprocity rule with the same understanding as in Ethiopia, the very purpose of reciprocity is defeated. Each side refuses to enforce the judgment/award until the other side blinks first and, in point of fact, enforces the judgment or award of the other. In such situations, the purpose of reciprocity is better attained by backing down rather than adhering to one's position.

Overall, the approach taken by the Ethiopian courts is not only unhelpful but could also be counterproductive. We come across cases in which even Ethiopian nationals are victimised just because of the insistence on reciprocity that is narrowly

---

[65]Telephone interview with Mr. Reta Alemu, Director, Legal Affairs Directorate, the Ministry of Foreign Affairs of Ethiopia. The interview was conducted on 25 June 2013.
[66]Tecle (2011), p. 122.

understood. So, it is submitted that the reciprocity rule be understood in light of the purpose it is meant to achieve. A teleological interpretation will lead to the recognition and enforcement of awards made in some foreign jurisdictions. A number of countries have domestic legislations drafted along the lines of the *UNCITRAL Model Law* providing for the recognition and enforcement of foreign awards irrespective of their country of origin. These countries should be regarded as having fulfilled the reciprocity requirement for purposes of Ethiopian law. Limiting the undesirable effect of the reciprocity rule by deeming reciprocity established where it is expected that the courts of the rendering state would extend recognition and enforcement to the judgments of the forum is not unheard of. This line of interpretation has been followed by the courts of Germany, Japan, Korea, Taiwan and the like, in relation to foreign judgments.[67] It is submitted that this line of interpretation be taken to the recognition and enforcement of non-convention foreign awards in Ethiopia.[68]

At this juncture, the mutually ratified treaty between the Peoples' Republic of China and Ethiopia providing for the recognition and enforcement of arbitral awards comes to mind. The treaty was ratified by the Ethiopian Parliament on 2 May 2017.[69] Article 28 of the treaty imposes reciprocal obligation on Ethiopia and China to recognise and enforce arbitral awards made in the territory of each party.[70] This bilateral treaty will be complemented by the New York Convention as far as recognition and enforcement of awards is concerned, because Ethiopia has now acceded to the Convention, and China too is a party. Awards made in either country before Ethiopia's accession to the New York Convention can be enforced based on this treaty.

The country does not have ratified bilateral treaties providing for the recognition and enforcement of foreign commercial awards and judgments except with the Peoples' Republic of China.[71] The treaty with the Republic of Djibouti was ratified by Ethiopia in early 1990s but has not been ratified by Djibouti as yet according to Ato Yusuf. Hence, negotiation is underway to develop a new treaty.[72] So, the

---

[67] Elbalti n.d..

[68] Another point that perhaps goes without saying is that the cross reference Article 461(2) of the Civil Procedure Code of Ethiopia makes to the provisions dealing with reciprocity in relation to foreign judgments should not be taken literally. In other words, in gauging foreign practice, for the purpose of enforcement of foreign awards in Ethiopia, we look at whether that country enforces or would enforce Ethiopian awards, rather than Ethiopian judgments.

[69] Interview with Ato Yusuf Jemaw, Director, Directorate for International Cooperation, Human Rights and Anti-Trafficking in Humans, Office of the Attorney General. Interview was conducted at his office on 14 November 2017. *See also,* Tecle (2011), p. 123.

[70] Treaty Between the Peoples' Republic of China and the Federal Democratic Republic of Ethiopia on Judicial Assistance in Civil and Commercial Matters, signed on 04 May 2014, Article 28.

[71] *Id.*, Article 21.

[72] Interview with Ato Yusuf Jemaw, Attorney General's Office, Head of the Department for International Cooperation. Ato Yusuf noted that many people including judges have cited the treaty with Djibouti thinking it has been ratified by Djibouti as well. Article authors cite that treaty, see for example, Tecle (2011), p. 123.

recognition and enforcement of non-convention awards other than Chinese awards is subject to 'reciprocity' as discussed in this section.

7.2.2.2   Beyond Reciprocity: Grounds for the Denial of Recognition and Enforcement

Establishing that the country in which an arbitral award was made enforces Ethiopian awards is a necessary but not a sufficient condition for a non-convention award to be enforced in Ethiopia. Several other conditions must be cumulatively met. Particularly, according to Article 461(1) (b) to (f), a foreign award may not be enforced unless:[73]

(b) the award has been made following a regular arbitration agreement or other legal act in the country where it was made;

(c) the parties have had equal rights in appointing the arbitrators and they have been summoned to attend the proceedings;

(d) the arbitration tribunal was regularly constituted;

(e) the award does not relate to matters which under the provisions of Ethiopian laws could not be submitted to arbitration or is not contrary to public order or morals; and

(f) the award is of such nature as to be enforceable on the condition laid down in Ethiopian laws.

A comparison of the foregoing provisions with the grounds for refusal of recognition and enforcement of foreign arbitral awards under Article V of the New York Convention reveals some level of similarity in essence despite the disparity in the language used. For example, Article 461(1)b above and Article V(1)(a) and (c) of the Convention, which state that the award must have been made in conformity with and within the scope of a valid arbitration agreement entered into by persons with capacity to do so, are similar. There is also some similarity between Article 461(1) (e) above, on the one hand, and Article V(2)(a) of the New York Convention which provides that recognition and enforcement may be denied if '[t]he subject matter of the difference is not capable of settlement by arbitration under the laws of that country' and Article V(2)(b) of the Convention which states that recognition and enforcement may be denied where that would be contrary to the 'public policy' of the state in which that is sought.

Notwithstanding the similarities, the grounds for the denial of enforcement of non-convention foreign awards under the Civil Procedure Code are not really coextensive with those under the New York Convention. We will, in what follows,

---

[73]Civil Procedure Code of Ethiopia Decree No. 52/1965, Article 461(1)b–f.

raise a few points that may potentially pose problems or require interpretation when the enforcement of a non-convention foreign award is sought in Ethiopia.

7.2.2.2.1 Constitution of the Arbitral Tribunal

A non-convention foreign arbitral award is not enforced in Ethiopia unless the tribunal that rendered the award had been 'regularly constituted.'[74] The English phrase 'regularly constituted' is not that clear. The Amharic version of the provision is plainer. A better translation of the controlling Amharic version would have been— the arbitral tribunal must have been 'constituted in compliance with legal requirements.' The closest that the New York Convention comes to this requirement of the Civil Procedure Code is when it states that a foreign award may be refused recognition and enforcement if: '[t]he composition of the arbitral authority . . . was not in accordance with the agreement of the parties, or, *failing such agreement, was not in accordance with the law of the country where the arbitration took place.*'[75] (Emphasis added). From this, it may be concluded that, the law of the place of arbitration is to be considered only where the parties have not provided for the composition of the arbitral authority. In other words, 'party autonomy takes priority over the law of the place of arbitration' under the New York Convention.[76]

The rule under Article 461 of the Civil Procedure Code differs from the Convention rule on this point in two important respects. First, mandatory legal requirements, regarding the composition of an arbitral tribunal, if any, prevail over the agreement of the parties on the subject. Secondly, according to Article 461(1)(d), whether the arbitral tribunal was 'regularly constituted' is, to some extent, determined by reference to Ethiopian law, the law of the country in which enforcement is sought, rather than the country in which the award was made. This latter point is not obvious because Article 461(1) d itself does not have any language to that effect. It rather results from a different provision of the Civil Procedure Code which reads, '[f]oreign arbitral awards may not be enforced in Ethiopia unless: . . . the parties have had equal rights in appointing the arbitrators . . . .'[77]

Too much should not, however, be read into 461(1) (c) that requires equality of the parties in constituting the arbitral tribunal. The essence of it is not really unique to Ethiopia. Putting a party to arbitration in a privileged position in constituting the tribunal itself is prohibited in probably all countries, in some explicitly and in others

---

[74]Civil Procedure Code of Ethiopia Decree No. 52/1965, Article 461(1)(d).

[75]UN Convention on Recognition and Enforcement of Foreign Arbitral Awards of 1958, Article V (1)(d).

[76]Kronke et al. (2010), p. 282.

[77]Civil Procedure Code of Ethiopia Decree No. 52/1965, Article 461(1)(c). We have a similar rule in the Civil Code. Article 3335 provides the Arbitral submission 'shall not be valid where it places one of the parties in a privileged position as regards the appointment of the arbitrator.'

as a matter of the application of the general principles of law.[78] Besides, an arbitration agreement that puts a party in a privileged position as regards the appointment of arbitrators is likely to be found invalid and the resultant award unenforceable owing to Article V(1)a of the Convention, itself. In consequence, the disparity between the Civil Procedure Code and Article V(1) (d) of the Convention on this point is unlikely to pose practical problems.

7.2.2.2.2   Opportunity to Appear and Present Defence

According to the New York Convention, the recognition and enforcement of a foreign award may be refused where '[t]he party against whom the award is invoked was not given proper notice of the appointment of the arbitrator or of the arbitration proceedings or was otherwise unable to present his case.'[79] The same conclusion may be reached regarding non-convention awards reading together Articles 461 (1) (c), 461(2) and 458(c) of the Civil Procedure Code. Article 461(1)(c), a sub-article of Article 461 that lists the grounds for refusing the enforcement of non-convention awards in Ethiopia, provides that a foreign award cannot be enforced in Ethiopia unless the parties 'have been summoned to attend the proceedings.'

This provision, read alone, gives a wrong impression that being summoned is sufficient. Read together with other provisions of the Code, however, clearly it envisages a broader 'due process exception', similar to that under the New York Convention. Particularly, Article 461(2) states that the grounds for refusal to enforce foreign awards under Article 461(1) are to be complemented by the rules on enforcement of foreign judgments, *mutatis mutandis*.[80] Article 458(c) of the Civil Procedure Code, which, therefore, applies by analogy, provides that a foreign judgment will not be enforced in Ethiopia unless 'the judgment-debtor was given the opportunity to appear and *present his defence*.' So, taken in their totality the rules under the Civil Procedure Code produce similar effect as that of the New York Convention, Article V(1)(b).

7.2.2.2.3   Public Order, Morals and Non-arbitrability

A non-convention foreign award may not be enforced in Ethiopia where the enforcement of the award is 'contrary to public order or morals'[81] according to the English

---

[78]Zekarias (2007), p. 140.

[79]UN Convention on Recognition and Enforcement of Foreign Arbitral Awards of 1958, Article V (1)(b).

[80]Civil Procedure Code of Ethiopia Decree No. 52/1965, Article 461(2) reads: '[t]he provisions of the *preceding Articles* shall apply by analogy when the enforcement of a foreign award is sought.'

[81]*Id.*,Article 461(1)(e).

version of the Civil Procedure Code. The New York Convention provision that comes closest to this is Article V (2) (b). The 'recognition or enforcement' of a foreign award may be refused where that would be 'contrary to the public policy' of the state in which recognition or enforcement is sought, according to this Convention provision. Now, it is not clear whether 'public order' the term the English version of the Civil Procedure Code uses is the same as 'public policy' of the New York Convention. Though in relation to a totally different treaty, Professor Catherine Kessedjian muses over whether there is really any distinction between the French expression '*ordre public*', on the one hand, and 'public order' and 'public policy', on the other, the terms into which it is often translated in treaties.[82] Whether these concepts are identical or different in content and methods in the French and common-law systems is a subject that continues to baffle experts. Suffice it, for the current purpose, to note that the terms are used interchangeably at least in some treaties.[83]

That said, things get murkier when we look at the phrase 'public order' in the Amharic version of the Code. The Amharic version of Article 461(1)(e) uses a phrase which can more accurately be translated as the 'security of the people.' So, according to the Amharic version, the enforcement of a foreign award will be refused if the 'implementation of the award' poses risk to the 'security of the people.' Noteworthy, at this point, is the fact that it is the 'implementation' of the award rather than how the award was made that should be contrary to the 'security of the people.' In sum, it appears that 'public order' under Civil Procedure Code is narrower than 'public policy' under the Convention. Unfortunately, no judicial interpretation of this phrase that elucidates the similarity and distinction between the Amharic and the English versions could be found. Incidentally, the Amharic versions of federal laws prevail over English versions in cases of disparity, since Amharic is the 'working language' of the Federal Government.[84]

'Public policy', the Convention ground for the refusal to recognise and enforce foreign awards, seems to be a much broader concept than the 'security of the people', its counterpart in the Amharic version of Article 461(1)(e) of the Civil Procedure Code. Judge Borrough's observation that public policy is 'never argued at all but when other points fail' indicates it is invoked, though often not accepted, to cover a wide set of circumstances.[85] Cognizant of the resultant possible abuse, the International Law Association has adopted recommendations aimed at a restrictive interpretation of 'public policy' with the objective of upholding international arbitral awards. According to its recommendation, 'public policy' includes: '(i) fundamental principles of justice and *morality* that a state wishes to protect, (ii) rules designed to protect essential social, political, or commercial interests of the state concerned, and

---

[82]Kessedjian (2007), p. 26.

[83]*Id.*

[84]Constitution of the Federal Democratic Republic of Ethiopia, Proclamation No. 1/1995, Federal *Negarit Gazeta*, 1st Year, No. 1, Article 5(2).

[85] Schramm et al. (2020), p. 365.

(iii) the duty to respect obligations towards other states . . . or international organizations.'[86] Even this purposively restrictive interpretation shows that 'public policy' in the Convention is quite a broad concept as compared to the protection of the 'security of the people,' the standard adopted by the controlling Amharic version of Article 461(1)e of the Civil Procedure Code. In fact, 'public policy' is such a broad concept that it, arguably, subsumes 'public morals,' yet another Article 461(1) (e) ground, for refusing enforcement of non-convention foreign awards in Ethiopia.

Coming to the issue of arbitrability, a foreign award will not be enforced in Ethiopia if the award relates to matters 'which under the provisions of Ethiopian laws could not be submitted to arbitration. . . .'[87] We have dwelt, at length, on the issue arbitrability under Ethiopian law[88] in Chap. 3. Hence, there is no need to reproduce the discussion here. Suffice it to say that this requirement of Ethiopian law is consonant with the Convention provision which provides that, the recognition and enforcement of a foreign award may be refused if the competent authority in the country where these are sought finds that '[t]he subject matter of the difference is not capable of settlement by arbitration under the law of that country.'[89]

To sum up, a non-convention foreign award will be refused enforcement in Ethiopia, if its enforcement is contrary to 'public order,' more precisely 'the security of the people', 'morals' or where the award relates to a matter that is non-arbitrable under Ethiopian law.[90] The grounds for the refusal to enforce foreign awards in the English version of Article 461(1) (e) are arguably coextensive with the grounds under Article V (2) of the Convention.[91] The grounds for refusal to recognise and enforce a non-convention foreign award are arguably narrower than those available under Article V (2) of the New York Convention in the Amharic version of Article 461(1) (e) of the Civil Procedure Code.

---

[86]*Id.*

[87]Civil Procedure of Code of Ethiopia Decree No. 52/1965, Article 461(1)(e).

[88]We have dealt with arbitrability under Ethiopian law under Chap. 4. We saw that according to 315 (2) of the Civil Procedure Code, provides administrative contracts are not arbitrable. Other than that there is no explicit rule dealing with arbitrability. We further saw other areas like bankruptcy law, competition law and consumer protection law may pose issues of arbitrability despite the silence of the law.

[89]UN Convention on Recognition and Enforcement of Foreign Arbitral Awards Convention, Article V(2)(a).

[90]Civil Procedure Code of Ethiopia Decree No. 52/1965, Article V(2)(e).

[91]UN Convention on Recognition and Enforcement of Foreign Arbitral Awards of 1958, Article V (2)(a) provides recognition and enforcement may be refused were the subject matter of the difference is non-arbitrable, while Article V(2)(b) allows refusal to recognize and enforce foreign awards where that would be contrary to 'public policy' of the country in which these are sought.

7.2.2.2.4   Award Must Be of Enforceable Nature Under Ethiopian law

A non-convention foreign award may not be enforced in Ethiopia unless it 'is of such nature as to be enforceable on the condition laid down in Ethiopian laws.'[92] The New York Convention provides no comparable ground for refusal to recognize and enforce foreign awards.[93]

The rule under Article 461(1)(f) of the Civil Procedure Code raises the question—when is an award of such a nature that it cannot be enforceable under Ethiopian law? Perhaps the best starting point to answer this question is identifying the possible remedies that an arbitral tribunal may give. An award may provide remedies like 'monetary compensation, punitive damages or exemplary damages, specific performance, injunctive relief, declaratory relief, interest, [and] costs.'[94] Now the question is which of the foregoing remedies is not enforceable under Ethiopian law? Most, if not all, of them are available under Ethiopian law. Only punitive damages and specific performance may possibly raise issues of enforceability under Ethiopian law.

Neither tort law, referred to as the law of extra-contractual liability in Ethiopia, nor the law of contracts of Ethiopia provides for 'punitive damages' as a remedy. The starting point, in the tort law of Ethiopia, is the principle of equivalence of compensation to the damage caused. The law provides that damages due by the person liable 'shall be equal to the damage caused to the victim by the act giving rise to the liability.'[95] This rule is subject to exceptions. There are cases of compulsory mitigation and discretionary mitigation by judges.[96] Coming to compensation for breach of contract, the starting point for the assessment of damages due for breach of contract is not equivalence. It is rather a more abstract question of what injury would one *normally expect* from the non-performance of the contract.[97] The answer to this question may result in the award of compensation that is less than actual damage or equal to actual damage, but not more.[98] 'Compensation' in excess of actual damage will be awarded only where the contract itself provides for a penalty fixing the amount to be paid in case of breach.[99] In short, punitive damages are not provided for under Ethiopian law as a remedy in both the laws of contract and extra-contractual liability. That does not, however, mean that this remedy would not be

---

[92]Civil Procedure Code of Ethiopia Decree No. 52/1965, Article 461(1)(f).

[93]UN Convention on Recognition and Enforcement of Foreign Arbitral Awards of 1958 York Convention, Article V.

[94]Tecle (2011), pp. 120–121.

[95]Civil Code of Ethiopia, Proclamation No. 165/1960, Article 2091.

[96]*Id.*, Article 2098–2104, for example.

[97]*Id.*, Article 1799.

[98]*Id.*, Article 1801.

[99]*Id.*, Article 1889 cum 1892(1).

'enforceable' under Ethiopian law, though Tecle Bahta takes a different view.[100] The law is simply silent about this matter. Given that Ethiopian law does not prohibit this, a better interpretation would be to enforce foreign awards that give punitive damages. Denying enforcement to a non-convention foreign award that provides for punitive damages available under the law applicable to the case does not seem to serve any legitimate purpose.

Coming to the enforceability of a foreign award giving specific or 'forced' performance as a remedy, the answer depends on the particulars of the case. Specific performance may not be ordered under Ethiopian law 'unless it is of special interest to the party requiring it and the contract can be enforced without affecting the personal liberty of the debtor.'[101] So, a non-convention award ordering a specific performance of a contract may not be enforced in Ethiopia if either specific performance affects the personal liberty of the award-debtor or the party seeking forced performance of the contractual obligation has no special interest in getting such performance.

The enforcement of an international commercial award is unlikely to adversely affect the 'personal liberty' of the award-debtor. This requirement for specific performance seems to have human debtors in mind rather than commercial entities. At least, the illustration given by René David, the drafter of the Civil Code, points in that direction.[102] Coming to the second requirement for the award of this remedy, it is not impossible to imagine situations in which the award creditor can prove it has special interest in specific performance of the contractual obligation rather than getting compensation.

In sum, the requirement of Article 461(1)(f) of the Civil Procedure Code that an award should be 'of such nature as to be enforceable on the condition laid down in Ethiopian laws' is not necessarily a big obstacle to the enforcement of a non-convention foreign award in Ethiopia.

7.2.2.2.5   Award Must Be Final and Enforceable

Yet another condition for the enforcement of a non-convention foreign award is that which results from the cross-reference made by Article 461(2) to the provisions on the enforcement of foreign judgment. Article 458(d) of the Civil Procedure Code, dealing with the enforcement of a foreign judgment, provides that a foreign judgment must be 'final and enforceable' for it to be executed in Ethiopia. So, this requirement applies by analogy to a non-convention foreign award for it to be enforced in Ethiopia.

---

[100]Tecle (2011), p. 121. According to Tecle that Ethiopian law 'does not recognize' punitive damage is sufficient reason to not enforce foreign awards that provide for it. Our submission is the silence of the law does not amount to not recognizing a remedy.

[101]Civil Code of Ethiopia Proclamation No. 165/1960, Article 1776.

[102]David (1973), p. 59.

This requirement is not unique to Ethiopian law. The New York Convention itself puts in place a similar requirement. It provides that recognition and enforcement may be refused if '[t]he award has not yet become binding on the parties, or has been set aside or suspended by a competent authority of the country in which, or under the law of which, that award was made.'[103] In reality, setting aside is the only recourse from an international arbitral award in most parts of the world, in part, owing to the widespread adoption of the Model Law.[104] Hence, the practical import of the cumulative reading of Article 461(2) and 458(d) is denying enforcement to a foreign award that had been set aside at the seat of the arbitration. This requirement is not, therefore, an unwarranted obstacle to the enforcement of non-convention foreign awards in Ethiopia.

7.2.2.3   Burden of Proof Regarding the Grounds for Refusal to Enforce Awards

The biggest challenge to the enforcement of non-convention foreign arbitral awards in Ethiopia is not so much the grounds for refusal of enforcement as the burden of proof. Under the New Convention, it is the party resisting enforcement that bears the burden of proof regarding all the grounds for resisting enforcement listed under Article V(1). The Convention makes this point clear as it reads: 'recognition and enforcement of the award may be refused, at the request of the *party against whom it is invoked, only if that party furnishes* . . . proof that'. . . and lists down the grounds that have to be proven.[105] In contrast, the Civil Procedure Code is silent but appears to put the onus of proof on the party seeking the enforcement of a foreign award. Article 461(1) reads: '[f]oreign arbitral awards may not be enforced in Ethiopia unless' and then lists down the grounds that must be met by such awards to be enforceable.

No court case dealing with the question of burden of proof in the context of the enforcement of a non-convention foreign award could be found. However, Ethiopian courts do put the burden of proof on the party seeking enforcement of foreign judgments despite the comparable language of Article 458.[106] For instance, in *Yusra Abdulmuein, et al v. Abdulkeni Abdulmuein*,[107] the respondent resisted the

---

[103]UN Convention on Recognition and Enforcement of Foreign Arbitral Awards of 1958, Article V (1)(e).

[104]We have discussed this in Chap. 6 at length, and specially under Sect. 6.2.

[105]UN Convention on Recognition and Enforcement of Foreign Arbitral Awards of 1958, Article V (1).

[106]The *chapeau* of Article 458 reads, '[p]ermission to execute a foreign judgment shall not be granted unless' and then the specific grounds that must be met are listed down. Court practice as seen previously is to require the party seeking enforcement to prove the fulfilment of the requirements listed, reciprocity, for example.

[107]Yusra Abdulmuein, et al v. Abdulkeni Abdulmuein, Federal Supreme Court, Cassation File No. 78206.

enforcement of a Yemeni judgment alleging the parties seeking enforcement did not prove Yemen enforces Ethiopian judgments and also claiming he was not given the 'opportunity to appear and present his defence' before the Yemeni court. The Supreme Court found in his favour, stating the parties seeking enforcement did not prove Yemen enforces Ethiopian judgments. It did not rule on the issue of opportunity to present defence. May be it did not find this necessary since it decided for him, though only on grounds of Article 458(a) (i.e., absence of proof of reciprocity). The Cassation Bench reversed the decision of the Supreme Court and instructed that the parties seeking enforcement be given time to adduce evidence to prove the requirements under Article 458(a) and (c). In short, both the Cassation Bench and the Supreme Court were in agreement that the burden of proof lies with the parties seeking enforcement. Their difference was only in regard to the sufficiency of time given to the party that bears the burden of proof.

7.3 Recognition and Enforcement of Awards Covered by the New York Convention

Ethiopia has acceded to the New York Convention subject to the 'reciprocity' and 'commercial' declarations.[108] Making these declarations is permissible under Article I(3) of the New York Convention.[109] Ethiopia has also crafted its own temporal reservation. The Convention, therefore, applies to 'arbitration agreements concluded and arbitral awards rendered after the date' of Ethiopia's accession to the Convention.[110] Ethiopia acceded to the Convention on 24 August 2020, 5 months after the passing of the ratification proclamation.[111] We have discussed, under Sect. 7.2.2 of this chapter, the legal regime that applies to foreign arbitral awards excluded from the scope of application of the Convention as the result of these declarations and reservation.

Coming to foreign awards which are not excluded by the declarations and reservation it made, Ethiopia is under obligation to 'recognise' them as 'binding' and 'enforce' them pursuant to its rules of procedure.[112] The Convention imposes a similar obligation as regards arbitral awards that are not deemed domestic in the state

---

[108]The Convention on Recognition and Enforcement of Foreign Arbitral Awards Ratification Proclamation No. 1184/2020, Federal *Negarit Gazeta*, 26th Year, No. 21, Article 2.

[109]UN Convention on Recognition and Enforcement of Foreign Arbitral Awards of 1958, Article I (3).

[110]The Convention on Recognition and Enforcement of Foreign Arbitral Awards Ratification Proclamation No. 1184/2020, Federal *Negarit Gazeta*, 26th Year, No. 21, Article 3.

[111]www.newyorkconvention.org/countries. The Ratification Proclamation was passed on the 13th of March 2020.

[112]UN Convention on Recognition and Enforcement of Foreign Arbitral Awards of 1958, Article III.

where recognition and enforcement is sought.[113] This rule envisages the possibility of an award being not regarded as domestic despite being made within the territory of the same country. Ethiopia has no laws, as yet, which consider awards made within its territory as non-domestic awards.

The obligation to recognize and enforce foreign arbitral awards is subject to certain exceptions that have been exhaustively listed under Article V of the New York Convention. They are divided into two categories. The first category are grounds to be proven by the party resisting recognition and enforcement. These are: (a) incapacity on the part of the parties to conclude an arbitration agreement, or invalidity of the arbitration agreement under the relevant applicable law; (b) violation of due process resulting in the inability of a party to present his case; (c) excess of authority of the tribunal; (d) the composition of the tribunal or the arbitral procedure being at variance with the agreement of the parties and (e) the award not having become binding yet, or it having been suspended or set aside by a competent authority of the country in which or under the laws of which it was made.[114]

The second category, grounds that can be raised by a court on its own initiative, to decline recognition and enforcement are: (a) the subject matter of the dispute not being capable of settlement by arbitration and (b) recognition and enforcement being contrary to the public policy of the country in which they are sought.[115]

We have already made, under Sect. 7.2.2.2 of this chapter, a comparative analysis of these convention grounds for resisting recognition enforcement and the non-convention grounds. Ethiopian courts have not, as yet, got the opportunity to analyse the convention grounds for resisting recognition and enforcement of foreign awards.

7.4 Conclusions

This chapter appraised the challenges involved in seeking the recognition and enforcement of foreign awards in Ethiopia. It found that Ethiopia acceded to the New York Convention on the Recognition and Enforcement of Foreign Arbitral Awards as recently as 24 August 2020. Ethiopia acceded to the convention subject to the 'reciprocity' and 'commercial' declarations. Besides, it crafted its own reservation restricting the application of the Convention to arbitration agreements and arbitral awards made after Ethiopia's accession to the Convention. The cumulative effect of all these is that the Convention does not fully supplant the legal regime that applied prior to Ethiopia's accession to the Convention. In fact, the old rules will

---

[113]*Id.*, Article I(1) and Article III read together.

[114]UN Convention on Recognition and Enforcement of Foreign Arbitral Awards of 1958, Article V (1).

[115]*Id.*, Article V(2) (a) and (b).

apply to most arbitral awards for a couple of years to come. The same rules will also remain relevant for many years to come, at least, as regards awards that are not deemed "commercial" under Ethiopian law. Similarly, they will remain applicable to awards that are made in countries that are not parties to the New York Convention, which include three of Ethiopia's own neighbours with whom it has significant economic ties.

The Civil Procedure Code that applies to non-convention awards is simply silent regarding the recognition of foreign awards in Ethiopia. Moreover, there are no reported cases in which the recognition of foreign awards was sought. That said, the Cassation Bench of the Federal Supreme Court has reached decisions regarding the recognition of foreign judgments that may be applied to foreign awards by analogy. These decisions are inconsistent. The Cassation Bench stated, in one of the cases, that recognition may be sought only in the context of an enforcement action, and not in a defence. This seriously curtails the right of an award creditor that wants to raise the award for defensive purposes such as *res judicata*, counterclaim and set-off.

Regarding enforcement of non-convention awards in Ethiopia, it must be proven that the country in which the award was made enforces Ethiopian awards. Though the courts are inconsistent as regards the modality of proof, the most recent cases suggest that showing the country concerned has a treaty obligation to enforce Ethiopian awards or actual practice of enforcing Ethiopian awards is required. In either case, establishing that is a tall order. Prior to Ethiopia's recent accession to the New York Convention, China was the only country that had assumed a treaty obligation to enforce commercial awards made in Ethiopia. So, establishing actual practice of enforcing Ethiopian awards needed to be shown regarding awards from all other countries. The problem is that there is no established mechanism for proving whether the country in which the award was made, in point of fact, enforces Ethiopian awards.

Establishing that the country in which the award was made enforces Ethiopian awards is a necessary but not a sufficient condition for a non-convention award to be enforced in Ethiopia. Article 461(1) of the Civil Procedure Code lists the exceptional grounds on which enforcement of a foreign award may be refused. Despite disparity in wording, these grounds are not that different from the grounds for declining recognition and enforcement of foreign awards under Article V of the New York Convention. A difference of far-reaching consequence is in the approach taken regarding the burden of proof. Under the New York Convention, Article V (2), it is the party resisting enforcement that shoulders the burden of proof about all the grounds for refusal of enforcement, except as regards public policy and arbitrability. In contrast, the party seeking enforcement bears the onus of proof to show all the requirements for enforcement of a non-convention award have been fulfilled under Article 461 of the Civil Procedure Code.

References

Balthasar S (ed) (2016) International Commercial Arbitration: international conventions, country reports and comparative analysis. Verlag C. H. Beck oHG/Hart Publishing

Coyle JF (2014) Rethinking judgments reciprocity. NCL Rev 92:1109

David R (1973) Commentary on contracts in Ethiopia (trans: Kindred M). Haile Selassie University

Elbalti B (n.d.) Reciprocity and the recognition and enforcement of foreign judgments, p 3. http://www.law.cam.ac.uk/repodocuments/pdf/events/PILConf/Reciprocity_and_the_Recognition_and_Enforcement_of_Foreign_Judgments_pdf. Last visited on 20 Nov 2016

Greenberg S et al (2011) International Commercial Arbitration: an Asia Pacific perspective. Cambridge University Press

Kessedjian C (2007) Public order in European law. Erasmus Law Rev 01(01):25

Kronke H et al (eds) (2010) Recognition and enforcement of foreign arbitral awards: a global commentary on the New York Convention. Wolters Kluwer

Michaels R (2009) Recognition and enforcement of foreign judgments. Max Planck Encyclopaedia of Public International Law

Samuel T (2000) Reciprocity with respect to enforcement of foreign judgments in Ethiopia: a critique of the Supreme Court's decision in the Paulos Papassinous Case. Afr J Int Comp Law 12:569

Schramm D et al (2020) In: Kronke H et al (eds) Recognition and enforcement of foreign arbitral awards: a global commentary on the New York Convention. Walters Kluwer, Austin

Tecle HB (2011) Recognition and enforcement of foreign arbitral awards in civil and commercial matters in Ethiopia. Mizan Law Rev 5(1)

Zekarias K (2007) Formation of arbitral tribunals and disqualification and removal of arbitrators under Ethiopian Law. J Ethiopian Law 21

Zeynalova Y (2013) The law on recognition and enforcement of foreign judgments: is it broken and how do we fix it? Berkeley J Int Law 31(1):150

Chapter 8
The Institutional Setting for International Commercial Arbitration

8.1 The Role of the Judiciary in Arbitration

Though arbitration is chosen to oust the jurisdiction of courts which would have otherwise been competent to resolve a dispute, paradoxically it needs the cooperation of the very courts it seeks to displace.[1] Despite the often voiced protestations of 'party autonomy', arbitration is dependent on the support of courts who alone have the power necessary to rescue it from sabotage by a party to it.[2] Even the Model Law, which at first sight seems determined to exclude courts from involvement in arbitration, does call for assistance and supervision from a competent court regarding several matters.[3] Particularly, it acknowledges the possible need for assistance and supervision from courts, among others, in regard to referring the parties to arbitration; appointment of arbitrators; challenge of arbitrators; termination of the mandate of arbitrators; determination of jurisdiction of an arbitral tribunal; enforcement of interim measures granted by arbitrators; issuance of interim measures; assistance in taking evidence; setting aside awards; as well as recognition and enforcement of awards.[4]

Besides, the parties' choice of arbitration, itself could raise issues of public policy. Hence, the state imposes limits to this freedom of choice, for instance, as regards which type of disputes are arbitrable and which others are not. Such boundaries of arbitration prescribed by the state are enforced through the

---

[1] Williams (2012).

[2] Redfern and Hunters (2004), p. 328.

[3] *Id.* at 329–330.

[4] See for instance, UNCITRAL Model Law on International Commercial Arbitration of 1985 as Revised in 2006, G.A. res. 61/33, U.N. Doc. A/40/17. Articles 8(1), 11(3)(4), 13(3), 14, 16, 17 H I J, 27, 34, 35 and 36 respectively. Note that Article 5 of the Model Law gives the impression that it proscribes court involvement very strongly when it provides: 'in matters governed by this law, no court shall intervene except where so provided in this law.' All the same it cannot help calling for support by competent court in many areas indicated above.

© The Author(s), under exclusive license to Springer Nature Switzerland AG 2021
S. Y. Tesfay, *International Commercial Arbitration*, European Yearbook of International Economic Law 12, https://doi.org/10.1007/978-3-030-66752-8_8

instrumentality of the national courts.[5] Therefore, the role of courts in arbitration goes well beyond 'support and supervision'. Overall, the conduct of arbitration is possible only when courts and arbitrators work in partnership. That said, one observes that this is, in fact, not a partnership of equals. Arbitration depends for its very existence on national courts, but the reverse is not true.[6]

Therefore, the successful conduct of arbitration presupposes not only the existence of law that strikes the right balance in its allocation of roles between arbitrators and national courts but also a competent judiciary that understands the laws, respects the laws and ensures respect for the same. Arbitration will succeed only when a harmonious relationship exists between courts and arbitral tribunals.[7] Hence, an assessment of a domestic environment for the conduct of commercial arbitration, international or otherwise, cannot ignore discussing the judiciary of the country under study. It is for this reason that we attempt to shed some light on the Ethiopian judiciary in what follows.

However, we have to emphasize right from the outset that a comprehensive discussion of the Ethiopian judiciary is beyond the scope of this book. An in-depth study of the judiciary and other institutions of relevance to arbitration would require an extensive empirical study which could in its own right be a topic for a different book. The aim here is limited to providing the context in which arbitration takes place and the resultant awards enforced in Ethiopia. We also try to shed light on the extent of support the judiciary lends to the success of arbitration and give general information of relevance.

8.2 Courts with Jurisdiction in Matters of International Arbitration

The Constitution of Ethiopia mandates the establishment of federal and state judiciaries.[8] Further, the Constitution specifies the 'structure and powers of courts'. More particularly, it envisages 'regular' three-tier federal and state court systems.[9]

Based on the powers vested in it by the Constitution, the Federal House of Representatives, which is the highest federal legislative body, has issued proclamations to determine the powers and operation of federal courts.[10] Federal Courts have

---

[5]Redfern and Hunter (2004), p. 328.

[6]*Id.*

[7]Williams (2012), p. 1.

[8]Constitution of the Federal Democratic Republic of Ethiopia, Proclamation No. 1/1995, Federal *Negarit Gazeta*, 1st Year, No. 1, Article 50(2).

[9]*Id.* Articles 78–74.

[10]*Id.* Articles 51 and 55, Federal Courts Proclamation No. 25/1996, Federal Negarit Gazeta, 2nd Year, No. 13; Federal Courts Amendment Proclamation No. 138/1998; Federal Courts Amendment Proclamation No. 321/2003 and Federal Courts Proclamation Reamendment Proclamation 454/2005.

jurisdiction over cases arising under the Constitution, federal laws, international treaties, places and parties specified under federal laws as well as places indicated in the Constitution as territories in which federal law applies.[11]

The Federal Government has the power to issue laws aimed at regulating twenty one major areas including finance, monetary matters, foreign investment, and transportation by air, waterways, major roads, inter-state commerce, foreign trade, communications, patents, copy rights and labour. It may also issue civil laws which the House of Federation[12] deems necessary to 'establish and sustain one economic community.'[13] So, where the arbitration involves the interpretation and application of such laws or where an international treaty is relevant, it is the Federal judiciary that has jurisdiction to support and supervise the arbitration.[14]

Similarly, the Federal judiciary plays supportive and supervisory roles where arbitration takes place in Addis Ababa, as this is the federal capital administered under federal law.[15] Likewise, among others, cases in which a foreign national is a party, suits involving two persons permanently residing in different regions, suits relating to business organizations registered or formed under the jurisdiction of the Federal Government fall within the jurisdiction of Federal courts.[16] So, it is the Federal judiciary that supervises and supports arbitration where the arbitration involves any of the foregoing.

In sum, in light of the Federal Constitution and the other relevant laws seen above, one can conclude that an arbitration that takes place in Addis Ababa or has a foreign element, either because of the identity of the parties or because the transaction involves two or more countries is supervised and assisted by the Federal Courts. In other words, the competence to support and supervise international commercial

---

[11]Federal Courts Proclamation No. 25/1996, Article 3. Some contend that this Proclamation encroaches on the powers of regional states. Particularly, some maintain that 'federal law' cannot freely designate 'places and parties' over which Federal Courts will have jurisdiction. The Contention is that the Federal law must be limited to matters over which the Federal Government has Jurisdiction under the Constitution.

[12]This is an assembly consisting of member of the various ethnic groups of the country. Each ethnic group has one representative and one more representative for every one million members of the ethnic group. The members are not directly elected by the people. It is the assembly of the state concerned that sends the representatives. The mandate of the House of Federation is essentially interpreting the constitution, promote harmony, unity and equality of the various ethnic groups, See Constitution of Federal Democratic Republic of Ethiopia, Proclamation No. 1/1995, Article 61 and 62.

[13]Id., Articles 51, 55(6).

[14]Id., Article 80(1) and Federal Courts Proclamation 25/1996, Article 3.

[15]Constitution of the Federal Democratic Republic of Ethiopia, Proclamation No. 1/1995, Article 49.

[16]Federal Courts Proclamation 25/96, Article 5. Some hold that the Proclamation has no constitutional basis to give jurisdiction to Federal Courts over disputes just because a foreign national is a party or a business organization is registered or formed under the jurisdiction of the Federal Government.

arbitration is vested by law in the Federal Judiciary. Hence, in what follows we will deal only with the federal judiciary.

8.3   Standard Parameters for Assessing the Judiciary: How Do the Federal Courts Fare?

The Constitution gives Ethiopian courts powers that are typically vested in the judiciaries of democratic countries. For example, it confers on Ethiopian courts all judicial powers. It also guarantees the judiciary freedom from interference by officials of the government, institutions of the state and any other source.[17] Judges are guaranteed security of tenure. They are to discharge their duties in full independence, directed in the exercise of their function only by law.[18] In sum, as far as formal structure, organization and operation are concerned the judiciary is as good as it can get in any democracy.[19] Hence, in this section, the focus will be on the reality on the ground in terms of independence, competence, integrity, accountability and the judiciary's overall capacity to support and supervise international commercial arbitration rather than its formal structure and organisation.

8.3.1   Independence

Judicial independence refers to the complete liberty of a judge to decide a case before him free from all sorts of influence and pressure that may come, among others, from pressure groups, government and even individuals, including other judges.[20] Though related to 'impartiality', 'independence' is a distinct concept. The former pertains to the attitude or state of mind of the tribunal towards a particular issue or party before it whereas 'independence' refers to status or relationship vis-à-vis others, especially, the executive branch of government. So, 'independence' refers to traditional constitutional value.[21] Judicial independence can be looked at from

---

[17]Constitution of the Federal Democratic Republic of Ethiopia, Proclamation No. 1/1995, Art 79 (2).

[18]*Id.*, Article 79(3).

[19]*Id.*, Articles 78–81.

[20]United Nations Commentary on the Bangalore Principles of Judicial Conduct 39. Available at: https://www.unodc.org/documents/corruption/publications_unodc_commentary-e.pdf, accessed on 20/9/2015.

[21]*Id.* at 40. Independence of the judiciary is the one principle that runs through the entire fabric of a democratic constitution. It inspires the entire constitutional scheme. It is the foundation on which rests the entire edifice of the constitution because it the judiciary which is entrusted with keeping every organ of the state within the law. *See also* 'Canons of Judicial Ethics', 2 Speech by Chief Justice Y.K Sabharwal, MC Setalvad Memorial Lecture Series. Available at: http://tnsja.tn.nic.in/article/Cannons%20of%20Jud%20Ethics.pdf, accessed on 20/9/2015.

institutional and individual perspective. The former refers to the relationship of the judiciary as an institution to others while the latter concerns an individual judge's factual independence.[22] The Bangalore Principles regard judicial independence as a prerequisite to rule of law and a fundamental guarantee to fair trial.[23]

Ensuring judicial independence requires more than putting in place constitutional and statutory guarantees to that end. Though very useful, such guarantees do not necessarily translate into actual independence of the judiciary. Judicial independence is realized only when all the branches of government, and particularly the executive, are genuinely committed to it.[24] In evaluating whether or not judicial independence is respected in point of fact, usually regard is had to the manner in which judges are appointed, promoted, their term of office, and conditions of service. Financial security and independence in matters of administration that is directly related to the exercise of the function of the judiciary are also important yardsticks for assessing the independence of the judiciary.[25] At the level of the individual judge, material and intellectual autonomy are also prerequisites for judicial independence.[26]

Coming to the specific condition in Ethiopia, much remains to be done for the judiciary to be truly independent. Even studies commissioned by the Government confirm that there are serious problems that hinder the actual independence of the judiciary as an institution and at the level of individual judges. Particular problems exist in the selection and promotion of judges. As regards selection, for example, a study commissioned by the Ministry of Capacity Building finds the criteria[27] for selection are too general. The study further concludes besides the process being insufficiently transparent, the input by the public is minimal. The law in place does not provide for details such as announcement of openings, search procedure, screening of potential candidates, and meaningful standards of evaluation.[28] To remedy this situation a directive was issued in July 2010 by the Judicial Administration Council. This directive provides a degree in law (LL.B) as a minimum eligibility requirement to be appointed to the Federal Judiciary.[29] It also provides that candidates are to sit for written and oral exams.[30] Moreover, the law did not provide for

---

[22]United Nations Commentary, *supra* note 20, p. 39.

[23]*Id.*

[24]*Id.* p. 41.

[25]*Id.*, p. 41.

[26]Provincial Court of British Columbia, Code of Judicial Ethics, Revised in 1994, Considerations 1.01 for Rule 1, available at: http://www.provincialcourt.bc.ca/downloads/pdf/codeofjudicialethics. pdf, accessed on 20/9/2015.

[27]Federal Judicial Administration Commission Establishment Proclamation No 24/1996, Article 8 lists the criteria. These are: having 'legal training' or acquiring adequate legal skill through experience, being loyal to the Constitution, being 25 years or older, having good reputation for sense of justice, diligence and conduct and consenting to assume the position.

[28]Ministry of Capacity Building Justice System Reform Program Office, 'Ethiopia: Comprehensive Justice System Reform Program, Baseline Study Report', 162–163 (March 2005).

[29]Directive to Provide for the Selection of Judges for the Federal Judiciary, Article 14 (July 2010).

[30]*Id.*, Articles 17–21.

participation by stakeholders such as bar associations, legal professionals, civil society, law schools, and the citizens at large.[31] The Directive issued in July 2010 provides limited scope for screening. It provides that announcement of vacancies shall be transparent and made in ways that ensure nationwide accessibility to potential candidates.[32] According to the Court Administrator, vacancies are now announced in Addis Zemen, a newspaper with nationwide circulation, and the names of candidates that have been shortlisted is announced on the website of the Federal Supreme Court.[33] Though this is a welcome development even practicing lawyers do not seem to be sure that this is consistently done. Besides, since most appointees are fresh graduates or people with very limited experience the legal community knows very little about them. There is also a culture of apathy. Few people, if any, monitor consistently the website of the Supreme Court and give credible information in big enough numbers. The appointment of judges to the federal judiciary is subject to the approval of the Parliament. This in practice is no more than a formality. It neither guarantees the transparency of the process itself nor ensures the best are selected.[34]

A poorly designed system such as this may allow incompetent, unskilled, unmotivated individuals of doubtful integrity to populate the judiciary. This type of judges cannot defend the independence of the judiciary as an institution. They are unable to protect even their own personal independence. They succumb to the faintest of pressure from any source.

8.3.2   Training, Competence and Work Conditions

Modern legal education was introduced in Ethiopia in 1963 when the Law Faculty was established in the Addis Ababa University College. The Faculty that used to be the only institution providing legal education at degree level for over 30 years graduated an average of 45 students annually till 1998.[35] In 1995, a second law school was established in the Civil Service College.[36] The aim of this new institution was addressing the acute shortage of administrators and other professionals with the necessary legal training.[37] The Law School at the Civil Service Collage of Ethiopia graduated students at the level of degree for the first time in 1997/1998. What

---

[31]Ministry of Capacity Building, *supra* note 28, at 162.

[32]Directive to Provide for Selection of Judges, *supra* note 29, Article 11.

[33]Ato Amare Ashenafi, Administrator of the Federal Courts, Interview held in his office in Addis Ababa on 24 September 2018.

[34]Ministry of Capacity Building, *supra* note 28, pp. 162–163.

[35]www.aau.edu.et/clgs/, accessed on 20 August 2017.

[36]www.ecsu.edu.et/establishment, accessed on 20 August 2017.

[37]Ministry of Capacity Building, *supra* note 28, pp. 121–122.

happened since the year 2000 is a different story.[38] Ethiopia now has over two dozen institutions that have launched degree programs in law.

Generally, legal education is beset by a number of problems ranging from ill prepared teaching staff, poor teaching methods, inadequate facilities, poor human resource management, shortage of funding, unmotivated teaching and administrative staff and quality control issues.[39] The judges that sit in the federal courts of Ethiopia are the product of this educational system.[40] As if this were not a bad enough problem judges are frequently rotated between criminal and civil benches. Even on the civil bench, they hear a variety of cases involving diverse areas of private law. This makes it difficult for judges to build up particular expertise in any area, be that an area of commercial law or otherwise.[41]

The problems in the quality of formal legal education are fully recognized by stakeholders of the justice system. Hence, various initiatives have been attempted. A judicial training centre was, for instance, established in 2003 to upgrade the training of judges. The aim was to give additional training to new graduates that are selected to be judges and upgrade the capacity of those already in the bench.[42] Initially, the courses lasted for 2 years and focused on candidate judges and new judges. That is no longer the case now. Judges are appointed without any training other than a university degree. While on the bench those that had no prior experience as judges in any court, for example state courts, are given short trainings lasting up to 2–3 months only.[43] Unfortunately, neither the curriculum nor the staffing of the Center is well planned and executed.[44] In the past, at least, the training tended to be re-delivery of courses taken in a university setting *albeit* by less competent instructors. In any event, there are judges sitting in the Federal courts today who have not undergone the training provided by the Center. Judges do take part in some other training from time to time. But these are mostly sporadic, and donor driven.[45] In sum, one can conclude no systematic, sustained, well-founded and well-thought-out program aimed at improving the skill and legal knowledge of judges is in place.

Poor working conditions, too, have adverse consequence on the quality of judges that the judiciary can retain. Well-trained, knowledgeable and skilled judges find it extremely difficult to stay in a judiciary that does not provide a clear career path and

---

[38] *Id.*

[39] *Id.* pp. 201–205.

[40] According to 2006 statistics there were 110 judges sitting in the Federal Bench. Almost all had first degree in law, LL.B but only 7 had LL.M degree. Now there are about 400 judges sitting in Federal courts since 120 were appointed in 2018. *See* USAID, Ethiopia: Commercial Law and Institutional Reform and Trade Diagnostic, 69 (January 2007), Available at: http://egateg.usaid. gov/sites/default/files/ethiopia.pdf, accessed on November 28, 2013.

[41] *Id.*

[42] Ministry of Capacity Building, *supra* note 28, p. 200.

[43] Interview with Mr. Amare Ashenafi, *supra* note 33.

[44] Interview with Mezmur Yared, Head of the Judicial Training Center till 2012. Interview conducted on November 21, 2013.

[45] Ministry of Capacity Building, *supra* note 28, p. 200.

decent standard of living. Judges in Ethiopia have very low salary. A first instance court judge used to draw till very recently a monthly salary of about 84 Euros and a housing allowance which generally was way below the rent prevailing in the market while a judge sitting in the Federal Supreme Court used to get a monthly salary of 240 Euros per month, free housing and a car.[46] Salary raises have been given since then. Because of the latest raise now a Federal First Instance Court judge draws a gross salary of Birr 10,700 and a housing allowance of Birr 2500. While a judge sitting in the Federal High Court gets a gross monthly salary of Birr 12,700 and a housing allowance of 2800. A judge sitting in the Highest Court of the country draws a gross monthly salary of Birr 15,000 and a housing allowance of 4600.[47] Talking of the net pay after taxation and other deductibles a judge sitting in the High Court told me that his monthly net pay is 12,000 Birr, inclusive of transportation and housing allowances.[48] That is about 372 Euros at the official exchange rate on 03 December 2018.

Clearly, the salary and other benefits do not meet international standards. In fact, putting enough food on the table used to be very difficult even for a judge with no family responsibility.[49] With the current salary, things have improved slightly. Regarding workplace, judges mostly work in dilapidated buildings.[50] They have neither research assistants, nor easy access to legal materials including laws.[51] Thus, generally new graduates join the judiciary to acquire training, reputation, and connections for future private legal practice. Very few who are really competent remain in the judiciary for longer than a couple of years. Though no recent statistics is available, that the majority of judges, especially from the lower courts, leave the bench after acquiring some experience is a fact that few dispute.[52]

Owing to the foregoing, in part, the competence of judges even in the highest court of the country, the Cassation Bench of the Federal Supreme Court, is doubtful.

---

[46]Hammergren (2012), p. 223. A Supreme Court judge drew a monthly salary of Ethiopian Birr 6000 only about 8 years ago. There had been three raises since this study. Now a Supreme Court judge draws a net income of about 500 Euros per month.

[47]Interview with Ato Amare Ashenafi, *supra* note 33.

[48]Zerai Woldesenbet, Judge, Federal High Court, Short interview held on December 10, 2017 in the compound of the Federal Supreme Court.

[49]A colleague of mine who used to be a judge in the Federal First instance court till 2002 told me that the monthly salary at the time was 835 Birr, less than 90 Euros though it is difficult to establish the exchange rate now after almost two decades. It was not uncommon for a judge to have a banana with a loaf of bread for dinner because even at that time when the cost of living was low, the salary was not enough to buy enough food after paying house rent. Informal talk with Mr Yazacew Belew.

[50]Ministry of Capacity Building, *supra* note 28, at 178.

[51]According to Judge Zerai Woldesenbet, federal judges have access to internet at their office. Generally they are expected to use that for researching any developments in law, such as issuance of new laws. Ato Amare Ashenafi, the Court Administrator, states there are no research assistants at the First Instance and High Court level. At the Federal Supreme Court there is a research department which has about five junior lawyers. Even at the level of the Supreme Court a judges and even a bench has no dedicated research assistant. Interview with Ato Amare Ashenafi, *supra* note 33.

[52]USAID, *supra* note 40, at 69.

An audit of judgments of this Bench, some of which have been discussed in the preceding chapters of this work, is a testament to this. In any event, the perception of those practicing law is that, most judges, especially those sitting in the highest courts of the country are of questionable competence.[53]

Yet another challenge is the number of cases that judges are expected to decide per year. A performance report of the judiciary for the Ethiopian fiscal year ending on July 7, 2018 indicates that there were only 39 judges in the Federal Supreme Court. The report further indicates that a total of 20,521 cases were pending before these judges during the year. Moreover, it states that a total of 17,698 cases were decided by these judges in the same year.[54] This is an extremely large number of cases. These judges sit in a panel of three in ordinary appellate matters and in a panel of five, if they have to review on cassation a final decision of a court. Even if all the benches consisted of three judges, this would mean each bench decided an average of 1361.38 cases in a year. Assuming they worked 7 days a week throughout the year, every bench had to give an average of 3.72 decisions per day to achieve this level of performance. In other words, on average reviewing a file, hearing the arguments of the parties, research and consultation among the judges, and write up of an average decision took about two hours only. This is a herculean task.

Perhaps, owing to the foregoing, many lawyers allege that judges do not work on a file together even when reviewing the file on cassation for basic error of law. They allege that each judge works on a file by himself, at best briefing the other judges on the same bench, and seeking their opinion from time to time. He/she writes up the decision and all the judge on the Bench sign the decision. The level of annual performance reported by the Supreme Court can be achieved, it seems, only under this kind of arrangement. The back-breaking workload and this kind of modus operandi seriously affect the quality of judgments even at the level of the highest court in the land.

Though an in-depth study of the judiciary is beyond the scope of this work, a questionnaire was disseminated to professionals to get the feel of the institutional context for arbitration in Ethiopia. One of the questions addressed to practitioners and academics familiar with arbitration and the judiciary was aimed at soliciting their opinion regarding the level of understanding that judges have about commercial arbitration. The question was 'whether or not judges have, in your opinion, a sufficient understanding of the rules and principles governing international

---

[53]Interviews conducted with Ato Teshome Gebremariam, a leading practitioner, especially in the area of commercial law. Interview conducted on 12 June 2013 in his office. Filipos Aynalem, formerly Federal High Court Judge, currently a practicing lawyer and part-time teaching staff at Addis Ababa University Law School, Interview conducted on November 21, 2013, in Addis Ababa University, *Sidist Killo* Campus.

[54]Performance Report of the Federal Judiciary for the Ethiopian Fiscal Year Ending on 7 July 2018 made available to the Author by Ato Amare Ashenafi, Court administrator, *supra* note 40.

commercial arbitration'. All the five practitioners that responded to the question answered no.[55]

8.3.3   Accountability

That judges should be independent does not imply that they should be unaccountable to the society in which they serve. If an elaborate mechanism for ensuring accountability without undermining independence is not put in place the judiciary is likely to lose the public's confidence and ultimately lose its independence.[56] Ensuring transparency such as by creating 'channels of non-controlling communication' between judges, professional associations, media, NGOs and the public is one of the mechanisms for attaining accountability.[57] In Ethiopia such informal communication that contributes to the attainment of accountability of judges does not exist. For example, there is no association of judges in which judges informally communicate. Periodic publication of judgments with criticism by academics or other legal professionals is nearly non-existent.[58] One does not see the media reporting court cases. In the rare cases when this is done, it is journalists without the necessary legal background that report on court proceedings. Hence, the public is unable to properly understand what the issues were let alone form opinion on the performance of the judges involved.[59]

Another mechanism for ensuring accountability is carrying out periodic judicial performance evaluation.[60] The Federal Supreme Court officially launched in 2015 a judicial performance evaluation program that shifts the emphasis from a productivity-focussed approach to a multi-dimensional approach gauging performance by mixed methods.[61] The new method uses three components for periodic data collection. Balanced scorecard, the first component, uses indicators drawn from

---

[55]Four of the five who answered this question have intimate knowledge about the judiciary and have also published articles on commercial arbitration in Ethiopia. Those who answered are: Professor Tilahun Teshome, formerly a Supreme Court judge, who practices arbitration; Yazachew Belew, formerly a judge in the Supreme Court of Oromia National Regional State who also practices and teaches arbitration; Tewodros Meheret, formerly Head of Legal Services of Abyssinia Bank, Currently, a practicing lawyer who also taught arbitration; Hailegabriel G. Feyissa and Muradu Abdo, both academics with significant knowledge of the practice of arbitration and the judiciary in Ethiopia.

[56]Ministry of Capacity Building, *supra* note 28, p. 163.

[57]*Id.*

[58]A handful of law journals are published by universities but they seldom contain more than two or three case comments. The decisions of the Cassation Bench of the Federal Supreme Court are published with regularity but without any comments.

[59]Ministry of Capacity Building, *supra* note 28, pp. 161–164.

[60]Perker S, *Judicial Performance Evaluation in Ethiopia: Local Reforms Meet Global Challenges,* in Indicators in Development, Safety and Justice, 4. Available at: http://www.hks.harvard.edu/criminaljustice/indicators-of-safety-and-justice, accessed on 19 August 2017.

[61]*Id.* p. 1.

the case management system of the Federal Supreme Court based on its strategic plan.[62] The second component is customer satisfaction. It gauges performance based on data generated by a survey of lay people and legal professionals that participated in legal proceedings before a judge.[63] A court room observation by designated officials takes place to check the overall reliability of this component though its results are not used to measure the performance of individual judges.[64] The third component of the performance evaluation gives the individual judge opportunity to provide benchmarks for his evaluation. Particularly, every judge prepares his own judicial performance plan which is taken into account when evaluating her/him.[65] The customer satisfaction evaluation, the second component above, take place twice a year and accounts for 15% of the individual judge's performance evaluation.[66] The balance of the evaluation is comprised of the judge's self-evaluation and evaluation by peer judges and the president of the court.[67]

Challenges like the need to balance performance evaluation with judicial independence and autonomy were at least initially causes for concern to judges. Outstanding challenges include limited technical, infrastructural and human resource especially to conduct court room observation.[68] The introduction of the multidimensional system of evaluation of judges is a step in the right direction. Unfortunately, 3 years after its introduction the results of this evaluation have not been used to incentivise or demote any judge according to the administrator of the federal courts. To date, they are simply filed.[69]

Yet another mechanism for ensuring accountability is having an appropriate entity that holds judges accountable for breach of discipline. A Judicial Administration Council has been established to this end. It has nine members. Its membership consist of three members of the House of People's Representatives (parliament), the president and vice president of the Federal Supreme Court, the presidents of the Federal High Court, and Federal First Instance Court and two most senior judges from the former two courts.[70] It has power to decide on disciplinary complaints against judges and recommend their dismissal to the House of the People's Representatives as envisaged by the Constitution. Pending investigation and final decision it can suspend judges whose integrity and impartiality is in question.[71] Though this body has all the powers necessary to ensure integrity it has not yet attained reputation

---

[62]*Id.*, p. 5.

[63]*Id.*

[64]*Id.*

[65]*Id.*

[66]*Id.* p. 7.

[67]*Id.*

[68]*Id.*, pp. 7–8.

[69]Interview with Ato Amare Ashenafi, *supra* note 33.

[70]Federal Judicial Administration Commission Proclamation No. 24/96, Article 4.

[71]*Id.* Art 5(5), 9(4, 5 &6). *See also* Constitution of Federal Democratic Republic of Ethiopia, Proclamation No. 1/1995, Federal *Negarit Gazeta*, 1st Year, Mo. 1, Article 79(4).

for living to the standard expected from it. Particularly, lack of transparency, predictability and professionalism are raised as the main concerns creating the appearance of politicization and favouritism in the workings of the Council.[72] Participation in proceedings before the Commission by judges whose cases is being investigated is not clearly provided for hence raising concern by judges.[73]

8.3.4   Impartiality, Integrity and Corruption

8.3.4.1   Impartiality and Integrity

Litigants before a state justice forum, especially a court, expect a fair dispute resolution. This is possible only if the judges are impartial and act with integrity.[74] Impartiality is a moral value which is a reflection of the judge's inner self. In the context of the judiciary, it pertains to the judge analysing the facts of the case at hand in view of the applicable law in a balanced manner 'without prejudice and predilection' and without favouring the interest of any of the parties before him.[75] The European Court of Human Rights has observed that there are two dimensions to impartiality. First, the court must be 'subjectively' impartial. That is, no judge seating on the bench should hold any personal prejudice or bias. In the absence of proof to the contrary a judge is deemed to be subjectively impartial. Second, the court must also be objectively impartial. Going beyond the judges' actual personal conduct, effort should be exerted to avoid any ascertainable facts that raise legitimate appearance of partiality. In other words, effort should be made to inspire confidence in the public including in the litigants before the court.[76]

Just like impartiality, integrity is an inner characteristic. It manifests itself when a person acts in compliance with certain principles and values without compromising them. In the context of the judiciary, a judge is said to act with integrity when he discharges his judicial duties industriously, correctly, honestly and meeting statutory requirements. Where a judge sells justice in return for favour or payment, impartiality and integrity are lost. Corruption erodes these values.[77] We look at this particular stain on integrity below.

---

[72]Legal Vice Presidency, World Bank, Ethiopia: Legal and Judicial Sector Assessment 18 (2004).
[73]Id.
[74]Danilet (2009), p. 1.
[75]Id., pp. 1–2.
[76]UN Commentary on Bangalore Principles, *supra* note 20, p. 58.
[77]Danilet (2009), p. 2.

8.3.4.2 Corruption and Perception of Corruption

In spite of the mechanisms for ensuring accountability discussed above, corruption is identified as a serious problem in the Ethiopian judiciary. That said, there appears to be a significant gap in views regarding the extent of this problem. Particularly, some studies find a considerable gap between public perception of corruption and the reality. Other studies suggest the problem is more real than apparent. To get a general feel of the situation, we look at the findings of studies conducted by Transparency International, the World Bank and the Ethiopian Government in this particular order.

The corruption perception index released by Transparency International in July 2013 ranks Ethiopia 111 out of 177 countries, scoring 33/100, in the year 2013.[78] The survey of 1000 respondents, conducted by Transparency International, reveals that the judiciary ranks third in corruption in the perception of Ethiopians following the police and health services. The survey, however, discloses that there was a significant improvement in the perception of the Ethiopian judiciary. The perception of corruption of the judiciary had decreased by about 20% compared to the previous survey.[79] The ranking of the country has not improved much since then. The 2016 rank of Ethiopia is 108th out of 176 countries surveyed by Transparency International. Ethiopia scores 34%, and hence is considered a country with serious corruption problem.[80] A World Bank Study[81] conducted upon the request of the Ethiopian Government finds corruption in the justice sector in general, and in the judiciary in particular, is much lower in reality compared to the perception of the public. It concludes that while corruption does exist in the Ethiopian judiciary, it is less rampant as compared to its prevalence in other countries in the region and outside the region where informants could state the 'price' for a 'judgment' at different levels of the judiciary.[82] Even in civil disputes, which are the most susceptible to

---

[78]Transparency International, Ethiopia: Corruption Perception Index, available at: http://cpi.transparency.org/cpi2013/results, accessed on December 4, 2015.

[79]Capital, English Weekly, July 17, 2013, available at: http://www.capitalethiopia.com/index, accessed on December 4, 2015.

[80]www.ey.com/Publication/vwLUAssets/EY-Transparency-International-Corruption-Perception-Index-2016, accessed on 21 August 2017.

[81]Hammergren (2012), p. 224. The study was focused on the Federal justice sector institutions. Structured questionnaires, interviews and two focus group discussions were conducted. Interestingly, members of the public who have no particular exposure to the sector did not participate. The participants of the study were 60 individuals from the Police, Office of Public Prosecutor, judges, private attorneys, NGOs, Donors and 'others'. Equal number of participants from each of the above categories was drawn for the purpose of this study. Clearly, these are the kind of people with the most intimate knowledge as regards the level and existence of corruption in the judiciary. So, they can give more reliable information than any other group about the type and prevalence of corruption in the judiciary. This is the positive side of the sample. The downside of this methodology, in my opinion is that the majority of the participants of the study are people who, by reason of their affiliation to the institutions that are being assessed, have motive to downplay the incidence and degree of corruption.

[82]Id.

corruption, the World Bank Study finds corruption is largely a function of individual susceptibility to monetary inducement, friendship and kinship. Within this category, it identifies two types of corruption as the more prevalent. These are[83] spontaneous and often small bribes to judges to alter decisions and the parties' reliance on attorneys with special relationship with judges. A third scenario that was certainly visible though not stressed by informants, according to the study, is large suits involving foreign clients that instruct their attorney to 'make the judge happy.'[84]

Overall the World Bank Study finds that there is no evidence of an internal corruption network within the judiciary. Particularly, there is no indication that monetarily induced corruption was a top-down controlled phenomenon.[85] Further, the study finds that the phenomenon of judges buying their position and engaging in corruption to recoup their investment is totally absent unlike in some other comparator countries.[86] In sum, the study finds that the perception of corruption is much higher than its actual existence, perhaps because of the general lack of transparency on the side of the government and citizens forming perceptions without first-hand experience such as on the basis of anecdotal evidence or few highly publicized cases.[87]

A study conducted by the Policy Studies and Research Center and the Ministry of Civil Service, in 2015, just 3 years after the publication of the foregoing World Bank report, paints a different picture. It finds that corruption is actually widespread and the top leadership plays a role in that. The study touches upon all the sectors that impact on good governance, focusing on top leadership. It does not generally single out the federal judiciary, the institution of particular relevance to international arbitration. Yet, it sheds light on the challenges that the justice sector, including the judiciary, face. Among other things, the findings of the study are as follows.

(a) Acquaintance, or even better friendship, with judges confers a distinct advantage on lawyers seeking clients. Hence, in hiring attorneys for legal representation, those who joined legal practice recently after resigning from the bench are much sought after;[88]
(b) Appointment to positions of leadership in the justice sector is not based on competence and knowledge of law in many parts of the country, including in Addis Ababa;[89]

---

[83] Id.

[84] Id.

[85] Id., p. 225.

[86] Id., pp. 225–226.

[87] Id., p. 226.

[88] Federal Democratic Republic of Ethiopia Policy Studies and Research Center and the Ministry of Civil Service, Challenges Faced by the Leadership in Ensuring Good Governance: Causes and Ideas for Solution, p. 112 (Unpublished document authored in Amharic, available on file with the author) (August 2015).

[89] Id., p. 114.

(c) Intervention in the administration of justice by those in leadership position exists[90] and

(d) Nepotism, rent seeking behaviour, lack of professional independence, and lack of accountability are common in the justice sector including in Addis Ababa.[91]

The foregoing indicates that corruption is a systemic problem in the justice sector, including in the judiciary. This impacts adversely the success of arbitration in Ethiopia.

8.4 Support and Supervision of Arbitration: Perceptions and Anecdotal Evidence

Attempt was made in the preceding sections to throw light on the state of the judiciary that plays a critical role in the success of arbitration. In this section, we will try to bring the discussion even closer to arbitration and assess the extent of support the Federal Courts of Ethiopia extend to arbitration, in reality, and their understanding of arbitration law. To assess the reality in this regard, arbitration practitioners, former judges and practicing lawyers, deemed most familiar[92] with the pertinent issues, were approached. Besides, anecdotal evidence resulting from two cases that passed through all the strata in the court hierarchy will be used. Obviously, one cannot reach a definitive conclusion about a court system based on their handling of two cases. But these cases, taken together with the number of other cases discussed in the preceding chapters, and the views of experts can give a picture of the state of the judiciary and the extent of support courts give to arbitration. So, below we will first discuss the perception of arbitration practitioners and then look at the two cases.

8.4.1 Judicial Support to Arbitration: Views of Practitioners

To start with the perception of arbitration practitioners, we find that their views are mixed and vary significantly from issue to issue. One of the issues their views were sought on was whether the federal courts, which have jurisdiction regarding international arbitration, extend a helping hand to arbitration. In their view, the courts are

---

[90]*Id*

[91]*Id.*, pp. 129–130.

[92]Respondents were Ato Teshome Gebremariam, Professor Tilahun Teshome, both the leading arbitration practitioners in Ethiopia, Yohannes Woldegabriel, Director of the only Arbitration Institute in the Country, Yazachew Belew, former judge, Hailegabriel Feyissa, who has published an article on the 'Role of Courts in Arbitration', two practitioners with moderate experience in arbitration, Dr. Muradu Abdo and Tewodros Meheret.

inconsistent in extending support to the conduct of arbitration. For instance, asked whether or not courts 'generally' compel the parties to an arbitration agreement to arbitrate,[93] four out of the six that responded to this question answered yes.[94] Similarly, four out of the five respondents said courts 'generally' lend the necessary support in the appointment of arbitrators. Asked about support to an ongoing arbitration, two out of the five respondents answered courts 'generally' give the necessary support to an ongoing arbitration, such as by compelling witnesses to testify and helping with provisional measures, such as the attachment of property when necessary.

Other questions addressed to the respondents[95] were aimed at soliciting their opinion on whether or not the courts 'generally refrain from unduly interfering' in an ongoing arbitration and whether or not they 'generally uphold awards' rendered by arbitrators. Three out of the six respondents answered that courts generally do not unduly interfere in arbitration. As regards awards, five out of the six respondents answered that courts generally do uphold awards. So, it does seem that overall experts believe awards are generally upheld by courts, but opinion is divided as regards unwarranted interference by courts in an ongoing arbitration.

Unanimity of opinion does exist regarding some other issues of relevance though. Asked whether or not judges in the federal judiciary have 'a sufficient understanding of the rules and principles governing international commercial arbitration', all seven respondents[96] answered in the negative. Similarly, all seven experts agreed that there is 'overall no sufficient institutional support' for international commercial arbitration to take place in Ethiopia. This appears to be in line with the 2017 Doing Business Report of the World Bank, which gives Ethiopia 5/18 for quality of judicial process.[97]

Against this backdrop, in the sub-section below, we will look at two cases that provide anecdotal evidence regarding the level of support courts extend to arbitration and their understanding of some of the issues involved.

---

[93]Hailegabriel Feyissa agrees that courts generally compel parties to arbitration agreements to arbitrate. But he says there is a practice that can effectively defeat the agreement to arbitrate. Particularly, when a party applies to court to disqualify an arbitrator Ethiopian courts have suspended the arbitration pending decision by court on this. This may indirectly result in the non-enforcement of the agreement to arbitrate. See Hailegabriel (2010), pp. 320–321.

[94]Yohannes Woldegabriel, the Director of the secretariat of an Addis Ababa Chamber of Commerce and Sectoral Association (AACCSA) arbitration institute (AI).

[95]The five respondents that answered these two questions are Professor Tilahun Teshome, Ato Yazachew Belew, Hailegabriel G. Feyissa, Tewodros Meheret, Muradu Abdo, and Zimita Beyene, Senior Legal Expert at the Addis Ababa Chamber of Commerce and Sectoral Association (AACCSA) Arbitration Institute (AI).

[96]Professor Tilahun Teshome, Hailegabriel G. Feyissa, Yohannes Woldegabriel, Tewodros Meheret, Zimita Beyene, Yazachew Belew and Muradu Abdo.

[97]World Bank 2017, Doing Business 2017: Equal Opportunity for All, p. 206, available at: www.doingbusiness.org/reports/global-reports/doing-business-2017, accessed on 24 August 2017.

8.4.2 Judicial Support for Arbitration: Court Cases Indicating Problems

Arbitration may require judicial support at various stages. The cases below focus on the establishment of a tribunal and whether courts consider issues that should be left to an arbitral tribunal.

8.4.2.1 Gebru Kore v. Amedeo Federeci

In *Gebru Kore v. Amedeo Federeci*,[98] the facts of the case were as follows. A contract between the parties had an arbitration clause. Mr. Amedeo Federeci sought assistance from the Federal First Instance Court in the formation of an arbitral tribunal. Particularly, he prayed the Court to appoint the presiding arbitrator and order the commencement of arbitration. The Court appointed for them the presiding arbitrator while the parties appointed one arbitrator each. So, the tribunal was successfully constituted with the help of the Court.[99]

The tribunal deemed it appropriate to determine the fee of arbitrators at the very outset, though there is no legal requirement to this effect. Hence, it instructed the parties to submit their pleadings. The parties were told clearly that the aim was to weigh the intricacy of the case with a view to determining the appropriate fee for the arbitrators, though the pleadings would eventually be used in settling the dispute. The parties did comply. The arbitrators then determined that a grand total of Birr 60,000 (roughly 2400 Euros at the exchange rate prevailing in 2016) would be a fair fee.[100] So, the total expected from each party, at the exchange rate in 2016 was about 1200 Euros. The arbitrators instructed the parties to deposit half the amount (about 600 Euros each) in advance. The balance was to be paid at the end of the arbitration proceeding. But the lawyer representing Mr. Amedeo Federeci did not show up before the tribunal on the date fixed for making the required deposit. Hence, the arbitrators closed the file.

Mr. Amedeo Federeci then applied to the Federal First Instance Court seeking the constitution of a different arbitration panel that would be willing to work for a lesser fee. The Federal First Instance Court rejected the petition. It relied on Art 317(1), 318(5) and 319(1) of the Civil Procedure Code. Particularly, Article 318(5) reads '[w]here the fee to be paid to the arbitrator has not been fixed; a reasonable fee shall be fixed by the arbitrator in his award.' The court reasoned the decision of arbitrators fixing the fee at the outset of the proceeding is to be regarded as an interlocutory

---

[98]*Gebru Kore v. Amedeo Federeci*, Federal Supreme Court Cassation Bench, Cassation Case No. 52942, Decided on 28 October 2010, Published in Cassation Court Decisions, Vol. 12 (2011).

[99]*Id.*

[100]A decade ago when the tribunal fixed the fee the exchange rate of the Birr to Euro was smaller. Though we cannot with certainty establish the amount, the total required from the two sides was slightly less than 5000 Euros, at the exchange rate prevailing at the time.

matter. It cannot be appealed from till the arbitrators finally give an award. According to the First Instance Court, once the award is given then an appeal may lie from the arbitral fee pursuant to Art 350–357 of the Civil Procedure Code. These are provisions that deal with appeal from award and setting aside of awards discussed at length in Chap. 6, Sects. 6.3.1 and 6.3.2.[101] In short, the First Instance Court held it could not order the establishment of a new panel of arbitrators on this ground, though parties may appeal to the court on the issue of arbitral fee once an award is given.

Mr. Amedeo Federeci appealed from this ruling of the First Instance Court to the Federal High Court. The High Court reversed the decision of the First Instance Court and instructed the latter to assist the parties in the formation of a different panel of arbitrators. Mr. Gebru Kore appealed this time around. But the Federal Supreme Court confirmed the decision of the High Court, whereupon Mr. Gebru Kore sought review on cassation for basic error of law.[102]

The Cassation Bench of the Federal Supreme Court framed the issue as, 'what is the course of action open to a party to arbitration that finds the service fee fixed by arbitrators *unacceptable*'?[103] It then ruled a different panel should be formed since it cannot be said the formation of a different panel will affect substantively the rights of the party who found the arbitral fee acceptable.[104] The Cassation Bench reasoned:[105]

> . . . just because a party has concluded an agreement to arbitrate it cannot be concluded that he should be compelled to continue arbitration despite being unhappy with the procedure being followed by the tribunal. Coming specifically to the case at hand, though one cannot fully conclude the decision of the tribunal fixing the fee is not interlocutory, the establishment of a new panel of arbitrators does not adversely affect the petitioner's [Mr. Gebru Kore's] substantive rights. Because the decision requiring the establishment of a new panel does not impact on the substantive outcome of the case we do not think that decision [the Supreme Court's decision instructing constitution of a new panel of arbitrators] involves a fundamental error of law. So, we confirm the decision pursuant to Article 348(1). (Translation mine)

This case shows several things about the extent and quality of support courts extend to arbitration. It also sheds some light on the reasoning and quality of decisions even by the highest court of the land. To start with the most obvious problem, the courts that found in favour of the establishment of a new panel of

---

[101]Civil Procedure Code of Ethiopia, Decree No. 52/1965, Article 351 exhaustively lists down the grounds for appeal while Article 356 does the same regarding the grounds on which application to set aside an award may be made. The ground which comes closest to covering the situation in this case is Article 351(a). It provides appeal is possible, if 'the award is inconsistent, uncertain or ambiguous or is on its face wrong in matter of law or fact.' We submit this provision does not cover the case at hand because the fee the tribunal fixed, or proposed was clear. It was not on its face wring on a matter of law or fact. We need not really dwell on this subject more as we have discussed these provisions at length in Chap. 7, Sects. 7.3 and 7.4 when discussing appeal and setting aside.

[102]*Gebru Kore v. Amedeo Federeci*, Cassation File No. 52942 (28 Oct. 2010).

[103]*Id.*

[104]*Id.*

[105]*Id.*

arbitrators did not themselves assist with the formation of the tribunal though they could. Instead, they kept on instructing the First Instance Court, the only court that found against this course of action, to help constitute a new tribunal. The High Court did that when it could simply assist in forming the new arbitral tribunal. The Supreme Court similarly did that. And the Cassation Bench just confirmed the decision of the Supreme Court instead of helping constitute the arbitral tribunal. The effect is that years were wasted trying to establish a new arbitral tribunal, and as the saying goes, justice delayed is justice denied. That the three appellate courts did not assist in the constitution of a new arbitral tribunal, though they could lawfully do that, is not a sign of effective support to arbitration.

Coming to the merit of the decisions of the courts, they are equally not beyond reproach. According to Article 318(5) of the Civil Procedure Code, where the fee to be paid to arbitrators has not been fixed, the arbitrators shall 'in the award fix a reasonable fee'. In this particular case, the arbitrators chose to fix the fee right at the outset of the case, though they could delay this till the time of award. They required the parties to submit their memorials only with a view to help them make decision on the fee. No substantive proceedings were, thus, started other than the submission of the memorials which would have also been used later in the process. Noteworthy is the fact that the party that requested the constitution of a different tribunal did not allege the fee fixed by the tribunal was *unreasonable*. Nor did he allege that he was unable pay the amount. In other words, the issue was neither the inability of the party to pay nor unreasonableness of the fee fixed by the tribunal. All that party wanted was a cheaper tribunal. So, effectively, to the High Court, the Supreme Court and the Cassation Bench of the Federal Supreme Court a party's interest in shopping for a cheaper panel of arbitrators is a good enough reason for a party to pull out from an arbitration and spend years litigating the matter at various levels of the judiciary, thus derailing the contractually agreed arbitration. The decision, which has the power of precedent, gives a free hand to a party that wants to derail arbitration. A service fee fixed by an arbitral tribunal can always be found subjectively unacceptable. Besides, even when a party does know the fee is fair in his heart of hearts, he can always declare it unacceptable.

Incidentally, the grand total expected from the party that was seeking a cheaper panel was approximately about 2000 Euros, in two instalments, at the exchange rate that prevailed at the time of the litigation. The parties were represented by lawyers.[106] So, one is left wondering whether securing reduction in the service fee of the arbitral tribunal was the real motivation behind hiring a lawyer and litigating the matter at different levels of the court system. Would any reduction in service fee be worth the cost of litigation and the delay in the settlement of the main dispute? It

---

[106]One cannot rule out the possibility that the lawyers were working for a fixed fee. In which event, the appeals in the court system would not necessarily entail extra cost to the party. But even then, it would be difficult to justify, the waste of time and emotional cost of the litigation, in light of the relatively small sum of reduction in service fee that could possibly be secured. Besides, is cheap 'justice', something to pursue this much?

appears the aim was to derail the arbitration for some reason. Yet, the courts did not seem to consider this possibility.

The reasoning of the Cassation Bench, the highest court in the country, gives cause for concern. It says, among other things, ' . . . just because a party has concluded an agreement to arbitrate it *cannot be* concluded that he should be *compelled to continue arbitration despite being unhappy regarding the procedure being followed* by the tribunal.' This statement appears unwarranted, and even worse random. The Cassation Bench did not have to make that remark given no procedural issues were raised, before the arbitral tribunal. The arbitral tribunal did not go beyond 'making an offer', if that may be said in the context of arbitration, regarding the fee it is willing to accept. The fee was 'rejected' by a party. So, the tribunal closed the file. No proceedings relating to the dispute itself took place other than exchange of memorials. The reasoning also raises another issue. Particularly, even assuming some procedural issues were involved, can a party pull back from arbitration because he is 'unhappy regarding the procedure followed' by the tribunal? This is a worrying statement, to say the least.

The reasoning of the First Instance Court that ruled in favour of a speedy arbitration too raises some issues. It treated the request for the constitution of a cheaper tribunal as an interlocutory appeal. It is doubtful that the decision of the arbitral tribunal fixing its fee is really an 'interlocutory' matter. According to the Civil Procedure Code, parties may appeal against 'any *final* judgment of a civil court.'[107] The Code gives an illustrative list of 'interlocutory' matters from which appeal is not possible until the *final* judgment is given. These include orders on adjournment, preliminary objections, admissibility or inadmissibility of evidence and permission to sue as pauper (not denial of the request to sue as a pauper).[108] A person against whom the interlocutory order goes can still prevail in the same court on the substance of the dispute. Hence, allowing appeal on these matters would be wasteful.[109] Unlike in the foregoing examples, future orders and decision of the arbitral tribunal cannot have the effect of rendering the tribunal's determination on its fee redundant. So, the characterization of the remedy sought as 'interlocutory' is disputable to say the least. We cannot, however, dwell on this further without digressing too much from the main subject.

The First Instance Court's holding that the party who is aggrieved by the arbitral fee fixed by the tribunal has a chance to challenge that on appeal once an award is given too seems untenable. Article 351 of the Procedure Code exhaustively lists permissible grounds for appeal from an arbitral award. Nothing on the list covers dissatisfaction with the service fee fixed by an arbitral tribunal. The ground for appeal that comes the closest to it is the one that reads 'when the award is on its face wrong in a matter of law or fact'. These words do not capture the case at hand. The arbitral fee determined by the tribunal was not in violation of any law. There is no

---

[107]Civil Procedure Code of Ethiopia Decree No. 52/1965, Article 320(1).

[108]*Id.*, Article 320(3).

[109] Sedler (1968), p. 221.

law dealing with the matter. The party that found the fee 'unacceptable' did not allege any breach of law. Besides, the determination of service fee by a tribunal cannot possibly be wrong in a matter of 'fact'. The grounds for appeal from arbitral award have been discussed at length in Chap. 6, Sects. 6.3.1 and 6.3.2. Suffice it to say, therefore, that even the court that was pro-arbitration in its approach follows legal reasoning that is questionable.

8.4.2.2 Solomon Negash v. Bahir Dar University

Solomon Negash v. Bahir Dar University[110] is yet another case demonstrating inadequate judicial support in the constitution of an arbitral tribunal. The parties had signed a consultancy agreement. The agreement contained an arbitration clause. Disagreement arose between the parties as regards the implementation of the contract. Hence, Dr Solomon Negash petitioned the West Gojam Zonal High Court to compel Bahir Dar University to appoint an arbitrator per the arbitration clause. The High Court did not call upon the University and hear what it had to say regarding the matter. It rather dismissed the petition alleging the petitioner had 'no cause of action'. The petitioner, thus, appealed to the Supreme Court of the Amhara Regional State which confirmed the decision of the Zonal High Court.[111] Dr. Solomon Negash, therefore, sought review on cassation by the Cassation Bench of the Federal Supreme Court. Until this point in time Bahir Dar University had not even been summoned. So, the Cassation Bench ordered it to respond to the petition, whereupon the University raised the issue of arbitrability alleging the contract was an administrative contract and hence inarbitrable. The University did not contest the existence of the arbitration clause.[112]

The Cassation Bench framed the issue in dispute as 'is the dismissal of the petition on the ground of absence of cause of action appropriate?'[113] It held the courts of the Regional State erred. It found the petitioner had cause of action. The Cassation Bench reasoned when Article 33(2) of the Civil Procedure Code says 'no person may be a plaintiff unless he has vested interest in the subject matter of the suit', it should be understood as requiring the plaintiff to show that he has interest or right based either in contract or law. In this case, the petitioner had shown that the right he was trying to vindicate is based on a contract. It cannot, therefore, be said that the allegation he made in the suit shows no cause of action. The Cassation Bench then quashed the decisions of the courts of the Regional State and instructed the Zonal High Court to 'hear what the parties may have to say about the basis of the suit and reach an appropriate decision.'

---

[110]*Solomon Negash v. Bahir Dar University*, Federal Supreme Court Cassation Bench, Case No. 56368 (10 November 2010).

[111]*Id.*

[112]*Id.*

[113]*Id.*

The handling of this case demonstrates the party seeking the constitution of the arbitral tribunal did not get the necessary support. Firstly, the Zonal High Court raised the issue of cause of action despite an uncontested arbitration clause in the contract. A court will find a statement of claim does not state a cause of action if, 'the allegations [made by the plaintiff], even if true, do not entitle the plaintiff to relief under the law.'[114] That means that the determination of whether a claim states a cause of action entails inter-relating the alleged facts with the law, or a contract, if the relief sought is based on a contract. Only then can one make a determination as to whether an allegation made by a party entitles him to a relief. A court requested to assist with the constitution of an arbitral tribunal should not go beyond making determination as to whether there is an agreement to arbitrate. That the contract contained an arbitration clause was not contested in this case. Hence, the High Court had no jurisdiction to evaluate the substantive merit of the claim of the party that sought support from it, in the constitution of an arbitral tribunal. Whether the claim stated a cause of action should have been left to the arbitral tribunal.

Second, none of the appellate courts considered the fact that the High Court inquired into whether the claim stated a cause of action as overstepping its jurisdictional boundary given the uncontested existence of an arbitration clause. The Regional Supreme Court simply confirmed the decision of the High Court. Even the Cassation Bench of the Federal Supreme Court did not find the fact that the regional courts considered the question of cause of action objectionable. It rather differed from them in its finding that the claim did, in fact, state a cause of action.

Third, the Cassation Bench of the Federal Supreme Court did not assist by helping form an arbitration tribunal. Nor did it determine that a tribunal should not be formed, such as by ruling on the arbitrability issue Bahir Dar University raised for the first time before the Cassation Bench. Instead, it referred the case back to the Regional High Court with a vague instruction. It ordered the High Court to make sure the University gets the pleading of Dr. Solomon Negash, 'hear what the parties may have to say about the basis of the claim and reach an appropriate decision.' So, after spending over a year seeking assistance, with the constitution of an arbitral tribunal, from regional courts and the highest court in the country, Dr. Solomon found himself back in square one. This kind of 'assistance' will not help international commercial arbitration thrive in Ethiopia.

---

[114]Sedler (1968), p. 141.

8.5 Arbitration Institutions

The Addis Ababa Chamber of Commerce and Sectoral Association (AACCSA) Arbitration Institute (AI) is the first ever and the only arbitration institute[115] established in accordance with the law[116] to facilitate the conduct of commercial arbitration in Ethiopia. It was established on 26 January 2002 with the objectives of facilitating the resolution of commercial disputes by arbitration pursuant to its rules of arbitration; to act as a body appointing arbitrators; to see to it that arbitrations conducted under its auspices follow the rules of arbitration of the institute and to generally promote the settlement of disputes by alternative dispute resolution mechanisms.[117]

The AACCSA Board of Directors has adopted rules that may be applied to both institutional and ad hoc arbitration. The rules that have been adopted by the Board so far are:[118]

(a) The Arbitration Institute Procedural Rules (16 June 2009),
(b) The Revised Arbitration Rules (25 November 2008);
(c) Adjudication Rules (14 September 2007) and
(d) Code of Ethics for Arbitrators/Adjudicators/Conciliators and Mediators (14 September 2007).

Cases that are arbitrated under the auspices of the Institute are increasing in number every year. In 2012 the number was about 40 cases. Thanks to this development the AACCSA Arbitration Institute (AI) is nearing the achievement of its goal of covering its expenses from service fee collected from disputants using its service.[119]

Overall the rules of the AACCSA Arbitration Institute (AI) provide parties to arbitration wide latitude in the selection of arbitrators, delimiting the scope of arbitration. Its rules of procedure are similar to those of other internationally renowned arbitration institutions.[120]

---

[115] Addis Ababa Chamber of Commerce and Sectoral Association website, available at: http://addischamber.com/arbitration/arbitration_detail.php?id=4, accessed on November 20, 2015.

[116] The Chamber of Commerce Sectoral Associations Proclamation No. 341/2003. A second arbitration institute, The Ethiopian Arbitration and Conciliation Center run by an NGO had to be closed after 6 years of existence on the ground. It could not continue because it was told that it is unlawful for an NGO to host arbitration institution.

[117] Id.

[118] Id.

[119] Interviews with Yohannes Woldegabriel, Director of the Secretariat of the Arbitration Institute and Zimita Beyene, Senior Legal Expert at the Secretariat of the Arbitration Institute, Interview was conducted on 28 June, 2013, at the Office of the Secretariat of the Arbitration Institute.

[120] USAID, Ethiopia: Commercial Law and Institutional Reform and Trade Diagnostic 70 (2007).

The main challenges of the Institute are finding highly qualified arbitrators in sufficient number and the general lack of awareness among Ethiopian businesses about the benefits of settlement of disputes by arbitration.[121]

8.6   Conclusions

This chapter reviewed the institutional setting for international commercial arbitration in Ethiopia. It noted that the success of arbitration is a function of the quality of institutional support it gets. Particularly, the judiciary and arbitration institutions play distinctly important role in arbitration. In Ethiopia, it is the federal courts that have jurisdiction to support and supervise international arbitration and enforce foreign arbitral awards. Hence, international arbitration depends for its success on the quality of assistance it gets from them.

Unfortunately, federal courts in Ethiopia today do not play their role in arbitration to an internationally acceptable standard. It does seem that their inability in this regard is the result of lack of adequate knowledge of the rules and principles that govern international commercial arbitration, deplorable working conditions, and the absence of mechanisms of accountability, especially when it comes to quality of judgments, and corruption to some extent.

Coming to arbitration institutions, there is only one arbitration institution established some 16 years ago. It is functioning more or less well. That being said, it does face challenges because of the overall constraining environment in which it operates.

References

'Canons of Judicial Ethics', Speech by Chief Justice Y.K Sabharwal, MC Setalvad Memorial Lecture Series. http://tnsja.tn.nic.in/article/Cannons%20of%20Jud%20Ethics.pdf. Accessed 20 Sept 2015

Addis Ababa Chamber of Commerce and Sectoral Association. http://addischamber.com/arbitration/arbitration_detail.php?id=4. Accessed 20 Nov 2015

Capital, English Weekly, July 17, 2013. http://www.capitalethiopia.com/index. Accessed 4 Dec 2015

Danilet C (2009) Corruption and ant-corruption in the justice system. Editura C.H. Beck, Bucharest

Hailegabriel GF (2010) The role of Ethiopian courts in commercial arbitration. Mizan Law Rev 4(2)

Hammergren LA (2012) Justice sector corruption in Ethiopia. In: Plummer J (ed) Diagnosing corruption in Ethiopia: perception, realities and the way forward for key sectors. The World Bank, Washington

Legal Vice Presidency The World Bank (2004) Ethiopia: legal and judicial sector assessment

---

[121] *Id.*

Ministry of Capacity Building Justice System Reform Program Office (2005) Ethiopia: comprehensive justice system reform program, Baseline Study Report

Perker S. Judicial performance evaluation in Ethiopia: local reforms meet global challenges. In: Indicators in development, safety and justice. http://www.hks.harvard.edu/criminaljustice/indicators-of-safety-and-justice. Accessed 19 Aug 2017

Redfern A, Hunter M (2004) Law and practice of International Commercial Arbitration, 4th edn. Sweet and Maxwell, London

Sedler A (1968) Ethiopian Civil Procedure. Haile Sellassie I University in association with Oxford University Press

Transparency International. Ethiopia: corruption perception index. http://cpi.transparency.org/cpi2013/results. Accessed 4 Dec 2015

UN Commentary on the Bangalore Principles

United Nations. Commentary on the Bangalore principles of judicial conduct. https://www.unodc.org/documents/corruption/publications_unodc_commentary-e.pdf. Accessed 20 Sept 2015

USAID (2007) Ethiopia: commercial law and institutional reform and trade diagnostic

Williams D. Defining the role of the court in modern International Commercial Arbitration, Herbert Smith Freehills-SMU Asian Arbitration Lecture, Singapore 1 (2012). https://www.arbitrationconference.com/download/file/218. Accessed 8 Dec 2013

World Bank (2017) Doing business 2017: equal opportunity for all, p 206. www.doingbusiness.org/reports/global-reports/doing-business-2017. Accessed 24 Aug 2017

Printed by Printforce, the Netherlands